THE LIBRARY
ST. MARY'S COLLEGE OF MARYLAND
ST. MARY'S CITY, MARYLAND 20686

U.S. Policy and the Security of Asia

Published volumes in the series,
"THE UNITED STATES AND CHINA IN WORLD AFFAIRS"

U.S. Policy and the Security of Asia

FRED GREENE

A VOLUME IN THE SERIES,
"THE UNITED STATES AND CHINA IN WORLD AFFAIRS"

PUBLISHED FOR THE COUNCIL ON FOREIGN RELATIONS BY THE

McGRAW-HILL BOOK COMPANY

New York · Toronto · London · Sydney

The Council on Foreign Relations is a nonprofit institution devoted to the study of political, economic, and strategic problems as related to American foreign policy. It takes no stand, expressed or implied, on American policy.

The authors of books published under the auspices of the Council are responsible for their statements of fact and expressions of opinion. The Council is responsible only for determining that they should be presented to the public.

U.S. POLICY AND THE SECURITY OF ASIA

Copyright © 1968 by Council on Foreign Relations, Inc. All Rights Reserved. Printed in the United States of America. This book, or parts thereof, may not be reproduced in any form without permission of the publishers.

Library of Congress Catalog Card Number: 68-11606

Third Printing   24333

To my wife, Ruth

Foreword

This is the eighth volume in the series on the United States and China in World Affairs, which is being sponsored by the Council on Foreign Relations through a generous grant from the Ford Foundation. In supporting this research program, the Council seeks to encourage more active and better informed considerations of one of the most important areas of foreign policy for the United States.

The Council program was under the able direction of Robert Blum until his untimely death, and it was he who envisaged the total project, arranged for the authors of the separate studies, and counseled them during the formative stages of their work. The appearance now of the completed studies constitutes appropriate memorials to his deep concern for a more enlightened public understanding of Asia.

This project, which has been guided by a Steering Committee under the chairmanship of Allen W. Dulles, has not sought to produce any single set of conclusions on a subject as complex as that of America's relations with China. Each study in the series, therefore, constitutes a separate and self-contained inquiry written on the responsibility of the author, who has reached his own judgments and conclusions regarding the subject of his investigations and its implications for United States policy. The list of authors includes persons with a variety of backgrounds in Chinese affairs and foreign policy. Some have had long personal experience in China. Others have studied China and Far Eastern problems during recent years or dealt with them as officials and administrators. In each case, they have been able to consult with a group of qualified persons invited by the Council on Foreign Relations to meet periodically with them.

In this study, Professor Fred Greene has undertaken the exceedingly difficult assignment of examining American security interests in Asia. Quite properly, he has rejected a narrow and purely military concept of our national security interests. Similarly, he has avoided the pitfall of trying to evaluate in an absolute, and hence static, sense the importance of different geographical locations in Asia for American security. His approach has been to see the problems of national security within the context of a dynamically changing Asia.

Historically, the instabilities of Asian political life have constantly placed new demands on American foreign policies. Professor Greene, therefore, arrives at the conclusion that the American national interest would be best served by a stable, coherent Asia. He advocates that we seek this objective by quite explicitly keeping in mind the advantages of creating a stable balance of power in all of Asia.

In a systematic fashion, Greene reviews the complex system of both bilateral and multilateral treaty commitments which we have built up over the recent years in Asia. His analysis is sensitive to the political realities and peculiarities of each of the countries in Asia with which we have such obligations. It includes also an understanding of complex points of view of the different neutralists or non-aligned powers in the area. It is, however, the emerging strength of Communist China and the problems surrounding Asia's entry into the nuclear age which dominate much of Greene's analysis.

Other studies of the China Project address themselves more specifically to China's military capabilities, her foreign policies, and the direct relations between the United States and Communist China. An outstanding feature of this book is that it treats American policies toward Communist China and our relations with non-Communist Asia as a single problem area. In recent years, there has been a strange dichotomy in American studies of policy in Asia. One school has focused on Communist China, sees our problem of policy almost entirely in terms of direct relations or confrontations with the Chinese, and has little regard for the development problems of the rest of Asia. The other school has concentrated on the problems of India, Southeast Asia, and Japan and is little concerned with the dynamics of development within Communist China. Each school feels that it is dealing with the essential issues, but it is, of course, the combination of the two focuses that can encompass all the elements which constitute United States policy toward China.

In this study, Professor Greene displays an appreciation of this broad and complex view. The result is a work of far-ranging interest which should be informative to all who are concerned with our policies in Asia.

Lucian W. Pye, *Director*
The United States and China
in World Affairs

Preface

American policy with regard to Asia has always held a fascination for me, as a romance viewed through adolescent eyes in the latter half of the 1930s, through the grim reality of war in which I served as a language officer in the Pacific during the following decade, and as a teacher and researcher ever since. When the late editor of this series, Robert Blum, first discussed the prospect of this book in 1963, I was attracted by the challenge of undertaking a study that would endeavor to place the American security effort in its historical setting and seek to determine its scope in the present era. This second goal also involved some evaluation of the policy-makers' standards as well as of the results attained. This, in turn, demands some projection ahead, especially in discussing the issues raised by the emergence of China as a nuclear power.

The book seeks to place American security policy in Eastern Asia in a meaningful setting for the interested general reader, hopefully offering some insights into the nature of contemporary problems to specialists as well. I have endeavored to weave three major themes —the historical pattern of America's evolving interests, balance-of-power analysis of the national interest today, and the peculiar sub-system that still prevails among Communist states (however mutually antagonistic they may be)—into the study, for each has had a profound impact on the evolution of this country's security commitments and undertakings in Asia today.

The book was written during 1964–66 at Williams College and, as the bibliographical footnotes attest, relies very heavily on the scholarship of the academic community as reflected in the books and periodical literature analyzing political and military developments in the Far East. Shortly after the manuscript was completed, I was offered and accepted in mid-1966 a temporary assignment in the Department of State dealing with East Asian affairs. Save for minor editorial changes and updating, the study stands as it was completed in the spring of 1966.

I should like to acknowledge very gratefully the kind assistance of Bob Blum whose unfailing kindness and patience were invaluable in helping me develop the scope of the study. His untimely death was mourned by all of us involved in this project. To Lucian Pye my thanks for advice in the late stages of the manuscript. I wish to thank in particular Lawrence Finklestein, Abe Halpern and General Richard A. Yudkin for their helpful comments on the manuscript in its early stages. Acknowledgments also extend to Frank Armbruster, James P. Baxter, 3rd, Joseph I. Coffey, Melvin Conant, Col. Edward P. Foote, George S. Franklin, Jr., Col. Robert W. Ginsburgh, Townsend Hoopes, 2nd, William Henderson, Robert H. Johnson, Col. William R. Kintner, S. A. Loftus, Jr., James W. Morley, Lewis M. Purnell, Maj. George Osborn, Joseph E. Slater, and Albert Wohlstetter for their considered observations. To David Albright, Robert Valkenier and Phyllis Freeman, my special gratitude for aid cheerfully and effectively rendered. Finally, I dedicated the book to my wife for help rendered far beyond the call of the stern demands of family duty.

July 1967
Williamstown, Mass.

Contents

PART III.   THE COMMUNIST THREAT IN ASIA

PART V.   PATTERNS AND PROBLEMS
FOR AMERICAN SECURITY POLICY IN ASIA

U.S. Policy and the Security of Asia

Introduction

With a war raging in Vietnam, involving hundreds of thousands of American servicemen, it hardly seems necessary to justify a study that centers around American security interests in Asia. Furthermore, this is the second war the United States has fought on the Asian mainland since 1945—and this is the only area in which it has been engaged in large-scale military conflicts during the past twenty years. Criticism was intense during the Korean War and the same is true of the Vietnamese campaign today. The arguments that have been generated against the first conflict essentially from the right, and against the second from the left, provide immediate and sobering evidence of basic disagreements on the proper approach toward the security problems of the United States in Asia. First of all, the issue involves but goes much deeper than how best to cope with threats to its interests there. Second, and more fundamentally, it concerns Asia's importance in the broader defense calculations of the United States. Moreover, the validity of a "security approach" to foreign policy in general has emerged as a third major issue underlying these national debates in the 1950s and 1960s.

This book seeks to determine the extent to which the United States has major security interests in Asia, and whether these should be considered "vital." The experience in Asia, an involvement dating from the start of this century, has known more than its share of outstanding triumphs, tragedies, and surprises. Indeed, since 1900 the United States has been engaged repeatedly in Asian security affairs, at times as a result of conscious policy decisions but often unexpectedly and seemingly against the national will. This region of the world has been second only to Europe in absorbing diplomatic attention, military effort, and economic activity and in provoking a

1

keen sensitivity regarding threats—real or imagined—to United States security.

Security problems have persisted in Asia with remarkable tenacity, though their nature has been profoundly changed by new ideological forces sweeping the world, radical shifts in power relationships, and revolutionary changes of regimes on the continent. In responding to the contemporary thrust of Asian politics, the United States has drawn heavily on its substantial historical experience there—a heritage that has both helped and hindered.

What case can one make for a U.S. security interest in Asia based on analyses of both past experiences and the present situation? The argument, briefly set forth here, is that outside of Western Europe no other area generates so vast a potential for political and military power as does the region encompassing Japan and China. If we add the Indian subcontinent to this grouping, we are considering states that form a major land mass, contain over one-third of the world's population, and have demonstrated a capacity—present or future—for considerable economic development. On this power base rest highly developed forms of government, ruling social entities that stem from some of the oldest and most powerful cultural traditions in recorded history. This is the stuff of greatness, as the past achievements of Japan, the awesome efforts of contemporary China, and the high promise of India readily attest. Should all three states, and the important lands adjacent to them, become hostile to the United States and follow a coordinated policy of enmity, its position would most certainly be weakened. If similar attitudes were adopted in Europe, U.S. security could be seriously jeopardized.

China is the centerpiece, though a considerable measure of its importance derives from the significant geographic setting in which it functions. Its militant advocacy of ideological hostility toward the United States, its commitment to undermine all opposing political orders, and its ready reliance on instruments of violence and coercion give a cutting edge to the power potential that its leaders claim lies within Peking's reach. China hopes to acquire the capacity to gain hegemony over Japan and India and to validate its operational concepts for the communization of other nearby lands. Peking's leaders further hope to prove their right to lead the rest of the non-Western world—the nations of Africa and Latin America in particular—and set it on a course for revolutionary political warfare while holding the United States and all other opponents at bay.

Given this Chinese orientation, the present situation in Asia threatens to breed major security crises. The region's great powers may soon engage in an intensive struggle for advantage and rely heavily on violence in their national and ideological competitions. Asia's latent strength and America's traditional involvement combine to induce Washington to participate in this region's affairs in defense of its own interests. How this came about and how America envisions or should envision its national interests are thus central issues for this book. Beyond this—as threats to be averted—are the more hypothetical dangers that could arise if the security situation should deteriorate: e.g., if Asia should become organized under Chinese leadership or if a substantial portion of the Afro-Asian world should become aligned with China on the latter's terms.

This approach to American security requirements does give great weight to ideological and political factors, but it rests just as heavily on a territorial-power orientation. It may therefore be criticized for failing to place sufficient emphasis on the grave social issues, related problems of revolutionary dynamics, and the challenge of political modernization that lie at the core of any security dilemma we face in the non-Western world. With its vast population, industrial capacity, historic cultural alienation from the West, and tradition of political discipline, Asia may well have the potential to damage greatly the security of the United States. But can we expect to gain even partial control of the problem through power analysis and a balance-of-power perspective? Can one pursue a policy with such modest intellectual tools? Are we relying too heavily upon American operational choices, even after acknowledging their limited impact on the course of events?

Affirmative answers appear increasingly reasonable the more scrupulously we circumscribe American objectives and recognize that this is a modest analytical approach, reflecting the restricted capacity of the United States to control events. To begin with, this country does have a major presence in Asia—and can probably retain a substantial position there in the near future—because of past endeavors and because many states fear the Chinese Communists. Unlike the situations in Africa, in Asia the United States has been able to forge firm and wide-ranging treaty commitments; in 1966, nine states in eastern and southern Asia, including South Vietnam, had formed security agreements with the United States. Second, the United States has the capacity to sustain a substantial security effort, though the business of balancing capabilities and commitments is admittedly very tricky. It is a function of available power, the relative importance of certain areas and issues, and the nature of existing and probable challenges to American interests. From the perspective of Asian needs, limitations on Chinese power, the capacity of the United States to respond, and its controlled responses—at least thus far—the long-term record does not point to a serious disequilibrium between American strength and undertakings. Third, many states have a sufficiently developed political infrastructure—in terms of national sentiment, political cohesion, administrative organs, capacity for social and economic evolution—to sustain hopes that they can progress along the path of modernization and blunt Communist challenges to their political integrity. The record is uneven, as the recurrent changes in appraisals of the security situation in South Korea and Thailand indicate. And the Vietnamese crisis, which stems in great part from the lack of political cohesion, is a warning that even a single exception to this essentially valid generalization bears the seeds of grave danger. On the whole, however, the majority of China's Asian neighbors have displayed relatively consistent policies in security diplomacy. Many of them can also boast of substantial economic progress in recent years. And their over-all record concerning internal political cohesion can readily stand comparsion with other non-Western regions.

In general, then, an active American security policy operates on friendlier soil in this area than elsewhere in the underdeveloped world. Washington's capacity and will to act here seem greater than anywhere else in Afro-Asia. Nor is there any doubt that United States security policies have profoundly influenced Asia's history during the past generation. Of course, security policy is but one branch of foreign affairs, and military instability is not the only threat to American interests. Other manifestations of instability also require careful attention, and American efforts in Asia have profited greatly from studies in political modernization, cultural change, economic growth, political institution-building, and the like. The point is that security questions deserve close study in their own right, for they play a crucial role in the general problem of instability, and the manner in which they are handled can profoundly affect the other aspects of Asia's political evolution in our turbulent epoch. This is especially relevant today in view of China's reliance on force, both to advance its ideological cause and to serve its substantial national interests.

In our times, Asia has undergone massive and traumatic military conflicts. Great international and civil wars have raged on its soil, and acts of violence on a smaller scale have been occurring seemingly without pause. The continent has had considerable experience with security diplomacy, much of it admittedly far from encouraging. Many alliances have flowered since the Anglo-Japanese accord of 1902, with markedly varying consequences and results. Successes and failures in arms-control arrangements have had a serious effect on the course of events since the Washington naval agreement of 1922. In threading its uncertain way through a series of momentous events, the United States has sometimes acted with limited aspirations firmly in mind. Yet on other occasions, it has moved ahead with high expectations—at least in declared official policy—and in the service of grand causes, such as preserving China's integrity under the Open Door notes or defending the principles of collective security in the Korean War. Frequently, the United States acted far more cautiously than it spoke; but at other times it became deeply involved, often to its own surprise.

Part I of this study endeavors to establish the setting in which American policy has operated: the place of security policy in foreign affairs, the evolution of American policy in Asia, and the contemporary significance of a balance-of-power approach in light of the past record and present interests of the United States. Part II stresses the instrumentalities of American defense policy as they have developed, especially through the establishment and modification of alliances. It includes a survey of the American military presence—in bases, machines of war, and armed forces—and the advantages and problems that flow from such dispositions and their modifications. The other side of the coin, Chinese security and military policy, is considered in Part III, which investigates Peking's ideological premises and strategies, its national objectives, and its view of the role of force—its own and that of indigenous revolutionaries. The position of North Vietnam, in the great-power context and in its own right, is considered as one counterpoint to the Chinese position. With the emergence of China as a nuclear power, questions of nuclear strategy, nuclear diplomacy, and arms control will attract increasing attention and concern. Part IV deals with aspects of the nuclear-weapons problem in view of China's use of nuclear strength in the support of its objectives, the difficulties posed for Japan and India, the problem of nuclear proliferation, and America's options. Finally, the implications for American security policy of current and possible future trends are explored in Part V. Changes in commitments, alignments, national policies of other states, dispositions of forces, and strategic doctrines receive primary consideration. However, these are examined in relation to American policies that might reduce tensions or even achieve limited accommodations with Peking in the future.

Naturally, such a study must make allowances for major imponderables, especially the courses to be followed by the Soviet Union and the states of Asia. For these countries will determine their policies from among the various options that they believe are open to them. Since the issues will be framed in terms of their own ideological orientations, national goals, and historical experiences, as well as their own values, the United States will have only a limited ability to exert influence on them. The severity of such limitations will continuously vary, but it will always be appreciable.

American options, too, will hardly appear clear-cut. Hence a good part of the analysis that follows is intended to clarify the problems, determine the choices that are open, identify key restrictive factors, and explore the consequences of alternative decisions. On many occasions, the author's preferences are clearly stated or apparent, though judgment is left open in an equal or greater number of instances. Caution in expressing an opinion seems advisable, especially when situations appear so complex. Also, when the pursuit of any course of action requires a major sacrifice of other values, a statement of individual preferences may do little more than becloud the issue further. Still, the imposition of a writer's values is inescapable—in establishing the framework for analysis and in estimating a threat, as well as in the way in which he analyzes a situation or a problem, or presents the available policy options. Even when judgments are made, the reader is well aware that others, even those working from the same premises and sets of facts, could in good faith reach quite different conclusions. The primary purpose of this study, therefore, is to clarify the issues and the choices open to the United States.

PART I

U.S. Security
Interests in Asia

CHAPTER ONE

The Scope of
Security Considerations

In the chapters that follow, we shall discuss American security interests in Asia both in general terms and in specific applications. We shall approach this subject from two perspectives—analyzing the balance-of-power potentials in the past and present and appraising Washington's record of experience and participation in Asian affairs. Before doing so, we should clarify the range of "national security interests" as well as certain aspects of their relation to other foreign-policy considerations. In scope, the term extends somewhat beyond purely military calculations, yet it stops far short of encompassing all major aspects of foreign relations. These limitations give rise to a dynamic interplay—the conflict of interests that may develop between defense and foreign-policy concerns. And it is these disparities that make the relationship among military, political, and economic considerations complex and, at times, baffling. Finally, we must recognize that other nations will inevitably have security perspectives quite different from those of the United States. This holds true even for those nations whose over-all approach to the current situation closely resembles that of the United States. In sum, we must proceed with a sobering realization of the stringent limitations that impose themselves on the concept, as well as the operational scope, of the national-security policy of any state, however richly endowed.

National Security Considerations

Although national security involves a spectrum of issues broader than those usually included in discussing military requirements, we

9

need not go to the other extreme of defining the term as a euphemism for all major foreign-policy considerations. We can avoid too narrow an interpretation by recognizing that American security interests are frequently and profoundly affected by the attitudes and considerations of other nations, even in their dealings with third parties on issues that do not affect Washington directly. Still, the essential threat that ties—and confines—many issues to the security field is their effect, however indirect, on a nation's military strength and on its willingness to use such power. Conditions that substantially affect the terms under which states are willing to commit themselves militarily, and the degree of effectiveness of their commitment, are of primary concern to security interests. As a result, the diplomatic relations of Asian states with third powers, their varying attitudes toward Communist China in particular, their ideological orientation regarding neutralism, and other related issues frequently become as essential to Washington's security calculations as their views regarding alliances or base arrangements.

Very often, problems that seem only distantly related to our security interests can seriously restrict our maneuverability in developing an adequate policy in Asia. Such issues may have a crucial impact on the area's security against a Chinese or other Communist threat, yet they may take unexpected and subtle forms because this relationship is not immediately apparent. Among the several surprisingly potent repercussions of internal political considerations, those in Japan have perhaps been most apparent. There the struggle for power between the country's two major parties involved the American alliance, the constitutionality of U.S.-backed rearmament, and the issues of nuclear weapons. To a lesser extent, the ideological beliefs of the opposition Australian Labor Party may seriously affect ties with America. Similarly, questions of economic and political nationalism in Manila may affect the key American alliance-base system in the Philippines. Communist revolutionary doctrine and the belief of certain neutralists that their view of foreign policy should become the writ of an entire region are two illustrations of the relevance of ideological considerations to American security interests. Even parochial problems between non-Communist states, such as the Afghan-Pakistani territorial dispute or the nationality problem regarding Indians living abroad, can take on significance in a moment of crisis. More directly, military confrontations such as the Indian-Pakistani or Indonesian-Malaysian campaigns have plagued American security efforts for some time. Less overtly, historical tensions, such as bedevil Japanese-Korean affairs and Cambodia's relations with its neighbors, can assume major importance. Thus, in this book, security questions cover a somewhat broader scope than the conventional meaning of this term would permit. As a consequence, it may appear that we are linking American military considerations to a large number of Asian issues that seem essentially political or of no significance to American interests or needs. But we hope to show that the connection is meaningful and that this is not an exercise in "imperialism," academic or otherwise. In fact, the existence of multiple links between American security interests and a host of Asian political and military issues does not argue for the primacy or even the pervasiveness of security values. Rather, this study should demonstrate how a vast number of political factors limit the options open to American security planners, and reduce the capacity of the United States to control events by its own policies and actions.

Defense and Foreign Policy

The relationship between security and other foreign policy interests is subject to many interpretations. To one concerned essentially with national defense, security enjoys a self-evident priority and seems to preserve or advance other American interests. In reality, however, security interests are usually difficult to define or to disentangle from the complex of other national interests. Those who focus on defense policy must recognize that they are dealing with but one aspect of a very broad field.

A defense-first advocate cannot expect to win his case simply by saying that all else will fail if security deteriorates. Security also may fail if political or economic interests deteriorate; and if security considerations conflict with other interests, we cannot assume that the former will predominate. The 1946 arrangements establishing Philippine independence, for instance, involve economic interests. The Americans gained equality with Filipinos in many economic activities in the Philippines, including the exploitation of natural resources. Today Philippine nationalists find this special treatment a "servitude," and the resultant hostility harms U.S. relations with an ally essential to the American military base system in the Pacific. In another example, the United States values highly its good relations with Japan, with whom it has delicately balanced and important mutual security interests. Yet the limitations on Japanese textile imports, the tax on Japanese efforts to raise capital in American markets, and the restrictions on defense purchases in that country to strengthen the United States balance of payments all tend to undermine other major interests. These include the maintenance of American treaty rights in Japan, fostering its full re-entry into the free world market and monetary systems, and minimization of its trade with Communist China.

Diplomatic requirements can also complicate the task of satisfying security interests in the Far East. For example, to maintain diplomatic warmth in Europe—for many purposes, including security—the United States might decide to make concessions to French or British interests in Asia. If they disagree with U.S. policy, the European or other allies might insist on dealing with the question through SEATO channels, which would enable them at least to threaten a veto. Or this country might agree, for a variety of reasons, to discuss certain issues at the United Nations or some other international forum (e.g., a Geneva conference on Indochina), when bilateral or independent lines of action might involve fewer complications or embarrassments.

More frequently, the opposite contention is heard that American foreign policy in Asia is excessively oriented toward immediate military needs to the detriment of other considerations. As a result, according to this criticism, the United States fails to recognize the significance of influential political forces, prosecutes security objectives to the point of diminishing returns, and ends by failing to fulfill military as well as other requirements.

This viewpoint has played an important role in the protracted debate over Vietnam. As the situation there deteriorated in the early 1960s, some asserted that American objectives were becoming unobtainable. These critics held that the scope for military operations had been severely restricted by the lack of social cohesion and political competence in South Vietnam. But a durable solution to the problem of governmental instability would probably entail concessions to the Buddhists despite the fact that Buddhist political dominance could run counter to more immediate American security goals.

In fierce clashes over Vietnam, advocates professing devotion to American national security interests reach opposite conclusions concerning the area's importance or tenability. The amazingly different views of the strength and motivation of the forces involved and the extraordinary difficulty in estimating the costs and consequences of recommended courses demonstrate how elusive a proper security policy can become at its point of greatest need. In any case, it must be recognized that neglect of political and diplomatic concerns in Asia can lead to major security setbacks, including withdrawal of American forces, expanded Chinese influence in allegedly neutral states, and perhaps even some Communist advances.

In addition to the general complaint that American security policy often flows dangerously against powerful political currents, a more specific and familiar criticism frequently arises: that concern with security has led the United States to sustain authoritarian regimes from Korea to Pakistan. The emergence of authoritarian civilian regimes in Korea and Vietnam, military coups in those two lands and in Pakistan, and the intensification of traditional authoritarian orders in Thailand and on Taiwan are adduced as significant departures from American ideological commitments. Suspicions exist that the United States actually encourages rather than passively tolerates such developments in the hope of stabilizing the internal affairs of these vulnerable lands. In reality, this criticism does not square with Washington's evaluation of its interests or of the requirements for political stability. A brief glance at the post-1945 record is sufficient to demonstrate that authoritarian regimes are not necessarily more stable or pro-Western than democracies. Moreover, the authoritarian usurpation of power, civilian and military, has occurred not only in aligned states but in neutral countries (Indonesia and Burma) as well. A powerful force like nationalism, with its anti-American overtones, has infected the democratic Philippines and semi-authoritarian Pakistan at the same time. Nor do authoritarian regimes that come to power in neutralist lands become pro-American.

To support the spread of anti-democratic regimes for security purposes would be doubly self-defeating. Such governments would give little or no help to the United States, even in the short run, and the policy would have a ruinous long-term effect on its ideological position in the Cold War. The United States has insistently urged the retention or restoration of democracy in Korea, Vietnam, and Pakistan, and its development in Taiwan and Thailand. For the most part, this has also been the American position, with varying degrees of effectiveness, regarding coups in Latin America during the 1960s. Indifferent results indicate not a lack of democratic commitments but how severely American influence is limited, even in states heavily dependent on American protection for survival. In fact, it can be argued that the area historically under Chinese cultural influence—particularly Korea and Vietnam—has such a deeply rooted tradition of authoritarian rule (under a leader-for-life), that attempts to create a democratic order are quixotic and possibly damaging to American security interests.[1] Since the United States rejects this argument and remains committed to the promotion of democratic rule, the greatest danger may lie in the desperation and intemperance that could result from the belief that this country should be able to accomplish more in fostering democracy outside its borders.

Another major concern derives from the fear that military requirements too frequently take precedence over welfare and economic development. This, it is argued, further reduces political stability and so becomes self-defeating. India frequently advanced this view during the 1950s, in its general argument against Cold War alignments. Yet events a decade later demonstrated that nonaligned states could also find themselves saddled with costly military burdens—as in the cases of Egypt, Ghana, and Algeria, all for quite different reasons. Nor has the United States been remiss in aiding its allies in the economic field. It has supported land reform, welfare projects, and the implementation of development strategies. Many allies have achieved striking economic gains without a heavy military effort. Japan contributes less than 2 per cent of its gross national product annually to defense. Nor have friendly African states, such as Tunisia and Libya, developed large armies, though confronted by powerful and dangerous neighbors. In recent years, with Japan the world pace-setter in the "economic growth stakes," lightly armed American allies in Asia have shown creditable economic development, as have Pakistan and Taiwan, despite their relatively extensive defense programs.[2] Nor has American economic help been restricted to allies. India has been receiving about $1 billion a year in foreign assistance since 1958, and Nigeria attracted a large share of America's relatively modest African aid program during 1960–65.

The general level of welfare in allied lands has tended to improve in the past decade. If anything, the neutralist lands have fared worse. India, like Communist China, has an overwhelming population problem. Though it followed quite different economic and political policies, New Delhi ran into difficulties similar to those that hobbled Peking: inadequate food production, a foreign-exchange crisis, transport bottlenecks, uneven industrial growth, shortages of raw materials, and idle industrial plants. When India had to raise defense expenditures from a low 2.5 per cent to a still modest 5 per cent of the national product, it found that this put a severe inflationary strain on the economy. Under Sukarno, Indonesia stressed foreign ventures and a large military establishment to the detriment of any serious effort to modernize its society or industrialize the economy. Both Ceylon and Burma suffered from ineffective governments whose doctrinaire plans for modernization proved far beyond their capacities to implement.

In states that face special security problems stemming from partitions or territorial divisions—Korea, Vietnam, Taiwan, and Pakistan—military expenditures are fairly high. Yet even here the economic record is mixed, with Taiwan and Pakistan doing quite well. Not until the mid-1960s did South Korea begin to progress on the economic front, leaving South Vietnam the only one of the area's Western allies with a poor record. In part, the troubles encountered by Seoul and Saigon stemmed from wars that sapped their strength. But they also reflect an inability, characteristic also of some neutralist lands, of the regimes to organize their societies effectively in formulating and executing development plans. A reduction of the military burden alone would not necessarily benefit Korea. Suffering from low productivity and disguised unemployment on the land and a high rate of visible unemployment in the cities, it would find a drastic cut in its force of more than 500,000 servicemen difficult to absorb under present conditions. Economic growth may ease, even speed, the transition to a smaller, more efficient defense establishment.

It appears, then, that military expenditures are only marginally related to economic achievement. At least it is difficult to correlate size of defense effort with results in economic development. It has been estimated that if Japan bore a more normal defense burden (around 5 per cent of its gross national product), its rate of growth would drop no more than 1 per cent from its phenomenal 9.2 per cent annual average. Nor has the economic competition between the Communist states and their neighbors, which so captured our imaginations a decade ago, proved to be the pivotal battlefield of the Cold War. If it had, the non-Communist side might now be resting comfortably. Instead, despite their economic advances, the states in the general vicinity of China are now in perceptibly worse security positions, even while China has been suffering staggering setbacks in its development plans. Security in Asia does not vary directly with a nation's degree of political stability or economic progress, however important these considerations may be.

The Security Perspectives of Other States

Only with the limitations on American action clearly in mind can we examine the security interests of the United States and judge the possible means of attaining them, or appreciate the dangers involved and determine the best way of reducing risks. Further, this country cannot act effectively unless it recognizes that the states of the area often have a significantly different view of what the dangers are. For example, both India and the United States now view Communist China as their primary security problem in Asia. But New Delhi treats this threat as directed almost exclusively in nation-state rather than ideological terms, insists on its traditional policy of nonalignment, and, in its weakness, seeks to avoid confrontations with Peking elsewhere in the region. By contrast, the United States considers ideology a vital component of the threat, operates through alliances, and seeks to confront Peking all along its periphery.

The states of the area differ markedly from us in describing their security needs. For many years after 1945, many states treated Japan as their greatest concern, because of the war experience and Tokyo's continuing potential to recreate its air and sea power. Even when China became a fearsome power, suspicion of Japan persisted in less prominent form. It underlay the security treaties the United States made with the Philippines, Australia, and New Zealand in 1951 to gain their acceptance of a Japanese peace settlement. The old imperial-colonial relationship has so poisoned relations between Japan and South Korea that the establishment of diplomatic relations eluded the two states until 1965. Only with the pact of 1965 on aid, trade, and fishing-right agreements, did substantial cooperation develop in economic matters, so essential to the stability and development of South Korea. Any combined defense effort lies in the distant future, however beneficial Japanese military assistance would be to the security of both states. Along with deep isolationism, retrospective hostilities still impede Japanese diplomacy and prevent Japan from playing a security role commensurate with its power.

Deep-rooted fear and distrust between neighboring countries are endemic in Asia. Cambodia has repeatedly identified attack and subversion from Thailand and South Vietnam as its main security concerns. Indonesia adopted a thoroughly hostile attitude toward Malaysia in 1962–63, at the time of the union of Malaya, Singapore, North Borneo, and Sarawak. The Philippines, because it claimed part of North Borneo, also opposed the new federation. But unlike Jakarta, Manila did not resort to violence. By the end of 1964, moreover, the Philippines regarded Indonesia as a menace to the security of its Muslim south, especially the island of Mindanao. The desire to control all of Borneo and, more broadly, to overturn the *status quo* in Southeast Asia led Indonesia to side with Peking until control was wrested from Sukarno.

In South Asia, India appears as a problem to its many neighbors. To Pakistan, it is a mortal enemy who may someday seek to undo the partition of 1947. The Muslim Pakistanis, therefore, accept support from any quarter, first from Washington and, after the Sino-Indian dispute erupted, from Peking. Ceylon has generally remained on good terms with India, though the vexing problem of Tamil-speaking Indians on the island disturbed relations until the settlement of 1964–65. The Singhalese also fear the loss of their national identity in the shadow of this huge neighbor. As a result, Ceylonese neutralism reflects a determined independence in foreign affairs that only gains in intensity when New Delhi runs into trouble that might embroil Ceylon. To the north, Nepalese-Indian relations deteriorated during the 1950s, when that mountain kingdom's ruler concluded that New Delhi sought to obtain a protectorate over his land. When he established his authoritarian rule at the end of the decade, he moved toward China, in aid and trade relations, and to a lesser extent toward Pakistan. Only after the 1962 Chinese demonstration of power did he swing back toward a more amenable India. Finally, Burmese-Indian relations have not been close. Fearful of China, certain that India would offer no security assistance (after New Delhi stood by with hands folded during a Chinese border invasion in 1955), and hoping to avoid involvement in India's problems, the Burmese have kept their distance from everyone.

This is not to imply that the states of Asia do not see China as a danger. Rather, many do not treat it as the outstanding menace, against which they and all other states should rally in disregard of other considerations. And responses to the threat, even when acknowledged, differ markedly. Among the neutrals, Burma and Ceylon retreat deeply toward neutrality as difficulties increase and Indian weakness becomes more apparent. Cambodia aligns itself with

Peking as Prince Sihanouk becomes more certain that China will dominate the area; it expresses great friendship for Peking, hoping to gain a "tolerated independence." India becomes determined to resist China but not in collaboration with other states, at least not if this means protecting anyone else's interests.

Allies of the United States, such as Thailand and Japan, wish to avert concessions to China that would diminish their own security. Yet they avoid involvement in measures not of direct concern to themselves that would anger Peking. Of all the allies, only the Philippines and South Korea have expressed support for America's determination to defend Taiwan, the most sensitive issue in the confrontation between Washington and Peking. Australia recognizes that China may well become a threat, but geographical considerations dictate that its main concern center upon Indonesia—although Canberra has recently begun to contribute substantial material and manpower aid to the war in Vietnam. Pakistan has become more "other-oriented" than ever, seeking close ties with Communist China, though this cuts across its American tie.

Equally complex ("distracting" to Americans) are the security relations among the smaller states of the region. South Korea has to contend with the threat posed by North Korea, which now primarily assumes subtle forms as well as a military challenge. Pyongyang offers unity proposals that play upon national feelings without impugning the integrity of the Communist segment. This appeal combines with the attraction of a successful program of economic development to disturb the Seoul regime. Any improvement in North Korean-Japanese relations, as occurred in the early 1960s, also poses a threat to South Korea.

Even within Taiwan, there are important cross-currents of interests and fears. The Nationalist Chinese leaders have a fixed resolve to return to the mainland, yet even they are vulnerable to propaganda calls for unity as the power of Peking mounts. Many cannot help feeling a pride in Peking's capacity to augment national power. More immediately, the indigenous population, while eager to remain free of the mainland, does not favor a military counteroffensive. Instead, it seeks a larger degree of self-rule and perhaps autonomy or independence from Nationalists and Communists alike. The role of the Japanese here illustrates the dilemma confronting the Nationalists. Close ties with the former imperial ruler (Japan controlled the island from 1895 to 1945) will help the island's economy and strengthen its international position. Yet they might also lead to a resurgence of Japanese influence and stimulate separatist feeling on Taiwan. Thus, even the Kuomintang, the most determined foe of the Peking regime, finds itself enmeshed in conflicts of interest that cause defense policy to deviate from its most effective path. It is in this restrictive and puzzling setting that American security interests have taken form and evolved.

CHAPTER TWO

Perspectives of the U.S. Involvement in Asia

No other continent in the last half-century has experienced more dramatic and substantial changes in power and politics than has Asia. The stability of European colonial empires has yielded to the uncertainties and confusion of new nationalisms. The great Chinese land mass, once important but disorganized, is today a disciplined center of world revolution and a nascent nuclear power. And Japan, which entered the world stage by defeating Czarist Russia and a scant forty years later was master of vast conquered domains, has survived the loss of empire and atomic attack with renewed economic vigor and political leverage. Perspectives have blurred as old realities became mere memories—whose influence remained pervasive—while the unimaginable has become the new reality.

The United States has had to marshal a succession of responses to these rapid and often bewildering upheavals. Policies that were rational and appropriate for one situation had to be revised swiftly to meet a wholly new and unpredictable development. The various changes and fluctuations throughout the region have also generated a particular blend of sentiments about our friends and foes. Thus, change has taxed emotions and commitments. In addition, each new investment in policy has had its champions, many of whom had little appreciation of the previous perspectives on Asia.

At the end of the nineteenth century, when America first felt the need to give any consideration to security matters across the Pacific, the dominant reality there was the disintegration of the Chinese empire and the possibility of vigorous foreign powers dividing the mainland of Asia among themselves. The U.S. response of the Open Door soon became a classic principle of American diplomatic policy. Around the First World War the rise of Japanese naval power emerged as the new theme, and for three decades, the apparently permanent characters were a strong Japan and a weak China. In the wake of the Japanese surrender in 1945, China was swiftly transformed by 1949 from a helpless prey into a new and powerful force allied with the Soviet superpower. Scarcely had American policy painfully adapted to this new Communist bloc on the Eurasian land mass than Peking and Moscow began their momentous dispute. Now America must come to grips with a new central opponent, a China that boasts that it will "go it alone," advocates a course of revolutionary violence, and remains potentially aggressive. Peking has a major opportunity to further its cause in Asia because the states on its frontiers are militarily weak and loosely organized; those to its south are especially vulnerable since they are in the early stages of the long process of developing into coherent political entities.

To counter the first postwar threat in the Pacific—a resurgent Japan—the United States concluded a group of pacts in 1951–52 designed to reassure Australia, New Zealand, and the Philippines. In Washington's view, however, Japan offered far less menace than did the Soviet Union. For only Moscow had the capacity to damage or invade Japan, and the Japanese Communist Party, a potential instrument of subversion, was still under Soviet control. Unlike its Pacific allies, Washington considered the treaties' chief value to lie in providing defense against the Soviet Union. For this reason, Washington frequently stands accused of introducing Cold War divisions to the Far East. But it must be remembered that these alliances came only after the thirty-year Moscow-Peking security treaty of February 1950, which aligned the two Communist powers defensively against Japan and any state allied with it.

Since the 1950s, the military aspects of the Soviet contest with America have diminished. The Russians have expanded their historical theme of peaceful coexistence considerably.[1] Even though they still emphasize an unremitting struggle to overturn Western political systems, their rejection of inevitable war, stress on economic development as the chief path to communism, and acceptance of the possibility of peaceful transition to the new order have all helped to enhance the credibility of coexistence. (The Chinese, for their part, find this Soviet tendency puzzling and hypocritical since these two "Western" states launched great armament programs in 1961 and engaged in substantial military muscle-flexing over Berlin and Cuba in 1961–62, all the while warning of China's reckless willingness to plunge the world into war.)

With awesome disregard of the odds, and with some success, China continues to press its campaign against American and Soviet foreign policy interests, on broadly separate fronts. Though the Soviet Union is now more heavily engaged than any other country except the United States in constricting Chinese power and influence, the Sino-Soviet alliance remains intact, at least as a reinsurance treaty of guarantee against attack. The profoundness of the dilemmas confronting both Washington and Moscow can be measured by an inability to predict which proposition will seem more ludicrous to future generations: (1) that anyone expected the United States and the Soviet Union to call off their deep-rooted Cold War because of China or (2) that Moscow and Washington failed to take essential joint steps so clearly required to confront the grave common danger emanating from Peking. Such uncertainties stem in part from the American experience of facing a succession of three major rivals within the span of one generation. The need for frequent shifts in focus compounds the difficulty of determining vital American interests in Asia.

Although the dominant theme has been change, there has also been an element of continuity in America's search for security and stability in Asia. Commitments made under one set of conditions often proved relevant in confronting new situations. And the accumulation of American obligations has in itself been a major factor in altering the power configurations of Asia. An examination of the record of reaction and response suggests the longer threads of continuity in American policy. But first, to gain a sense of perspective and proportion, it would be useful to briefly compare the United States course in Asia with that in Europe.

Comparisons with Europe

United States security policy in Europe in this century has differed considerably from its policy in Asia, and despite appearances to the contrary, the Atlantic policy does not emerge as consistently superior. The American position regarding Europe has been both more erratic and more clear-cut, and the degree of participation has fluctuated sharply as a consequence. The powerful pre-1914 tradition of isolation, barely affected even by the energetic

Theodore Roosevelt, re-emerged in full triumph following America's brief but intense participation in the final years of the First World War, the significance of which for American security escaped our understanding at the time. In contrast, after the Second World War, the threat of Soviet expansionism led to a profound involvement in Europe and brought an epochal revolution in world diplomacy.

The new era began with aid programs motivated by deep security considerations—the loan to Britain in 1946, the Truman Doctrine for Greece and Turkey in 1947, and the Marshall Plan of 1948, and culminated in the first alliance since the French treaty of 1778. The NATO pact of 1949 became the symbol of a binding obligation—at least to Asians, who later contrasted the "automatic" nature of its commitment, the establishment of a central command, and the presence of an American army in Europe, with what they described as a lighter security involvement in the Orient.

Even the Korean War of 1950–53 seemed to reinforce the preeminence of Europe. It contributed to: the dispatch of four American divisions to Germany, the appointment of Dwight Eisenhower as SHAPE commander, a substantial military assistance program and modernization of armed forces in Europe, the creation of a NATO infrastructure, the NATO Council's establishment of a high (and unattainable) target of 96 divisions, and finally, the determination to re-arm West Germany and bring it into NATO. America's more limited commitment in Asia was a key point in the debate that raged about the recall of General Douglas MacArthur in 1951. The testimony of the Joint Chiefs of Staff pointed up the priority they gave to Europe.[2] General Bradley's comment that a major war in Asia would be the wrong war in the wrong place at the wrong time with the wrong enemy reflected the judgment that the United States lacked the force to fight two major wars simultaneously. The Joint Chiefs feared that the Asian war might be a decoy and decided to keep their limited reserves available in case the Russians struck at the most vital point, Western Europe. Its industrial capacity, skilled populace, relative nearness, developed transport network, port facilities and terrain, as well as a common civilization, all placed Europe at the head of the priority list.

Since the struggle in Korea apparently reinforced Europe's strategic primacy, Asians emphasized the key differences in the American military posture on the two continents. The large force deployments in Europe because of the vast strategic obligations and the treatment of Berlin as a vital interest impressed Asians, for the Soviet Union had the capacity to damage the United States severely. By contrast, many Asians doubted America's willingness to run even lower-grade risks on their behalf because of their great distance from the New World and lack of substantial industrial power. Even the Europeans have repeatedly demonstrated nervousness over the durability of our commitment.

Paradoxically, American policy has been more consistent toward Asia than toward Europe, despite the smaller degree of involvement. Some inconsistencies in action and gaps between declaratory policy and actual behavior have clouded this important point. This lesser yet steadier display of interest has been too subtle to dispel Far Eastern confusion and doubts, though the two wars the United States has fought since 1945 have been on the Asian mainland.

Yet despite their professed anxiety over the durability of the American involvement, U.S. allies and friends in Asia, as elsewhere, depend on it for freedom of action to pursue their own interests that may even be in conflict with regional or American security requirements. The Japanese effort to open economic and cultural ties with mainland China, South Korea's long Cold War with Japan, Filipino claims against a vulnerable Malaysia, Thai complaints of inadequate allied support and concern over involvement "east of Laos," Pakistan's obsession with an Indian menace, and India's insistence on nonalignment exemplify Asian pursuits of national policies that, Washington feels, undermine the security of the entire region.

The Record of American Involvement

It is only in recent years that the United States has been asked to balance its interests between Europe and Asia. Historically, many American doctrines and strategies of foreign policy were developed in the Asian rather than in the European context. The record of American statements and actions in Asia during this century suggests a continuity of security interests, however unclearly defined. Since the first Open Door note of 1899, the United States has never abandoned its posture of diplomatic or strategic involvement in the major diplomatic issues of Asia, but until the Second World War, its declaratory policies were rarely corroborated by physical involvement. In particular, the profound commitment of the second

Open Door note of 1900 to the preservation of China's territorial and administrative integrity was not honored militarily until Japan attacked American territory four decades later.

Even during the administration of Theodore Roosevelt, the United States followed a modest course, recognizing from the first that it did not have the power to compel Russia to respect Chinese sovereignty in Manchuria. Without making a secret agreement, Washington and Tokyo assured one another that they would uphold their respective positions in the Philippines, Manchuria, and Korea. Only during the Taft administration did the systematic effort get fully under way to extend the concept of the Open Door to protect China against Japan.[3]

Under the pressure of the First World War and the withdrawal of European power from the Pacific, Washington recognized in 1915 and again in the Lansing-Ishii agreement of 1917, that territorial "contiguity" and "propinquity" created special relations, primarily in economic affairs, between Japan and those parts of China adjacent to its possessions. To Japan, America seemed to have accepted its paramount interests in China, though Washington continued to declare support of China's integrity and denied agreement on anything but Tokyo's economic interests. Still, the Versailles Treaty gave Japan a special position in Shantung Province, Germany's former leasehold area.

The end of the European war left America with a large naval force in being and under construction, theoretically available for Far Eastern action. Though the United States did not wish either to fight a war across the Pacific or to sustain a large navy, American power and commitments to China sufficed to bring Japan to the negotiating table for the Washington Conference of 1921–22. The naval agreement of 1922 gave Japan naval superiority and security in the Western Pacific, its home waters. Both sides agreed to a compromise: the U.S. navy sought a 10:10:5 ratio for American, British and Japanese capital ships, respectively; the Imperial Japanese Navy desired 10:10:7; and they settled for 10:10:6. In return, Japan undertook a solemn diplomatic pledge to respect the Open Door in China (including Shantung Province) in a nine-power treaty that formally internationalized this American obligation. Without judging the wisdom of the experiment in arms limitation, one can credit this "Asian settlement of the First World War" with enabling the United States to use a passing advantage in the balance of power to stabilize conditions in the Far East. Washington seemed to gain multilateral diplomatic backing for its obligations to the Chinese while obviating the necessity of a military effort.

When the Japanese seized Manchuria in 1931, President Hoover followed tradition in refusing to take security measures. At most, he allowed Secretary of State Stimson to proclaim America's refusal to recognize the legality of this conquest. A decade later, in the abortive American-Japanese discussions that eventually led to war, the question of Manchuria did not emerge as a major stumbling block. Rather, it was the Japanese army's insistence on retaining some presence in North China that proved beyond negotiation.[4] Yet when Japan attacked China proper in 1937, America again was unwilling to use force to sustain the Open Door. The signatories to the 1922 multilateral commitment had to "act," which they did at the Brussels Conference, by following the American lead of making merely an oral protest. No international diplomatic front took shape, and over the next few years the United States moved very cautiously and unilaterally toward hostility while Japan occupied a great portion of China.

The prolonged negotiations that ended with Pearl Harbor produced deviations from the basic American posture in the Far East, but also revealed its staying power. During the mid-1930s, with Japan's star on the rise, the U.S. army advocated dropping the long-standing commitment to the Philippines by a grant of independence to the country. Even the navy, though anxious to prolong the commitment, saw it as only peripherally related to the physical security of the United States.[5] But despite a heated debate and despite a questionable ability to defend the area, the security link survived; and when America rearmed after 1938, moving from continental to hemispheric defense commitments by 1940 and then beyond, even the army came to consider the defense of the Philippines feasible.

A more crucial incentive of American involvement was maintenance of Great Britain, with its key Asian interests, as a major Atlantic power in the dark days of 1940 following the fall of France. Germany became the primary threat to be engaged first in any two-ocean war, according to long-established doctrine. With Britain the prime bastion of defense in the Atlantic, it became vital for the United States to preserve the security of Britain's Asian colonies, regarded as essential to over-all British power.

With Japan menacing Southeast Asia, the Philippines unavoidably became involved. Had Japan abstained from an attack on the Philippines, the United States might have been seriously divided over a military repsonse to an invasion of nearby colonial lands. However, the American buildup in 1941, especially the approximately 100 B-17 strategic bombers that comprised one of the greatest concentrations of striking power in the world at that time, made such a Japanese strategy totally unrealistic. For the Japanese dared not move to the southwest against the European colonial strongholds with this formidable and growing American force astride their lines of communications. Expecting war with the United States in any event, the Imperial Japanese Navy decided to attack American naval power at its main Pacific base, Pearl Harbor. The operation succeeded in destroying the capacity to retaliate instantly against Japan or to relieve the Philippines according to standing plans.

Though the Philippine and British involvements drew the United States toward a military confrontation with Japan, it took the traditional, ambiguous commitment to China to make the conflict "inevitable." Despite its traditional refusal to fight for the Chinese on the Asian mainland, the United States nonetheless could not recognize Japanese territorial rule in China proper. This refusal did not deter Japan, but it established a moral obligation that prevented a compromise acceptable to Tokyo in 1941. Ironically, the Japanese occupation of certain bases in South Vietnam in July 1941, a move directed away from China, proved a point of no return. The United States did not react sharply to the occupation of North Vietnam in 1940, because it could be considered as part of the on-going Sino-Japanese conflict, in which Americans had refused to become involved. Whereas the 1940 move cut an important rail link between the South China coast and the southwestern interior, the thrust in South Vietnam was the first that clearly menaced the British position in Southeast Asia.

The three great concerns—Britain, the Philippines, and China—reinforced one another in the sweep toward a showdown. The China issue did not involve American security interests as directly as the other two, yet it proved the one point on which the negotiators could not give ground. The Japanese—to the extent that their army would accept a settlement—were willing to withdraw from southern Indochina and compromise their 1940 Tripartite Pact with Germany, obliging them to fight if America declared war against the Reich. But the militarists would not withdraw from sensitive Southeast Asia without compensation—some recognition of their position in North China. Despite the relatively low American security interest in this area, Secretary Hull would not consider such a possibility, given China's vulnerability, the opposition of London and Chungking to major concessions, and American public sympathy for these *de facto* allies. Yet, until this point in mid-1941, both he and U.S. military leaders favored such a cautious policy in dealing with Tokyo that our Embassy had to urge a firmer stance lest this attitude encourage the expansionists.[6]

The Joint Board of the Army and Navy hoped to avoid a collision before March 1942, when the Philippine garrison would reach the strength required. But with Germany the major concern, the Board at no time showed any eagerness for a Japanese war. Like the German General Staff of modern times, American planners viewed a two-front war as their most dread nightmare, and they too determined to give top priority to one theater. However, the Germans, with their long-term emphasis on offensive operations, planned to overwhelm the more vulnerable foe first. American strategic plans from 1919 onward aimed at the defense of the homeland or overseas territories in their first stages. In a two-front war, the stronger opponent, in the Atlantic, was to receive first priority. The weaker Japanese would be held off, hopefully, west of Hawaii, until the defeat of the European enemy. Plans for a two-front war in the interwar period could hardly contemplate a successful defense of the Philippines. Rather, security policy hinged on defending the great triangle of Hawaii, Alaska, and the Canal Zone.[7] Only with a post-1938 armament effort did these calculations change substantially, allowing the United States to project its power into the western Pacific. By September 1941, the Joint Board did indicate again an interest in the preservation of the balance of power in the Pacific, but did not detail the justification for this or spell out the relationship Washington sought among the major powers.[8] A strange convergence of interests therefore brought the United States to a Pacific war in 1941—a fading imperial role, protection of a major Atlantic power, and moral obligations to China.

The Asian mainland came well behind the European and the Pacific campaign in strategic priority. The Pacific front received as much military support as the Atlantic during the crucial years 1942–43, despite popular belief to the contrary, but very little went to the China-Burma-India theater.[9] Given the distance involved, difficulty of access, and its own low level of military competence, China could never convince the Western powers that it lay at the center of a vital and major war effort.

To the United States, China was an important theater to tie down

Japanese strength and to provide a base for attacking the home islands. For these purposes, America went to great trouble to fly in a considerable amount of equipment and supplies. But it did not overcome its great reluctance to land major forces in China or fight a large-scale engagement on the vast plains of Asia. After island bases captured in 1944 brought Japan within range of the new B-29 bombers, strategic interest in China waned further. Taiwan lost its priority as a theater of operations in 1944, when General Mac-Arthur successfully pressed his recommendation that the Philippines be liberated. Finally, a projected landing in South China in 1945 never came to pass when the war ended suddenly.

In the latter stages of the war, the Nationalists received substantial help in modernizing their army; but following the surrender of Japan, the United States reaffirmed its determination to avoid a major military entanglement on the mainland. American units, with considerable assistance from Japanese prisoners, helped the Nationalists regain control of most of China proper. But Washington avoided armed confrontation with the Communists and did not significantly step up its military assistance and advisory program when the war went against the Nationalists. A similar unwillingness to fight on the mainland led the Joint Chiefs of Staff to remove U.S. forces from Korea in 1949 after the Communist triumph in China, even though the peninsula protected Japan and thus could be considered a forward buffer for a major American security interest.[10]

Imperial Japan had created a great-power center in 1941, comprising the Japan-Korea-Manchuria complex plus parts of North China, which afforded Japan the possibility of dominating the entire Asian mainland. But in 1947–49, the American government evidently did not think there was an imminent possibility of a hostile power getting control over this area. The Joint Chiefs pressed for a retrenchment in Asia. They concluded that the American army, with only fourteen divisions and "twenty-division" global commitments, could be more rationally deployed in central locations to sustain beleaguered Europe. The statement by Secretary of State Acheson of January 1950 that identified U.S. vital interests along the off-continent Aleutians-Japan-Ryukyus-Philippines line seemed to reinforce this position.[11]

The return to Korea in 1950, with a ground war on the mainland, reversed this general orientation sharply. Still, the American military leadership contained this operation and vigorously opposed any extension to the territory of mainland China. The defense commitment to South Korea, assumed in the aftermath of an unexpected war, was an unsought burden, a partial compensation for President Rhee's acceptance of a stalemate. The Korean experience had a doubly ironic consequence. The Russians evidently learned that the Americans had a greater will to fight than they had supposed, for they pursued a more cautious policy thereafter. In America, it gave rise to the "never again" school, of which General Maxwell Taylor was a powerful and determined advocate. Adherents of this view argued that the United States should, in the future, avoid another major land engagement on the Asian mainland, especially under such restrictive and unfavorable terms of combat. General Taylor retained this view later, as Army Chief of Staff, architect of counterinsurgency policy in Vietnam, and Chairman of the Joint Chiefs. And as ambassador to Vietnam in 1964–65, he appeared to favor a lesser degree of American combat commitment than did the Military Assistance Command in Saigon.

Even before Taylor assumed these offices, his predecessor as Army Chief of Staff, Matthew Ridgway, played an important role in the decision not to enter the Indochina war in 1954. The government's reasons included an unwillingness to side with a colonial power and the absence of other allied support. But an old refrain was also heard—reluctance to commit sizable ground forces that, General Ridgway argued, were essential for effective intervention.

Both the Korean and Indochinese wars ended in partition—which meant the *status quo* in Korea and a partial Communist victory in Vietnam with a new regime in Hanoi. Yet conditions had changed by 1955, when these two wars had ended, and the U.S. alliance system took its present shape. The United States had demonstrated its staying power with a bitter three-year war, suffering 137,000 casualties, and afterward undertook treaty obligations to defend advanced positions against Communist aggression. With regard to the mainland, the United States signed a bilateral treaty with South Korea in 1953 and a multilateral accord, SEATO, that included Thailand and Pakistan in 1954. A protocol to this treaty involved us even more deeply, by unilaterally extending SEATO's mantle to South Vietnam, Laos and Cambodia. Although the treaty with the Chinese Nationalists on Taiwan in 1954 was not a direct involvement with the mainland, it did freeze Washington-Peking relations, and increased the possibility of America's entanglement in the prolonged Chinese civil war.

The mainland areas around the periphery of China form a twilight security sector. They now involve American military commitments but of a different character from the commitments toward the islands to the east. In its treaties of 1951–52, the United States had firmly extended its security zone from the Hawaii-Alaska-Panama triangle to the off-continent line of Japan-Philippines-Australia. The security of these lands became vital American interests that Washington thought it could protect with its predominant air and sea power. The new 1953–55 line of obligations seemed less forthright: these lands are relatively less important strategically than the Japan-Philippines-Australia group, more vulnerable politically, and more likely to require ground combat on the mainland very near the borders of China. Outside Korea, no American ground combat formations were on station in these exposed lands for about a decade after 1953.

The historic theme of limitations to American commitments—either in obligations or implementation—persisted even in this new alliance pattern. Peripheral to the main defensive interests, these alliances of 1953–55 reflect in part a diplomatic glacis to establish the credibility of American determination to defend the more important line immediately to the east and south. Despite the efforts of Thailand, Pakistan, and the Philippines to require a SEATO response to any aggression, the United States firmly limited its commitment to Communist thrusts. By contrast the 1951–52 accords with Japan, the Philippines, Australia and New Zealand guarantee protection against any acts of aggression, regardless of the source. These pacts also differed from the SEATO obligation in that America had no expectation of shouldering the SEATO burden alone. It hoped that Britain and France, maintaining substantial military postures in the region, supplemented by local forces, would provide for a truly multilateral undertaking. However, the United States avoided the formal arrangements of a command headquarters, infrastructure, and allocation of units as established under its multilateral accord in Europe, NATO.

Secretary of State Dulles also hoped to link Southeast Asia with the other sectors around China in a cohesive security arrangement that would activate the separate defense pacts in case of aggression at any point. But the fragmentation that caused this scattering of treaties persisted. In 1958, the United States vainly sought to involve SEATO in the Quemoy-Matsu dispute, but even Thailand, the state most interested in enhancing the alliance, refused its backing. Similarly, Japan isolated itself from all issues involving territories outside its jurisdiction, including its own, Okinawa, which was under American control. The United States avoided commitments not only to neutrals but also to territories of its allies. Just as Britain steered clear of the Taiwan problem, so America did not wish to commit itself on Hong Kong or, after 1957, on Malaya, when that country disassociated itself from the SEATO arrangement upon gaining independence.

A further instance of America's limited involvement is seen in the matter of resort to atomic weapons in repelling aggression. Nuclear deterrence to protect Japan became necessary in the 1950s with the development of a modern Soviet arsenal and will become even more important when China acquires a short-range missile potential. A less dramatic global issue than the defense of Europe during the post-sputnik crises, Japan can still be grouped with the American homeland and the NATO area as a target vital enough to require all-out protection. But what of the rest of Asia? There, except perhaps for the Indian subcontinent, the enemy does not seem likely to use such weapons. Significantly, the United States has demonstrated a similar degree of reluctance in the use of nuclear weapons, though in the last stages of the Korean War, it had threatened to employ them against China if the war continued.[12]

American forces on Okinawa and the Philippines, as well as the Seventh Fleet off Taiwan and in the Indian Ocean, have both a conventional and an atomic capability. But nuclear power has remained sheathed, with conventional weapons prevailing in combat and as instruments of diplomacy. In Indochina, despite the rapid intensification of America's military role since 1960, its strategy has remained limited. The United States settled for neutralization in Laos in 1962 and has given the neutralist regime limited but consistent combat air support since the Communist Pathet Lao broke the truce in 1963. In the more complex Vietnamese situation, the threat is greater, the stakes are larger, and American involvement has become far more substantial. Yet U.S. policy in Vietnam indicates the pursuit of goals below even the "limited war" level of Korea, which required seven combat divisions and at one point included as an objective the elimination of the North Korean regime.

Still the dispatch of large numbers of military personnel, rising from less than 1,000 in 1960 to 23,000 in 1964 and reaching more than 375,000 in 1966, makes this a major effort. The strain on a moderate-sized Europe-oriented army in dispatching first a sizable cadre and then major combat units to Vietnam is far greater than the numbers indicate. New air bases at Bienhoa and Danang, along with similar installations in Thailand, anchored the United States firmly on the Southeast Asian mainland. The war became a major focal point of international tension, causing considerable anxiety in Europe that this "distraction" would weaken the American commitment to the primary theater. The struggle, particularly the bombing of North Vietnam, seriously impeded efforts to further a *détente* with Moscow. Worst of all, a defeat in Vietnam might have global implications for American prestige and staying power and, consequently, for its capacity to sustain interests elsewhere.

Nevertheless, despite these serious strategic-diplomatic considerations, the extensive nature of the Communist effort, and the danger of escalation, the American response has remained within the framework of limited undertakings along this inner belt of Asian states. The United States very reluctantly dispatched ground forces as line combat units, and then only to defend South Vietnam, which otherwise might have been overwhelmed. These forces did not invade the North. Nor has the United States, as the Communists have done, made the overthrow of the enemy regime a national objective. Even the bombing of North Vietnam was delayed until 1965, and it was then treated as an instrument of pressure to hamper Hanoi's infiltration, cause a withdrawal of guerrillas from the South, and induce the enemy to negotiate a settlement. With the appearance of sizable North Vietnamese contingents south of the 17th parallel, the United States also sought to use the cessation of bombing in the North as a bargaining counter to gain the withdrawal of these regular forces. Further, targets were carefully chosen, and even as the bombing escalated, the United States sought to avoid points of such strategic importance that their loss might have threatened the survival of the Hanoi regime. Otherwise, it was feared, Communist China might feel impelled to intervene directly in the war. Finally, the United States repeatedly offered to remove its formidable military presence from South Vietnam if that state could be secured. It even seemed, at times, to be willing to accept a compromise political settlement if it could retain even part of its security objective.

In summing up the record of formal United States security obligations in Asia, we should observe that they have been shaped somewhat haphazardly to meet specific needs that emerged during the efforts to liquidate the effects of three wars—with Japan, in Korea, and in Indochina. Even the link to Taiwan arose from an accident in timing: the North Koreans attacked their neighbors to the South before Peking could launch an invasion of the Nationalists' island. Until that moment the United States had no obligation to the Nationalists, and only after the Korean War had started did President Truman interpose the Seventh Fleet between Taiwan and the mainland.[13] Nevertheless, the fragmented and restricted undertakings that emerged by 1955 hardened over the next decade.

Hopes of mutual allied cooperation, coalition forces, and a general nuclear posture to deter local wars, especially in the south, soon faded. Yet the history of the origins of these treaties should have provided ample warnings against optimism. Even in Korea, where an unambiguous act of aggression was condemned by the U.N., there was little rallying of allied forces. America and South Korea had to provide more than 90 per cent of the defending combat strength, and forces from other states of the region were conspicuous primarily by their absence.

Hesitant states, such as Ceylon and Burma, decided to avoid alignment; and the active neutrals, India and Indonesia, became more antagonistic than ever as the 1950s progressed. Jakarta actually proposed to India that the neutrals form their own bloc and declare their friendliness to Peking. India refused, but its antipathy to SEATO persisted because the alliance strengthened Pakistan and brought the Cold War to Southeast Asia when New Delhi was trying to mollify its dangerous Chinese neighbor. Cambodia by unilateral action, and Laos through an international accord, renounced SEATO protection for neutrality. While retaining its SEATO tie, Pakistan has intensified its drift to a quasi-neutralist policy because of Western help to India since 1962. In view of past experiences and the disarray in South Asia, it is doubtful whether the United States would wish to assume additional obligations, except perhaps in India, even if it could acquire additional bases.

The United States has had a long tradition of involvement in Asian security affairs without clearly identifying or justifying its interests in terms of a coherent policy. Though at times the engagement has been very extensive in prestige and effort, from the pre-1941 confrontation with Japan to the war in South Vietnam, the United States has tried to restrict its physical commitments. The American stance has been shaped in a series of responses to aggression or immediate threats. The United States still has to devise a defense pattern based on its own concepts and initiatives and in harmony with its view of its own major interests.

CHAPTER THREE

The Vital Interest:
A Balance of Power in Asia

This review of the diplomatic-military record during this century indicates that American security interests have in most instances been closely tied to the stability of relations among the Asian countries. When some Asian power has displayed the potential to threaten and absorb weaker Asian countries, that threat has also posed at least a potential danger to American security interests in the Pacific. Even when the United States has not been involved, it has had to deal in subsequent crises with the lingering repercussions of divisiveness and intra-Asian alliances. Often, of course, the danger to U.S. interests has been direct and immediate.

The initial American concern in the region was aroused by the impotence of China, and the United States became increasingly involved as the Japanese Empire began to overshadow Eastern Asia. The present commitments again focus on China, which, through the changing fortunes of history, has today become capable of menacing all its neighbors.

Now, as in the past, the United States has fashioned its commitments not only to secure its own national objectives, but also in reaction to the fears of American allies in the Far East. This is not to assert that past U.S. actions in this region constituted consciously patterned responses to recognized security threats. They were not based on a sophisticated balance-of-power rationale, such as one that saw a danger to American interests in the rise of any power seeking hegemony in Asia or that stressed the value to the American position of a free and independent China. The uncertain nature of American obligations and the gap between specific undertakings and the means provided to implement them are sufficient testimony on that score. Furthermore, the clear lines of policy have often become blurred because of the discrepancies between Washington's estimates of a given or potential situation and the estimates our allies might make.

Still, in retrospect, American actions did follow a course that, with all its inconsistencies, was pointed toward the maintenance of a balance in Asia. Despite a lack of conscious design, this unstructured policy operated in the service of major American security interests by focusing upon the preservation of an independent China while seeking to avoid a deep military involvement on the mainland, particularly in China itself.

We can, in other words, derive an interpretation of American interests and needs from historical experience, even though we are imposing this view on the past from the perspective of the present situation and requirements. A rational theory for contemporary American policy in the Far East can thus reflect continuity with past actions, centering upon keeping China and other states politically independent of one another. In developing major U.S. strategies in pursuit of this objective, it is to be hoped that accumulated experience will enable this country to demonstrate more consistency and greater purposefulness than we have in the past. Still, certain major issues from the past will remain with us and will be especially influential in determining what specific actions are essential and in aligning commitments with a will and readiness to execute such burdensome operations.

Since it is the hypothesis of this book that U.S. security is closely linked to Asia's ability to avoid domination by any one power or political system by means other than voluntary association, the most crucial feature of U.S. security policy must be the preservation of Japan, Pakistan, and India, as well as the strategically essential access states, the Philippines and Australia. This objective also involves most intimately the independence of the smaller states that form an arc around the mainland of Asia from Japan through Southeast Asia to the subcontinent of India and Pakistan. The task calls for the cooperation of the United States with Asian states and, hopefully in the future, for cooperation among the Asian states.

Analysis of these American security interests must include an examination of the security relationships among Asian states. Not every clash among Asians necessitates an American response; but during the modern era, while Asian societies are experiencing the unsettling effects of social change and modernization, even modest difficulties become major sources of international instability.

These considerations mean that our inquiry into American security interests in Asia must be expanded to encompass the entire dynamics of interstate relations in Asia. Central to these relations are those of Communist China toward all the other Asian states, and thus we must in later sections examine China's foreign policies in some detail. But we must also, at different points in our analysis, deal with the problems of India and Pakistan, of Indonesia and its neighbors, of South Korea and Japan, as well as with other major potential sources of instability.

The key to a balanced continent today, as in the past, is China. In the half-century before 1949, the United States fitfully endeavored to preserve it from foreign domination—by Japan primarily, by Russia potentially—which might have enabled the conqueror to dominate the entire Far East. In these efforts to protect China, the United States did not act on the basis of power calculations, though effective maintenance of the Open Door policy would have harmonized with U.S. security interests. The converse possibility—a powerful China in control of the Soviet Far East and/or Japan—seemed totally unlikely at the time. Despite the profound diplomatic-power revolution in Asia, the optimal American objective would still reflect continuity with the past: an independent China, strong enough to preserve its security but prevented from gaining control over its major neighbors.

Eastern Asia has never experienced even the relatively brief interludes of diplomatic stability enjoyed by Europe in modern times because it has never approached a durable balance of power. Domestic political instability in Asia is much to blame for the volatile shifts of power relations between nations. But as the colonial era recedes in memory and the new states gain valuable experience in government with each passing decade, a relatively stable diplomatic environment becomes increasingly possible. With political institutions assuming a greater degree of permanence, we can expect somewhat more favorable conditions for the quest for order in the Far East.

The obstacles to stability, however, are also increasing. This politically more sophisticated age must confront not only overt aggression, but the rise of indigenous Communist power or camouflaged aggressions in Vietnam and elsewhere. Imbalance can also arise from a compact between ideological allies to overturn the existing order.

The Sino-Soviet treaty seemingly represented such an effort until differences over ideology, weapons, and diplomatic policy rendered it virtually inoperative. The two powers may avert a complete split, and Soviet ideological commitments may bind Moscow to give some support to a violence-oriented Communist state against its own better judgment. Yet as long as Moscow and Peking divide over fundamental policy, the danger of an overwhelming Asian power bloc recedes.

With the breakdown of Communist solidarity, it might follow that China would be unable to dominate Japan and India even if pro-Peking Communists came to power in those countries. New national differences, also based on substantive policy, doctrinal inventiveness, and psychological needs of national self-assertion could triumph over China's efforts to create a bloc under its leadership. Such a development may be even more likely now that a doctrine of "national relativity"—i.e., applying communism to each state in accordance with its specific needs—has emerged in the Communist world.

North Vietnam's effort to walk a tightrope between Moscow and Peking, and the Indonesian Communists' stress on national policy-making during the early 1960s indicate that this is possible. Yet one cannot count on this moderately favorable outcome, especially in an environment of upheaval throughout Asia. Peking-led unity could thrive under the impetus of success, fanaticism, an ability to compromise to preserve fundamental cohesion, and even a degree of voluntary acceptance of prestigious Chinese leadership. It should be recalled how earnestly the Soviets tried to sustain unity with China, with assistance programs and a doctrinal papering-over of disputes. Moscow has retained the reinsurance feature of the defense treaty despite the shaky moments of the Tonkin Gulf affair in 1964, when Khrushchev seemed to be threatening to stand aside in a crisis related to Peking's doctrines. Given doctrinal agreement among the Asian Communist leaders and shrewder handling of "fraternal parties," Peking might succeed in a determined effort to maintain the unity of its own camp under China's banner. In fact, the Vietnamese War indicates how difficult it is for the Soviet Union to sustain a moderate course; though it has actually intensified the Sino-Soviet split, a later crisis of this sort might result in driving the rivals together. In order to protect a socialist state, retain influence in other Communist lands, perhaps control and dampen the course of a conflict, and continue the quest for that elusive unity of the movement, Russia might find itself compelled to match Chinese displays of virulence against the West. One cannot, in short, write off the possibility of a relatively cohesive group of "national Communist" states emerging in Asia, sufficiently organized around Chinese leadership to communize the rest of the region.

The large segment of Asia that has China at its core must be treated as an integral diplomatic and security area. The lands of this region respond quickly and with great sensitivity (albeit often negatively) to important events anywhere on the arc. The four major centers of power are China, Japan, the Indian subcontinent, and the Soviet Far East, which is a special case. Two other states, Australia and Indonesia, can also affect events beyond their frontiers, though to a much lesser degree. The primary long-range American purpose is to keep Japan and the Indian subcontinent from falling under Chinese domination.

Against this background, there is intellectual consistency in the reversal of the traditional American policy of protecting China against Japan in favor of securing Japan and India against the multiple pressures emanating from Peking. But the question of the intermediate areas and their fate remains unresolved. In this marginal power zone, no single segment appears absolutely crucial to the over-all balance. Acts of violence and aggression in any one of these smaller states, therefore, seem less risky, especially when begun as civil strife or proxy guerrilla infiltration. Each major antagonist can accept some territorial setbacks and make adjustments without suffering a grave loss in power or in the competition for influence. Leeway may be provided for settlements without resort to major confrontations. But the very fact that the aggressor concludes that the opponent need not consider a loss vital may induce it to further, dangerous initiatives. Meanwhile, the opponent may decide to resist a further concession at some point in front of its vital defense line in order to arrest a drift toward deterioration. Thus, an objective that of itself does not have intrinsic significance may provide the setting for a strategic test of wills. This, in turn, can lead to a grave crisis, with compromise most difficult to reach, especially when the smaller powers have vital interests at stake and pressure their large allies to take inflexible stands.

Although a consolidation of Chinese influence in North Korea and North Vietnam would not upset the over-all balance, it could give Peking a base for further thrusts in the two partitioned lands. Stability even at this modest level of expansion may depend on a Russian counterweight within this Asian bloc, and eventually on local opposition by Japan and India to an expansion of the Peking-oriented realm. Japan did sympathize to some extent with the Korean War effort, primarily because it was a response to overt aggression in an area vital to Japanese security. Today, a Communist thrust against South Korea, in response to American assaults on North Vietnam, might well find Tokyo hesitant or even hostile toward the U.S. position, because of the distant source of the conflict. The spread of war under these circumstances might strengthen rather than undermine the intense Japanese desire to avoid military action outside their homeland, even in Korea. Like Japan, India avoids foreign involvement even when the security of its closest neighbors is menaced. It would no more become involved in the collective defense of Northeast Asia than Japan would in Southeast Asia. Hence the United States can expect no immediate help in this twilight zone from these two pivotal states whose protection is of primary concern to Washington and who could, theoretically, contribute to the security of the area.

At this time, then, only China, the United States, and possibly Soviet Russia can be considered to have commitments, involvements, and ambitions that reach to all areas of Asia. They are the only powers that are centrally involved in the working of an Asian power system. In time, possibly both Japan and India will be able to assume broader roles throughout Asia to counterbalance the influence of China. But even if Japan and India alter their current approach drastically and seek to become regional security powers, they are certain to encounter opposition, for the memories of Japanese conquest die slowly in Southeast Asia; and in South Asia, there are states that consider Indian power far from benign.

Despite its manifold weaknesses, a balance-of-power approach can be applied fruitfully to Asia. Historically, the United States has not employed this guideline systematically in its quest of a proper security policy. Admittedly, techniques of analysis must differ from those applied to Europe in the "classical past." Ideological considerations, intangibles of cultural and racial dissimilarity, strategies of development, and the power differential between Washington and its distant allies all present grave obstacles. However, the situation still bears conceptual resemblances to Britain's historic effort to keep any one European power from forcibly dominating the others.

The assertion that a balanced relationship among the major states of Asia is a vital American interest rests on the belief that serious dangers would ensue from the forcible establishment of a unified power system centered on China. Let us examine what repercussions this eventuality could have:

1. To an important degree, the physical security of the United States would be impaired by such an aggregation of power. Though not comparable to the threat that a similar situation in Europe would pose, the military strength and political momentum generated from the start would be formidable.

2. Creation of a Communist-dominated region under Chinese suzerainty would profoundly alter the fundamental pattern of the nation-state system. It would deal a devastating blow to the hope of creating a global order of sovereign states able to coexist and harmonize their policies despite competing political systems. Such a development would create a grave crisis of confidence, born of the realization that the United States has suffered a serious defeat in the struggle to create a workable pattern for a world order. A failure of this magnitude might also undermine the adherence of the United States to the live-and-let-live ethic that has contributed significantly to its policy of self-restraint.

3. In addition, America would have to make an enormous countereffort outside of East Asia that would make present expenditures and commitments seem small in comparison. A great triumph by expansionist Communist ideologies, so basically hostile to the West, could precipitate an ideological and military offensive of unprecedented fury. To illustrate its intensity, this challenge, though centering in the underdeveloped world, might push the West belatedly into the Atlantic Union it now considers unrealistic and unnecessary. In Asia, it might push states like Japan and Australia, confronted with threats to the communications and trade systems on which they depend so heavily, into closer collaboration with one another. But despite the possibility of marginal benefits, the over-all result would probably be sharper divisions not only in Asia but throughout the world. If the Cold War were intensified, life in most societies would become much more disciplined, and for America this would mean a strain on its democratic values.

The Russian Dilemma

Since the Soviet Union has important ideological and power interests throughout this area and a great capacity for policy initiatives, Moscow's policies can have a profound impact on American security interests.

At present, the Soviet role in Asia reflects serious ambivalences and contradictions. Despite intense Chinese hostility, Russia's doggedly friendly policy toward India has been a crucial feature of its global diplomacy. Russia's unprecedented neutrality in the Sino-Indian confrontation since 1959, sustained economic aid to New Delhi, tacit support of the Congress Party, lavish praise of Prime Minister Nehru, and intensified military assistance after 1962 appeared inexcusable to Peking. The basic Soviet design remains to separate India from the West, win it over to communism, and so validate the Soviet claim that the gospel can be spread without war. Yet for the short term, the balance-of-power consequences of this Moscow policy indicate a degree of parallelism between certain American and Soviet interests—notably in containing the expansion of Chinese influences and power in southern Asia. New Delhi would like the nuclear powers to extend individual, unilateral guarantees of protection to the non-nuclear states. This would extend the "parallel collaboration" of the superpowers even further and amount to an informal ratification of Soviet-American common interests in this matter. Yet any appearance of closeness between Washington and Moscow would gratuitously antagonize Peking and expose Russia to the criticism of falling in with the "imperialist aggressor." And the ultimate objective behind Russian actions in New Delhi still remains sharply at variance with American aspirations for a non-Communist independent India.

In Russia's relations with Japan, China does not occupy such a central position as it does in Russian-Indian relations. In Japan, Moscow's prime immediate objective is to end that country's alignment with America, while the Indian government has long been totally committed to neutralism. The Sino-Soviet dispute does generate live issues in Japan, as in Moscow's effort to retain some influence when the Japanese Communist movement was oriented toward Peking. Russia also seeks to improve trade and other formal relations with the Japanese government so as to match the growth in Japanese-Chinese contacts. But its main concern is to break the American alliance, here as in all other nations around the vast Soviet periphery that have such defensive treaties and base arrangements with the United States. National security, fragmentation of the opponent's camp, and implementation of the doctrine of gradual communization motivate this effort.

From a security perspective, Japan and the Soviet Union seem to have a mutual interest in protection against a Chinese threat. But in view of Moscow's power position and ultimate objectives, neither Washington nor Tokyo will jettison their mutual alliance, the bedrock of Japan's security, in return for a vague assurance of friendship. How Tokyo would respond to a credible offer of Russian protection against China remains another, currently hypothetical, question. From Washington's perspective, the conflicting Soviet aspirations—to check China and yet to oppose "imperialist" America—clash openly in the case of Japan, with the benefits accruing only to Peking. Perhaps the Soviet Union will come to view the American-Japanese Alliance as a lesser evil that helps contain the Chinese threat.

Soviet policy in the area between Japan and India has wavered between the two extremes of opposing the United States and cooperating with it. The latter approach was pursued at some risk to Soviet standing in the Communist camp. Soviet advice to Communist China to exercise restraint regarding Taiwan aroused considerable antagonism in Peking. Moscow consistently supported a neutralist solution for Laos after 1958, though the regime that emerged in 1962 moved closer to the United States in security matters while retaining its formal neutralist orientation. In the Vietnamese War after 1960, Premier Khrushchev sought to avoid involvement; he certainly offered little encouragement to the Vietcong. By mid-1964, shortly before his ouster, Moscow seemed ready to wash its hands of all connection. The Soviet reaction to the naval incidents in the Gulf of Tonkin in August 1964, the occasion of the first American air assaults on North Vietnam, was extraordinarily mild, despite denunciation of the "imperialists" and praise of the "just war." Only after Khrushchev's ouster did Moscow express vigorous support for Hanoi, including offers to extend defensive military equipment. When systematic American bombing began, coincidentally almost simultaneously with these new Moscow-Hanoi arrangements, Soviet denunciations of Washington became more intense. However, despite their inability to stop the air attacks, Russia's new leaders continued to stress the dangers of global war and the value of peaceful coexistence. Toward the United States they adopted a new intermediate stance of tempered hostility—refusal to sponsor compromise negotiations and warnings of dire consequences should the United States step up its war effort.

The Soviets decided in the mid-1960s to remain involved in Southeast Asia because they hoped to improve their position inside the Communist world, protect North Vietnam, and compete with

China for influence in Hanoi. At the same time, they hoped to check escalation, prove that it was possible to extend communism without engaging in major wars, and preserve a quasi-normal relationship with the United States in the pursuit of peaceful coexistence. When Premier Kosygin visited North Vietnam and North Korea in February 1965, he obtained from their leaders statements in support of peaceful coexistence, though they apparently changed none of their specific policies. Washington also wanted to keep close ties with Russia and sustain the doctrine of peaceful coexistence, but it sought to do so while preventing the communization of South Vietnam. Here emerged a true case of contradiction between "peaceful coexistence" and "wars of liberation," however much Moscow tried to avoid acknowledging the existence of such a crucial dilemma.[1]

Though desirous of compromising with China, Premier Kosygin did not capitulate to Peking's demands for a radical policy of hostility to Washington, or accept the view of Mao and his colleagues that war was inevitable. Adopting a firm posture against the United States, the Russians still stressed the dangers of war and the need to avoid a major confrontation. Thus, like Khrushchev before them, the new leaders of Russia wish to maintain the struggle against the West on their own terms. This leads them to approaches that vary extensively, from cooperation with the United States to intense antagonism, often depending on world conditions beyond the control of either power. Changes in American policies and actions add other imponderables to this erratic and unpredictable relationship. In sum, the original enemies of the Cold War continue their Asian confrontations, though at times these appear less ominous than during the 1945–55 era. Both seek to restrain Peking, but China's allegations to the contrary notwithstanding, even rudimentary cooperation remains at an exalted level beyond their reach.[2]

China's Threat to the Balance in Asia

Whenever a major crisis erupts overseas, the United States must ask whether a triumph for great power X would adversely affect its security interests. If the answer is affirmative, balance-of-power doctrine holds that one should confront the opponent as far away from one's homeland as possible. There are security benefits in facing the danger at a distance and in checking the enemy before he accumulates additional strength.

However, there is always the risk of making trouble for ourselves by applying the balance-of-power doctrine against a state that means us no harm, in order merely to maintain a balance abroad. Many held that this basic fault underlay American opposition to Japan before 1941.[3] Britain's effort to check the growth of the United States in the nineteenth century on these grounds appears ludicrous in retrospect. Then, too, such extensions of a nation's commitments seriously strain its available power, especially in time of peace, and the strain is increased by the tendency of a nation's power to diminish as its forces move away from their homeland and by the need to disperse efforts to distant and widely scattered peril points. Finally, in a particular crisis, American efforts—regardless of their character or extent—may be virtually nullified by indigenous political considerations, as in the classic instance of South Vietnam in the 1960s.

Although from a broad historical perspective a Chinese assumption of regional authority in Southeast Asia would seem to parallel its assertions of suzerainty in past centuries, the historical experience is of little relevance to the current situation. Moreover, several fundamental changes in Peking's role and objectives increase the importance of containing its power.

1. Since the Communist victory of 1949, China has demonstrated both a will to dominate the entire region and a surprising ability to augment its power rapidly.

2. Because of its ideological interpretation of history, the Peking regime has come to regard the United States as its major and unchanging enemy in a struggle explicitly designed to communize the world through a heavy reliance on force, especially by Communist-led elements in the underdeveloped world.

3. This ideological framework means that the United States does not confront simply a national or territorial expansionist but a more dangerous opponent who can cloak his ambitions with political legitimacy and acquire an internationalist coloration denied to previous seekers of hegemony.

4. The creation of a base of power in Asia would vindicate China's emphasis on employing force against great physical odds, give luster to Peking's claim to have found an infallible and scientific path to world revolution, and establish the material and psychological setting for a reinvigorated effort to win over Communist parties and radical regimes to its cause in Africa and Latin America.

During the Second World War, in order to sustain the battered

Nationalist regime, the United States insisted on treating China as a great power and gave it firm diplomatic support. In consequence, China, with its vast area, resources and potential, received a permanent seat on the U.N. Security Council. Ironically, the achievements of the successor regime validated this estimate of China's inherent capability. While Washington cannot assume that the neighboring states, if communized, would cooperate with Peking in furthering its view of the world revolution, it can assume that such states, however autonomous, would be hostile to "imperialist" America.

Moreover, non-Communist Asian states, confronted with such a sudden shift in the continental balance of power, might tend to overestimate the resultant threat—even to the point of precipitating a new crisis, if only to clarify the portentous but unpredictable new conditions of their existence. Should India and Japan remain truly independent while other rimland states fell under Peking's influence, tensions would still be far greater than at present. The issue of security links with America would become such a burning political question that it could endanger domestic order in both countries.[4] The United States would face a tremendous task in proving that it would stand by them. Tokyo and New Delhi would find it almost impossible to resist domestic pressures to develop their own nuclear power, perhaps even if the United States made bilateral ironclad commitments to use nuclear weapons in their defense.

In sustaining their antagonism to the Soviet doctrine of peaceful coexistence, the Chinese have had to treat the United States as the archenemy of mankind. The frightening logic of their fanatical ideology rests fundamentally on the argument that Marxism-Leninism "proves scientifically" that the United States is by nature aggressive. Essentially, the Chinese believe, the behavior pattern of capitalism-to-imperialism-to-aggression operates "through a process independent of the human will." It is, therefore, irrelevant to speak of avoiding provocations; it is misleading even to imply that the United States might prefer peace. The Chinese leaders carry their conviction that class forms the whole basis of history to terrifying extremes: they believe that people with different class backgrounds are incapable of sharing the common traits of human nature. Consequently, they ridicule the Soviet hope for peace between "socialists and capitalists" under a nuclear stalemate that allows the Communists to extend their realm, preferably by nonviolent means.

The Chinese have, of course, negotiated with the West and reached many settlements, regarding Korea (1953), Indochina

(1954), and Laos (1962), to mention only those that provided for the end of hostilities. They claim freedom to execute such tactical compromises because, being pure of doctrine, they could never delude themselves ideologically about the ultimate purposes of their opponents, as the Soviets have done. The central trouble from an American perspective is that the act of negotiation, even when it leads to important settlements, does not seem to change the basic Chinese posture.

China's leaders treat settlements as proper tactics to avert a grave danger or as a great victory over the other side. They also interpret any compromises as the most advantageous course available at that moment to further their revolutionary objectives. They carefully avoid compromising on major strategic issues, such as arms control. To them, conciliatory American gestures are capitalist devices to trick the Communists into lowering their defenses. A true concession from the West becomes proof that the enemy is weakening, that its people want peace, and that further Chinese intransigence will carry the day.

Americans must recognize that the Chinese have many reasonable grounds for fearing the United States. We must always attempt to see what defensive considerations induce them to view their actions purely as responses to bellicose American policies and statements and the dangerous presence of American forces near their homeland. Still, we must also recognize that the empirical record in these matters does not seem vital to Peking. In plotting its course, the Chinese leadership does not distinguish between situations in which it has a reasonable argument and those in which its grievances rest on doctrinal belief.

Although the United States labors under difficult circumstances in trying to thwart Chinese ambitions, there are several reasons it must keep the paths to negotiation open on specific issues: (1) to gain allied support for the policy of firmness by demonstrating reasonableness, (2) to reach settlements on their own merits whenever possible and avoid needless crises, and (3) to demonstrate to *some* Chinese the errors of their official ideology and the feasibility of eventual strategic compromise. Such openness and receptivity are extremely difficult to maintain in a democracy whose government becomes increasingly convinced that its opponent presents the greatest menace to its own security and to the peace of the world.

Americans must also recognize that the greatest dangers are long-term in nature and that China has a limited capacity to influence events on these vital points. Moscow's refusal to place its power at the disposal of Chinese purposes further reduces Peking's capacity to mold the strategic outline of world diplomacy. Japan and India, however ambivalent and wavering, still present formidable obstacles to the growth of Chinese power. It is also painfully clear that the developed states have been increasing the gap in productivity and wealth that separates them from the less-developed lands, including China.

Even in military technology, both the United States and the Soviet Union will undoubtedly increase their superiority over China in the next decade. However, they face two crucial difficulties. First, they will continue to allocate the bulk of their strength and direct a large proportion of their attention to ends dictated by their mutual antagonism. Second, the Chinese breakthrough in attaining a capacity to produce combat aircraft, nuclear weapons, missiles, and communications equipment comprises a qualitative jump of great significance. It puts them in the same class with the others; though comparably weaker, they have become *comparable*. Given Peking's determination and proved ability to turn its limited physical capacity to great diplomatic advantage, this qualitative change may be proportionately more decisive in the balance of power than even a striking increase in America's military superiority. Nevertheless, the United States is on doubtful ground in viewing China as dedicated solely to the rapid increase of its aggressive capability, and concluding from this that Peking's relative power will continue to grow at its present impressive rate.

Leeway and Limitations

Both the historical record and a balance-of-power analysis demonstrate the persistence of American security interests in Asia. Yet, to a certain degree, events in other areas have had a major influence on the Far Eastern policies of the United States: notably, the First World War and its aftermath, the security needs of Britain in 1940–41, the consequences for Europe of the Korean War a decade later, and grave dilemmas confronting Moscow's Cold War strategy in the 1960s. Yet, as we have repeatedly become engaged in Asia's diplomatic and military crises, we have acquired many interests there, and our actions have shown that we consider certain of these interests vital to our security.

If Washington looks at its defense needs essentially in terms of

Asian considerations, it seems clear that the United States must keep a single power from attaining a position of dominance there. This requires that:

1. China be strong and independent, able to preserve itself against aggressors, but not exercising control over its neighbors.

2. The two other indigenous main power centers, Japan and the Indian subcontinent (as well as the Soviet Far East), remain independent of Chinese control, direct or indirect.

3. The smaller states in the general area remain an intermediate power zone within which Chinese power and influence can be contained. There is no absolute security requirement to hold any one line in this region, provided that the entire area does not become submerged. Theoretically, at least, there is leeway here for compromise and mutual concessions that could enhance the security of all concerned. (Yet, this sector has become a prime zone of violence, partly because the need to hold firm is not as clear as elsewhere, and partly because of local political conditions that facilitate internal war.)

To some extent, the United States can use the leverage of the Sino-Soviet dispute to advance these security objectives. Still, it must recognize that Chinese use or sponsorship of violence may well inhibit Soviet efforts to reach accommodations with the West and even undermine the doctrine of peaceful coexistence. Russia might eventually even decide to try to outdo Peking in specific anti-Western propaganda.

American security efforts must operate in a difficult political environment in relation to the non-Communist states of the region. Allied-neutral hostilities, fragmentation of security interests, conflicting national interests, and fear of Chinese power frequently inhibit U.S. efforts to create a broader and more stable defense alignment against China.

These conditions provide the background for operational decisions. Actual policies of implementation, especially their manner and timing and the treatment of complicating factors (e.g., Indonesian expansionism and the Indian-Pakistani antagonism), can come only from intensive study of the forces at work and the consequences of their interplay. It is toward this purpose that we shall consider the American-sponsored security and alliance systems, the policies and capabilities of the Chinese and other Asian Communist states, the nuclear problem, and the problems of altering American security policy in the area.

CHAPTER FOUR

Problems of Implementing
a Balance of Power in Asia

We have argued that balance in Asia is a vital American interest and that, for our generation at least, this means primarily checking Chinese power. Since Peking draws great strength from both its national power and ideological orientation, as well as from the interplay of these two forces, this task is most formidable. It is made more difficult still by the fragmentation and weakness of the region, the deep ambivalence in the Soviet position, and American uncertainty about the importance of the states lying between Japan and the Indian subcontinent.

Moreover, general agreement on this basic approach to Asia does not of itself ensure agreement on specific operations. Even in the highly unlikely case of a consensus regarding the approaches and tools to be used, there remains the problem of their proper mix at any one time. Basic guidelines do not tell us whether or how to defend the intermediate states, or what key will resolve the dispute between Pakistan and India. They provide only marginal insights on weapons policy and offer even fewer clues on policy toward the neutrals of various types on the fringes of China. Nor do they help much in deciding whether the United States should take the political initiative or adopt a more prudent line of counterthrusts against specific dangers. Since a defensive stance imposes less strain on diplomatic relations than does an offensive posture, it facilitates the organization of a firm political base on which to mount a response. But this advantage may be overbalanced by the disadvantage of constantly yielding the initiative to Peking. This drawback may be compounded by the Chinese belief, stubbornly held despite substantial contradictory evidence, that possession of the initiative somehow gives them ultimate control over events.

50

Although guidelines cannot solve such problems, it remains necessary to clarify basic interests and purposes. For these play a vital role in determining the degree and location of American commitment, and the importance of the stakes.

In seeking to implement a balance-of-power strategy in Asia, we must dispel the confusion on a wide range of operational questions that have often been intensely debated by American policymakers. Should the United States draw firm territorial lines in Asia and deploy its forces so that its intentions are unambiguous? How can the calculation of a balance-of-power strategy be related to the fluid and revolutionary societies of Asia, which are so inherently unstable? How is "flexibility" balanced with "firmness"? Should Washington not try to establish a clearer sense of priorities in its approaches toward Asia to be able to distinguish between points that are vital and points that are marginal? What about the "domino theory" that has appeared so frequently in recent discussions of the security of Southeast Asia? Above all, what should be the basic posture of the United States in its dealings with Asia, and how can it estimate the threat of Communist China?

Before turning to a more detailed analysis of both the record of American security commitments in Asia and the challenge that China poses, it would be appropriate to deal briefly with this sizable list of questions. Viewing the problem of security in Asia in terms of a balance of power will, we believe, help not only to clarify these operational issues but also to provide a coherent perspective for relating and assessing the heavy and often conflicting demands on American policy. This discussion will also attempt to provide some insights that will bear on our subsequent analyses of both the recent history of American security commitments in Asia and the policy problems confronting the United States.

Drawing Lines and Peripheral Mainland Defense

In recent years, one of the main issues of Asian strategy has been whether the United States can and should define precisely and unmistakably its limited security interests in Asia. For example, can the United States establish a firm territorial line, extending it from the old Pacific triangle (Hawaii–Alaska–Panama) to Japan–the Philippines–Australia, as Secretary of State Acheson indicated in his famous speech of January 1950? His critics subsequently charged that he invited the aggression in South Korea because he did not specifically include it within his description of America's defense perimeter. Should the United States now add those states with whom it signed defense treaties in 1953–55, even if not all are vital to American security? Must this country preserve any neutral, especially India, which comes under pressure and seeks assistance? What prime motives should underlie U.S. policy? Should Washington focus on the importance of thwarting any Communist advance because victories "prove" the efficacy of Peking's revolutionary approach and feed the flames of its global ideological aspirations? Or should Washington stress narrower power considerations—that any territorial loss undermines the sense of security of all states around China?

In seeking clarification on such issues, we may begin by noting that a broad territorial commitment loses its value unless there is an accompanying estimate of the costs involved and forces available. One form of commitment would involve only strategically important segments of the Asian mainland—e.g., the Korean Peninsula, the Mekong Delta, other delta and port areas, and selected strong points.[1] Its advocates argue that the United States could maintain this position with limited efforts that rest primarily on air and sea power. This approach is realistic in seeking to align capacity with objectives and in reflecting the traditional American view that much of this area is of substantial but not vital importance.

Yet politically, such a limited commitment is extremely unrealistic, particularly as declared policy. It would destroy all mainland alignments, for no state could settle for less than the complete defense of its territorial integrity from external aggression. Without such a commitment, enforced by an American military presence, states would flee to neutralism or succumb to enemy pressure. In a crisis, the United States might be denied access to important areas altogether. Britain, for instance, could hardly have told Malaya during the 1950s that it would secure only part of the peninsula against the guerrillas that terrorized it for ten years. The same would apply to an American refusal to protect the vulnerable northern and northeastern reaches of Thailand.

Moreover, a belated decision to intervene, like perimeter defense, runs the risk of political disaster. If much time has been permitted to elapse, the opposition probably will have won military victories; it is likely to control much national territory; it may have established a government and hold the propaganda initiative. The United States would then join the fight under the worst of military, political, and diplomatic circumstances.

American defense strategy must also take into account the transnational currents at work in Asia and should not bind itself to the compartmentalized requirements of individual states. The United States should make aggregate territorial calculations in evaluating its security position. Fundamental military considerations, including force and base requirements, lend themselves more efficiently to regional planning. Similarly, area-wide political movements (e.g., Buddhism in Southeast Asia) or regional development schemes (e.g., the Mekong River valley project) may become highly significant factors. Nevertheless, the operational point remains the territorial state, although its own interests may be internally contradictory, may be burdened with purely national requirements that run counter to the security needs of others, and may mesh imperfectly with important regional defense needs. Yet it is in this discrete setting, on a state-by-state basis, that most of the vital decisions are made. The main focus of effort must remain the nation-state, with other factors exerting their critical influences within this setting.

Levels of Violence

It is true that the focus in a balance-of-power approach has classically been on the nation-state as the basic unit of world politics, but is this applicable to the situation in Asia, where old societies are only gradually becoming effective new states? Asia is manifestly a highly volatile region; this means that stability within nations is as uncertain as stability among the nations. This means also that in Asia we must recognize new dimensions of violence in which conflicts take the forms of internal wars, indirect aggression, and border clashes, with the danger of escalation always present. How can United States power be related to these levels of violence?

Though this country has participated in some of the pivotal engagements, many of the crises and conflicts in Asia have not involved the United States. Had the United States entered them and employed larger military forces, threatened escalation, and introduced a nuclear factor, could these dangerous outbreaks have been stemmed?

In Europe, the presence of nuclear power and the bipolar confrontation, directly and through an alliance system, may have helped contain the use of force. It might, therefore, be logically argued that unambiguous Cold War confrontations of a dangerous sort would clear the atmosphere and, after a dangerous period of adjustment, contribute to Asian stability. Our Asian allies, however, would be dismayed by heavy American dependence on nuclear power, preferring to restrict the United States to an essentially "diplomatic" rather than a military reliance on such weapons to deter a showdown. From the American viewpoint, such an attitude is self-contradictory since one cannot *simulate* political will and military competence in this field against a determined and competent opponent. But, as a result of China's development of nuclear power, American declarations of a will to respond in kind to nuclear blackmail may appear less abhorrent or provocative in Asian eyes than they would have in the past. And the United States may find such declarations a diplomatic necessity, in order to reassure certain allies, despite Peking's repeated statements that it will not be the first to use nuclear weapons in warfare.

We must recognize that a Sino-American nuclear confrontation runs a serious risk of Soviet intervention, despite the deep split between Moscow and Peking. This is not simply 1949 revisited. Although China is about where Russia stood then in nuclear capability, the Russians may feel compelled to respond to an American nuclear assault against China with major defense assistance or even with counterblows, perhaps confined to the Pacific theater. Moreover, to prevent matters from coming to such a critical pass, Moscow may intervene diplomatically in the early stages of a strategic Sino-American confrontation. Fear of an American power ascendancy, concern over relations with other Communist states and parties, and estimates that silence would lead to a dangerous escalation could all play a role in inducing a Russian response. The Soviet Union might even feel compelled to act militarily within the territorial confines of China, for example, if this "fraternal brother" came under even a limited attack, such as a blow against its nuclear installations.[2]

It will be some time before U.S. nuclear policy vis-à-vis China will be centered on such problems as strategic surprise, pre-emption, and American counterforce capabilities. China's comparative weakness will make the political and diplomatic value of its nuclear weapons more significant for the present.[3] A key question becomes the political capacity and willingness of the United States (1) to have in position and ready a broad range of responses, including graded nuclear escalations, and (2) to employ these at the lowest level of damage necessary to check the advance of Communist power. Moreover, the United States must keep Peking somewhat uncertain of its intentions regarding the possible use of nuclear weapons. An ambiguous stance, if essential for its deterrent effect, could become deliberate American policy.

Such a course of deterrence and possible action, with all its potential dangers, would become necessary when the United States could not check aggression within the target state. By having a group of graded responses—with more intensive options in reserve—the United States might be able to bring an opponent to terms without necessarily threatening its vital interests. But this policy would require a radical departure from America's long-standing reluctance to commit substantial conventional forces on or near the Chinese periphery except as an emergency measure. Ironically, though the United States has demonstrated the will, ability, and ingenuity to employ a variety of low-intensity responses to aggressions since 1950, its reluctance to act has been apparent to all. The credibility of the American spectrum-of-response remains in doubt.

The Need for "Flexibility" and "Firmness"

The problem of coping with different forms of violence and of strengthening the credibility of American responses is closely associated with the basic issue of how to balance firmness and flexibility in foreign policy. Firmness is essential to ensure the credibility of a U.S. commitment, but flexibility is also basic to any sense of realism.

It is, of course, in America's direct confrontation with Communist China that the issue of flexibility and firmness has become most critical. Future critics may well conclude that this country wore a variety of intellectual blinders in its efforts to contain China over the last fifteen years. For example, during the 1950s, many of us may have seen only three major sides to the Chinese puzzle: the grand ideological foundation of China's foreign policy, the global aspects of the Sino-American confrontation, and the permanence of the Moscow-Peking tie.

The protracted failure to discern the existence of a serious split within the Communist monolith was particularly injurious, for it led the United States to deny or disparage the great policy consequences that the split generated: the contest for influence in Hanoi, disagreements over the Vietnamese War, antagonistic policies regarding India, a sharp division on the partial nuclear test-ban, and important shifts in the basic pattern of foreign trade (the Communist bloc's percentage of the China trade fell from 75 to 40 after the split). Such developments are of great significance to the preservation of an Asian balance of power and influence both national and ideological motivations in China's foreign policy. Only in Chinese propaganda do all actions appear logically related to one another and point toward inevitable success in accordance with an infallible doctrine.

But adoption of a radically different policy toward China is obviously far easier to propose than to accomplish. For example, Peking's current determination to avoid economic dependence on Moscow would seem to afford inviting opportunities for a U.S. policy designed to isolate and weaken China. Without Soviet support, China has no assured source of economic assistance, technical help, trade, and planning advice. It must, therefore, seek such help from other industrial lands in order to maintain a vigorous rate of growth. But the United States has not been able to utilize this dependence on the non-Communist world to exert leverage on Peking in disarmament affairs or in the Vietnamese War, and whether it could do so even with greatly intensified efforts is questionable. At present, the United States has even neglected to revamp its own trade policies, especially in agriculture, on the global scale needed to make others change their policies toward China. Moreover, America has not explored the possibility that an agreement between the West and Japan on a tough economic policy toward China might force Peking to end its split with Moscow on terms favorable to Russia. Nor has the United States determined how such a development would affect American interests.

American diplomacy will also have to come to terms with other consequences of the split. As the American-Chinese confrontation deepens, the Russians may enjoy greater opportunities to gain influence in Pyongyang and Hanoi. Only Moscow can protect the two smaller Communist states effectively against American power and supply the economic and defense assistance they both need. If Moscow can exploit these advantages, the result might be increased armed strength for the smaller Communist powers and a stronger Russian diplomatic position in the bloc. The net effect on American interests would be problematical since the Soviets give some support to these small aggressors even while trumpeting peaceful coexistence. But other developments are possible. These lesser Communist powers might turn the tables on Moscow and use the leverage offered by the Sino-Soviet split to gain more Russian aid and grudging Soviet acceptance of their aggressive policies. Much depends on the depth of the Moscow-Peking split, Russia's diplomatic skill in dealing with its Asian allies, ultimate Soviet purposes, and the policy motives of these small states.

By adopting the maintenance of an Asian balance as policy, the United States may intensify an inclination to contain communism in the doctrinaire and rigid manner that has already proved costly and inefficient in the fields of diplomatic recognition and trade policy. Thus, though it opens new perspectives and perhaps provides a clearer focus for policy, the effort to balance China could become a self-defeating obsession, especially if all other actions in the Far East are judged in light of their contributions to this dominant requirement.

Despite the acknowledged inertia in policymaking quarters that often blocks attempts to temper "firmness" with "flexibility," there is a countervailing tendency. Governments generally prize freedom of maneuver very highly. It gives them the capacity to adjust more readily to the unexpected; it may enable a state to keep opponents guessing; and it may prevent friends from collecting too large a diplomatic ransom for their support in a crisis. Yet adjustments on our part may lead to gross miscalculations on the part of a foe whose interpretation of reality is distorted by rigid ideology, and who prizes the initiative in his drive toward a fixed strategic objective.

The Asian policy of the United States in the late 1930s demonstrates how one can be blamed, after the event, for adopting either a flexible or a firm approach. Over-all military plans changed repeatedly in accordance with bewildering global events and the pace of America's rearmament effort. During 1935–38, Franklin Roosevelt used what little leeway he had to move slowly in adopting a new security policy for the Philippines after they gained independence (scheduled for 1946). In 1938, while condemning Japan's aggression in China, he allowed the army to withdraw the last remnants of the small military garrison—a heritage of the Boxer Uprising—from the Tientsin-Peking region. The United States hesitated on the issue of whether and when to confront Japan, hoping to avoid a two-front war, if possible. Had the United States been bound by a fixed power purpose, especially one linked to a moral obligation to fight all aggression and thwart an ideological foe, it would not have enjoyed such freedom of choice in these essential matters. A policy of cautious adjustment seemed essential at that time in view of the "Atlantic first" strategy and general military unpreparedness. Yet American flexibility appeared to some as evidence of Roosevelt's dangerous indecisiveness, related to his failure to take a firm stand that might have deterred aggression following his famous "Quarantine" speech of 1937.[4]

For the years 1940–41, however, many analysts have held the opposite view, imputing to diplomatic rigidity Washington's failure to reach a political settlement with Japan. Though military advisers favored a cautious approach, Secretary of State Hull stood fast against major concessions to Japan and so hastened the final breakdown. Clearly, protagonists in a dispute can put the label that suits their view of the national interest on any policy decision: firmness or dogmatic rigidity, flexibility or indecisive drift.

Ideally, the United States should devise and support a basic set of policy objectives, but it should be possible, nevertheless, to change them drastically if required. And rigidity in implementation should be avoided—in timing, types and sequences of actions, and priorities of objectives. The United States must constantly evaluate its national interests in light of new developments and uncover any conflicts that may develop in the relationships among its various policies. And Washington must judge whether its goals are roughly commensurate with the magnitude of the effort they entail.

Beyond our ideal conception, we must always bear in mind the numerous inevitable "distortions"—the momentum of existing policies, the emotional involvement in time of crisis, the ideological fanaticism of some protagonists, inaccurate intelligence information and appraisals, and miscalculations regarding the other side's determination. Only by recognizing and dealing with these limitations can we hope to approach a rational policy.

The Priorities Approach

If prudence and flexibility are essential for a rational security policy, and if a fixed fundamental commitment to "balance China" could reduce the likelihood of such attitudes, then the United States must seek an alternative approach that, at the very least, would highlight the variety and conflicting nature of its aspirations. It could rank its goals in importance, estimate the costs of attaining them, determine the relative likelihood of threatening developments, and decide how well capabilities accord with needs. It would then have a basis for judging the extent to which objectives are in conflict and for discerning the possibilities of cutting costs.

Hopefully, the "priorities approach" would enable this country to avoid dependence on a single theory, such as the balance of power. By itself, however, the "priorities" method cannot provide the basis for rational policy-making, for it cannot satisfactorily weigh short-range against long-range goals. Nor can this judgment be derived from calculations of cost, of the likelihood of developments, or of the capacity to respond. A priority approach tends to accept policy goals as fixed, but, in fact, they must change frequently to cope with the kaleidoscopic world situation. To cite just two examples, the determination of the United States to exorcise communism from Cuba waned markedly after the missile crisis of 1962, for communism had, in effect, been contained on that island. A decade ago, the ostensible American aim toward China altered from replacement to containment of the Peking regime, in accord with the options that were open. In short, the priorities often prove insufficient guidelines to fluid circumstances.

Even in a stable situation, with priorities established and agreed upon, their application might be inadequate for determining our response in an actual crisis. The Korean policy after 1945, based on husbanding strength for the main theater, Europe, illuminates the dilemma of choosing whether to hold forces in reserve or to take the risk of committing them early in the emergency at hand. When the attack on Korea came in 1950, the United States hedged its bets by moving decisively—on the assumption that inaction would have caused a broad erosion of its Asian security position—but at the same time withholding strategic reserve for possible use in Europe.

Today, Washington accords the security of Japan a much higher priority than that of Laos. Yet because a crisis in Laos could affect the U.S. posture in Tokyo, we must marshal at least a measured response in that small kingdom. As Vietnam has shown and Laos may yet show, Washington finds it very difficult to judge the cost of an effective response and whether rising tensions—or even the absence of tensions elsewhere—will increase the comparative importance of a given area. An effective and timely response, even in a low-priority locale, may improve the American position throughout the region simply because it represents a successful demonstration of U.S. power and will. These results might more than compensate for the "inefficient" expenditures involved.

Our intensive engagement in distant Indochina and our peripheral impact on Castro's Cuba, in defiance of the logic of geography, underline the importance of intangibles in security diplomacy. Because of general acceptance of the present rules of conduct among states, the United States could not use its vast physical powers effectively to overturn Castro. It also had to reckon with the absence of several essential factors: an effective doctrine of intervention, the support of an international organization, and an alternative regime that could claim legitimacy.[5] In Laos, not only could America stay at the request of an established regime, but it had the freedom and capacity to intervene at low cost after 1962 to thwart innumerable coups from the right and military pressure from the left. Facing a hostile Pathet Lao Communist force, which had North Vietnam's backing, Premier Souvanna Phouma could justify his call for outside assistance and still technically preserve his country's neutralized status.

The "domino theory" is a variation on the cost-value theme of priorities. It gained prominence during the Indochina crisis of 1954, when it was applied by President Eisenhower. He feared that the loss of all Vietnam would have disastrous material and psychological effects on the security of nearby states, which might then be toppled like a row of dominoes. A decade later, the same argument focused on South Vietnam.

As early as 1961, it was feared that a Communist victory in Vietnam might wreck SEATO, cause Laos to crumble, drive Thailand to neutrality, reduce Cambodia to a Chinese satellite, lead to a rapid growth or revival of insurgency in Malaya, Luzon, and Northeast Thailand, widen the gap between the neutral states and the West, and result in the expulsion of all Western bases from Southeast Asia. Peking, gaining further confidence in its doctrine that violence is indispensable for the expansion of communism, would probably sponsor such efforts even more vigorously in other parts of the world. The Chinese could assert that sustained pressure brings victories, citing the pattern of: China, 1949; North Vietnam, 1954; Cuba, 1959; Algeria, 1962; and finally South Vietnam. They would win an important debating point with the Soviet Union on taking risks against the American "paper tiger," while denying Moscow any credit for deterring the United States.

The domino theory (or Secretary McNamara's modified "wave" effect) rests on the persuasive argument that the implications of the South Vietnamese situation have become a determining factor in the future of Asian politics. However, even so powerful a concept remains only a hypothesis and should not be considered as more than a reasonable—but partial—estimate of the consequences of a debacle in Vietnam. The effects of such a defeat would be far more complex. For example, if in the course of the struggle, North Vietnam should suffer considerable damage or if extensive escalation threatened, the rest of the world might conclude not that America is a paper tiger, but that the next time (perhaps in Thailand), the United States would work more determinedly than ever to avert a similar collapse—even to the point of broadening the war. Further, in neighboring lands, there might not be the special circumstances that favor the guerrillas in Vietnam: their strong position in the South before 1959, the Saigon bureaucracy's weak administration, a partitioned state whose other half is run by a triumphant nationalist Communist party, and easy routes of access and infiltration into the defender's heartland. We should recall that the fears of a domino effect in Latin America which followed Castro's rise in Cuba proved wholly premature, even in regard to his closest neighbors, in the Caribbean. In democratic Chile, identification with Castro proved a grave handicap to the leftists in the critical election of 1964. Whatever the outcome in Vietnam, Peking will probably redouble its efforts, especially in Africa, in proportion to the growth of its resources. It will work to undermine weak states, build Communist parties, and maintain close formal ties with radical regimes. Within a few years, the results of the Vietnamese War might play only a marginal role in other local revolutionary movements.

Such instances reveal the complexities of establishing priorities. The price of intervention in South Vietnam eluded precise calculation in 1961, and the burden since then has annually exceeded the most pessimistic official projections. Even if the government were agreed on cost calculations, it might become deeply divided on the course to follow, as in the Indochinese War during April 1954. Though the priorities approach can help to order our thoughts and illuminate difficulties and opportunities, our judgments ultimately depend on more fundamental considerations.

What Basic American Posture in Asia?

A determination to contain China by creating a new balance of power in Asia without sacrificing other urgent interests still leaves the United States with a major problem: whether to remain involved all along the Chinese perimeter to the fullest extent that is diplomatically feasible, or whether to disengage somewhat, accepting setbacks and partial defeats, in the hope of inducing the states of Asia to fend for themselves more effectively—with American help becoming only supplementary.

Advocates of the present policy of almost total engagement have a powerful, realistic argument on their side: the United States is the major, if not the sole, support of the area's security. In the event of an American pullback—no matter how controlled and measured—disunity, weakness, and psychological insecurity, already endemic among the free states, might intensify to such an extent that these lands might easily collapse under the pressure of even a divided Communist movement. The American presence alone provides the cementing common link in this fragmented region. Without assured American power, economic help, and encouragement of regional cohesion, there would be little to halt the rapid disintegration of the entire area.

Yet America's very deep involvement has also contributed to its difficulties. Neutrals retain their critical attitude toward our forward defense posture in the "certainty" that the United States will bail them out in case of aggression. Allies use the engagement to pursue their own goals.

Under classical balance-of-power theory, the states on the front line bear the brunt of the burden. Those to the rear, theoretically, merely give the help needed to sustain the defenders, while extracting maximum benefit from these marginal inputs. Because of the grave threats posed first by Russia and then China, however, the United States has often been compelled to engage itself completely in Asia with less than maximum benefit, while the vulnerable target countries sometimes show surprisingly little concern for American policies or views of the common interest. The Japanese, for instance, still refuse to rearm sufficiently or undertake any diplomatic obligations that might strengthen the region's defense posture. The United States has, therefore, been forced to adopt a *policy of interposition*, in which it places itself between a target state and a potential aggressor.

The Vietnamese affair illustrates other dangers that accompany interposition of power from afar. The United States finds itself with no powerful supporters in regional security diplomacy. At one extreme, before the dramatic events of 1965, Indonesia professed fear of Chinese expansionism to justify its own Malaysian aggression, but treated the American effort in Vietnam as neocolonialism. Other major powers wish to avoid direct involvement—because of the costs, fear of China, concern over driving Moscow closer to Peking, or the requirements of "more immediate" problems. But they do not hesitate to give advice—emitting warnings, or asserting, as Japan does, that they should play a greater role in determining the course of events since proximity makes the issue more important to them.

The massive American deployments have also had their effect on Vietnamese domestic politics. Admittedly, the country has a long history of factionalism, and almost no experience with democratic self-rule. Nevertheless, the American presence has served as a protective shield that has enabled military officers to compete with one another for political power, religious sects to press for their own objectives, and other groups (students, labor unions, provincial leaders) to place their interests seemingly before national survival. The students, for example, have demonstrated for greater democracy and a larger voice for themselves in public affairs while ignoring the war, avoiding the draft, and showing little concern for the peasantry—in spite of the fact that they would stand to lose heavily with a Vietcong victory. Though such an irresponsible behavior pattern probably would have emerged in any case, the presence of U.S. troops has certainly facilitated and may have intensified these developments.

Opponents of the theory that any American retreat in Asia will lead to disintegration argue that the United States has failed to explore the possibilities of a graded scale of involvements. In linking commitments to the performance levels of the recipient countries, America might achieve better results and a healthier relationship with its allies in the long run, turning fears of withdrawal to an advantage. A threat to withdraw aid from Vietnam would be very risky but, if credible, might have a desired effect at a critical moment. Such a gambit must be used sparingly, and it begs the question somewhat, since it presupposes the existence of a substantial American commitment and an obligation to remain on the scene over the long haul. Otherwise, the threat to withdraw might boomerang and lead to a total collapse of confidence in Washington. On the other hand, a lesser threat—to curtail a particular aid program, for example—though more credible, will be far less effective in changing a nation's basic policy than a threat to eliminate aid or dismantle our alliance.

A reduction in American involvement might follow a natural course, much as the alliance system arose through an unplanned series of responses to crises. Or it could result from an explicit decision to fall back upon a less extended offshore position—perhaps the line of Japan, Okinawa, Taiwan, the Philippines, and Australia. This island perimeter does encompass a large portion of the vital American security interests and could be held even if mainland states fell to the Communists. Although a withdrawal would entail risks, it would have several positive repercussions: it would mitigate tensions with neutral states, curtail American embroilment with recalcitrant and Machiavellian allies on the mainland, and end the recurrent nightmare of continental military entanglements. The states of the area might respond by reducing their mutual hostility and giving regional defense efforts against the threat from Peking more adequate consideration, at least to the point of closer collaboration in diplomatic security policy.

Nevertheless, on balance, the costs of a pullback would be staggering. If the area fell to the Communists, maintenance of the island line would become far more burdensome than the present effort to remain in certain parts of the mainland. Collapse of the will to resist on the mainland would raise the likelihood of a similar, if less intense, development in the offshore lands. And ultimate American obligations might actually expand through the commitments of allied governments, although Washington would enjoy even less ability than at present to influence events. For example, a Tokyo-Seoul accord, a continued Australian commitment to Malaysia, or a settlement between India and Pakistan (especially if backed by Britain) might involve the United States more deeply in mainland security problems than ever before, since these allies could not fulfill their obligations on their own. Moreover, any decision regarding the Pakistani tie must take into account the strategic importance of the Indian subcontinent. Nor can Washington contemplate retrenchment from the mainland without considering its impact on Thailand and South Korea, which have remained loyal to their American commitments, and which, along with the other states of Asia would view a broad withdrawal as a betrayal. Such an abdication of responsibility would impugn American reliability everywhere and lead our opponents to doubt that even the island defense line would remain stable for very long.

American foreign policy of the period 1950–65 may be open to criticism for leading to excessive involvement on the Asian mainland. "Real estate" may have become important mainly because we said it was. This study, however, maintains that India and Pakistan are vital, and that events in other parts of the mainland affect the fate of vital areas. As our China policy demonstrated in 1941, involvement acquires a dynamic of its own.

Even those Europeans who oppose American policy toward China, who think that Washington has botched affairs in Vietnam, and who dread an Asian war that might escalate, would be alarmed by an American failure to hold fast. Surely, few would fail to draw significant conclusions from the contrast between a Soviet commitment to Cuba, in the face of enormous American power that can interdict direct Russian defense efforts, and an American withdrawal from Asian positions that it can reinforce. At a time when Peking lacks combat mobility, distant striking power, or Soviet support for aggressive initiatives, American retreat from the mainland might well presage, in the minds of Asians, a further retreat tomorrow when China's weaponry would make an offshore position as difficult to hold as our present lines are now.

The United States can do much to improve specific military policies, aid programs, and diplomatic efforts, and to enhance the flexibility of its position in the future. But for the moment, the basic U.S. security position and any hopes for a broad settlement in Asia will depend on the current alignment posture. Significant changes may be both possible and necessary—with regard to Indochina, nuclear diffusion or control, and the treatment of neutrals. But we cannot conclude that a cool appraisal of our national interests points to a large-scale withdrawal. Nor can we justify such a course by arguing that the United States is overcommitted in a distant continent, overrigid in its policy, or overemotional in its responses.

The Complex Diplomatic Setting

China's mighty shadow complicates the problems of Asian diplomacy in a somewhat paradoxical way. Other major Asian states seem to lose their international status in proportion to the degree to which they pursue policies antagonistic to Peking.

The Japanese at present have a surprisingly tenuous relationship with the other states of Asia. A wartime legacy, this condition also reveals the nation's inward and self-centered orientation. Though America has for years encouraged Tokyo to become more self-assertive, its belated gestures of "independence" often show indifference to American interests, reflecting an inclination toward closer economic and cultural ties with mainland China. Perhaps, however, only such a risky approach can enable Japan to gain trust and influence, both economic and diplomatic, among the underdeveloped states, who look with suspicion on all industrial powers. Moreover, new departures in Tokyo should not obscure the fact that China recognizes Japan as its only serious Asian rival.

It is relevant that Pakistan also found itself unable to extend its influence in Asia as long as it conveyed the image of a loyal U.S. ally, and its diplomatic forays into the Middle East encountered stiff resistance from neutralists there. In recent years, Pakistan has sought to exert greater influence in South Central Asia while adopting a course that the United States considers detrimental to the general security: friendship with Peking, isolation of a now anti-Chinese India, coolness toward SEATO, and pressure for an independent policy among the Asian CENTO powers. Meanwhile, India's fortunes have suffered reverses, including the loss of much prestige and leadership in the underdeveloped world following the Chinese border victory of 1962. This defeat, the enmity of Peking, and dependence on both Moscow and Washington for protection have caused India's influence to decline just as Indian and American policies have become somewhat more compatible.

We must recognize that the major states of Asia today cannot or will not assume the roles of counterweights to China. Rather, our Asian allies argue that undefinable long-term advantages will flow from accommodations with China. Though the United States cannot agree that they will compensate for painfully evident immediate security costs, it must be recognized that only through the pursuit of self-defined national interests can these states ultimately adopt stable foreign policies with any degree of self-confidence. And until they become stable and confident, they cannot participate effectively in a common security policy regarding China. Admittedly, this will take a long while, but no reliable shortcut exists. As we have learned in Europe, even coalitions formed by sophisticated, experienced powers against an acknowledged threat can fall into disarray under the battering of changing conditions and conflicting national interests.

The United States cannot resolve the problem of relations with the allies simply by supporting their basic interests in return for solidarity on China. The need for independent policies on China may lie at the root of the problem. Or the security price for solidarity might be too high—for instance, a Pakistani demand that the United States not arm India against China and that Washington should compel New Delhi to yield on the Kashmir issue. Moreover, we ourselves remain most reluctant to extend new guarantees against non-Communist aggressions or even to extend to neutrals our protective umbrella against Communist threats.

In its efforts to have allies provide a greater portion of the economic support and defense of the region, the United States has tried to reduce its burden and, at the same time, enhance allied cohesion through multilateral endeavors. But we have not adequately grasped the consequences of greater allied support: states that participate more fully will demand a larger voice in policy making. Any power making a substantial contribution in South Vietnam, for example, would expect to have a voice in decisions regarding escalation, negotiation, and support of a particular regime in Saigon. In 1966, with more than a division of troops engaged in combat in Vietnam, South Korea demanded a role in the strategic direction of the war. Even with a much smaller force engaged, Australia probably felt that its advocacy of a hard-line policy toward Communist threats should entitle it to carry greater weight in Vietnamese councils than other powers that were not involved. As was learned in the effort to get more flags into Thailand during the Laos crisis of 1962, considerable friction is generated when the United States tries to get allies to participate under purely American terms.

The reverse difficulty persists as well—allied "guidance" with little or no burden-sharing. France and Pakistan have become extreme examples of this attitude since 1961, after their disaffection from American policy reached significant proportions. The desire to avoid involvement in an ally's costly problems led Britain and America after 1961 to engage in two parallel, almost uncoordinated efforts to protect Malaysia and Vietnam, respectively.

Finally, the present condition of the Sino-Soviet split also suggests opportunities and limitations for American policy. Should the United States judge that its national interest lay in sustaining and widening the split, it could make this a formal policy objective. But such a decision could require thorough-going modifications of many policies, even to the extent of sacrificing other interests.

The decision to bomb North Vietnam, including the manner and underlying purpose of the raids, illustrates this point. From one perspective, the United States simply validated the long-standing Soviet warning that America is not a paper tiger, that Peking has placed an excessive emphasis on violence as the key to social change, and that even just wars of liberation can escalate dangerously. On the other hand, these attacks gave North Vietnam an opportunity to compel Moscow and Peking to converge somewhat in their policies, thereby contributing, however slightly, to one of Hanoi's most important objectives—the restoration of Communist unity. However, restrictions on targets and types of bombs, and a determination to preserve South Vietnam without destroying North Vietnam, may eventually intensify differences between Moscow and Peking.

The great Communist dispute has led, at times indirectly, to the partial test-ban treaty, some increased security for India, and a degree of stability in Laos, as well as shattering the image of communism as a monolithic unit. A longer-range dividend of the split may be that Moscow will move toward a policy of fruitful cooperation with the West, such as Rumania alleges it has been advocating for the past few years. Peaceful coexistence thus could become something more positive than a truce enforced by the balance of nuclear deterrence. But the crisis in Vietnam has demonstrated how difficult it is to sustain even a minimal common ground in an otherwise deeply hostile relationship. More specifically, it has revealed that a high degree of diplomatic skill, often absent in the key capitals of the world, is essential if the United States is to avoid a dangerous regression in its relations with the Communist states.

The American Treaty System

CHAPTER FIVE

The Chronology
of Treaty-Making

In the preceding chapters, we have traced the historical development of United States involvement in Asia, suggested that in general terms a balance-of-power strategy has served American interests in this region, and reviewed some of the principle themes and issues common to debates on Asian policy. Against this background, the stage is set for us to turn now in Part II to a more systematic and detailed examination of the formal structure of this involvement: American security treaties in Asia.

It is in these treaties that we find the most authoritative definitions of what constitute our current national commitment in Asia. American cooperation with Asian states in maintaining the balance of power and the physical bases for our military cooperation in the region are governed in no small degree by treaties. Thus, although foreign policy and the calculations of security interests must involve far more than formal treaties, such pledges of intention and commitments for future contingencies do constitute the ultimate fundamentals of policy.

Undoubtedly, the United States might like to wish away some of its commitments. Several times they have required Washington to deal with willful and unresponsive leaders, who made difficult and unreliable allies. Yet U.S. national policy cannot be determined by the temperament of allied leaders; it must respond to the imperatives of our national interest. Apart from these often long-range considerations, the United States must also choose between conflicting priorities. In the confrontation between unaligned India and the treaty ally Pakistan, Washington had to weigh Pakistan's requests against a variety of other pressures and probabilities—including po-

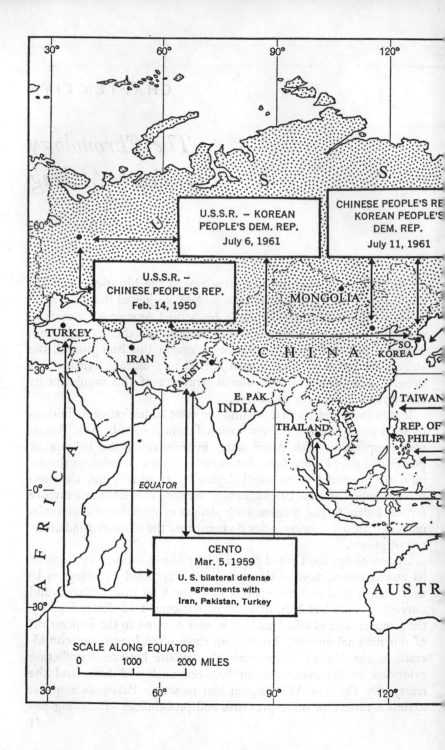

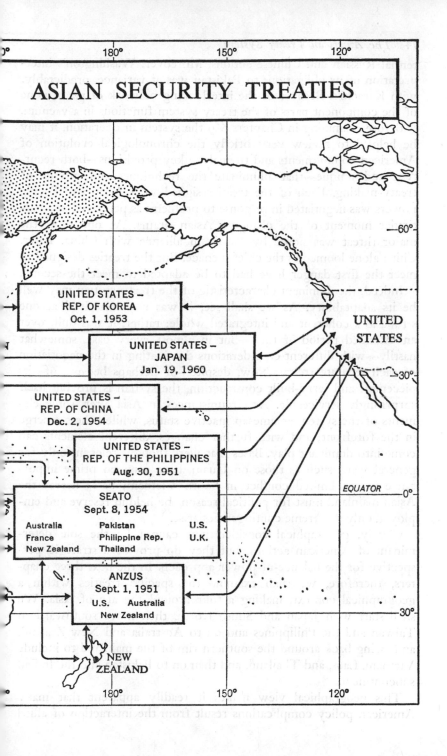

ASIAN SECURITY TREATIES

UNITED STATES –
REP. OF KOREA
Oct. 1, 1953

UNITED STATES –
JAPAN
Jan. 19, 1960

UNITED STATES –
REP. OF CHINA
Dec. 2, 1954

UNITED STATES –
REP. OF THE PHILIPPINES
Aug. 30, 1951

SEATO
Sept. 8, 1954

Australia	Pakistan	U.S.
France	Philippine Rep.	U.K.
New Zealand	Thailand	

ANZUS
Sept. 1, 1951

U.S.   Australia
New Zealand

UNITED
STATES

EQUATOR

NEW
ZEALAND

180°   150°   120°

—60°

—30°

0°

—30°

tential Russian and Chinese actions. Moreover, Washington's interpretation of its obligations to Pakistan was at variance, predictably, with Karachi's. Because of the interlocking network of pacts, none of the component parts of the treaty system functions in a vacuum.

Before examining in Chapters 6–9 the system in operation, it may be helpful to review very briefly the chronological evolution of American commitments and to analyze key provisions—both recurrent and unique—that illuminate the techniques and pitfalls of treaty-making. Each of the treaties signed with Asian and Pacific powers was negotiated in response to problems as perceived at a particular moment of the changing Asian drama. At one time, the major threat was posed by Russia in alliance with China. Later, China alone loomed as the chief menace. But the treaties designed to meet the first danger have had to be adapted to meet the second.

Indeed, the dominant characteristic of the treaty system may well be its adaptability. As we shall see, it was not conceived at one stroke as a coherent and integrated whole; rather, it was built over an extended period of time—but in almost every case, somewhat hastily—with different considerations dominating in the negotiation of each separate treaty. Now, despite—or perhaps because of—its piecemeal and jerry-built construction, the system is proving itself surprisingly serviceable. As circumstances in Asia alter, some elements of the system assume an inactive status, while others emerge in the forefront; and with further changes, different elements can come into dominant play. Bases that were thought relevant only for general wars, such as those on Guam, have assumed prime importance in the limited conflict in South Vietnam; bases nearer the Asian mainland must for political reasons be held in reserve and employed only if extreme contingencies arise.

Clearly, geographical considerations cannot be the sole determinant of American actions, but they do provide a strategic perspective for the balance-of-power approach. In the next three chapters, therefore, we shall examine the specific treaties within a geographical context, making a tour around the arc of Asia. We shall start with Japan and South Korea, then move southward to Taiwan and the Philippines and on to Australia and New Zealand, and swing back around the southern rim of the mainland to include Vietnam, Laos, and Thailand, and then on to Pakistan and the Indian subcontinent.

This geographical view makes it readily apparent that many American policy complications result from the interaction of allied and neutralist states. Since these relationships have often decisively influenced the evolution of U.S. alliance policies, we shall have to expand the analysis to include the role of the neutrals, particularly India, for its dispute with Pakistan has affected American policy.

After our geographical tour, we shall be ready to look at the treaty system of the United States from a slightly different perspective in analyzing the problems that arise out of the presence of American personnel and bases in Asian societies. We shall also evaluate the extent to which military bases may affect U.S. capabilities for maintaining a flexible military posture and may allow or inhibit change and adaptation in U.S. security policies.

Usually, shifts in policy have been accomplished without formal treaty modification. In a few significant cases, however, the United States or allied governments have exercised their prerogative for unilateral restriction or expansion of a treaty's scope. In the case of the United States, the traditional reluctance to be involved in a war on the Asian mainland has persisted, despite the Asian involvements undertaken during the Second World War, and the Congress has, on several occasions, put a checkrein on treaty commitments. In fact, the first major powers to make postwar security arrangements in Asia were the Soviet Union and Great Britain. U.S. participation lagged some years behind.

In 1949, Britain, Australia, and New Zealand began coordinated defense planning in the informal manner that is the hallmark of Commonwealth cooperation. The region covered—called ANZAM —encompassed British territories in Malaya, Borneo, and adjacent areas. Though a guerrilla war was taking place in Malaya, Australia and New Zealand did not undertake a firm defense commitment there until 1955.

The first Russian commitment was a defense treaty with Mongolia in 1946, presumably to safeguard its independence from Nationalist China. (However, when the two signatories renewed the pact in 1966, the threat they had in mind was Communist China.) The critical pact, however, brought Moscow and Peking into alignment in 1950, when a Treaty of Friendship abrogated previous accords and established a new defensive alliance. The 1950 pact extends for thirty years, and obliges the Soviet Union and Communist China to fight together against aggression by Japan or any state collaborating with Japan. Like other postwar Soviet security treaties, this arrangement invoked Article 107 of the U.N. Charter, which authorized alliances against former Axis powers. This approach allowed the Russians to derive some propaganda advantage from commitments against the West without appearing overtly hostile or provocative.

Although the Truman Administration had rebuffed British attempts to involve the United States in the defense of Southeast Asia, the June 1950 invasion of South Korea—far to the north of any Commonwealth territory—evoked a swift U.S. response. It evoked, as well, recognition of the new diplomatic and power situation in Asia. In 1951 and 1952, the military effort was bolstered by a group of treaties, among which the U.S. bilateral security pact with Japan played the pivotal role. This treaty, which came into force April 28, 1952, allowed American forces to remain in Japan to protect that country against outside attack and also, at Tokyo's request, to help in putting down externally instigated riots and large-scale disturbances. The assessment of Japan's capabilities is evident even in the preamble to the treaty, which depicted a weak country, unable to defend itself and requiring American protection. The treaty forbade Japan to grant military bases to a third power without U.S. consent. It was open-ended in two senses: it had no terminal date and permitted the United States to use its armed forces stationed in Japan in any way that Washington deemed necessary to keep the peace in the Far East.[1] Both parties found the treaty in need of modification and revised it extensively in 1960.

In light of the new realities in Asia, the United States also launched a thorough-going reversal of its hands-off policy in Southeast Asia. In 1951, the United States completed a defense pact with Australia and New Zealand (the ANZUS treaty) and one with the Philippines. These took effect on April 29 and August 27, 1952, respectively. Their timing, so close to that of the treaty with Japan, reflected an inescapable political fact: only by making pacts with them could the United States win the support of these countries for a settlement with Japan. All three feared and distrusted Japan, but Australia in particular had lost confidence in the security value of the Commonwealth and was not sure how much to rely on American assistance. In New Zealand, as well as in Australia, there was considerable uncertainty over the proper security stance to take in Asia and how to square this with professed political interest in improving relations with the lands to the north[2]—notably Japan, which they feared might gain diplomatic freedom to maneuver between the two major blocs and bargain its way to an impressive power position once more.

ANZUS was a collective defense arrangement, under which "each party recognizes that an armed attack in the Pacific area on either of the parties would be dangerous to its own peace and safety and declares that it would act to meet the common danger in accordance with its constitutional processes." The reference to constitutional processes, a standard clause in all these treaties, was inserted in reaction to the NATO arrangement, with its seemingly automatic commitment which had led the U.S. Congress to insist on a clear recognition in future treaties of its power to declare war.[3]

Australia considered the treaty less than ideal, for Washington refused Canberra's request for a guarantee of the island barriers, lying just north of Australia. Australia also thought the treaty's diplomatic machinery somewhat inadequate. But there was a provision for annual meetings of the three Foreign Ministers, and useful military staff consultations have evolved.[4]

The almost concurrent Philippine treaty had the same joint defense clause—a promise to act against any armed attack on either state in the Pacific area, in accordance with each signatory's constitutional processes.[5] This bilateral accord did not provide for consultative machinery equivalent to the tripartite ANZUS apparatus, though a U.S.-Philippine Mutual Defense Board was established in 1958.[6] On the other hand, while no American forces were stationed in Australia or New Zealand, U.S. air and naval forces did remain in the Philippines after it gained independence, and their status was unaffected by the 1951 treaty.

The next addition to the treaty system came in 1953, when Washington pressed Seoul to agree to an armistice to end the Korean War. The treaty represented an American concession to President Syngman Rhee in return for his agreement to support the truce and to moderate his campaign to "go north." The pact, signed in October 1953, provided for consultation in response to a threat against either party and a commitment to act in case of attack, "in accordance with [the signatories'] constitutional processes."

The pact also allowed the United States to dispose its forces in and about the Republic of Korea as determined by mutual agreement. The wording of the treaty covered all Korea, provided that unification was attained by peaceful means.[7] This last proviso reflected and underscored the delicate balance between President Rhee's aspirations to end Korea's division by force and the limited extent of American commitments and interests. A 1954 agreement pursuant to the treaty placed South Korean forces under the U.N.

Command, giving the United States operational control of the Korean army as long as the Command remained responsible for the country's security.

The last two American treaties were arranged about a year after the Korean accord. The Southeast Asia Treaty Organization (SEATO) pact took effect February 19, 1955, and the treaty with Nationalist China entered into force March 3, 1955.

Although the SEATO alliance marked a new departure for U.S. policy, involving commitments with nations on the mainland of southern Asia, the wording of the treaty in many respects resembled that of the previous pacts: Article 4, Paragraph 1, states that armed aggression in the treaty area against any signatory menaces the safety of all and binds the others to act against this common danger in accordance with their constitutional processes. Originally, all action required unanimous consent of the parties, but this provision was later modified to permit abstentions.

From the outset, the United States had carefully qualified its commitment with an "understanding" limiting its response to cases of *Communist* aggression and armed attack. In the event of other aggressions or attacks, Washington affirmed merely its willingness to consult, referring in such instances to Article 4, Paragraph 2, which deals only with the *threat* of armed attack or with a "situation which might endanger the peace of the area." In this provision, the SEATO treaty paralleled the U.S. accord with South Korea, reflecting traditional American reluctance against being dragged into an Asian land war.

Article 4, Paragraph 2, was also designed to provide the legal justification for action against subversion, calling on members to "consult immediately" on measures "for a common defense" if the integrity of the territory or sovereignty or political independence is "threatened in any way other than by armed attack." The concept of obliging treaty members to help "prevent and counter subversive activities directed from without against their territorial integrity and political stability" (Article 2) represented an important extension of the traditional coverage of defense arrangements.

In other ways, however, the treaty was somewhat circumscribed. Australia added its understanding that it would not intervene in a conflict between two Asian Commonwealth powers. No combined Command and headquarters system, such as NATO, was provided —despite the urging of Thailand, Pakistan, and the Philippines—and the signatories restricted the treaty further by setting its northern limit at latitude 21°–30″N.[8] This demarcation, excluding both Taiwan and Hong Kong from its jurisdiction, confirmed the earlier failure of Secretary of State Dulles to weld all fronts facing China into a firm anti-Communist coalition ready to act in every sector in response to Communist aggression at any one point. On the other hand, there was a proviso that the treaty area could be extended to cover "any state or territory which the parties by unanimous agreement may hereafter designate" (and with the consent of that state and territory). Following this procedure, the original signatories—the United States, the United Kingdom, France, Australia, New Zealand, the Philippines, Thailand, and Pakistan—designated Cambodia, Laos, and "the Free territory under the jurisdiction of the State of Viet-Nam" as coming under the pact's protective mantle. By unanimous agreement, this guarantee was incorporated into a Protocol that came into force simultaneously with the treaty. Though all three Indochinese states at first favored this protocol, Cambodia soon rejected SEATO protection, and its ruler embarked on a course of neutralism that became more stridently anti-Western in tone with the passing years. The neutralization of Laos in 1962 left only one Indochinese state—South Vietnam—under SEATO's umbrella.

Though it still has no supreme field command with assigned forces, SEATO has had some success in military planning and coordination at the conventional-war level. Its Military Planning Office and its senior planning and advisory bodies have been functioning with reasonable effectiveness. They produce contingency plans, updated as conditions change, for dealing with possible acts of aggression in the area, assigning obligations and functions to each treaty member. Various military exercises, standardization of training, and experience in coordinated planning have had a favorable cumulative impact—even inducing some Asian members to adjust their own national military plans to SEATO concepts.

Beyond this military effort, which is associated primarily with the American position in Thailand and the Philippines, SEATO conducts technical and political operations. Expert committees in technology, intelligence, and the like—most of them affiliated with the Secretary General's office in Bangkok—meet regularly and make significant if limited contributions. SEATO's political operations, apart from the annual meetings of the Council itself (usually attended by Foreign Ministers), are maintained by the diplomatic mission heads in Thailand, who meet frequently as representatives of the Council, and by the first secretaries of these embassies, who are formed into Permanent Working Groups for continuity. In addition, there are three expert committees—on economics, security, and educational-cultural-labor affairs—plus various *ad hoc* bodies.

In the last new security treaty to enter into force—the pact with Nationalist China—the United States limited its formal territorial commitment to the islands of Taiwan and the Pescadores. The United States assumed the standard obligation to meet the common danger of an armed attack in accordance with its constitutional processes. Employing language very similar to that of the SEATO pact, the treaty also provided for mutual help in resisting Communist subversive activities directed from without against either signatory's territorial and political stability.[9]

The Senate Committee on Foreign Relations attached three very important understandings or reservations to the treaty, to spell out the limits of American obligations. The first concerned claims by both Chinese camps to clear title to Taiwan and the Pescadores. The Senate noted that the treaty in no way modified their legal status, thus leaving the United States uncommitted on the question of ultimate sovereignty. Further, it stated that Washington would act only if the Nationalists had to fight in self-defense. In this way, it hoped to protect the United States from a sequence of events in which a Nationalist effort to return to the mainland would lead to counteroffensive endangering the security of Taiwan, and so involve America in a war. However, a strong Nationalist military position on the offshore islands prevented this limitation from becoming clear-cut. Since the treaty was completed in the midst of a Chinese Communist assault against the offshore islands of Quemoy and Matsu, the question of American commitments to repulse attacks against these targets plagued Washington from the outset. Finally, to avoid a unilateral widening of the conflict beyond the treaty area, the Senate made its approval a precondition for any expansion of the commitments to other territories.

In effect, this Senate action "released" Chiang Kai-shek two years after President Eisenhower, in his first inaugural address, had freed the Nationalists from any restraints against their military activities. Eisenhower's 1953 statement had been an attempt to fulfill the desire of the Republican party to support Nationalist objectives and remove the restrictions imposed in 1950 when President Truman had stationed the Seventh Fleet as a barrier against military actions by the Communists and Nationalists against one another.[10] By

1955, since the Nationalists' inability to sustain a unilateral effort on the mainland had become evident, the defense treaty then coming into force served as a compromise arrangement that simply ratified the obligation undertaken in the aftermath of the North Korean invasion of 1950.

A decade of making security treaties was climaxed in 1960 by the Japanese Diet's passage—after a stormy session and prolonged street demonstrations—of a revised Japanese-American security pact. This capped years of careful and difficult negotiations in which each party strove to protect its own interests while moving toward a more equitable and durable military arrangement.

As these efforts were taking place, Sino-Soviet relations were undergoing a series of dramatic developments unknown to the outside world. It was the Chinese who revealed in 1963 that Moscow and Peking had concluded an agreement in October 1957 on "new technology for national defense," but that the Russians had unilaterally abrogated this in June 1959 "and refused to provide China with a sample of an atomic bomb and technical data concerning its manufacture." [11]

Nothing so spectacular was involved in the American-Japanese treaty revisions, but they brought a considerable change in Japan's status. They restored full sovereign powers to Japan in its four home islands, but American control over the Bonin and Ryukyu islands remained as before. The preamble's reference to a weak and submissive Japan was eliminated, and Japan assumed the obligation of full responsibility for its internal security. Although the pact allowed American forces to stay on in Japan, they were no longer permitted to intervene in riots and disturbances. Japan regained the right to negotiate security arrangements with other powers. However, the revision reflected Tokyo's desire to restrict its involvement in Asian security problems to its own territory, stating that an attack on either party *in Japan* constituted a common danger that the two signatories would meet together. [12] Unlike the previous accord, this pact was made subject to abrogation after 1970 by either party upon one year's notice.

Tokyo and Washington could not agree on their respective rights concerning two key issues: the basing of nuclear weapons in Japan and the redeployment of American forces from Japanese bases to combat areas. Clearly, American freedom on these points could involve Japan in foreign crises against its will, yet Washington refused to tie its hands in advance by giving Japan a veto. In an uneasy compromise, the two signatories exchanged notes in which Washington pledged "prior consultation" before acting on these matters.

Since 1960, there have been no fundamental changes in the Asian treaties, though various modifications have been made on the periphery of the great-power confrontations. In 1961, the North Koreans signed separate defense treaties with the two major Communist rivals—Moscow and Peking. In the spring of 1962, at Bangkok's urging, Secretary of State Rusk negotiated an agreement with the Thai Foreign Minister, Thanat Khoman, that recorded an American understanding to come to the aid of Thailand in case of an attack, regardless of the response of other SEATO members. Thailand believed a direct and bilateral American tie—in no way conditioned upon unanimous agreement of all signatories—was essential to its security. With good reason, Thailand had begun to doubt SEATO solidarity. France and Pakistan had demonstrated a profound disenchantment with the allied treaty system after 1960, and as the decade wore on, both gave numerous indications of their *de facto* disengagement from their commitments. Finally, under the Geneva agreement of 1962, Laos was neutralized and removed from the SEATO umbrella. Though the three-part domestic coalition under neutralist leadership that was to have sustained this accord quickly broke down, the governent of Souvanna Phouma maintained the formality of this arrangement. Laos remained technically neutral even while the war for Vietnam raged across its eastern border.

Thus, the United States by the mid-1960s had a variety of security commitments around the arc of China. In some areas, it was protecting an ally who had been subjected to military assault at one time or another, as in the divided lands of Korea, Taiwan, and Vietnam. It had military units stationed in most of these lands; in fact, by 1965 all treaty and protocol states except Australia and Pakistan had had U.S. forces based in their territory. However, in the northern Asian states of South Korea and Japan, the size of these contingents gradually diminished, whereas in Southeast Asia a significant buildup occurred in conjunction with the Vietnamese war. While ties of alliance with some (especially Pakistan and France) frayed almost to the breaking point, relations with others (for example, Thailand) improved after a period of tension. Still other connections—such as those with Japan, Australia, the Philippines, and Nationalist China—remained on a relatively steady keel despite continued public uncertainty or policy disagreements.

A study of the evolution and current status of these alliances by geographic region—going from Northeast to South-central Asia—highlights one further problem: the difficulty of bringing about even rudimentary cooperation in the security diplomacy of non-Communist Asian states. The best prospect for some kind of indigenous Asian diplomatic front against China now depends on the possibility—admittedly slight—of collaboration between aligned Japan and neutral India. That we now contemplate such a problematic development, which incidentally would afford very little hope for substantial progress in the security field in the immediate future, illustrates both the complexities and difficulties of planning and implementing a coherent regional security policy.

CHAPTER SIX

The Western Pacific Allies

From this historical overview of American treaty obligations, we now proceed to a more detailed examination of the implications of each of the treaties in themselves and as dynamic parts of the whole. Since our analysis should be in a strategic context, we shall retain the geographic approach. In doing so, and by beginning with Japan, we shall also be starting with the country with which the United States initiated its system of alliance.

From almost every vantage point, Japan is the most important American ally in the Pacific. Recognized by China as its main rival in Asia, an independent Japan, with its enormous industrial capacity, is absolutely essential to the preservation of any regional balance of power. The Japanese, still strongly nationalistic, have rejected communism at home and have repeatedly demonstrated a fear of Soviet and Chinese intentions. They have no desire to break their strong political and economic ties with America and seek to strengthen their connections with Western Europe. Yet their security tie with the United States has been under strain from the start, racked by profound countervailing emotions: fear of involvement in war, an inclination toward neutralism, and hostility to a revival of militarism. Moreover, many Japanese are determined that their country shall live harmoniously with its neighbors in Asia—a determination that springs not only from their feeling of guilt toward China and their desire to make amends for earlier wrongs, but also from their apprehensiveness over American withdrawal.

These sentiments reflect basic inconsistencies in the Japanese assessment of their security position: (1) The American treaty has involved Japan in dangerous power politics and may invite an assault; yet Japan fears its neighbors and wishes an assured, though less evident, American protective mantle. (2) Japan does not desire a large military force and seeks to avoid both the risks of a revival of militarism and the economic burden rearmament entails; yet without the presence of adequate forces, its leaders believe, the country could be subjected to blackmail from mainland China and would be an exceedingly attractive target for aggresion. Such various and sometimes contradictory attitudes, many antedating the peace treaty of 1951, helped to trigger the explosive riots that accompanied the treaty's revision in 1960, while at the same time limiting the riots' scope and impact.

Ending the Japanese Occupation

The divergent views within the American government on how to deal with postwar Japan in the unprecedented Cold War environment reflected American ambiguities as complex and persistent as those in Tokyo. The debate centered on the problem of ending the Occupation.[1] The argument for swift termination, supported by the State Department and General MacArthur, rested on the premise that only through independence and a reassertion of initiative could Japanese friendship toward the United States become a reliable factor in diplomacy. However, the Department of Defense did not wish to jeopardize existing security arrangements, and until the Korean War, it opposed any significant reduction in Occupation powers.

Similar hesitations arose over the establishment of a national police force and of a security force for Japan. Since Article 9 of the Japanese Constitution forbade "land, sea, and air forces, as well as other war potential," General MacArthur hesitated to increase the number of Japanese police, despite a recommendation in 1948 by the U.S. National Security Council for creation of a 150,000-man force. Only after the start of the Korean War did a 75,000-man group—later to evolve into the Self-Defense Force—come into being.

Further, because of neutralist sentiment in Japan and the limited security capabilities of the American Occupation force, some Americans even questioned whether Japan was defensible and whether it was advisable to undertake any substantial security obligation whatsoever there. In 1949, in a widely reported off-the-record press conference with American newsmen in Japan, Secretary of the Army Kenneth Royall alarmed the Japanese by favoring withdrawal of American troops.[2] Royall termed U.S. Occupation forces inadequate to protect the country against a major Soviet attack and stated that America's major concern was Europe, whose defense would tax the limited forces then available. The reaction to Royall's statement from leading American military officials was sharply negative, and there was a prompt reassertion of the American commitment to Japan.[3] Both the speech by Secretary of State Acheson in January 1950—excluding Taiwan and Korea from the sphere of vital U.S. interests but specifically encompassing Japan in the area America would safeguard—and the security arrangements of 1951–52 validated this historic American commitment. However, with the emergence of Communist China as a major potential threat, in addition to the more immediate danger from the Soviet Union, the problem of defending Japan became acute. At issue were the size of the American presence, the nature of U.S. installations, and the re-establishment of a Japanese armed force. All these, in turn, depended on Japanese domestic politics, as indeed did the security pact itself.

In November 1949, General MacArthur, as Supreme Commander for the Allied Powers (SCAP), raised the possibility of a separate peace treaty without Soviet participation and linked to an American defense treaty. The Japanese response was extremely hesitant, for the pro-American Premier Yoshida Shigeru doubted that the Japanese public would support such a move.[4] Yoshida moved very cautiously through this political minefield, aware that only a minority (20.5 per cent in a November 1949 poll) favored dependence on the United States for the nation's security. He first spoke of a treaty involving all the powers and specifying continued disarmament. Only gradually in 1950, and with election victories behind him, did he claim the right for Japan to have self-defense forces, imply a willingness to sign a separate peace, and favor a new security-base arrangement with Washington.[5] Meanwhile, the advocates of a neutralist Japan had been expounding their views vociferously. In 1950, under the leadership of the Peace Problem Council, they demanded withdrawal of all foreign forces, economic independence, and security through neutrality, inviolability, disarmament, and membership in the United Nations.

The Korean War acted as a major catalyst for the decisions about Japanese sovereignty and security. The firm American response to North Korea's aggression resolved Japanese doubts, at least temporarily, regarding the American will and commitment to protect what was ultimately a Japanese vital interest, the security of South Korea. Though America stripped its security forces to the bone in

Japan, that country remained a loyal base, aiding the war effort with a minimum of friction. The establishment of a national police force, the quashing of Communist agitation, the decline in Communist popularity, and the continued strength of the Yoshida Administration all reinforced Japanese support. Public-opinion polls in September 1950 revealed a pro-American sentiment (55 per cent favorable to the United States, as against o per cent for Russia, 22 per cent neutralist, and 23 per cent other or don't know). A majority (54 per cent, against 28 per cent opposed) agreed that Japan needed military forces. Approval of American bases was at its all-time high, 30 per cent, with 38 per cent opposed and 32 per cent uncertain.[6] Though the Socialist Party favored neutrality and opposed a security pact with America, the issues of a separate peace and rearmament led to a split into Right and Left factions over the peace treaty of 1951. The Right-wing Socialists supported the separate peace settlement and recognized the need for self-defense forces; the Left-wingers stood for neutralism, a peace treaty signed by all, and no rearmament.

In September 1951, both the peace and the security agreements were signed. The peace treaty liquidated the war as far as the Western powers and their allies were concerned and restored Japanese sovereignty. Japan committed itself to the principles of the U.N. Charter, though it was not yet a member of the organization, and accepted the territorial losses of 1945. It also agreed to reach reparation accords with its old enemies and to refrain from using force in international relations. The security pact allowed Americans to remain in Japan to fight "against armed attack from without" and to aid Japan, upon Tokyo's request, "to put down large-scale internal riots and disturbances in Japan, caused through instigation or intervention by an outside Power or Powers."

The Post-Occupation Era

Japanese attitudes toward the American alliance after the end of the Korean War took a new turn, reflecting a feeling of weakness and dependency, a nationalist restiveness, and irritation over a series of issues, including the constitutionality both of American bases and of Japan's growing but still small self-defense effort.[7] The issue of the bases was actually litigated, and a lower court ruled them unconstitutional but was overruled by the Supreme Court of Japan on December 16, 1959. Though the Court was unanimous, ten of the fifteen justices felt impelled to give their divergent reasons. Essentially, the Court held that the right of self-defense, retained by Japan, implies the right to obtain security guarantees and forces from others. It also ruled that this high policy decision, arrived at constitutionally, fell outside the scope of judicial review. This crucial decision ended the legal arguments and thus dissipated much of the political pressure against the defense treaty.

The Socialists endeavored to sustain a feeling of neutralism and an anti-American "Pro-Asian" sentiment during the 1950s. The resurgence of nationalism, inevitable with the end of the American Occupation, afforded them a major opportunity, linked to the new national aspirations for prosperity and reform. To a great extent, however, they found their appeal blunted by Hatoyama Ichiro, a conservative who succeeded the pro-American Yoshida as Premier. Playing on desires for independence in order to steer an opportunistic course between the true neutralists and the advocates of close cooperation with Washington, he sought with modest success to improve trade with China and regularize relations with Moscow. In 1955, Moscow and Tokyo re-established diplomatic ties, arranged fishing rights, and cleared the way for Japan's entry into the United Nations. But Japan's claim to some of the Kurile Islands and her request for a formal peace treaty were denied by the Russian negotiators because Hatoyama would not agree to the Soviet demand for an end to the American security connection. The Premier never intended to break his ties with the United States, but he hoped to use the greater leeway Japan then enjoyed to bargain for better treaty terms from the Soviets. Though he played down the American-oriented aspects of his diplomacy at home, he stressed friendship with the United States abroad. He was also willing to press rearmament, even more vigorously than Yoshida, provided the United States financed the greater share of the burden.

Egged on by both Moscow and Peking, Left-wing Socialist leaders had decided around 1957 that militant anti-Americanism was good politics, for the Socialists had been gaining ground in each national election. After the two wings had reunited in 1955, the radical segment gained ascendancy within the party and now hoped to use this issue to win a national election against the conservative Liberal-Democratic Party that had also united in 1955. While visiting in China in March 1959, Asanuma Inejiro, the Socialist Party leader, even went so far as to concur with his hosts that "American imperialism is the common enemy of the Chinese and Japanese peoples."

This unofficial statement appeared too extreme even to his supporters and was effectively exploited by the opposition in the months
that followed. Moreover, the statement split his own party, and in
January 1960, the Socialist right-wing formed its own Democratic
Socialist Party.

Neutralist attitudes also persisted among the conservative right. A
combination of nationalist sentiment, interest in the China trade, and
unwillingness to become engaged in America's broader defense
problems led many conservatives, businessmen, and military thinkers to espouse a separation from the United States. A former military officer, Colonel Tsuji Masanobu proposed development of a
force without offensive potential that nonetheless could impose
unacceptable penalties on an invader, the most likely being the Soviet Union, which would not wish to divert power from its primary
objective, the United States. In effect, he was counting on American
power but offering nothing in return. Though this view did not receive any significant conservative political backing, it did reflect a
strand of isolationist conservative thought.

General public sentiment reflected, though less sharply, the uneasiness behind these extreme positions. Premier Kishi Nobusuke,
whose public stand on America fell between the Hatoyama and
Yoshida positions, held office from early 1957 until after the passage
of the revised U.S. security treaty in 1960. Much like Yoshida before him, he had to move carefully in improving Japan's position
within the framework of a continued American tie, for polls during
1953–57 showed its growing unpopularity. When asked the best
way to maintain their security in 1957, 37 per cent favored Japanese
forces, 27 per cent were for collective security, and only 4 per cent
wanted American forces. Meanwhile, those who thought that Japan
needed military forces in any event totaled 64 per cent, a rise of 10
per cent since 1950. As to amending the Constitution to allow rearmament, however, only one-third approved this during 1952–57,
whereas the opponents increased from 42 to 52 per cent during that
period.[8]

Such revision of the Constitution, which would require a two-
thirds majority in the legislature, has become a powerful issue for
the Socialists. They can rally opposition support from pacifists and
neutralists, as well as from those who fear a resurgence of militarism
and cultural authoritarianism in the wake of any large-scale rearmament. Although many conservatives favor such a chauvinist resurgence, they recognize its unpopularity, and have not dared to at-

tack the Socialist position. So pervasive is the fear of a revival of militarism that needed reforms in the military establishment, which might have been construed as steps in this direction, were slow in coming. As late as 1965, Premier Sato Eisaku, though deeply concerned about Japan's military vulnerability, did not feel it politic to try to raise the National Defense Agency to Cabinet level.

American bases found little favor, with the approve-disapprove percentages changing, respectively, from 27-48 in 1953 to 18-60 in 1957 and 8-58 in 1958. In 1958, the main reasons given for opposing the bases were: they constituted an offense to national pride, Japan's own forces were adequate, and the bases might bring involvement in war. Such views were also expressed in 1955, when 19 per cent thought that bases aided Japanese security and 43 per cent held that they endangered the peace of Japan. More significant for the future was the fact that in 1957 only 16 per cent favored and 60 per cent opposed a promise by the Japanese government to allow American bases to remain on Okinawa in the event of its return to Japan.[9] The 1951 treaty had left the island under American jurisdiction, permitting the United States complete freedom to use it as a military base.

In broad political terms, the Japanese people continued to be predisposed toward America on global questions. In 1957, 39 per cent said that America worked harder for peace while only 3 per cent named Russia, and with 38 per cent answering both; the United States also won handily the popularity contest as the most-liked nation, receiving 27 per cent, with India (cited by 6 per cent) next. On whether Japan should be pro-American or pro-Soviet or neutralist, the percentage tabulations went 35-1-38 in 1953 and 53-1-17 in 1959. Despite this marked pro-Americanism, recognition of Communist China won favorable though moderate support in 1958. Although only 4 per cent desired recognition of Communist China instead of Taiwan, 25 per cent wished to recognize Peking while expressing uncertainty regarding Taiwan; and 24 per cent desired relations with both. On the other hand, 30 per cent opposed recognition of Peking.[10]

Treaty Revision

With full awareness of these ambiguous attitudes, Premier Kishi sought agreements with the United States satisfying a variety of Japanese national aspirations. In 1957, he persuaded Washington to halve its forces in Japan to 65,000 (they were later halved again), turn over numerous military facilities to Japan, and release the last eighty war criminals held by the Americans. Japan ended its role as the only American ally making contributions to the maintenance of American forces. However, Japan's rearmament projections continued far below the level Washington thought necessary, though the force totals had been sharply reduced from Secretary Dulles' 1953 proposal of 350,000 men. By 1960, the army was below its projected size of about 180,000 soldiers and 1,300 planes. But it did comprise 13 divisions of about 8,000 men each, thereby attaining a capacity for expansion at a future date.

By 1959, negotiations over revision of the security treaty moved into the final stage. The Premier's party had won the crucial lower-house election of 1958 with 57.8 per cent of the vote (more than 63 per cent, with the backing of sympathetic independents). Kishi correctly gauged that the Socialists had overstepped popular bounds with the Asanuma statement in China and their bitter campaign against the American tie. Elections in 1959 reversed the trend of small but steady Socialist advances in the popular vote and legislators elected.[11] But if the Socialists were out on a limb, so was Kishi. For the people would tolerate the treaty only so long as it assured Japan's security without risk or significant cost. Majorities in surveys continued to oppose the bases, despite the fact that fewer favored neutrality and still fewer felt friendly toward Peking. Support for the government's policy of cooperation with America ran 21 per cent yes, 8 per cent no, with 43 per cent maintaining that there was no alternative. Many vehemently opposed the presence of nuclear weapons on their soil and continued to reject a significant rearmament effort, asserting that the weak Self-Defense Forces could do the job without outside help or new equipment.

The 1960 security treaty restored important rights to Japan. It removed all derogations of sovereignty in the 1951 accord. The treaty also mentioned respect for the Japanese Constitution—an implied American recognition that Japan could not legally send troops from its shores or engage in anything but self-defense.

The American position was that the United States had made two major concessions in the 1960 security pact: by acknowledging that Japanese forces could be used only for self-defense, it had reduced the danger of Japan's involvement in areas beyond the four home islands (even Okinawa or American naval vessels not far from Japanese home waters). In addition, America assumed the commitment to treat an attack on Japan as an attack on itself. Furthermore, Japan undertook no obligation to increase its very small defense expenditures by any significant degree.

Nevertheless, in Japan, the treaty's opponents, who had unleashed powerful street demonstrations in 1959, became even more vehement in 1960, when the treaty terms became public. Defending the new accord, Kishi maintained that it deprived America of substantial existing freedoms in Japan, and the accompanying note of understanding bound Washington to consult on the two most objectionable points: the stationing of nuclear weapons in Japan and the deployment of U.S. forces from Japanese bases. Kishi noted that this arrangement was both logical and effective since Washington could not act against Tokyo's will in a crisis without generating such hostility that it would make the American position untenable. This argument, though seldom explicitly advanced, is an underlying reality that Washington diplomats have had to face in dealing with even their smallest ally.

Nor was this factor resolved then or later in Japan. The spectacular riots that accompanied the ratification in June 1960 are an instance of the paralyzing impact such hostility can have. Though the riots are worthy of a study in themselves, here we can note only that the minority, bitterly opposed to the treaty, gained the temporary support of the uncertain majority by exploiting fear of unwitting involvement in dangerous American military operations and fear of Soviet missiles, then regarded—even among some American experts—as giving the Soviet Union strategic superiority.[12] Such fears seemed to be substantiated by the U-2 incident, by the lack of a veto over American actions, and later by the "move-first-inform-afterwards" type of "consultation" that the United States employed in moving airpower from Japan to Southeast Asia in 1962 and 1964. Japanese opposition toward the treaty was heightened by what many considered to be the high-handed tactics used by the Premier to push ratification through the Diet and to coordinate its effective date with President Eisenhower's projected visit.

With the passage of the treaty, the antagonisms subsided. The pro-American conservatives retained power, with the moderate Ikeda Hayato winning an election in 1960 after defending the treaty and criticizing neutralism. Yet Japanese-American security relations remained uneasy. Since the treaty may be legally terminated by either party in 1970 on one year's notice, any worsening in conditions before then may bring an end to the accord. There are several danger points.

1. Japan fears for its own security and is aware of the inadequacies of its defense. Yet, though it is modernizing and improving its defense establishment, it has not decided to arm to the level required for adequate self-defense. Most underdeveloped states spend around 5 per cent of their GNP for security; a much wealthier Japan allocates under 2 per cent, less than one-eighth of the proportion allocated by its far poorer neighbor China.

2. The Japanese recognize the importance of American protection. Yet their inability to control their protectors poses the danger of unwilling involvement in distant wars.

3. The emergence of China as a nuclear power confronts Japan with a grave choice: whether to develop its own bomb, to rely more heavily on the United States, or to try to maintain the present course of gradually increasing independence. A fourth choice, to enter China's orbit, is considered unacceptable today. Any of the other three routes presents grave security dangers. Japanese abhorrence of the weapon that wrought such great destruction in their land in 1945 makes the whole issue even more emotional and difficult to handle.

4. A specific problem, the future of Okinawa, remains a great point of possible danger in relations with Washington.

5. Japan desires to demonstrate its revitalized sense of strength and independence. Yet in the dangerous world of today, there are very few vigorous approaches Japan can make, given its weak military posture, without the possibility of suffering damage to its security position. Since Japan tends to compensate for its dependence on the United States by criticizing Washington's conduct of foreign affairs, relations between the United States and its most important Asian ally may come under increasing strains.

We shall return to these and related issues in considering the security problems of the alliance during the 1960s in its broader Pacific setting.

The Western Pacific as a Region

The second great treaty in the Northeast Asian area formed part of the over-all settlement of the Korean War, committing the United States to defend South Korea. Since the government of

Syngman Rhee feared being left without allies, Washington had agreed to discuss a defense treaty, and South Korea received its promised American alliance in October 1953. Two months earlier, on July 27, 1953, the sixteen members of the United Nations who fought in defense of South Korea had issued a declaration stating that

if there is a renewal of the armed attack, challenging again the principles of the United Nations, we should again be united and prompt to resist. The consequences of such a break of the armistice would again be so grave that, in all probability, it would not be possible to confine hostilities within the frontier of Korea.[13]

This allusion to a wider war barely veiled the threat of resort to nuclear weapons. It was a decade later that former President Eisenhower revealed his warning to Peking, through Indian diplomatic channels and other means, that the United States would employ nuclear weapons in case of a failure in the truce negotiations.[14]

Although overt military activity remained a possibility in Korea after 1953, neither direct aggression nor guerrilla war materialized. Rather, the main problems proved to be political instability and inadequate economic growth. Changes in regimes, corruption, and uncertain democratic processes—all punctuated by repeated student demonstrations—dominated the political scene after 1960. The failure of successive governments to control inflation, raise agricultural output, or sustain industrial growth led to a consistently high level of unemployment. Poor economic relations with Japan and an inability to match high imports with exports kept the country heavily dependent on American aid. Only in the mid-1960s did Korea begin to show marked improvement in matters of political stability and economic growth.

In this setting, North Korea's economic progress and subtle appeals for unity played on whatever nationalist-neutralist sentiment existed in the South. Couched in gradualist terms of first "confederating" the two autonomous halves of the country and eliminating all foreign influences, this approach presented the South Korean leadership with a major foreign-policy problem. Only the vexing matter of establishing at least formal relations with Japan surpassed it in urgency. Though essential for the development and stability of the Republic of Korea, the proposed reconciliation with Japan evoked so much antagonism, stemming from the bitter colonial heritage and the crosscurrents of domestic politics in both lands, that the negotiations did not succeed until 1965.

America incurred a third great obligation in the Far East in a treaty with Nationalist China, ratified in 1955 in response to the growing threat from Communist China. Peking was then bringing its full might to bear against Taiwan, its top-priority target after the wars in Korea and Indochina were over. The core of the pact was the mutual agreement to meet the common danger of an armed attack in the Western Pacific area, against Taiwan and the Pescadores, about 100 miles out to sea. Nevertheless, because of the persistent desire of the Nationalists to return to the mainland and their retention of groups of small islands just a few miles from the continent, this treaty seemed to entail the likelihood that the United States might become entangled to an extent unjustified by what Washington considered its own security interests.

As we have seen, the American commitments to Korea and Japan were complicated by the problem of Korea's partition and by the role of Japan as an American security base. With the Chinese Nationalists, it was the issue of the mainland and the strongly fortified offshore bastions that caused long-range concern. Despite Communist bombings in late 1954 and early 1955, which led to an evacuation of the Tachen Islands, Washington and Taipei agreed to defend Quemoy and Matsu. In 1953, the United States had apparently urged the Kuomintang to retain control of these islands, and in 1955, Chiang would not agree to even a partial withdrawal to reduce his combat and prestige commitments, notwithstanding an American offer to deploy air and marine forces on Taiwan.[15] The crisis, coming soon after the ratification of the treaty, led the Congress on January 29, 1955 (*i.e.*, about five weeks *before* the treaty took effect), to pass a joint resolution giving the President more freedom of action, temporarily, than the Senate had contemplated during its treaty deliberations. The resolution authorized the President to use armed force to protect "such related positions and territories . . . now in friendly hands," as well as to take other measures deemed appropriate to secure the defense of Taiwan and the Pescadores. Under such authority, in 1958 President Eisenhower committed the United States to help the Nationalists hold Quemoy and Matsu, where they had placed about 100,000 men—one-third of their total force—in anticipation of a new Chinese Communist attack.

At that time, Secretary Dulles made full use of the 1955 Congressional resolution authorizing the President to secure other positions in order to protect Taiwan and the Pescadores. An official statement on September 4, 1958, said that the President did not yet find that

American armed force was required, but it noted the increasing relationship between the security of the offshore islands and Taiwan and stressed that American military dispositions had been made to assure timely and effective action if needed.[16]

This type of deliberate ambiguity allowed the President to decide whether to consider an attack on Quemoy and Matsu as a prelude to an assault on Taiwan and the Pescadores. If he decided affirmatively, the President could order action to help the Nationalists defend their offshore positions. As matters actually developed, the Nationalists were enabled to hold the islands during the crisis of August-September 1958 through the presence of the American Seventh Fleet in the area, the superiority of Nationalist planes equipped with more effective air-to-air missiles, and the use of American naval power to escort Nationalist ships to within three miles of the coast, thereby assuring a safe supply line.[17]

Thus, ambiguities persist in the defense of American security interests in the most vital area of Asia—the Western Pacific—and complicate the three treaties that establish Washington's formal commitments. Nonetheless, the American security obligation to defend these lands in general is clear-cut, however tortuous the path to these undertakings may have been. The treaties cover all the territory in that sector not under Communist control. Admittedly, differences exist about the ultimate disposition of certain lands (such as Okinawa), which areas to defend (*e.g.*, the offshore islands), and how to reunify Korea. However, the treaties are bilateral and specific in their commitments and obligations. The reiterated American obligation to defend Japan is straightforward, backed by the presence of naval and air installations. The stationing of two divisions in Korea has been an earnest of American intentions. The Seventh Fleet remains on duty to protect Taiwan.

The passage of years has not reduced the importance of these engagements. Today, the psychological and material significance of a free South Korea to Japan is far more evident than it was in 1947, when the Joint Chiefs recommended the withdrawal of American ground forces from the Korean peninsula. And there is no prospect that a large military-assistance program can replace the American military presence in Korea. The renewal of small scale military activity by North Korea in the area of the demilitarized zone in recent years underscored this point. Even an effort to modify the types of forces Washington stations in Korea must now be treated as a highly delicate and sensitive subject. Moreover, with the Communist Chinese steadily increasing their modern airpower and the development of sophisticated defensive networks, the air defense of the Korea-Japan complex may require a single system that can cover both countries. For better or for worse, in a security sense, the fates of Seoul and Tokyo are more closely linked than ever before. And the American commitment to protect Taiwan remains as strong as ever, whatever questions arise about the means, the diplomatic setting, and the political burdens entailed. Indeed, in purely political and diplomatic terms, our treaty with Taiwan is a major factor in the whole Far Eastern policy of the United States, and we shall have to return to it again as we analyze the threat of Communist China. In purely military and strategic terms, however, the United States has depended very little upon Taiwan. It did not establish any military bases there before 1965, when it developed an air transport staging facility because of the war in Vietnam. Still, in terms of the system of security treaties, Taiwan does not rival those islands that do contain American bases—Japan, Okinawa, and the Philippines.

The Southwest Pacific and Insular Southeast Asia

The alliances in areas to the south have certain ambiguities that do not affect their counterparts to the north. The Philippines, Australia, and New Zealand, each of which has two security links to the United States, faced, at least until 1965, the unexpected problem of possible aggression from a non-Communist source—Indonesia. Though the 1951 treaties offer some security against this danger, Washington's commitments emphasize the more remote threat of Communist attack. Moreover, for these three states, security links to America (a communications base in Australia, and a major naval-air complex in Luzon) could bring entanglement in distant wars that might otherwise be avoided. Finally, there are no American combat forces stationed in or close to Australia and New Zealand.

These relationships are also more complex in nature than the bilateral ties America made with the states to the north. All the allied states in the southern region are linked together by SEATO in a multilateral accord. This situation has been further complicated by the continued participation in SEATO, earnestly desired by Washington, of two major European members and by SEATO's extension of unilateral guarantees of protection to the three Indochinese states. How to turn this unwieldy alliance into a coherent unit remains an unresolved problem.

Since the ANZUS accord gives the Australians and New Zealanders a broad guarantee of security against any type of attack—whether from a resurgent Japan, a bellicose Indonesia, or an expansionist China—it proved of greater value than the later SEATO arrangement, which was limited to combating Communist aggression. In addition, as the ANZUS organs of consultation have evolved, including military staff conversations and the Foreign Ministers' Council, the three signatories have integrated their security activities more closely than have the participants in the broader SEATO system.

The Indonesian confrontation with Malaysia, however, also raised questions about the extent of the ANZUS alignment. The two Southwest Pacific states, with an ever-deepening commitment to Malaysia, found the United States unwilling to make a firm military commitment in 1963–64—even to support them in the event their obligations brought them into open war with Indonesia. Although Indonesia has now abated its hostility toward Malaysia, if such an event had taken place, would the ANZUS Pact have been involved? On the one hand, an armed attack on Australian forces in Malaysia would be an act of aggression. On the other hand, although a question of self-defense, it would not be a matter of the direct defense of Australia. Indonesia, unless it receives substantial foreign help, does not now have the capacity to menace that state directly. We shall return to this issue in our examination of the current operations of the alliance system, but we should note in passing that under Article 5 of the 1951 treaty, armed attacks against "armed forces, public vessels, or aircraft in the Pacific" of any of the signatories, as well as against their territory or possessions, require the others to respond.

American relations with the Philippines, deriving, like the ANZUS tie, from a long-term special relationship, have been closer than with any other state in the Pacific area. The deep historic connection, the previous honoring of security commitments despite the disaster of 1941–42, and the termination of imperial rule left the Filipinos with few fears about America's willingness to come to their defense in a crisis. Yet despite their intimacy and durability, American-Filipino security relations have probably been more riddled with frustration than any other Asian defense tie. The original military-base agreement of 1947 enabled the United States to reserve rights to about 100 locations as potential bases.[18] Though the Filipinos do not object to the presence of bases as such or consider the base or alliance accords as a "mortgage on independence," a series of disputes regarding security and economic relations has arisen.

As to the bases themselves, the United States yielded its claims to the areas held in reserve during the 1940s, and today there are only two naval stations, one air base, and one rest camp. But friction over the size of these establishments nonetheless may induce the United States to reduce its position to Subic Bay and Clark Field. Furthermore, a reduction of the terms of the lease, from 99 to 25 years, was tentatively agreed upon in the accord negotiated by U.S. Ambassador Charles Bohlen and the Philippine Foreign Minister Felixberto Serrano in 1959. This also included an American promise to consult with the Philippine government regarding the stationing of missile and nuclear forces at the bases and the deployment of troops to other areas, or for purposes not covered in the 1951 defense treaty or the 1954 SEATO pact. A strong and mounting nationalist trend in Philippine politics, plus a fear of unwanted military involvement, led Manila to demand application of these restrictions despite a failure to settle the issue of a Status of Forces Agreement (SOFA), a basic condition for the implementation of the tentative accord.

In justifying these efforts to control American actions and thus indirectly limit Manila's involvement abroad, some Filipinos, noting that SEATO has not undertaken strategic planning for their defense, doubt that other allies, apart from America and perhaps Australia, would give them material support in a crisis. For example, there are fears that allied support might not be available in the case of a major re-emergence of the Huk guerrilla effort, suppressed by 1955, but showing signs of reviving in the mid-1960s. Pressures against the security arrangements and insistence on restrictions on American freedom of action reflect, in part, the work of a vigorous anti-American Nationalist, Senator Claro Recto, whose efforts led in 1958 to a resolution by the Philippine Senate against the establishment of missile bases on Philippine soil without the Senate's consent.

Finally, a base issue of a completely different sort led the Philippines to seek close ties with America—and more bases! With the rise of a threat to the southern Philippines from Indonesia in 1964–65, Manila sought to reverse a new Washington policy of reducing military assistance. Instead, it asked for more aid and requested help in establishing several Filipino bases in Mindanao. Ironically, this request followed by less than one year the Philippines' diplomatic support of Indonesia's hostile policy toward Malaysia, motivated by Manila's claim to part of North Borneo. Indonesian aggressions, particularly paratroop drops on the Malay Peninsula in 1964, upset the Philippine government, and it moved to improve relations with Malaysia, to the extent of exchanging consuls.

However, Manila could not end the dispute or extend full diplomatic recognition because President Macapagal, who had sponsored the claim to North Borneo initially, thought that a concession would cause him to lose ground in his race for re-election in the fall of 1965. Following Macapagal's defeat by Ferdinand Marcos, formal diplomatic relations were re-established with Malaysia; but the Borneo issue remained unresolved. Malaysia and the Philippines tried to negotiate their differences but reached a stalemate over Manila's demand that Malaysia agree in advance to submit the case to the World Court should all other methods fail. This the Malays were unwilling to do because any doubt cast on the status of North Borneo would further imperil their already precarious internal stability.

Despite this jumble, with its complications for American security interests, the United States firmly backed Manila in its concern over possible Indonesian aggression in the Mindanao area. In October 1964, Secretary Rusk stated "that if there is an attack on the Philippines from any quarter, that is an attack on the United States." Referring to the broad commitments of the 1951 accord, which encompassed protection against Indonesia as well as possible Chinese threats, American officials stated that the United States would help Manila strengthen its defense posture in the southern region.

Despite a considerable degree of American-Philippine consensus in military-security affairs and a basic Philippine loyalty to the American alliance, the rising force of Filipino nationalism has increased tensions between the two allies. A desire to seek an identity apart from the United States has led the Filipinos to a skeptical view of the cultural values of their former ruler and a quest for identity with other Asian lands and with the earlier Spanish tradition. Significantly, Independence Day has been shifted from July 4 to June 12, the date of the abortive declaration of a republic following the defeat of Spain in 1898.

This new nationalism can feed on several specific irritants, apart from jurisdictional questions, such as SOFA, and security issues, such as control over the use of the bases. A major source of rancor is the parity clauses giving Americans the right, enjoyed by no other foreigners, to develop natural resources; to own and operate public utilities; and to maintain retail outlets on the same terms as

Filipinos. These privileges are especially resented by the new young Filipino businessmen, protectionist-oriented and industrial-minded, who are competing for economic leadership with the old cash-crop exporters (in sugar, tobacco, and coconut oil), who have long been dependent on a U.S. market. Attacks focus largely on the Laurel-Langley accord, negotiated in 1955 to revise a 1946 trade agreement. Its provisions actually benefit the Philippines—particularly the exporters of traditional crops—by cushioning the transition away from colonial-era tariff preferences for Filipino products in the American market. Yet these arrangements are frequently denounced as a neocolonial trick, and many Filipinos are agitating for the immediate application to Americans of a discriminatory law against Chinese businesses passed in 1954.

American privileges, secured in a constitutional amendment (a price many Filipinos believe was extracted by the U.S. Congress in return for war-damage payments), expire in 1974. At that time, a Filipino controlling interest may be required in every enterprise. Such a development would affect 186 American-owned concerns and might be extended to involve 211 other firms with an American financial interest. In all, U.S. citizens have a total direct investment of about $500 million in the Philippines.

Thus, confusing crosscurrents now affect the Philippine diplomatic-security scene. A growing desire for self-assertion and acceptance by other Asian states exists side by side with a belief in American loyalty in time of crisis, which the Filipinos aver they reciprocate. Willingness to support Nationalist China and to honor SEATO commitments is balanced by fear of involvement in other conflicts not of direct concern to Manila. The interest of the Filipinos in a strong base system—including an agreement to allow well-stocked American supply vessels to anchor off Luzon—and their commitment against aggression were frequently undercut before 1965 by efforts to limit American use of base facilities and by an ambiguous policy toward Indonesia.

CHAPTER SEVEN

The Seato Area

The SEATO Accord

The origin and development of SEATO, the most ambitious of all the U.S. pacts in Asia, provide an even more dramatic illustration than do the earlier treaties of the complexities and ambiguities that can beset American security arrangements in Asia. Signed at Manila on September 8, 1954, and entering into force for the United States on February 19, 1955, the Southeast Asia Collective Defense Treaty and Protocol added two nations to the existing U.S. roster of Asian allies—Thailand and Pakistan, the sole treaty partners on the South Asia mainland. (The Protocol, however, extended unilateral guarantees to South Vietnam, Laos, and Cambodia as well.) The Philippines, Australia, and New Zealand already had links with the United States. The other treaty members, Britain and France, were NATO allies.

This complex eight-power pact has a far more elaborate organization and covers a far broader area than any other allied treaty in eastern Asia. Although it has greater scope and thus greater potential than the other accords, it contains at the same time far greater weaknesses. More and more, it has become a nominal multilateral framework for a series of bilateral American arrangements with the ANZ and Asian states—Australia, New Zealand, the Philippines, South Vietnam, and Thailand.

In probing the origin and the record of SEATO over its first decade, we hope to uncover the reasons why the treaty has failed to fulfill its promise—and yet has confounded many early critics.

Origins of the Pact

Since SEATO arose as a consequence of the disastrous French effort to hold Indochina and took shape in the course of Anglo-

French-American negotiations during 1952–54, the predominantly Western context of the treaty's arrangements and membership is not surprising. However, close examination of the developments leading to the treaty reveals differences in attitudes among the allies that were to influence the course of France's long and bitter struggle in Vietnam and persist over the next decade.

With that war exacting a terrible toll even before the Korean armistice, the French proposed in 1952 that a permanent military organization study the Southeast Asian situation and plan broad regional defense measures. Over the next two years, American assistance rose sharply as the French fought a losing battle, reaching a total of $825.6 million in economic aid and $709.6 million in military assistance for the years 1950–54. Negotiations among the Western Big Three moved into high gear as the war reached its climax in the spring of 1954 and led to the birth of SEATO. Their views differed sharply both on military policy in Indochina and on the kind of alliance that should emerge from this crisis.

Though never directly involved in the Indochina struggle, Britain had a record of military engagement on the mainland, with a Commonwealth Brigade in the Korean war, and with twenty-three battalions, totaling 40,000 troops, fighting Communist guerrillas in Malaya in the early 1950s. It also had 80,000 troops garrisoned in Suez. Despite British efforts at the start of the 1950s, the United States would not commit itself to a security pact for Southeast Asia. In fact, the desire to avoid entanglements on the mainland, especially in support of British interests, had led to America's insistence on excluding England from the ANZUS treaty.

The British held certain strong views regarding the Indochinese War. They opposed an explicit threat of retaliation against deeper Chinese involvement as long as Peking did not raise its level of assistance to the Viet Minh rebels. They believed that preparations for deterrent action, to be used only when needed, would suffice. Having concluded that victory was out of the question, the British thought that the war itself should be terminated with half a loaf if possible, though they doubted that even South Vietnam could be saved. Above all, they sought to protect Malaya by halting the southward spread of the war, and in their opinion, a truce in Indochina would improve their chances of isolating and ending the brutal struggle in Malaya. In their opposition to military intervention in Indochina, they argued that in order to have an effect, the effort would have to be so massive that it might well lead to implementation of the Russian-Chinese treaty of 1950, especially if the war expanded to a direct American-Chinese confrontation.[1]

In renewing their quest for a defense pact, the British sought as large a group of signatories as possible. But they did not wish to make this security arrangement an instrument of military pressure for negotiating a peace in Indochina. They also wanted broad Commonwealth participation in the Indochina settlement as well as in the security accord.[2]

Meanwhile, the French continued their grim and costly war, wavering between optimism and despair. Conducting military operations on their own with as little outside interference as possible, they did not even discuss the relief or defense of Dien Bien Phu with the Americans on the scene, despite the fact that the latter were trying to develop such plans.[3] Later, the desperate French calls for help reminded the British of the French pleas of 1940, made without any effort to develop a workable war plan.[4] The Americans considered the French colonial position politically untenable and viewed their military program as gravely defective in strategy and training. They cited the inadequate counterinsurgency tactics and the failure to train Vietnamese officers for leadership or to place them in responsible positions.

As in the 1960s, the Americans in the 1950s stressed the role of Communist China. In 1952, Secretary of State Dean Acheson expressed concern about overt Chinese intervention in Indochina and sought to warn Peking that America would respond with a blockade or attacks on Chinese lines of communications. At the same time, Washington, though handicapped by a desire not to weaken its NATO relationship with Paris, repeatedly pressed the French to undertake necessary military and administrative reforms and to allow the United States some control over operations. But for a variety of reasons, including domestic political pressures, France found those proposals unacceptable. Nonetheless, when the Republicans took over in Washington in 1953, the President, the Chairman of the Joint Chiefs, and the Secretary of State agreed to a limited but unspecified American military intervention, contingent on an allied cooperative effort in order to ensure congressional support. The new U.S. leaders felt that a compromise peace was impossible and that any settlement short of victory would mean the loss of all Indochina. In this context, Secretary Dulles viewed discussions to establish SEATO as an important diplomatic lever, combined with the threat of force, to deter the Chinese Communists and stabilize the region.

In a message to Prime Minister Churchill on April 4, 1954, President Eisenhower stressed the need to support France and proposed an *ad hoc* coalition of the United States, the United Kingdom, the Associated States of Indochina, the ANZUS powers, Thailand, and the Philippines. He stated that the United States was prepared to .fight but did not envisage the need for appreciable American or British ground forces.

Although the British favored a collective organization that would help secure Malaya and Hong Kong and would compensate for their rankling exclusion from ANZUS, they would not cooperate in this effort before a forthcoming conference in Geneva, at which they hoped to arrange a peace; and they opposed military involvement on the grounds that it would frighten off potential signatories to the proposed treaty. They insisted that mere threats would not compel the Chinese to withdraw support and that the bombing of China would raise the possibility of nuclear war without being locally effective.[5]

In return for a British agreement to begin coalition talks, the United States ceased its efforts to have Britain join in a warning to China. Britain wished to discuss membership carefully so as to avoid a deliberate barring of India or other Asian Commonwealth states, but the United States, though desiring a broadly based treaty, wanted only those states interested in a military-security pact. When Washington proposed the inclusion of Nationalist China, Britain agreed in the spring of 1954 to drop both India and Taiwan as potential members—a timely compromise that opened the way for five-power staff talks among Britain, France, the United States, Australia, and New Zealand at Singapore. In turn, negotiations for a military treaty were separated from the Indochinese bargaining process.

With Britain striving to bring in as many as possible of the Colombo Powers (an informal grouping comprising India, Pakistan, Ceylon, Burma, and Indonesia), Anglo-American differences persisted over three principal issues: the number of Asian members, the relative emphasis on military and on socioeconomic concerns, and the insistence (by the Americans) on the anti-Communist nature of the pact. The final compromise averted both a tightly knit arrangement and the loose nonmilitary system desired by Britain. Instead, a firm commitment to the defense of Southeast Asia was undertaken without spelling out the exact nature of the pledge—making SEATO more similar to the ANZUS arrangement than to the NATO treaty. SEATO also emerged with a socioeconomic program and with an accompanying statement, the Pacific Charter—adopted at the initiative of the Philippines—that stressed the importance of self-determination and an end to colonialism.

With a peace settlement in Indochina in mid-1954, the United States acquiesced in Britain's appeal to the Colombo Powers to consider joining in the collective defense arrangement. But at a September 1954 meeting of the group, only Pakistan accepted, thus dashing London's hopes for participation by Ceylon and Burma. The addition of Pakistan, the only major Asian land power to join, was a mixed blessing. Though militarily helpful, Pakistan also brought its feud with India into SEATO councils, and within a decade, this dispute produced a crisis of confidence in the Alliance.

These compromises in membership, purpose, and coverage, often reflecting the uncertain and conflicting interests of the treaty's sponsors, contributed to the ambivalence that continued to plague SEATO after its launching. Though a military alliance with the West seemed necessary at a time when Asian states saw themselves compelled to choose between neutralism and Western alignment, SEATO lacked the organizational structure and combat capacity to reassure Thailand and Pakistan. And there was no indication of how the promises of socioeconomic cooperation were to be honored. With the United States already committed to bilateral economic and military aid and to multilateral assistance through the United Nations and with the Commonwealth Colombo Plan already embracing several countries in the region, the SEATO channels seemed either a form of duplication or a form of discrimination. Over the years, the Asian SEATO powers argued that they deserved special treatment, and some additional economic aid did flow through SEATO, especially in engineering and education. But this aid merely supplemented existing bilateral or international economic programs financed by the Western powers. In this respect, too, SEATO has never demonstrated much vigor.

Erosion of membership, begun when Cambodia rejected the unilateral SEATO protection almost at the outset, continued in 1957 when Malaya gained its independence and dropped the participating role it had held as a British colony. Apart from the states of Laos and South Vietnam, over which SEATO had extended its mantle, this defection left only two mainland countries—Thailand and Pakistan—in the system, and the latter identified its security problems almost exclusively in terms of India. Only Thailand had a direct security interest of territorial protection through SEATO. Though it may be unfair to charge that SEATO was merely an elaborate arrangement to protect Thailand, many critics viewed it this way.[6] The Thais, ironically, found it unsatisfactory, not only because of the hedged obligations and inadequate military preparations, but also because they feared that individual SEATO members would not act unless all signatories were in accord. They quickly became suspicious of French intentions and later came to doubt Pakistani support. This, combined with SEATO's inaction in Laos and Vietnam, raised fears in Bangkok to such a pitch that only a bilateral understanding with the United States could mitigate them. The Philippine government was sympathetic to the security purposes of SEATO, but its military weakness made it a limited partner in defensive efforts on the mainland. The treaty, however, did clear the way for Manila to permit American military deployment from Luzon to mainland allies with a minimum of diplomatic or physical delay.

Neutralist Responses

How did the neutrals view this incursion of alignment onto the South Asian mainland, which seemed to involve Thailand in the Cold War without affording adequate on-the-scene protection? Though the British believed that their policy of consultations with the Colombo Powers in 1954 had prevented an outright Indian condemnation of SEATO, Burma and Ceylon also deserve some credit for India's response by expressing their deep fear of the Communist military danger. At Colombo, they tried to induce Prime Minister Nehru to sponsor an alternate scheme for the region's security. Since India refused to acknowledge SEATO's value or devise a different system, it accepted the task of persuading China to demonstrate its benevolent intentions regarding South Asia. Toward this end, India concluded that China would accept an unaligned Indochina and so supported a Geneva settlement that excluded American forces from that territory. India took on a role as a member of the three-power International Control Commission (along with Canada and Poland) to police this neutrality and sought to commit the component states in the former French colony to neutrality. Further, Nehru himself signed the famous Five Principles of Coexistence with Chou En-lai in June 1954. India considered the SEATO pact of September 1954 a grave error since it brought the influence of distant great powers to the region; it similarly opposed the Protocol extending SEATO's protection to the new Indochinese states.

While India concentrated on getting Chinese verbal promises, the two small Colombo states still sought more substantial protective assurances. On the other hand, Indonesia had become so antagonized by SEATO that it proposed formal creation of a neutralist bloc professing friendship for China. India vetoed the Indonesian suggestion and, to reassure the others, tried to induce China to show goodwill by entering into more regular diplomatic contacts with neighboring states. As a consequence, the Colombo Powers decided in December 1954 to invite China to the Bandung Conference of the nonaligned states. Pakistan, already a member of SEATO, objected at first but yielded when the other three backed India.[7]

In the end, Indian efforts may well have been crucial in the decisions of Ceylon and Burma not to join SEATO. However, it is doubtful whether either of these two strongly nationalistic Buddhist states could have adhered to a policy of alignment. After all, Burma had shed its Western ties previously, leaving the Commonwealth upon gaining its independence in 1948. The combination of xenophobia, which led it to curtail foreign contacts and even reject foreign aid on two later occasions, and fear of Chinese power ultimately drove Rangoon to a passive neutralism. The first army coup of 1958 brought no main change in this course, though Burma had observers at the 1959 SEATO maneuvers. However, after the 1962 coup, an intense isolationist neutrality became the country's predominant policy. Ceylon's mildly pro-Western government lost the 1956 election to a leftist-Buddhist coalition that promptly terminated the naval-base agreement with Britain and swung to a thorough-going neutralist course. Even when the moderately pro-Western elements returned to power in 1964, they continued this neutralist tack, though in a much milder vein.

India's policy of goodwill toward Peking rested on an uncertain foundation since it, too, feared the power to the north, as Peking consolidated its military position in Tibet. New Delhi yielded its special privileges in Tibet in 1954, partly to accommodate China and partly to concentrate on the threat from Pakistan, greatly increased by an American-Pakistani arms accord of that year that gave Karachi its first opportunity to develop a modern fighting force. Concern over China strengthened India's neutralist stand against

SEATO on the grounds that such an overt American influence could only force China to abandon its new policy of reasonableness and so endanger India's insecure northern front. Thus neutralist doctrine, hostility to Pakistan, fear of China, and a determined policy of accommodation with Peking all reinforced Indian opposition to an American alliance system in its vicinity.

China's appearance at Bandung capped New Delhi's campaign to convince others of Peking's peaceful intentions. Premier Chou Enlai had assured Nehru that his country would respect the internal autonomy of Tibet. Now at Bandung, India arranged meetings at which Chou informed Thailand, Laos, and Cambodia that China would not interfere in the domestic affairs of other states. More generally, he stressed China's desire to live in accord with all other states even to the extent of respecting the political and economic systems of Japan and the United States.

Despite such Chinese blandishments, the neutralists could not jar the aligned Asian states from their treaty connections. The Bandung Conference's formal communiqué was a compromise, recognizing the right of each state to defend itself singly or collectively, but recommending abstention from "arrangements of collective defense to serve the particular interests of any of the big powers." (Similar wording later appeared in the abortive Maphilindo agreement of 1963 that sought to end the disputes between Jakarta and Manila and the new state of Malaysia.) From Bandung on, the Colombo Powers disintegrated as a group that could link Southcentral and Southeast Asia as well as aligned and neutralist states.

The SEATO accord could not simplify the complex diplomacy within Southeast Asia, for it also reflected the tangled interplay of many Western and indigenous allied interests. The neutrals added another dimension, not only in their doctrinal objection to alliances and their specific policies toward the Asian SEATO powers, but also through their own special relations with Western lands other than the United States. France retained close cultural, political, and even military relations with Cambodia even when that state adopted a vitriolic anti-American position. Malaya clung to its British alliance after 1957, allowing Commonwealth military bases there for its protection. Even Indonesia tried to maintain good relations with Australia, and the two at one time held joint naval exercises. Australia, in turn, did its utmost to live on good terms with this large and potentially dangerous neighbor.

Southeast Asian countries took repeated initiatives toward creation of a regional organization that could bridge the gap between neutrals and aligned powers and perhaps obviate all other arrangements. Even before the Colombo Powers emerged, the Philippines in 1950 had sought a military association of all free South Asian states. But neutralist opposition to a formal arrangement prevented a six-power meeting at Baguio from going beyond declarations of the need to end colonialism and preserve the integrity of new states. In 1954, Thailand sought to establish a close relationship among all the Buddhist states of South Asia—also without success. Five years later, meeting an equally lackluster response in an attempt to conclude a Southeast Asian economic and friendship treaty, Malaya sponsored the Association of Southeast Asia (ASA), modeled on the Nordic Council, to link itself in a socioeconomic grouping with Thailand and the Philippines. As a neutral tied to Britain in a defense treaty, Malaya hoped to bypass other security arrangements and still give the area a regional structure. In 1963, along with the Philippines, the new Federation of Malaysia sought to join with Indonesia in a regional political organization—Maphilindo. But both the ASA and Maphilindo quickly foundered on the unwillingness of the Philippines and Indonesia to accept Malaysian jurisdiction over territories to which they laid claim. Such repeated initiatives, as, for example, the revival of ASA in 1966, reflected both the persistent desire of the Southeast Asian states—many of them Western allies—for an accord without Western states and the uncertainty about the permanence and adequacy of Western ties. Finally in 1967 the five states of Thailand, Indonesia, Malaysia, the Philippines and Singapore succeeded in establishing the Association of South East Asian Nations (ASEAN) which stressed social and economic cooperation and for practical purposes superseded these earlier efforts. The fact that a strongly aligned state like Thailand could join in the same organization with Indonesia, a state committed to neutralism, again revealed the durability of the urge for regional cooperation and the desire to become master of their own fate.

The Problem of Subversion

During the latter half of the 1950s, it was frequently argued that subversion, rather than direct aggression, had become the main threat to regional security, and this viewpoint was incorporated in Article 2 of the SEATO Treaty, specifically binding the signatories to act against an external assault of this nature. The second annual report of SEATO, in 1957, acknowledged this new kind of danger virtually outright.[8] At that time, armed attack had tapered off and Asia seemed to be moving into a more peaceful era; the armed insurrections of 1948, the two great wars in Korea and Indochina, and Peking's use of force in Tibet, off Taiwan, and on the Burma frontier all seemed part of history. Even the Taiwanese, Tibetan, and Burmese incidents were explained away as domestic or minor frontier issues. SEATO claimed that by neutralizing the rise in Communist military strength and helping to reduce the danger of external aggression, it had made possible the new emphasis on checking subversion.

Washington apparently concluded that, whatever its limitations, SEATO posed an effective warning to the Chinese against committing an overt act of aggression. The Asian treaty members concurred, adding the assertion that the neutrals also benefited, however ungrateful and hostile their attitude. The European states, however, did not credit SEATO as a deterrent, and viewed China as unlikely in any event to commit such a clear-cut violation of international law as a conventional assault across a frontier. Still other observers who feared Chinese intentions attributed Chinese restraint and Peking's reliance on more subtle indirect aggressions, not to SEATO, but to the general doctrine of collective security and, in particular, to the experience in Korea.

America's willingness to treat subversion as the main threat in the late 1950s seemed to indicate a growing maturity, based on greater experience. Yet it proved difficult to arrive at precise definitions of the terms "subversion" and "indirect aggression." They expanded to include insurrection, terror, political pressure, propaganda, underground operations, and even economic aid that caused excessive dependency on a totalitarian donor. Three forms of subversion appeared most important: (1) armed insurrection, such as had occurred in Malaya and the Philippines; (2) briefer and more restricted efforts based on force and pressure, such as the assaults and demonstrations then going on in Singapore; (3) actions within the law to win popular support, as in the case of the Communist party of Indonesia on Java. There were also a variety of moves from across a border that could have subversive effects: disruptive frontier claims, the smuggling of supplies to dissidents, the organizing of clandestine indigenous groups, and vigorous anti-government propaganda directed at ethnic or economic groups, to name a few.

Article 4, Paragraph 2, dealing with threats "other than by armed attacks," clearly reflected the type of threat then prevalent throughout Southeast Asia. SEATO's definition of terms and the Committee of Experts it established to cope with this problem seemed reasonable responses to a real need. However, its terms of reference were limited to blocking "subversion directed from without against the integrity and stability" of the member states, and no action could be taken without the consent of the target state. In consequence, the two coups in Thailand, in 1957 and 1958, were considered internal affairs beyond the jurisdiction of the treaty. Moreover, neither coup had any tinge of Communist backing, which Washington deemed a prerequisite to any action on its part.

SEATO's concern centered on subversion in lands where legal Communist parties were making strong efforts to gain popular support. But the prime targets of this approach—India and Indonesia—were not only outside the treaty's jurisdiction, but also the most determined neutralists of all. The major problems that were soon to emerge in Laos and South Vietnam—to which SEATO guarantees had been extended—did not receive central attention, and when their urgency became apparent, SEATO found that its capacity to act was sorely limited.

The Cases of Laos and South Vietnam

Subversion proved difficult to identify and isolate in the Laos crises of 1958–62. A civil war developed, with a complex struggle for power among rightists, neutralists, and Communists (Pathet Lao), but the question of subversion was problematical. At first, in 1957, the Communists joined the neutralist government and made a good showing in the 1958 elections, only to be driven out by a rightist counterthrust that caused many Pathet Lao to flee to their sanctuary on the border in North Vietnam. A civil conflict followed, with a neutralist-Communist coalition supported by Soviet air supplies gaining military success in 1961 against an American-backed rightist force.

To what extent subversion was being sponsored from beyond Laos' frontiers then became the issue. The Pathet Lao relied extensively on North Vietnam, which sustained the Pathet Lao forces and contributed an undetermined amount of guidance and cadre support. Moreover, the American advisory aid, and financial support in the late 1950s could also be considered acts that subverted an existing administration. In 1962, the great powers finally agreed to neutralize Laos with all three political elements joined together in the government. But this volatile combination degenerated again into civil war the following year. However, rightists and neutralists now found themselves allied in coalition against the Communists, who were still enjoying considerable support from Hanoi and were making a strong bid to gain supremacy in Laos.

Throughout this turbulence, SEATO refused to make any moves despite urgings from Thailand and, to a lesser extent, the United States. Bangkok declared its concern as early as 1955, when Pathet Lao and government forces were fighting in northern Laos, and again during the 1959 crisis. But with SEATO taking no action, in 1959 the United States stepped up aid to the rightists, and Thailand likewise contributed support.

SEATO's sole involvement came when its three Western members persuaded the U.N. Security Council, over Soviet objections that Moscow had veto power, to send a commission of inquiry to Laos to investigate charges of external aggression. But the commission reported that the problem remained primarily internal. The Americans and Thais continued their efforts to activate SEATO in 1960–61, but to no avail, even with Russia supplying arms to the neutralist and Communist forces. However, possibly because of the rightist regime's low international reputation and a consequent fear of its rejection, the United States discouraged Laos from applying for SEATO membership.

At its Council meeting of March 1961, SEATO did at least consider the problem and take a public stand. Noting "with grave concern the continual offensive by rebel elements in Laos who are continuing to be supplied and assisted by communist powers," it declared its readiness to take appropriate actions if there continued to be "active military attempts to obtain control of Laos." SEATO also referred to "the efforts of an armed minority, again supported from outside in violation of the Geneva accord, to destroy the government of Vietnam, and declared its firm resolve not to acquiesce in any such takeover of that country." [9] However, primarily because of French opposition, this outright accusation of subversion from without was not implemented by any specific action. Nor did the operational plans for the defense of Laos made by SEATO in 1959 go into effect. When the Pathet Lao launched an offensive in northwestern Laos near the Thai frontier in 1962, the United States and its English-speaking SEATO allies sought to restore the balance without going through treaty auspices, by moving forces into northeastern Thailand across the border.[10] Similarly, American military support for the neutralist regime after 1962 bypassed SEATO and went directly to Laos, since the neutralization settlement that year had ended its status under the SEATO Protocol.

South Vietnam had then become a major concern. After a lull in combat from 1954–57, guerrilla efforts, which had resumed in 1957, had moved into terror and combat operations during 1959–61 and by 1962 were becoming formidable. The Viet Cong had hoped to win control of the South through the elections promised in the 1954 Geneva settlement. Saigon at first expressed an interest in joining SEATO, and the South Vietnam Legislative Assembly sent a message to the SEATO Council disavowing the Geneva arrangements. SEATO proved unwilling to entertain Saigon's application, whereupon President Ngo Dinh Diem made an important statement in April 1956, refusing to hold elections or implement the armistice. But he also declared that South Vietnam would remain neutral, under the protective SEATO Protocol, without foreign troops or bases. Both the United States and South Vietnam adhered to this position—that a South Vietnam at peace would have no alliances or foreign bases—even after major American intervention in the war.

Unlike Laos and Cambodia, Saigon had kept its link to SEATO, with its interest in the organization rising sharply in 1958 as the guerrilla war mounted. Rather than press again for membership, Saigon settled for associate status and participated as an observer in various SEATO agencies and military exercises. The strong 1961 Council resolution of support was of some value to Saigon, especially since the French at that time firmly recognized South Vietnam's integrity. However, with no action sought or obtained under SEATO auspices, the main defense effort rested on American help pursuant to a military assistance accord of 1959.[11] Saigon again thought of asking for SEATO support in 1964, but by then, both France and Pakistan had expressed strong disinclination to become involved. SEATO's mandate against subversion and indirect aggression remained unfulfilled—despite its unilateral guarantee of protection to these Indochinese states.

Changes and Limits

In 1963, SEATO modified its original rule of unanimity which had made Thailand skeptical of the treaty's effectiveness. Though retaining the veto desired by France, the organization decided to permit a majority to take collective action provided no member cast a negative vote. Individual members still remained free to limit their commitments even after a vote, since their obligation to act applied only in accordance with their constitutional processes. As host of the 1963 Council meeting, France emphasized its views by failing to invite South Vietnamese observers, and that summer President de Gaulle began his campaign to have the Indochinese area neutralized. Yet at the April 1964 Council meeting, the French did not put forth any specific proposal to implement their views. South Vietnam returned as an observer but, possibly out of fear of French opposition, did not formally ask the alliance to intervene, though it charged North Vietnam with aggression and subversion. In what may have been a compromise arrangement, France abstained from signing a strong communiqué in support of Vietnam. The Pakistani representative voted for it, though to judge from a remark he made later, Foreign Minister Bhutto would not have done so had he been there. Ironically, Bhutto for the second consecutive year snubbed the meeting—this time choosing to attend an Afro-Asian Conference at Jakarta along with Peking's Foreign Minister.

As matters stood in 1965, France still pressed for the neutralization of South Vietnam, but remained in the SEATO system. For the moment at least, it agreed to discuss differences in private with the United States rather than precipitate a showdown in the Council. But while Paris did not repudiate its obligation to act against aggression in the area, it would not go beyond its traditional military contribution of a few officers for staff work and exercises, and soon cut down even this degree of participation. Demonstrating its strong opposition to the escalation of the war in Vietnam, France refused to send its Foreign Minister to the 1965 Council meeting, participate in SEATO naval exercises, or—now along with Pakistan—sign the communiqué.

Though SEATO has been inoperative in the region outside its territorial jurisdiction, even the neutralists who publicly denounced the organization have on occasion privately acknowledged their reliance on it to help maintain a stable balance in South Asia. Feeling itself under Chinese Communist pressure (over the demarcation of the border and the Chinese Nationalist remnants still hiding in its jungles), Burma in 1956 relied on the good offices of India and the existence of SEATO—despite the fact it could not invoke the organization in reaching a settlement—and even signed a friendship treaty with Thailand. In general, however, SEATO's record has been lackluster. In 1958, it failed to act on a rebellion on Sumatra against the Sukarno regime in Indonesia, despite considerable sympathy in Malaya, the Philippines, and Australia for the pro-Western rebels. Even Thailand, usually eager to extend SEATO's scope, failed to back American efforts to muster SEATO support for its position on the Quemoy-Matsu crisis. The only member to join America in attempting to make SEATO take a stand was the Philippines.

The Position of Thailand

Despite apprehensions regarding SEATO's ability to act, Thailand, of all the members, benefited most directly and extensively from the alliance. Thailand's vivid recollection of unprotected exposure to Japanese power in 1941 compelled it to cast off its tradition of neutrality, much as the Low Countries, Denmark, and Norway did in 1949 in joining NATO. Though Bangkok persists in the desire to combine the advantages of alliance with those of neutrality, it signed its first military aid pact with the United States in 1950 and dispatched a small contingent to Korea.[12] The SEATO system itself is very Thai-oriented; its headquarters are in Bangkok, and many of the ablest Thai officers participate actively in planning and other staff work. Moreover, Thailand takes part in frequent SEATO combat exercises.

The Thais themselves have sought to demonstrate support for fellow-allies, notably Pakistan and the Philippines. As relations with Pakistan cooled in 1960, ties with Manila grew more intimate, since both the Philippines and Thailand sought greater assurances against aggression. In offering to support allies in general, however, Thailand expected a larger degree of reciprocation than it received. After defending its Western link at Bandung (though not so vigorously as Manila or Karachi), Bangkok was acutely embarrassed by the Suez crisis, which lent credence to the charge that the country was aligning itself with imperialism. And as a rice-producing state, it also resented the 1960 American decision to aid India with considerable amounts of U.S. rice.

But military issues provided the central focus for Thailand's attitude toward the alliance. It conceived its role as limited to its own protection, including, at first, the defense of Cambodia and Laos, which it considered areas of primary importance to its own security. Early plans were developed on this basis, and allied air and naval backing was assured for the deployment of Thailand's small forces in defense of these neighbors. Up to 1955, Thai-Cambodian relations were good, with cooperation in transportation and trade and even a Thai grant of military aid. Then, Cambodia began to exhibit increasing hostility toward Thailand.

In 1954, Cambodia appeared anxious for an association with the West, particularly the United States, and expressed an interest in joining SEATO. With American support, it resisted neutralization at Geneva, refused to assure Peking that it would bar American bases, and—its security endangered by the Viet Minh—decided to accept American military aid in early 1955. In view of Cambodia's assurances of its nonalignment, the International Control Commission decided that this decision did not violate the neutrality provisions of the Geneva accords.

Later in 1955, however, with internal control assured and the North Vietnamese threat at least temporarily removed, Cambodia entered upon its present course of intense neutrality and revived its traditional enmity toward Thailand and, more especially, toward Vietnam. While visiting Peking early in 1956, Prince Sihanouk denounced SEATO protection as dishonorable. The following year, the Cambodian legislature made neutrality in foreign policy the law of the land. What chiefly worried Thailand, however, was Cambodia's recognition of Peking in 1958 and Treaty of Friendship with China in 1960. As Peking's power increased and India's waned, and as the guerrillas grew stronger in Vietnam, Sihanouk moved still closer to Peking.

Even before events in Laos and Cambodia had reached these menacing stages, the Thais had expressed their doubts about Western support. Making the oft-voiced complaint that Washington's economic-aid priorities favored neutralists over allies, Thailand demanded that neutralism be officially censured. Accordingly, in 1957, in a communiqué that outraged many neutrals, the SEATO Council indicated "concern that some governments have, in varying degrees, adopted a line of active opposition to collective security arrangements such as SEATO," and it expressed the hope that "those who criticized it [SEATO] today would eventually be willing to welcome it." But Thai anxieties had deep roots and could not be so easily assuaged. The country's need to depend for defense on distant great powers entailed reciprocal involvement on its part in distant crises that might provoke its powerful neighbor China. Therefore, though the Thais previously had desired an American military presence—possibly in reaction to American reluctance to grant it—they made a major point in the late 1950s of rejecting bases on their soil, as well as other obligations that would add to their duties or limit their freedom of action.

While consolidating his power around 1957, General Sarit Thanarat, Thailand's leading military authority, made much of his refusal to allow rocket bases. In fact, he allowed full expression of the strong neutralist sentiment that exists among some urban elements in Thailand. But after using this device to weaken his pro-American rival, Marshall Pibul Songgram, Sarit clamped down on such activities once in office. Yet this experience indicated a strong neutralist strain in Thai politics, a willingness to foster it for political purposes, and a hostility toward wide-ranging commitments—all in the country that held SEATO most important to its security. Similar patterns of behavior were to emerge more broadly and intensely in Pakistan in later years. When Thailand lifted its strict political controls in 1964 after Sarit's death, a vigorous, if narrowly based, neutralist sentiment immediately reappeared.

Thai-American relations improved during Sarit's regime. In the 1960s, extensive U.S. aid programs (a cumulative total of $315.0 million in economic aid and $423.3 million in military assistance by 1963) reached full stride, and important projects in communications and transportation were launched. Air base facilities in the central and northeast regions constructed in the early 1960s enabled the United States to send substantial and immediate support to the Indochinese states to the east.

Presumably, the Thais agreed to accept these bases because of the deteriorating military situation in Laos and Vietnam and because Bangkok was granted the right to restrict use of these facilities to the defense of Thailand and its vital interests. The appearance of allied air and ground forces during the 1962 Laos crisis, the retention of an allied air presence thereafter, and the more active military role played by the United States in Laos and Vietnam all helped make the Thai-American connection, strengthened by the Rusk-Thanat accord, more intimate than ever. The rise of a guerrilla threat in the mid-1960s further strengthened the country's interest in the alliance and the direct help it could provide for internal security.[13]

Thailand has now become the westernmost anchor of a network of U.S. military bases that extends all the way to Japan. Despite the lack of regional diplomatic integration in security affairs and despite various restrictions on America's freedom to treat its strong points around the Chinese periphery as a truly integrated defense system, the physical potential is there, and Thailand has made important contributions to it. Moreover, in practice, the United States has gained a surprising degree of area-wide mobility from its "diplomatically disconnected" base network.

Drawing a Balance Sheet

SEATO has provided legal sanction for much of America's freedom to maneuver in the region, and its members give the organization much credit for making Communist states recognize the danger involved in committing overt aggression. Though during the previous decade it was believed that the treaty's main function would lie in the field of subversion, its supporters now—ironically enough—doubt SEATO's utility in the antiguerrilla sphere but consider it effective in deterring direct attack, such as that suffered by neutral India in 1962. Anxieties on the subversion issue have been intensified not only by the immediate dangers of the Indochina War but also by a belief that Communist success in Vietnam might lead to new guerrilla efforts in both Thailand and the Philippines.

It is difficult to draw a balance sheet on SEATO because the treaty is limited in Asian membership, in territory covered, and in the commitments of the signatories. In such circumstances, changes in the policies of individual members—often produced by motivations irrelevant to the treaty's provisions—may have a profound effect upon the organization and its value.

A tentative appraisal at this date would have to include the following negative considerations:

1. Subversion and internal war continue to elude SEATO's operational scope and confront the alliance with its gravest long-term issue. This problem goes beyond the matter of determining when to act in a civil war or whether outside aggression has occurred. (However, the French contention of 1965 that the war in South Vietnam was primarily indigenous—although they had signed previous SEATO communiqués that held the North responsible—indicates that even this question can raise unanticipated difficulties.) Serious difficulties in the national politics in the threatened countries must also be taken into consideration. Reforms needed to thwart guerrillas in Northeast Thailand or Central Luzon, for instance, cannot be enacted without dealing with deep-rooted domestic political interests and issues on which an outside agency can have only a mar-

ginal impact. In any event, helping an Asian state maintain its internal security is at best a delicate act of diplomacy for a Western power. In the semiannual security reviews by SEATO experts, for example, Western representatives face the difficult problem of tactfully but effectively delving into the domestic affairs of the Asian signatories.

2. Loyalty to SEATO has never been high, and the recent aloofness of Pakistan, combined with France's anti-American positions, has diminished the confidence of the states that still wish to make the system work. This problem, to a great extent, is a result of policies not directly related to the organization. Yet SEATO is a vulnerable target against which Pakistan can project its displeasure over America's policy toward India, and France can assert its distinctive appeal to the underdeveloped world. And there is little the United States can do to keep members from using SEATO in this negative manner to implement national policies.

3. Constitutionally confined to a given area, the alliance has been unable to project itself as a force for stability in lands beyond its purview. Even within its territorial range, as its failure to act in Burma and Malaysia suggests, the alliance has not extended its coverage to nonmember states. The case of Malaysia is particularly instructive. Though its predecessor, Malaya, had refused to join SEATO in 1957, just six years later, Malaysia did seek external help —with little success—from the United States and the Asian powers to meet a threat from Indonesia. In such instances, the unwillingness of signatories to extend their duties, together with conflicts of interest among the Asian members, results in paralyzing inaction. SEATO's inability to act in Vietnam, an area within its original jurisdiction, provides even more telling evidence of the body's weaknesses.

4. The hostility of neutrals toward SEATO has seemed somewhat less pronounced since 1960, with some neutral states privately (but not publicly) acknowledging its security value. But Burma and Ceylon have adhered firmly to their neutralist course, and any trend of diminishing antagonism in India was directly proportionate to increasing Pakistani complaints that the alliance was not serving its national interests to the extent originally hoped.

5. The Western allies were just as reluctant to undertake a long-term obligation to station ground forces in the area in the 1960s as they had been in the previous decade. After 1954, with France's departure from Indochina, Britain and America repeatedly demon-

strated their willingness to employ force in Southeast Asia as needed, but only in response to crises. When it came to allocating any contingents to be kept under SEATO control, they both demurred. The United States has greatly modified its retaliatory concept since November 10, 1954, when Secretary Dulles told the Senate that the treaty did not affect the policy of deploying Pacific forces wherever the United States chose and striking back as it decided. The idea of massive retaliation had begun to give way to a measured or controlled response late in the Dulles era, but avoidance of prior commitment of extensive ground forces has remained a hallmark of American policy even in Thailand and the Philippines.

6. The United States repeatedly asserts its belief in the importance of coalition operations. Nevertheless, it has avoided operating through SEATO whenever possible. The 1962 landings in Thailand, the retaliatory strikes and escalation in South Vietnam, and the appeal for third-country assistance to Saigon are dramatic illustrations of this tendency. This policy has deprived some allies, especially the Philippines, of the opportunity to support or join in these actions under the legitimacy of the SEATO banner. Had the American forces been moved from Luzon to the mainland under SEATO auspices, there would have been no basis for Filipino nationalist complaints that the deployments were unilateral and, therefore, violated the host country's sovereign authority. Of course, resort to SEATO means running the risk of coming under a degree of alliance control. But if the United States wishes to avoid this, it can hardly appeal to an allied sense of duty to participate. Moreover, other states are also jealous of their prestige. Many call for multilateral SEATO aid, but whenever a member other than America gives aid, it makes certain to emphasize its role in order to garner full credit. Apparently, other states think that only American assistance should go through "multilateral" SEATO channels.

Though the organization's problems and the general instability of Southeast Asia, tend to overshadow the contributions SEATO has made to the region's security, its achievements are notable and important:

1. No signatory has suffered a direct attack, whereas Malaysia, despite its security pact with Britain, and neutral India have been far less fortunate. The U.S. commitment remains the outstanding factor in maintaining Southeast Asian security notwithstanding the Communist inroads in South Vietnam and the dangers of subversion in Thailand and the Philippines.

2. SEATO has provided an important framework for significant bilateral accords between Washington and Bangkok. Without it, a major treaty would have been required to validate the Rusk-Thanat accord of 1962. Similarly, the treaty's Protocol provided a formal basis for American military support of South Vietnam. (In originally justifying American military intervention there, however, Washington stressed its direct commitments to Saigon far more than the SEATO pact.) [14] In turn, the Asian allies find a multilateral treaty less onerous than a bilateral one in responding to neutralist opposition at home and abroad, and when combined with strong bilateral assurances of support, a multilateral treaty confers a strong sense of security.

3. Despite the severe criticism of American policy emanating from Pakistan and France and their refusal to undertake or execute significant military obligations, both powers have repeatedly reaffirmed their desire to remain in the treaty system. Until the mid-1960s, at least, both states retained a commitment to respond to an act of overt aggression, even if they denied the likelihood of such an event. The United States for its part still derives direct military value from its tie with Pakistan and desires to keep open the SEATO channels for cooperation with France should the opportunity arise.

4. The United States has a legal basis for deploying its forces and moving them about within the treaty zone without suffering from the restrictive national controls that could be imposed under a series of bilateral accords. Although, as the Philippine experience indicated, Washington has not taken full advantage of this asset, it remains potentially available. Only the unrestricted use of Okinawa, but at the high price of a strong nationalist reaction there and in Japan, gives the United States a higher degree of freedom and mobility than SEATO could theoretically confer.

5. Neutrals have gained some protection through the mere existence of SEATO as a counterweight to the Communist military presence. Their hostility toward the treaty as such has diminished in recent years. Instances of good relations between aligned and neutral powers, as in the case of Thailand and Burma and, sporadically, the Philippines and Indonesia, indicate that adherence to the treaty need not prove a major obstacle to cooperation among neighbors. In one case, however—Pakistan's effort to establish an anti-Indian front with the neutral states of Southeast Asia—such crossing of diplo-

matic boundaries has worked to the detriment of American security interests.

6. Finally, the SEATO connection may have had some restraining effect on the behavior pattern of our Asian allies. Pakistan might have gone to much further extremes, and much sooner, in its anti-Indian policy had it been unaligned. Without an American treaty and its reassurance, Thailand might have committed itself more deeply to the unstable rightist regimes in Laos during 1958–61 and to the abortive rightist coups that occurred after the neutralist leader, Souvanna Phouma, returned to power. Similarly, the Filipino position on Malaysia might have been even more divisive had it not encountered the dismay of its allies.

CHAPTER EIGHT

The Indian Subcontinent

American concern with Southcentral Asia—an area embracing Afghanistan, Pakistan, India, and Ceylon—developed slowly, even after the end of British rule in 1947–48. Though Britain's departure shattered the area's strategic unity, this aspect of independence received little attention because nation-building, anti-imperialism, and, somewhat later, neutralism seemed to be overriding values. Except for the enmity between India and Pakistan, no immediate security issues troubled the scene. With the West gone, only a highly unconventional belief in the possibility of threats from "nonimperial" fellow Asian states could have evoked a security orientation in these countries. And only Pakistan, fearing that New Delhi would not tolerate its survival, could imagine such an eventuality. Beset with vast Afghan territorial claims against its western sector, uncertain about the adequacy of its Muslim and anti-Indian sentiment as bases for statehood, and concerned about the 1,000-mile separation of its two vulnerable wings, Pakistan soon showed an interest in acquiring even distant allies.

The Lack of Strategic Unity

In the pre-independence era, the strategic unity of the region had rested on Britain's dominant political position, its control of the seas, and a strong Indian Army that could protect Burma and Afghanistan as well as project its force into the Middle East and Southeast Asia. With independence, all this changed. The new political divisions soon rivaled historic cockpits like the Balkans in their tangled complexity. At the core lay the deep Pakistani-Indian antagonism —over Kashmir, over the concept of communal states, and over the dismemberment of the subcontinent. Neutral Afghanistan had claims against Pakistan and looked to India and the Soviet Union for

124

support against the common opponent. Ceylon soon sought refuge in neutralism, fearing Indian cultural dominance and subversion from large settlements of Indian Tamil workers whom it considered potentially dangerous and unassimilable. Burma, too, feared Indian dominance and ultimately, in the early 1960s, expelled from its midst the despised Indian merchant community.

Although India was the central power, it did not try to establish security accords or to compose its differences with its neighbors. On the contrary, its own deep neutralism led it to disavow all alliances, with neighbors as well as the West, and to avoid creating even blocs of neutralists. Nor did it cultivate close and friendly relations with these states. In part, this attitude reflected a deep sense of nationalism, which found expression in nonalignment; in part, it reflected apprehension that others would recoil in fear and hostility from Indian attempts, as the largest power in the region, to force itself on others.

Yet India also aspired—in an abstract, universal way—to be a leader in world politics, particularly of the unaligned states. Animated by ethical traditions condemning violence, India adopted and propagated a peace-oriented neutralist philosophy. It advocated disarmament at the United Nations, pressed its views at nonaligned conferences, and—in less passive manifestations of its pacifist tendency—fostered truces in the Korean and Indochinese wars, administered the Korean truce, served on the International Control Commission (ICC) in Indochina, and sent a major force (4,500 men) to the Congo. Its contribution in the Congo came at the United Nations' moment of crisis in 1961 after other, more strident neutralists, such as Ghana and Egypt, had withdrawn their support. But India faced grave dilemmas in reconciling its nonviolent policy with the constraints on its position in South Asian politics. It used force to take Hyderabad in 1948, refused to compromise or allow a plebiscite over Kashmir, and (despite its professions to the contrary) deeply feared China.

To the two great changes in the region—post-colonial political fragmentation and the absence of Indian leadership—a third was soon added: the appearance of strong, dangerous powers to the north. Though at first Soviet power seemed more menacing, China shortly emerged as the greater danger. But India continued its attempt to accommodate China by opposing SEATO, accepting Peking's assurances regarding internal autonomy for Tibet, and sponsoring Peking at the United Nations, while treating Pakistan as its main military threat. To implement this policy, the Indian government even kept from its own people its knowledge of Chinese incursions into Indian territory and acts of suppression in Tibet during 1956–59.[1]

Pakistan, despairing of normal relations with India, viewed the rise of Peking as a godsend, and took constant care, as the Indians were later to observe bitterly, to assure Peking that it saw no conflict of interest between itself and China. While recognizing the benefits of their American tie, with its security assurances and substantial military aid, the Pakistanis repeatedly complained that neither SEATO nor CENTO provided a commitment of support against what they regarded as India's threat to their country's very existence.

In the view of the United States, the two great states of the subcontinent have uselessly dissipated their resources and prevented the formation of a regional alliance to contain Communist China (though the two countries might resist communism at home). As a result, one of the most significant strategic areas in Asia has presented the United States with a most intractable security problem. The strong national feelings in these great lands, the absence of any previous American involvement, and the incompatibility in the objectives of all concerned combine to make Washington's current influence on the course of events extremely marginal.

The saving grace, in a security perspective, is the relative remoteness thus far of the threat from the north, and the absence of an indigenous Communist military force within the subcontinent. Despite China's success in its 1962 invasion of India, both India and Pakistan are too massive, too developed politically, and too strong in relation to China's current level of power to fall victim to the degree of physical pressure that can be applied against them in the near future. Their safety is further enhanced by Moscow's policy of opposing violence in this region, extending large-scale assistance to India, and seeking better relations with Pakistan, which it hopes to win over to a position of nonalignment. Still, India and Pakistan suffer from profound weaknesses, and the present diplomatic maneuvering may have ominous consequences.

Pakistan Aligned

The hostility between India and Pakistan has produced a number of striking diplomatic shifts. In the early 1950s, Indian-American relations were at low ebb while Indian-Chinese and Pakistani-American connections flourished. But from 1955 on, a new pattern of relationships seemed to emerge.

Pakistan never had disguised its anti-Indian motivation for joining SEATO; and the United States, which viewed SEATO as a means of containing Peking, had not originally included Pakistan in the alignment. Even when at the behest of Britain, in August 1954, Pakistan announced its intention to join, it immediately made clear to Peking that it hoped to maintain their cordial relations. Pakistan hoped to isolate neutral India, by bringing the other Colombo Powers into SEATO, much as it would stress neutralism a decade later to isolate an India dependent on Western and Soviet military support. Though the attempt at aligning its Colombo partners failed, Pakistan did succeed in breaking the group's unity, helped greatly by Indian unwillingness to undertake treaty commitments to the other states. Pakistan's nationalistic thrust, powerfully fueled by the Kashmir dispute, thus proved compatible with the American policy in 1954 of expanding SEATO and opposing neutralism. But the different objectives of Karachi and Washington meant that even at the start, Pakistan's dramatic abandonment of nonalignment was far from clear-cut.

Meanwhile, Karachi had been drawing closer to the pro-Western states of Turkey and Iran, in a move that culminated in the Baghdad Pact of 1955 (with Britain and Iraq as the other full members). In fact, Washington had first discerned Pakistan's strong interest in a security link while canvassing for a stronger diplomatic posture in the Middle East. But when in November 1953 the United States informed India of its intention to offer Pakistan substantial military assistance, India withdrew an offer made to Karachi that August to consider a plebiscite for Kashmir and adopted a position of complete rigidity on the issue.

India argued that the Mutual Defense Assistance agreement of May 1954 between the United States and Pakistan [2] made its neighbor a major military threat, necessitated Indian rearmament, and put Pakistan in the "service" of American interests. India's anger even led it to demand the removal of American citizens from the U.N. peace observation mission in Kashmir. The Pakistanis charged India with efforts to control their foreign policy, prevent them from exercising the right of self-defense, and keep them neutral so that India could attain its alleged objective—domination of South Asia. Karachi also observed that India itself had signed a similar aid pact with the United States in 1951, which it later renewed in 1958.

The 1954 agreement stipulated that Pakistan would use the aid only for internal security, self-defense, participation in the defense of the area, or in U.N. collective security measures. Further, Pakistan affirmed that it would not commit aggression.[3] Nonetheless, India remained unmollified and took the same aggrieved stance— that these conditions did not protect its security interests and could readily be violated—that Pakistan was to adopt in 1962, when the Anglo-American powers began aiding India.

Pakistan joined the Baghdad Pact in 1955, arousing the ire of Moscow and leading it to change its stand on Kashmir from neutrality to support of India. Russia even vetoed a mild U.N. Security Council resolution calling on the two powers to settle their dispute through bilateral negotiations. The CENTO tie (as the Baghdad Pact was renamed following a neutralist coup in 1958 in Baghdad that ended Iraq's membership) had compensatory benefits, however, for the United States concluded separate Bilateral Agreements of Cooperation with the three remaining Muslim members. Under the American-Pakistani accord of March 5, 1959, the United States recognized that Pakistan's independence and integrity were vital to its own interests, and "in case of aggression against Pakistan, the Government of the United States of America, in accordance with the Constitution of the United States of America, will take such appropriate action, including the use of armed force, as may be mutually agreed upon."[4] At this time, President Mohammed Ayub Khan offered to form a common defense policy with India if New Delhi would settle the Kashmir dispute. But Prime Minister Nehru on May 7, 1959, vigorously rejected this offer, terming it "almost some kind of military alliance."[5]

Pakistan's Difficulties

Pakistan's view of the threat posed by communism is far from consistent, with varying estimates dominant over the course of time, but it was not indifferent to the problem. Although its primary worry was obviously India, Pakistan demonstrated some concern with Russian and even Chinese aggression from its early days of independence. Ayub's offer to Nehru of a common defense policy in 1959 reflects his recognition that a divided subcontinent constituted a vulnerable target to potential aggressors from the north. The accords with the West, moreover, embroiled Pakistan in disputes with

Moscow. Speaking at Srinagar, Kashmir, during his visit to India in December 1955, Nikita Khrushchev denounced the partition of India and accused foreign powers of exploiting the subcontinent's religious differences for their own ends. He asserted that Kashmir was a part of India, according to the wishes of the people of the area—despite India's refusal to allow a vote on this issue. Soviet pressure continued with a note of April 1958 that complained bitterly of Pakistan's participation in alliances, accused Karachi of allowing the United States to construct air bases and missile installations on its territory, and claimed that Pakistan had asked for atomic and rocket weapons at a recent CENTO meeting. Like India, the Soviet Union attacked the bilateral American-Pakistani accord of 1959, arguing that such links drew Pakistan into the military ventures of third powers and infringed on Moscow's security.

Karachi responded that despite Soviet bases near Pakistan, there were no American military combat bases or installations on Pakistani soil; it added that its defensive accords lay within the right of collective security and endangered no one. The abortive U-2 flight of May 1960 by Francis Gary Powers, however, brought the issue of bases to a climax. Premier Khrushchev threatened to destroy Peshawar, the admitted point of departure, and though Pakistan denied any role in the affair, its position had obviously been compromised. The importance of the base for such flights diminished sharply, as did threats from Khrushchev, when President Eisenhower announced the end of U-2 operations over Russia. From then on, Pakistan presumably exercised tight control over military facilities on its soil.[6]

Another major disagreement between Karachi and Moscow was instigated by Afghanistan. The Afghans had a long-standing claim to the region on the Pakistan border called Pushtunistan, which they later extended to preposterous length in claiming a major slice of West Pakistan extending all the way to the coast. During the mid-1950s, as various Middle Eastern Muslim states failed in attempts to mediate the dispute, Afghanistan became increasingly outspoken in its demands. In 1955, it even opposed Karachi's decision to consolidate the subdivisions of West Pakistan into a single administrative entity. The Soviet government supported Afghanistan's claim at that time, sending considerable economic and military aid.

Pakistan viewed the subsequent Soviet economic and military penetration of Afghanistan with deep suspicion. It feared that Moscow would gain a political stranglehold over the economy and use its comprehensive land surveys for espionage. Pakistan was further alarmed by Russia's construction of strategic roads and its increased influence over the Afghan army. Karachi became convinced that this was a Russian pressure tactic, since Moscow offered to better relations if Pakistan followed a more independent line in foreign policy. In 1960, the Soviets demanded self-determination, on the basis of the U.N. Charter, for the Pathan people who inhabit the Pakistani-Afghan border region. Pakistan angrily invoked its Western alliances as the basis of its foreign policy and the guarantee of its sovereignty. Denouncing the Soviet Union for its designs on the entire subcontinent, Karachi countered with a call—purely for the record—for a referendum among the Pathans in Afghanistan.

Even China presented problems during this period, though never a major threat. Pakistan followed the Commonwealth course, granting Peking early recognition and supporting its admission to the United Nations. Like India, Pakistan exchanged high ministerial visits with China, even in the prime years of its Western orientation. Peking never engaged in such direct pressure against Pakistan's alignment as Moscow did, and Karachi in turn stressed its desire at every opportunity to remain friendly with Peking. However, China did have a border claim of about 1,000 square miles against Pakistan, and Ayub's defense offer to Nehru in 1959 moved Peking to ask against whom the cooperation would be directed. Also in 1959, Karachi demonstrated sufficient general concern with Communist expansion to call upon Asian states to join in collective self-defense arrangements. It also supported the U.N. resolution that same year on Tibet, condemning Chinese violation of human rights.

In general, until 1962, Pakistan looked upon its Western tie as a guarantee of defense from an overweening Indian neighbor and from a threat, possibly through Afghan pressures, from the north. Pakistani leaders recognized the value of the West's military aid and security guarantees, while they retained the all-important right to conduct an independent foreign policy. But Karachi never lost sight of the price involved—Soviet support of India, exacerbation of the Afghan problem, loss of any chance to settle the Kashmir issue, and estrangement from Asian neutrals. Pakistan also considered its Western orientation partly to blame—along with Arab exclusiveness and Egyptian jealousy of a rival—for its inability to exercise any substantial influence in the Arab world. Furthermore, public opinion at home remained split, somewhat along the lines of the country's territorial division; most support for the alliances lay in West

Pakistan, whereas East Pakistan harbored a strong current of neutralism, which was vividly displayed in the 1954 election campaign and its hectic aftermath. Following Ayub's authoritarian coup in 1958, expressions of neutralism began to appear more frequently and persistently in the press and in the observations of national officials.

SEATO and the Subcontinent

In this context, SEATO held an insecure position in the Pakistani scheme of priorities. With the country's main security interests, military power, and support for the alliance centered in its Western sector, many East Pakistanis—along with some in the Western part --—regarded SEATO as an unnecessary and dangerous national commitment and felt that as long as the Indian problem remained unresolved, the country could ill afford to dispatch troops to Southeast Asia. Nonetheless, though the country had no American combat bases on its soil and did not participate in SEATO military exercises, Pakistan's leaders insisted through 1961 that they would meet their treaty obligations without hesitation.[7] With the largest force of any of the allies in the area, Pakistan had an important role in the contingency plans developed late in the 1950s, making an implicit commitment to provide the forces required in time of need. And in the Laos crisis of 1961, Pakistan sided with Thailand in calling for action.[8]

An important motive for the country's continued adherence to SEATO was the vulnerability of its eastern wing, which many Pakistanis considered indefensible without the cooperation of India —although a few of the military argued that the region could be defended by relying on amphibious operations.[9] Despite the fact that more than half its people live in East Pakistan and the region is gradually increasing its influence in national affairs, the regime has assigned few important forces there and the advocates of SEATO have employed the argument that the treaty is a shield to obviate the need to fight in East Pakistan.

Thus, those favoring the alignment held that it raised national self-esteem, provided insurance against Indian ambitions, and deterred possible attack. The opposition included advocates of neutralism, those who sought new ties with which to pressure India, and those who felt that Pakistan did not have the resources for involvement in Southeast Asia. Moreover, there was a general feeling that the alignment was bringing the Kashmir issue no nearer to a successful resolution. But all were united in their desire to use SEATO in relation to Kashmir and other non-Communist problems.

In this regard, SEATO at first proved of some value. For example, in the aftermath of Khrushchev's anti-Pakistan statements in December 1955, the SEATO Council the following March recognized the existing Durand Line as the legitimate Afghan-Pakistani border and stressed that the SEATO area, under Articles 4 and 8, extended to that boundary. (Britain had supported this boundary from the outset, in 1949.) Still, SEATO was not legally obligated to act in case of aggression on this frontier unless the operation was Communist-influenced. Pakistan therefore stressed the rise of Soviet influence in Afghanistan. At the same 1956 meeting, the Council deplored Khrushchev's pro-Indian statement on Kashmir and went on record with a mild affirmation of "the need for an early settlement of the Kashmir question through the United Nations or by direct negotiations." The only other time Pakistani interests received SEATO support was in 1957, when the Council made a critical reference to neutralism. But these actions did not satisfy Karachi's vital interests or appease Pakistani critics of the SEATO accord. Restiveness with the tie grew as the Western treaty members steadfastly refused to use SEATO as an instrument for effective pressure against India.

India, America, and Pakistan

The unstable equilibrium in South Asia became increasingly precarious as Western relations with India improved steadily during 1958–62. When Washington and London extended military aid to India in a systematic if modest way, Pakistani sentiment turned sharply against the West. This was reminiscent of the hostility against the West which India displayed because of the creation of SEATO, the West's unfriendly comments on neutralism, and its "intervention" in the Kashmir dispute. As the Indians saw it, SEATO had compelled them to reinforce their Pakistani frontier and end all pretense about allowing a plebiscite in Kashmir. Following Defense Minister V. K. Krishna Menon's policy, India treated Pakistan as its main threat and tried, with indifferent results outside its northern region, to make the Kashmir issue a major rallying point for national patriotic sentiment.

Even while the Pakistan-SEATO problem caused a strain in India's relations with the West, two significant issues were already compelling India to adopt a more moderate stance toward the United States. The first was the country's growing economic crisis, reflected in food shortages, inadequate foreign exchange, and difficulty in reaching planned rates of growth. Only substantial Western help, in the hundreds of millions of dollars, enabled New Delhi to complete its second five-year plan, and it took $1 billion a year in foreign aid to keep the third (1961–66) plan afloat. In addition, the United States began a huge agricultural assistance program in 1959, averaging about three million tons of wheat and substantial, if smaller quantities, of rice annually. This help was to prove crucial in averting famine, panic, and skyrocketing food prices. Even with such help, India found itself with recurrent food shortages during the 1960s.

The second development pushing India and the West closer together was the rising Chinese power and bellicosity. In 1958, the United States renewed its 1951 agreement to provide India with some military aid and softened its opposition to neutralism. Washington even acknowledged that in some instances, neutralism could serve American security aspirations inasmuch as it strengthened the determination of nonaligned powers to preserve their sovereign independence.[10]

The renewed aid for India and Washington's acceptance of neutralism caused great consternation in Pakistan, where hostility toward India had not abated despite settlement of differences on such important matters as trade, the development of the Indus River basin, and refugee control and compensation. President Ayub went so far as to interpret America's assurances to India in 1959 that the Agreement of Cooperation with Pakistan would never be used against India to mean that the United States would not aid Pakistan if attacked by India. Such an extreme distortion of the pledge extended in 1954 reflects Pakistan's obsessive antipathy toward a country that, it argued, had tried to prevent Karachi from joining an alliance and tried to dictate where and when it could receive military aid. Pakistan also held that India aspired to regional "leadership" that really meant domination, refused to settle territorial disputes, and carried within its body politic Hindu communalists who might some day gain power and try to destroy their Muslim neighbor.[11]

The great Himalayan crisis of 1962 brought matters to a head for Pakistan. Since the invasion set China and India at loggerheads, it offered Pakistan a golden opportunity to break out of its Asian isolation. Up to that time, Pakistan had been at odds with two great neighbors, Moscow and New Delhi, and enjoyed only tolerable relations with Peking. Now the Chinese confrontation with India offered Pakistan leverage in the Kashmir dispute, plus new protection against a future assault from New Delhi. It also provided Pakistan with its first opportunity to receive help from both sides in the Cold War. India had previously infuriated Karachi by using a nonalignment policy to obtain considerable aid from both Washington and Moscow.

The Anglo-American response of help to India (though a modest $120 million, primarily for mountain defense, in 1962–63 and an equal amount the following year, essentially for air defense and transportation) came as a staggering blow to Pakistan. The anguish mounted sharply in 1964 when the United States demonstrated its intent to continue military aid to India with a modest long-term program. To Pakistan, this decision was folly beyond belief; whereas to Washington, it reflected the simple virtue of helping a new-found associate (however limited the relationship) defend itself against aggression from Peking. Though the United States sponsored Indian-Pakistani talks in 1963, it would not make its new assistance to New Delhi conditional on a Kashmir settlement. Washington feared that such pressure, just as India was facing up to the Chinese threat, would deprive it of a great chance to establish a new alignment against Peking. Pakistan responded with bitterness over what it considered a totally misdirected American emphasis, and the two countries exchanged recriminations over one another's willingness to undermine the alliance in pursuit of objectives that the other considered harmful.

Though recognizing that its ultimate security depended on normalization of relations with India, Pakistan held that only if India yielded on the Kashmir question could Karachi operate as an effective member of the anti-Communist alliance. Such Pakistani reasoning, particularly as it led to attempts to exploit Chinese pressure on India to gain concessions on Kashmir, seemed illogical to Washington. For violent action to win Kashmir or even to wring concessions from India under foreign pressure could only strengthen the extremist communal parties in New Delhi that would seek to undo the partition of 1947. Yet the frustration of fifteen years could no longer be held back. The Chinese assault of 1962 had broken the old diplomatic order, seemingly unfavorable to Pakistan, and suddenly provided an opportunity for new maneuvering. To lose this momentary advantage, and in fact to see Indian strength rebounding to new heights through arms aid programs, was more than Pakistan could endure.

Pakistani and American Policies at Odds

It is apparent that Pakistan has shown tactical consistency in using its every resource to extract a settlement on Kashmir before Indian power and, as a consequence, Indian intransigence became prohibitive. At first, this policy meant exploiting the shock of the Chinese victory in the Himalayas to compel a settlement. At that stage, Pakistan sought to persuade the Americans and British to make Western help to India contingent on concessions regarding Kashmir. But Washington rushed in ground equipment and air protection, both to bolster India and to make certain that the Soviet Union did not preempt this field. In the futile Indian-Pakistani discussions of 1963, India agreed only to consider relatively minor boundary rectifications. Partition proved abhorrent to both sides, discussion of a condominium over Kashmir led nowhere (Pakistan viewed this as a transitional step to acquisition; India saw it as an uncompensated loss), and negotiations over control of headwaters in Kashmir ended in deadlock.

As India received military assistance, with promises of more to come, Pakistan showed increasing signs of a "now or never" mentality. New Delhi would soon have sufficient power to deter or turn back a new Chinese aggression, signifying a potential at some time to launch a successful assault on Pakistan. To retain any hope of salvaging a Kashmir settlement out of this new situation, Pakistan would have to embark on a drastic shift in policy—some alignment with China, and recourse to violence. By such activism, Pakistan apparently hoped to propel the issue onto the world diplomatic stage and force a solution that would stress the right of self-determination and thus the justice of its cause.

In 1963, Pakistan minimized the Chinese threat to India and the subcontinent in general and downgraded the role that India would play if a defense against Peking became necessary. Pakistan termed the 1962 Chinese assault not a sustained threat but a border demonstration that did not threaten India's vital security interests. It branded U.S. military aid to India premature and, in light of China's withdrawal, unnecessary. It treated continued Western help to New Delhi—despite India's failure to substantiate its claims of massive Chinese preparations in Tibet—as appalling and incomprehensible.

America received promises from India that the aid, primarily to equip mountain combat divisions, would not be used for aggressive purposes against Pakistan, and it assured the Pakistanis that the Indian promises would be enforced. But just as Pakistan's similar promise a decade earlier had not impressed India, so it was Pakistan's turn to derive cold comfort from these new assurances. Pakistan expressed doubt that the United States would act if at some distant date, when it had its hands full elsewhere in the world, India (perhaps having by then doubled its army to 22 divisions) exerted subtle pressure or launched a direct attack on Pakistan. From this perspective, the continuance of Indian-Chinese antagonism and of some protection from Peking seemed to be diplomatic imperatives for Pakistan. More than anything else, this assessment reveals how far apart America and Pakistan had drifted.

Pakistan moved closer to Peking with new commercial arrangements, cultural exchanges, a boundary settlement,[12] and an aviation agreement that gave China a route through Pakistan. Those in Pakistan who favored reliance on close relations with the Chinese may have argued that they could do much along this line—essentially to redress the balance against India—without losing Western ties. Karachi did not wish to terminate its membership in the CENTO and SEATO pacts since these were the bases for a vast American military-aid program, and China was apparently satisfied with obtaining an "ally of opportunity" in its effort to isolate India.[13] Peking therefore appeared content when Pakistan reduced its participation in the treaty organizations, adopted a neutralist tone, and, especially, expressed far from wholehearted support for the American war effort in Vietnam.

The greatest difficulty for Pakistan lay in sustaining the American tie while pursuing a policy so much at odds with American concepts, policies, and commitments. In fact, Washington's reactions became steadily more hostile as the 1960s progressed. As Pakistan's policy grows more nationalistic, it inexorably moves in the direction of neutralism—the powerful impulse that dominates most of the underdeveloped world. Apart from the former American colony, the Philippines, and a state the United States rescued from conquest, South Korea, only one of all the states that gained independence after 1945 became an American ally—Pakistan. The state that manifested the greatest desire to break the U.S.-Pakistan alliance was the Soviet Union, which in 1965 and early 1966 abandoned its policy of complete support for India on Kashmir to take a position of neutrality. But Pakistan probably calculated that Moscow would not pay a high enough price to make a break with the United States worthwhile.

A confrontation of sorts developed nonetheless between the United States and Pakistan, centering on the issue of economic aid, essential to sustain Pakistan's remarkable record of economic growth. Although, as in the case of India, a consortium of industrial powers rendered assistance to Pakistan under World Bank auspices, the United States was the prime mover in this effort. In mid-1965, Washington showed its displeasure with Pakistan's policy line by delaying a decision on assisting that country's third five-year plan.

The net overall effect for the United States was loss of support from the subcontinent for its defensive efforts in Southeast Asia. Pakistani participation and commitments under SEATO faded to the vanishing point; with official approval, its press leveled strenuous attacks on the United States; its government, like India's, took a strong stand against American military action against North Vietnam; and its Foreign Minister, Z. A. Bhutto, displayed a strong preference for the new tie with China. The United States regarded Pakistan's unrelenting effort to isolate India as a great tragedy, for it neutralized many of the benefits derived from India's new wariness of China and its determination to oppose further assaults. The subcontinent was more than ever divided, China had humiliated India, and Pakistan had detached itself to an important degree from the Western camp.

Pakistan sought to make its way as an independent and critical ally of America, perhaps on the French model.[14] Nevertheless, it felt obliged to depend on China for its security, whereas Paris did not need to take such a drastic measure, having American protection against Russia and a reasonably friendly relationship with its German neighbor. In 1963, Pakistan's Foreign Minister Bhutto asserted that "the largest power in Asia" would come to his country's assistance in case of Indian aggression. Under these circumstances, either the United States or Pakistan might have terminated the alliance. Yet through 1966 the United States showed no signs of contemplating such a step, perhaps because it thought that dissolution of a solemn defense accord would set a bad precedent, and perhaps because it recognized that in any case Pakistan's independence required U.S. military and economic aid. Moreover, a complete split would diminish the little existing U.S. influence to press for a settlement on the subcontinent and impose a gratuitous obstacle to the reestablishment of better relations should conditions change.

Thus, even during the Indian-Pakistani war of 1965, though begun by Pakistan's infiltration of Kashmir, the United States treated both sides impartially, at least to the extent of calling for a cease-fire and suspending major assistance programs. Each warring party, of course, considered this policy discriminatory. But probably because this surface neutrality could have hurt Pakistan more, since it was more dependent on American assistance for its basic defense posture, Pakistan reacted more sharply than India against the American position. Yet Washington had not even taken a strong and immediate verbal stand against Pakistan's extensive use of sophisticated military equipment in this war, though such an outright violation of the aid agreement left America's 1959 guarantee to India in shambles. This violation of earlier agreements, however, did make future acquisitions of new American equipment most doubtful and led Pakistan to turn—with some success—to Peking for tanks and jet combat planes. The Pakistanis justified this move on the grounds of much larger Soviet military assistance to India.

India: Cold-War Neutral Against China

One Pakistani argument proved correct: India would not join any Asian defense system. At the very best, it would defend its own positions. But it still would not join any alliances, encourage other states to do so, or even support American military actions in Southeast Asia. In the Vietnam crisis, for example, India wished to see Chinese power contained but feared that too strong an American response would drive Russia and China together again. India continued to adhere to its policy of nonalignment even toward its Southeast Asian neighbors who felt threatened by China.

As the Pakistanis also noted, India considered the national state of China, not communism, its major enemy and continued to treat communism as an ideological challenge not linked to any power threat. President Ayub argued that the entire basis of U.S. policy—the alleged durability of Sino-Indian hostility—would soon dissolve, as India settled with China. China has, in fact, repeatedly offered a complete settlement—on its own terms: New Delhi's acceptance of the *de facto* lines of territorial control that would ratify Peking's rule over the Aksai Chin plateau in India's northwestern frontier region. Nonetheless, an Indian-Chinese rapprochement would be possible in good part as a result of Pakistan's actions. If Pakistan's military challenge becomes so persistent that New Delhi feels obligated to cut its losses elsewhere, or, on the other hand, should the regime in New Delhi feel politically strong enough (*e.g.*, after a limited military victory over Pakistan), India might come to terms with China. However, the catalyst would be Pakistan itself.

It may be that despite his professions to the contrary, Ayub is fairly certain of the essential durability of Sino-Indian hostility. But he may well doubt the stability of Peking's association with what the Chinese must consider a landlord-dominated military Islamic state like Pakistan. For Pakistan to jeopardize or disavow its American tie may indicate, in addition to a certain rashness, a confident calculation that the tensions between New Delhi and Peking will persist. Should the Pakistanis conclude that India and China will reconcile their differences in the near future, they might also expect their friendly relations with Peking to be short-lived. Washington considers the Sino-Indian dispute very deep and real and believes that only its hostility to New Delhi blinds Pakistan (if indeed Pakistan is blinded) to the fundamental shift in world diplomacy that the conflict between India and China has produced.

Yet how much has Indian policy really shifted? For reasons of its own national interest and without significant American influence, India has assumed a hostile stance against China. India also insists on complete freedom to alter its China policy again, without feeling obliged to take the views of others into account. Moreover, India calls for aid on its own terms and offers no accommodation to American interests in return, holding that its anti-Chinese stance affords sufficient reasons for military assistance on a very large scale. It adheres to neutralism, provides no support for American policies, refuses to compromise on the Kashmir dispute, and obtains sophisticated Russian military help (though this may jeopardize the security of our own technical assistance). It refuses to allow bases on its soil, though foreign military experts consider them necessary for the effective defense of its territory against the Chinese attack that it fears.

To a certain extent, the United States benefits from this informal relationship, since a closer degree of cooperation would further aggravate its difficult relations with Pakistan. But Washington must judge the net value of extending combat aid to India under such circumstances, especially since it is this military assistance that lies at the root of American-Pakistani difficulties. For its part, India prefers informal assurances and military help from many sources to a formal alignment. The birthright of neutralism, strong domestic support for nonalignment, and the hope of reasserting its role of pivotal mediator in the Cold War keep India on this course. Realistic justifications for India's policy are many, including perpetuation of the Russian-Chinese split, Soviet diplomatic support, and a continuation of substantial economic and military assistance from Moscow.

To a certain extent, these objectives reflect a coincidence of American and Indian interests, but Washington still looks upon the growth of Soviet influence in India as a mixed blessing at best. It is true that Moscow regards tension in the subcontinent with great concern and strongly opposed the abortive war of 1965.[15] American fears, however, stem from a realization that the Russians still seek to reduce Western influence in New Delhi as well as push India eventually on the path to communism. More immediately and tactically, Russia will seek Indian backing for its objectives, most of which are still opposed by Washington. And India, adjusting its conduct to avoid affronting Russia, will refrain from supporting American policy initiatives or moving toward a closer working relationship with the United States.

Regardless of how we weigh the pros and cons of continued American aid to India, the format of an *ad hoc* relationship is the only one under which any arrangement can realistically be devised in the foreseeable future. More theoretically, some analysts hold that flexible relationships, suited to the requirements of all, make for stronger or more effective ties than ponderous, official accords. As the last two decades have shown, making, renewing, modifying, terminating, or even sustaining defense pacts can impose tremendous burdens on a nation's foreign policy. There is much to be said for informal ties that confer mutual benefits of some sort with minimal entangling obligations.

However, treaties do have special values, and informal ties are often hampered by serious restrictions. In moments of crisis, leaders of states cannot confidently determine policy on the basis of private assurances of support or even public sympathy without a formal commitment. Questions of speed, types, and amounts of assistance are of crucial importance, and here, too, alignment affords greater assurance and security. A neutral, even if on reasonably good terms with the United States, cannot anticipate American support to the degree that an ally can, regardless of any unstated assumptions its leaders may make. Moreover, an alliance that has any life to it also operates to keep the partners from sliding into bitterly antagonistic positions.

When a neutral is the opponent of an ally, as in the Thai-Cambodian instance, the United States faces an additional handicap in contemplating assistance to the nonaligned state; at best, Washington can offer only limited aid or require some compensating concession on the neutral's part. Even when we did give military help to India, Pakistan's opposition played a crucial role in our refusal to offer modern fighter aircraft that India sought in order to overcome the danger of Chinese airpower. To avoid negating important Pakistani defensive advantages, Washington concentrated on strengthening India's mountain divisions and passive air defense. The upshot was that Pakistan remained angry with Washington and the dissatisfied Indians depended more than ever on the Soviet Union for advanced military equipment.

The Indians for their part believe a Western alignment would pose grave risks for their special relationship with Russia. The Soviets have long made such a major point of Indian neutrality that Moscow would have to respond with a series of critical public statements that would further weaken Indian-Soviet ties and endanger whatever *détente* existed between Moscow and the West. It would also amount to a major defeat in the Russians' struggle with the Chinese, who have strongly criticized the Soviet Union's pro-Indian policy and stress on the importance of nonalignment. At least in the idcological polemics between Moscow and Peking, the Russians treat neutralism as a valid way-station to communism, signifying adherence to the "zone of the peace," with entry into the pro-Soviet camp a potential future development.

India probably assumes that a close tie with Washington, even if it is specifically directed against China and pointedly excludes Russia as a target, would jeopardize Soviet aid and friendship. However, here too India is vulnerable since Moscow retains the freedom to move to a more equivocal position, perhaps in order to win Pakistan to neutrality. Soviet neutrality in 1965 and its sponsorship of the Indian-Pakistani peace talks in Tashkent early in 1966 indicated that the Soviet Union, no less than the United States, opposes a military solution in Kashmir and will not necessarily side with India. Unless India can retain some degree of flexibility of its own—to settle in Kashmir, come to terms with China, or move closer to the West—it will yield the diplomatic initiative to its three neighbors. Since any change along these lines requires a major Indian concession—territorial or ideological—New Delhi anxiously supports the political *status quo*. However, it then remains heavily dependent on an insecure Indian-Soviet-American "front" against China. Yet the three "front" members have conflicting objectives and are essentially uncommitted to one another, and this, we have seen, makes for uneasy bedfellows.

If the ideological and diplomatic tenets of Indian foreign policy make for an inadequate security posture, and are unlikely to change soon, then the military problem posed by this policy becomes even more significant. Nonalignment has brought India a mélange of foreign airplanes, tanks, field guns, and anti-aircraft equipment. But a mélange poses formidable obstacles to efficiency in war. No foreign power may establish, let alone man, military bases on Indian soil. Though fearful of Chinese power, and sufficiently worried about possible Sino-Pakistani aggression to appeal for vast quantities of sophisticated military equipment, the Indians in their devotion to neutralism argue that such bases are not necessary. Yet as our experience in Thailand since 1960 indicates, only the advanced preparation of bases enables a state to render effective assistance or devise realistic mutual defense plans. At present, the American base network appears adequate for defense from Japan-Korea to Thailand, but not for a sustained effort on the Indian subcontinent.

American assistance to Pakistan enabled it to develop a homogeneously equipped and trained force, one that officials in West Pakistan believed, before 1963, could meet assaults from the north and more than hold its own against attacks from India. One unfortunate consequence of this sense of superiority was its contribution to a preventive-assault mentality. Pakistan became disposed to settle the Kashmir dispute by force or generate such friction that the issue would again come into the international arena with an urgent priority to find a settlement, presumably in Pakistan's favor. The 1965 war may perpetuate in both lands the most depressing aspects of the past: the deadlock over Kashmir, the quests for modern arms from all sources, the rise of religious communal extremism at home, and the competition for Soviet support. Washington's policies—to bolster the economies of both countries, foster a Kashmir settlement, attain strategic defensive unity for the subcontinent, and give both states arms to be used only against Communist aggressors—have, in short, run into puzzling and extremely grave difficulties in South Asia.[16]

The subcontinent retains its high strategic importance and can still make a substantial contribution to the security of southern and eastern Asia. It also remains the point of greatest long-run potential danger for stability in Asia. The antagonism aroused in both India and Pakistan toward the United States during 1965—because of its military aid to the rival side and its failure to use its alleged capacity to make this enemy yield the essential concessions—indicates the frustrating complexity of American security problems in this vital region.

CHAPTER NINE

Problems of the American Presence

Advocates of an active American security policy in Asia can make a strong case in support of the physical presence of U.S. military forces in the region. Such a "forward strategy," indicating a willingness to protect the entire homeland of an Asian ally, parallels our commitment to West Germany, where the military threat, though apparently in abeyance, is potentially greater. Extensive security commitments, when feasible, seem more conducive to alliance stability than a narrower territorial obligation or a treaty arrangement not backed by forces in the region. Though the United States has refused to commit ground forces in advance to South Asia, its repeated and substantial deployments around the periphery of China have given American defensive commitments a fair degree of plausibility in a region skeptical of treaty promises. As demonstrated in Vietnam in 1965, the United States can quickly deploy several ground formations, large naval forces, and hundreds of tactical aircraft with conventional bombing capacities as much as double that of the old B-17. Without this presence, it is feared, massive Chinese power concentrated against a single victim not only might compel it to yield on the immediate point at issue but also might cause a general crisis in the country and undermine the confidence of all other governments in the region. For the present, the impact of American on-site power is increased by Communist China's lack of a highly mobile modern force and its inability to threaten U.S. home territory.

In addition to the role of American military power as an operational force, its mere presence provides a guarantee of political intent and physical capacity to bring additional strength across the

144

Pacific. The United States has gained great influence over the Nationalist Chinese regime through the presence of the Seventh Fleet and its Taiwan station. Similarly, the sizable American ground forces in Korea increased Washington's leverage in attempting to induce Seoul's military leaders to return to democratic rule in the early 1960s; and the American presence probably played a crucial role in overcoming South Korean reluctance to work for a settlement with Japan, for it offered security against possible threats from this traditional enemy as well as from North Korea. Despite the rioting in Tokyo over the security treaty with the United States, Japan's underlying desire to retain American air bases was revealed by the widespread uneasiness over the removal of F-102 squadrons in 1964—even though the shift was made possible by a growing Japanese defense capacity.

Two weaknesses intrinsic to Asia provide additional arguments for the stationing of a U.S. presence there. First, it is doubtful that most of the Asian nations have the capacity to sustain adequate defenses. The underdeveloped states of the continent rightly fear that military requirements will divert resources from economic development or social progress, both of which are vital to national security and stability, and will enhance the power and prestige of the army at the expense of the civil authorities. Moreover, the need to develop conventional forces and at the same time undertake counterinsurgency training may lead a state to spread its military as well as social and economic resources too thinly. Such a state might become vulnerable to guerrilla war based on a discontented peasantry, whether located in pivotal or overcrowded regions like Central Luzon, or in the sparsely populated, peripheral area of Northeast Thailand. (At the other extreme, Japan's very low level of military expenditures has contributed at least marginally to its remarkable economic growth rate, which, in turn, has contributed significantly to its political stability.)

A second weakness in the Asian situation is the reluctance of these states to muster strength (even when they have the capacity, as Japan does) and surmount their antipathy to a collective-defense system. Although the assertion has been made that the American military presence itself inhibits development of a collective arrangement by the Asian states, Washington considers this only a marginal factor in their unwillingness, and believes that only a major American presence can actually help persuade the non-Communist states to compose their differences and face the common threat together.

Since cohesive and sustained Asian defense against the Communists remains well beyond reach and may be so for years to come, only the United States—as the single non-Communist state capable of establishing a presence in every sector from Korea to Pakistan—can provide the core for a sustained and integrated defensive effort.

Bases

When viewed as a single system, rather than a series of disconnected bilateral or multilateral arrangements, the American military deployment across the Pacific is impressive in its sweep. To the Communist mainland powers, despite all their propaganda about paper tigers, it must appear as a very menacing force. All three U.S. armed forces can function interdependently, and any one sector of the region can be reinforced by units from adjacent or nearby zones.

In general, U.S. ground troops and facilities in the Far East depend for their security on pivotal port facilities, air bases, and supply depots. Air facilities, though reduced somewhat in recent years, include installations in South Korea, Japan, Okinawa, and the Philippines and, more recently, in Thailand and South Vietnam on the South Asian mainland. Air force headquarters are located in Japan and the Philippines and are complemented by the strategic island base of Guam to the east.

The army maintains supply bases in Okinawa, Japan, and South Korea, with two divisions of ground forces stationed in Korea. Until deployed to Vietnam, the 25th Infantry Division served as a distant reserve in Hawaii.

The navy has major bases in Japan and the Philippines, with depots in Okinawa, and part of a marine division is based in Okinawa. The Seventh Fleet, numbering more than 130 vessels, is stationed as a protective force to shield Taiwan, but it also ranges far to the north and south, and in the aftermath of the Himalayan crisis of 1962, it was assigned to establish a presence in the Indian Ocean to the west. To the east, Polaris submarines made their first appearance in the Pacific in the same year, and the size of this force has mounted steadily. A new, important communications facility has been established at Exmouth, Australia, facing the Indian Ocean, to handle strategic communications primarily for the Polaris submarines ranging in these waters.

Control of the seas has become essential to the United States for force mobility, blockade operations, demonstrations of power, and deterrence of potential non-Communist aggressors. Consequently, American naval power now has an immense task—in area coverage, variety of sea missions, and range of potential combat operations (from the interdiction of small North Vietnamese infiltration boats to strategic-missile deployments).

The interdependence of U.S. forces is demonstrated by the Oahu base, which provides backup support and reinforcement for all services and installations, and by Clark Air Force Base, in the Philippines. In 1964, Clark received B-57s from Japan and served as a transfer point for planes conducting raids, begun in February 1965, above the 17th parallel in Vietnam. In addition to its proved value in the Indochina campaign, Clark Field also remains a strategic center for the deployment of airpower in case of a larger conflict and adds to the staying power of the other services.

From these and other established strongholds, it was possible to move forces into Thailand in 1962 without fear of overextension, and they also served as support points when the United States set up new air bases in central Thailand and at Udorn in northeast Thailand and later at Bienhoa and Danang in Vietnam. The Thai facilities broaden the American capacity to use land-based airpower over Laos and Vietnam, as well as to protect Thailand itself. To prepare for other contingencies, a special logistics program for the country has begun, consisting mainly of rolling stock, mobile pipelines, airfield improvements, and forward storage depots for ground forces.[1]

As the scope of operations in Thailand suggests, the U.S. base system cannot operate as an island within the host country. To the extent that the foreign policies or internal politics of the host country are unstable, the mere presence of the bases does not relieve U.S. anxieties. In fact, in such instances, the bases become hostages to the uncertainties of the region's politics. Intense domestic criticism has been aroused by the extensive American base options in the Philippines under the 1947 treaty, the maintenance and expansion of air fields in land-hungry Japan during the 1950s, and exclusive American control over communications facilities in Australia. The United States must constantly keep in mind that bases involve considerable economic cost, provoke nationalist feeling, and present excellent targets for an opportunistic opposition party.

There is also the risk that for the host country heavy reliance on American bases may bring disproportionate diplomatic vulnerability and Chinese hostility. In certain instances, hostile Chinese intentions appear so obvious and unappeasable that, as the Thais calculated, there is little to lose by accepting bases. The partitioned lands— Vietnam and Korea—have actually suffered attacks. The island states have less fear of immediate Chinese pressure and a less critical need for on-the-spot protection. But in all cases, an American presence gives China's neighbors greater leverage for bargaining with the United States while making the problem of their accommodation with Peking more difficult. For as the entire region's network of bases becomes essential to the security position of host states, it becomes increasingly difficult for all concerned to treat base arrangements as negotiable counters in seeking bilateral or general settlements.

To utilize its bases, the United States must have considerable freedom of movement for its forces. Because of this maneuverability, it was possible to deploy Philippine-based forces in the Quemoy-Matsu area during 1958, to use Japan-based aircraft in Southeast Asia in 1962 and 1964, and to rush air and ground forces into Thailand in 1962. However, here, too, the United States encountered serious political attacks, with local opposition leaders charging that these activities meant direct involvement in American combat operations. By using Clark Field in the Philippines as a way-station, the United States has often protected an original host government, such as Japan, from such charges.

Nevertheless, in certain international crises, the Japanese government might feel unable to guarantee adequate use of existing bases in the face of a hostile labor force. More dramatically, the American military force in South Korea, which has been of major value to successive regimes in Seoul, depends heavily on the cooperation of the indigenous army and thus on the Korean will to resist. Should a neutralist government emerge or should even an anti-Communist regime have a falling out with Washington (and relations with Seoul became strained several times during the political turmoil of the early 1960s), the American position might be gravely compromised.

Still another obstacle to effective use of the far-flung and complex system of bases is the unwillingness of neutrals to cooperate in the maintenance of firm transportation links, by air and sea. During the Pathet Lao thrust against the Thai border in the early 1960s, Burma refused permission to the United States to overfly its territory and thus made it more difficult to speed aircraft to Thailand. In recent years, as part of its anti-Indian campaign, Pakistan has criticized proposals for the establishment of an American naval presence in the Indian Ocean and has encouraged the neutralist states of South Asia to stand firm in their traditional opposition to such a move. India itself opposes a significant American presence for reasons of high policy, despite the evident price in Indian national military security. For with a troop presence, the United States could create and maintain the air bases, warning systems, radar nets, and supply networks that India—or indeed any country with gaps in its defense— requires.

Although both India and Pakistan, for different reasons, oppose the establishment of U.S. bases, their leaders recognize that the facilities would be necessary in a crisis. Consequently, both antagonists become enmeshed in inconsistencies. Pakistan stays in SEATO and seeks additional American military aid, though it denies the imminence of a Communist threat and focuses on India's belligerence. India emphasizes the Chinese danger but refuses to become involved in any political or military alignment. The United States is aware that aid to both can intensify their rivalry; but because of its concern over the area's strategic weakness, Washington maintains its commitments to Pakistan even without a supporting base system. It also continues moderate aid to India despite uncertainty about the extent of the American obligation and about India's ability to defend itself or acquire adequate support from other foreign sources in time of need.

Clearly, the disparate and varied internal, national, and international interests of all the countries involved make retention and maintenance of effective mutual-security arrangements across the Pacific a difficult and demanding challenge. Even the lands that stand to forfeit the most if the system should lose its viability press for changes that, in Washington's view, would erode its foundations. The preservation and protection of these crucial but highly vulnerable installations remain among the most difficult and delicate tasks of American statesmanship. Yet the question of alternative solutions must be considered, by diplomats as well as military thinkers. We shall return to this subject after exploring further the ramifications of the existing arrangements.

Personnel

The presence of American personnel, civilian and military, has many of the advantages and drawbacks associated with bases. On the one hand, the actual deployment of men provides psychological and diplomatic reassurance, a capacity for effective military action, an ability to react quickly in a crisis, and a secure platform for extended military endeavors. On the other hand, the presence of American forces arouses fears of involvement in Cold War confrontations and troop contact with the population often generates frictions. (Nevertheless, the converse fear of the security consequences of U.S. withdrawal persists.)

Military personnel stationed abroad, in combat and service units or military-assistance groups, generally present less of a problem today than they did in the days of the Second World War. Fewer in number, older, and more experienced, they are better prepared and better disciplined for the diplomatic aspects of their assignment in living abroad. When problems arise concerning the local populace, primary responsibility rests with the American Embassy. The overall record has not been uniform; the fairly small military establishment in Thailand has made a good impression, but difficulties have appeared elsewhere. The presence of large contingents of American economic- and military-aid personnel is especially likely to create problems if they live with their families in exclusive compounds and enjoy a standard of living much higher than that of the host people.

Although American military participation in civic-action or nation-building programs has had some favorable impact, particularly in rural areas, the Pentagon overestimates the good will that flows from such military contributions. The benefits tend to be overshadowed by the nationalist resentment and social friction a foreign presence evokes and by fear that the domestic military leaders will augment their power by moving into spheres that were formerly civilian, such as construction and social work.

None of the problems caused by the presence of American troops has been more abrasive than disputes over criminal jurisdiction, usually handled by status of forces agreements (SOFA). Nationalists both in the United States and overseas wish to see their own country retain the widest possible jurisdiction over criminal acts committed by Americans stationed abroad.[2] During the mid-1950s, Japan provided the focus for arguments over this issue with the Girard case of 1957, involving the off-duty but on-base killing of a Japanese woman scavenging for materials. As provided in the 1951 security agreement, a Japanese court exercised jurisdiction, and it returned a verdict more lenient than might have been expected from a U.S. court-martial. The nationalist fervor on both sides subsided and subsequent relations with Japan on this point have been good. Such cases in Japan are now governed by the NATO formula,[3] under which America and the other state enjoy concurrent jurisdiction over offenses punishable by the laws of both states, with primary jurisdiction resting with the state deploying troops abroad when the case involves offenses committed in the line of official duty or in the course of other security operations. In addition, the host state agrees to waive primary jurisdiction in the remaining cases unless the administration of justice in the country would be seriously inconvenienced.

Since Congress is extremely concerned over SOFA operations, it requires an annual hearing on them. There was particular apprehension over waiving any criminal jurisdiction in Asia (except in the Philippines and Japan, whose judicial codes are close to those of the United States), because of the fear that procedures of trial and standards of punishment in the region would display less regard for the individual than in the West.[4]

The greatest diplomatic strain over criminal jurisdiction in Asia has arisen in the Philippines, the only Asian state besides Japan and Korea with which agreement has been reached.[5] The 1947 arrangement with the Philippines provided an on-base, off-base formula for determining jurisdiction. The 1956–57 negotiations, provided for the NATO "duty" formula, allotting the Philippines control over certain on-base actions but reducing its advantage of full control over off-base actions. As a result, Manila made a strenuous effort to expand its off-base jurisdiction by narrowing the meaning of "duty" and obtaining the power to determine whether a specific act occurred in the line of duty. In the matter of waiver, especially with regard to on-base offenses, the Philippine government was less willing to make formal concessions in this regard than the United States was in defining off-base duty. Yet in 1963, Manila waived or dropped 52 of the 67 cases subject to its jurisdiction. In light of Washington's claim that it had already conceded greater jurisdiction than the NATO allies enjoy, the Filipino quest for as much formal jurisdiction as possible appeared to reflect a purely nationalistic desire to control all cases in any way involving Filipino nationals. An agreement was finally concluded on August 10, 1965, regarding criminal jurisdiction, following the NATO formula with certain concessions to Philippine nationalist sentiment.

The resolution of the SOFA dispute was a matter of considerable importance since the United States considers that the concessions it made to the Philippines in the late 1950s on other points—particularly weapons deployments and control over force movements—could not take formal effect until settlement of the dispute over criminal jurisdiction.[6] Not until 1966 did the accord signed by Secretary of State Dean Rusk and Foreign Minister Narciso Ramos ratify the Bohlen-Serrano understanding of 1959.

Economic and Political Effects of the U.S. Presence

It is not our purpose here to discuss U.S. aid programs in general, but in focusing on the impact of the U.S. military presence, we cannot overlook its economic and social effects and the role played by U.S. advisory personnel, as part of the complex that makes up the military presence.

In a relatively small recipient or host nation, a modest U.S. presence often appears so massive that it is considered to be a form of intervention. Well-meaning efforts at "nation-building," to help a state develop a more orderly administration or launch a program for economic growth, frequently entail an undesired degree of penetration in the cultural and ideological as well as the political sphere. Such pro-American leaders as Sarit in Thailand and Macapagal in the Philippines and suspicious neutralists such as Ne Win of Burma voiced strong opposition to this sort of American interference. U.S. attempts to foster democracy, sustain stable governments, and in some instances to reduce indigenous military controls can breed deep resentment and even endanger the security of certain regimes. The fact that Washington insistently stresses extensive political reform in lands like South Korea and South Vietnam, where it has a large presence, does not escape notice elsewhere. Coups in these two lands and American pressure for modification of the authoritarian regimes that followed cast an ominous shadow over the question of American intervention elsewhere, even among those who agree with U.S. ideological objectives.

In advanced states, especially Japan, the U.S. presence has clearcut economic effects. These nations depend on American off-shore purchases or imports of military equipment to help sustain their exports and thus reduce pressure on their balance of payments. Frequently, these lands can produce certain items more cheaply than the United States can and provide a further saving in transoceanic shipping costs. Such American purchases are of particular value to countries with which the United States runs a net surplus on bilateral trade and also to pay for military equipment when the United States seeks to get a state to increase its defense expenditures (and reduce its own). But in attempting to reduce a deficit in the over-all U.S. balance of payments and to stop an adverse gold flow, the United States often seizes upon the elimination or reduction of these arrangements as a quick means to effect savings in foreign currency. Yet by eliminating truck purchases from Japan, for example, Americans deal themselves a multiple blow—strengthening the hand of those in Tokyo who seek more diverse (i.e., Communist) outlets for trade, reducing U.S. ability to pressure Japan to speed its own defense effort, and adding to Japan's difficulties in finding dollars with which to buy American items. These adverse effects are especially likely when, as is often the case, the purchase agreement covers a large part of Tokyo's trade deficit on current accounts. Similarly, the removal of U.S. troops from Korea would effect a savings for the American balance of payments, amounting to tens of millions of dollars annually.[7] However, the United States has already cut down annual expenditures in Korea that reduce the balance of payments outflow from $80 million to $45 million. Further, it is not wholly desirable to save foreign exchange in Korea because Seoul needs this currency to sustain required imports. Export earnings in the past have continually failed, by a wide margin, to meet import needs.[8] Assistance not given through military cost payments would have to flow through a substitute channel. Even with striking improvements over Seoul's recent export record, the financial gap would widen with help in the form of loans.[9]

Thus, short-term benefits in the American balance of payments U. S. Policy-Greene—12578 10 Janson 25-12 O. Style Figures T-4 may come at a very high cost in terms of the general U.S. position and specific military and diplomatic policies. Here again, the issue of security must be viewed in a far broader context than the customary "military" considerations would imply.

CHAPTER TEN

Fear of American Changes and Withdrawal

Despite the political, economic, and military difficulties it entails, an American presence on allied soil generally achieves its primary objective: it provides a sense of security. But this asset diminishes so sharply with even a hint of military withdrawal that Washington cannot easily utilize this threat, either to swing negotiations its way or to prevent the ally from exploiting America's commitments to its own advantage. Since many Asians fear that the Americans view their own involvement as an aberration, any proposals for change arouse severe anxiety. For instance, although the departure of U.S. troops from Korea in 1949 was justified in terms of that nation's low priority in the scale of American strategic interests, the United States nevertheless had to return the following year in full force. And after an armistice was arranged in 1953, the American force in Korea dropped from seven to two divisions, and the promised substitute, a reserve for the Pacific, did not materialize. Consequently, there is great uncertainty in Seoul about how long Washington will adhere to a policy of overseas deployment so alien to its traditions.

All over Asia, the fear persists that the United States might again decide, for budgetary and technological reasons, to reduce its surface fleet, combat divisions, and air squadrons, as it did in the 1950s. And forces once removed from the area might not return because unexpected crises elsewhere might take priority. There might also be hesitation in time of crisis while the United States decided where to place its main effort, and even if the delay proved temporary, it could be extremely damaging to Asian morale. Forces on hand are obviously more reassuring than any treaty guarantees, especially in the early stages of a crisis.

154

Asia's overriding concern is that the United States, in the event of a choice, would opt to defend Europe and the West. After all, the decision to restrict the Korean commitment derived from the fear that the Rusians might precipitate a new crisis in the more vital European theater. It would not take much to revive apprehension in Asia today, especially if the United States thinned out its position across the Pacific while it maintained substantial forces in Europe and again modernized the armies of its Western allies, as it did at great expense in the 1950s. For that matter, any reduction of America's presence in Europe would also raise strong Asian fears that the United States was returning to an isolationist stance and fortress-America concept.

The Europeans, too, have manifested deep anxiety that America will abandon them. When additional American forces went to Germany during the Berlin crisis of 1961, Washington stated repeatedly that this was a temporary assignment. Yet as proportionate reductions later followed on schedule, Bonn expressed its concern. While impressed by the rapid airlift of one division in 1963, Europeans quickly voiced fears that this would lead to a thinning out of the powerful Seventh Army. Similarly, a statement to NATO in 1964 that the United States had augmented its airlift capacity was cause for both reassurance and concern.[1]

Whatever the resemblances in the problems generated by any alterations in American deployments on either side of the globe, the Asians remain acutely anxious about their priority in U.S. planning. Since the United States deploys both conventional and nuclear forces in Europe, even a change in the American posture in Asia that compensates for conventional reductions with a nuclear force would invite invidious comparisons. The fact that Asia is the only region where nuclear weapons were ever employed in combat would probably intensify the difficulty, especially if the United States should continue to stress the importance of a conventional force in Europe—although its purpose might be only to effect a "pause" and win a chance for second thoughts before combat deteriorates into nuclear war.[2]

Of course, there are valid reasons for placing great emphasis on Europe today: to reassure the Germans, to refute France's criticisms, and to keep pace with the modernization of the armies to the east. Impressive evidence exists that the Soviet security position depends heavily on a vast array of missiles deployed against Western Europe, which the Russians also tried to use for diplomatic blackmail during the Berlin crisis of 1961. But these very arguments for the importance of Europe have an adverse effect in Asia because the Chinese are now on the road to becoming a modern military power. However modest Chinese strength is in comparison to that of the European powers, it places China far ahead of all its neighbors.

As Peking's capacity to threaten its neighbors is rising sharply, the persistence of apprehensions about the continuation of the U.S. presence—despite powerful evidence to the contrary—becomes a major political consideration in itself. Should changes in deployments generally shift American forces away from the vicinity of China, the diplomatic underpinning of American base and lines-of-communications arrangements would be sorely shaken. At the very least, Peking would attack the American security network at its weakest point—the reciprocal uncertainty felt by America and its local ally concerning the other's reliability. Fears of being left alone to cope with China might impel its neighbors to contemplate coming to terms with Peking. Even if the Chinese thought an American response likely, they might not slacken their efforts to instill the opposite view in the minds of others. Asians may also consider it prudent to keep the path to future negotiations open in case the United States should leave. And they may even see the currently stable situation as a last opportunity to take advantage of the bargaining power afforded by the American presence.

A U.S. presence, however, can have a dramatically different result: it can lead Asians to believe that they can freely pursue their own interests, however risky or distasteful to the United States, without undermining American willingness to perform any necessary rescue or support operation. This attitude has been evinced not only by Pakistan but also on occasion by Thailand, the Philippines, and South Korea. Furthermore, even neutrals, confident of the durability of America's arrangements with its local allies, may rely upon Washington for defense against a potential Communist foe. Thus, the United States encounters two difficult and contradictory attitudes in beneficiaries of its military presence: a fear of its ultimate departure and a presumption of its unconditional short-run support.

If the United States should guarantee all countries a permanent commitment to their defense against aggression, more problems might well be created than would be solved. Not only would such a promise irritate Asian allies who have bound themselves by treaty, but it would also facilitate abuse of the commitment and embroil the

United States in innumerable local disputes in which it would be blamed by all parties for the failures of their foreign policies and the iniquities of their antagonists. Furthermore, some allies might feel that such an extensive American involvement was impelling them toward a more hostile policy toward China than they desired or could sustain in light of their domestic political situation. Neutrals might publicly accuse the United States of neo-imperialism and complain of involuntary entanglement in great-power disputes while privately rejoicing in Washington's assurances and redoubling their efforts to gain Washington's backing in their own disputes. Finally, such a general commitment might sharpen still further the antagonism between America and China, if that is possible, by bringing almost every territorial or security issue within its scope. American involvement all along the Chinese periphery and the growing importance of nuclear weapons in this region may have made a confrontation inevitable, but assumption of an unconditional commitment against China would reduce the freedom of diplomatic maneuver while offering only dubious compensations.

The task of the United States remains to convince others that its interest in Asian security is permanent but not unconditional and that its alliance commitments are as firm in Asia as they are in Europe. This will require a determined diplomatic effort by both Asia and the United States, for there is resistance to change in both areas.

American Ambivalence Regarding Change

The uneven distribution of American forces, the dependence on bilateral accords with mutually hostile allies, and the relative weakness of these Asian states all compound the difficulties of retaining flexibiity in U.S. military plans and deployments.

Nevertheless, because of changes in the international setting and in the domestic situation in allied lands, the security arrangements of the United States must continually be modified, as indeed they have been over the past decade. In light of China's new technical capacities, too, the United States must study the need for shifts in the composition and location of its forces. But it is here that a sort of roadblock within U.S. thinking itself is encountered. Because of the understandable—but chronic—tension between diplomatic and military security perspectives, civilians and soldiers constantly alternate as proponents or critics of change. They favor or challenge withdrawals, alterations or expansions in American force dispositions in accordance with their differing judgments of the security interests in each case. For the most part, the impetus for change in force dispositions comes from the Department of Defense. The reasons may stem from new strategic doctrines, changes in the availability of manpower, developments in technology, and/or the need for economy.[3] However, a "model" arrangement to give optimal satisfaction to both viewpoints can be extremely difficult to hammer out.

Currently, for example, the armed forces favor new deployments in the Indian Ocean area and a base structure along the entire arc around China. Although this would enhance American capacity to operate in the region of Southcentral Asia and East Africa, it also implies the possibility of further political and military involvement in these areas, with no assurance of force increases to keep power in balance at this high level of commitment. In the event that India had to be supported against a large-scale Chinese aggression, even such sea-based support, plus facilities now being developed in India, might not be adequate. Nor could the United States carry out a commitment along the northern Indian or Pakistani borders without bases to receive air and ground forces and to sustain their operations.

Acquisition of bases in India and Pakistan would, of course, require major diplomatic shifts that neither they nor the United States are prepared to undertake now. Despite this instance in which U.S. diplomats prefer to stand pat, they keenly appreciate the need for constant change in the composition of forces overseas, as well as for specific contractions and expansions of the American presence. Moreover, they also realize how frequently they oppose such change on political grounds, and they often find themselves hard-pressed to provide an adequate response to charges of immobilism. But political officials consider the flexibility desired by military leaders an improvement only if security is viewed from a somewhat restricted, combat-oriented, outlook, and they point out that the Pentagon itself often resists proposals for change in the overseas posture. Like the State Department, the Pentagon can present strong reasons for supporting a specific *status quo*—e.g., the base at stake is vital and irreplaceable, a reduction in force levels would leave insufficient strength to cope with responsibilities, or new technological developments will make a proposed change easier in a few years.

How does one measure the net impact of a change that may have an immediate and high military cost but that might avert serious diplomatic trouble with the states concerned in the long run? Both estimates are based on security considerations; but the military price is immediate and specific, while the political advantage, by contrast, may seem distant, possibly elusive, and difficult to validate. Judgment becomes even more difficult when we realize that a military concession might reduce pressure to give ground on another matter, whereas maintenance of the *status quo* could require unanticipated political expenditures.

In light of these various judgments, perhaps conflicting more than converging, we shall consider the implications of two specific possibilities for change in the American position in Asia: a reduction of U.S. forces in South Korea and a change in the *status quo* regarding Okinawa.

The Case of South Korea

South Korea presents a dramatic illustration of the political problems posed by military change—in this case, withdrawal. The two divisions stationed there represent an enormous allocation of scarce American combat formations, and many military and economic justifications can be adduced for their removal. With more than 12 per cent of its divisional strength assigned to Korea and the equivalent of approximately three more divisional cadres unexpectedly pressed into the Vietnamese conflict, the U.S. army in the 1960s faced a dire shortage of manpower to maintain its commitments. This problem became all the more acute since the army's major function and orientation remained in the European theater. Furthermore, the American treaty commitment to Seoul could be sustained by a military presence other than troops. Allocation of modern weapons (such as air defense systems, sophisticated fighter planes, and tactical missiles of the type placed in Europe) could both demonstrate America's defensive intent and deter an aggressor, while freeing U.S. infantry formations for more efficient use. The change could have unsettling effects, but in the Pentagon's view, these dangers would not outweigh the advantages. An alternative would be heavy Japanese involvement in the defense of South Korea, but neither Seoul nor Tokyo would agree to the stationing of the substantial forces involved. In fact, if it coincided with an American troops withdrawal, such a Japanese commitment might make the Koreans think that they were being abandoned to the Japanese.[4]

The Department of State has opposed troop reduction because it believes that the retention of a stable American posture gives Seoul a much-needed sense of security and continuity. The need to readjust relations with Japan, the economic successes of North Korea, the rising power of China, and the political instability and economic difficulties of its own system made South Korea extremely vulnerable to outside pressures during the early 1960s. A large-scale withdrawal of American troops might reduce the combat effectiveness of Repubic of Korea forces and cause the Koreans to feel that their country has descended into a twilight world like that of 1949–50, when U.S. troops did depart.

The U.S. army, though recognizing the problem, can still justify its position on the grounds that it cannot freeze itself into obsolescence and inefficiency because of "overriding" political considerations. However, a transitional compromise might be reached. For example, the army could redeploy units from Korea within the Far East, as a regional strategic reserve. Yet such a move would encounter significant problems: expense, the acquisition of an acceptable base of operations, and the establishment and maintenance of required facilities. If these troops were relocated where space is available, in Australia, it might prove difficult to redeploy them to the central or northern sectors if, as seems likely, the situation in Southeast Asia remains unstable. States in that storm center would soon consider such units as "their" supporting force, much as Seoul views the American contingent now stationed in Korea.

Another approach might be to replace one division with a smaller but powerfully armed contingent, leaving the other division in place. Such a mix could partially satisfy the conflicting political and military claims on security policy as well as the basic interests of South Korea. On the other hand, some experts think that this compromise could keep costs unnecessarily high, while failing to satisfy Seoul's concern about the ultimate intentions of the United States to maintain a deterrent dependable in a future crisis.[5]

The Role of Okinawa

While the Korean dilemma illustrates the armed services' eagerness for change, the Okinawan situation exemplifies its desire to continue the *status quo*. The root of the problem is the Pentagon's belief that only through unfettered American jurisdiction can the island retain its very high value to U.S. security. American freedom to move forces to and from the island, in any direction at any time, becomes increasingly important with every new move by the Philippines and Japan to restrict American use of bases in their countries. In 1965, the United States moved planes from Japan to Okinawa—establishing the island as the actual staging point—before transferring them to Vietnam. Thus Okinawa functions as a transit point to absolve a host country—particularly Japan with its vocal domestic opposition—of implication in U.S. combat activities. With the growth of Chinese nuclear power, the Okinawa base may become even more valuable. Sustaining all three services with its air fields, ground-force installations, and navy depots—the total facilities are valued at about $1 billion—the island, along with Taiwan, is a pivotal connection between the northern defense area and the battered Southeast Asian sector. As a missile site, it could give well over 1,000 miles of mainland coverage.

To Japan, Okinawa represents a major irredentist claim.[6] The treaties with the United States recognize Japan's sovereignty and its ultimate right to jurisdiction once security returns to the Far East. But as that era of peace is delayed into the future, Japanese pressure for return of official authority over the island increases. Yet with such powers, Japan would find it very difficult to allow the United States to maintain the military autonomy—especially regarding nuclear weapons—that it now enjoys on Okinawa, in sharp contrast to arrangements on the home islands. Even now, the Communists constantly warn Tokyo that it risks involvement in a conflict if it continues to permit American deployments from Okinawa, as well as from the four home islands, to sensitive zones like Vietnam.

Public opinion in Japan and Okinawa clearly favors a return of Japanese administrative authority. Okinawa's pro-Western Democratic Party holding (18 of the 29 seats in the legislature in 1965) and moderate leftists both pressed for reversion to Japan. They acknowledged that the crisis in Vietnam would first have to be resolved, and that some American military presence would still be required to protect the weak mother country as well as Okinawa itself.[7] In 1965 both in Japan and Okinawa, the date (April 28) of the peace treaty that gave the United States full administrative rights was designated Reversion Day. In Japan, national sentiment for Okinawan reversion has remained strong and consistent. But significantly, in polls taken in Japan during 1957–58, 60 per cent opposed allowing American bases to remain on Okinawa in the event of its return to Japan. Five years later in December 1962, the opposition to bases persisted by a margin of 56 to 11, with 33 per cent undecided.[8]

This reaction increases American concern about the fate of the Okinawan base in case of even a partial reversion. Washington takes little comfort from pro-base sentiment among the Okinawans, especially since these views are often qualified by the statement that the nuclear arsenal should go because it makes the island a prime target. Although after the 1960 treaty revision the Japanese government agreed to permit America to retain the base on Okinawa, Tokyo remained unwilling to broaden its responsibilities beyond the home islands—even though an extended military role would validate its claim to early restoration of full Japanese administrative powers on Okinawa.

The situation has been complicated by the long history of inept American handling of the Okinawans, which caused considerable ill-feeling in the mid-1950s and the early 1960s. The main problem concerned the conversion of scarce arable land to military purposes. Eventually more than one-third of the 900,000 inhabitants were displaced and given totally inadequate compensation. In addition to a standard of living well below Japanese levels, and slow economic growth, the island chafed under a heavy-handed military High Commissioner. Eventually, this discontent erupted in intense anti-American feelings, and at one point, a leading opponent of an American presence was elected mayor of Naha.

After 1957, the United States eliminated most of these grievances. It established a fairer and more generous method of land compensation, liberalized currency and trade regulations, and expanded its nation-building activities. Responding to new and strenuous complaints against American political controls, in the 1960s the United States placed a civilian directly under the High Commissioner, restricted his veto power over acts of the local legislature, and—in addition to raising its own aid level—encouraged and assisted greater Japanese participation in the island's economic development. At this point, the Okinawans felt that the Japanese government was remiss in its trade and aid policies and was actually discriminating against the islanders. By the mid-1960s, the internal political situation had calmed down, though there were still complaints about harsh restrictions on contacts with the Japanese home islands, including the right to visit ancestral graves. Despite its belated improvements, the record of American control was not inspiring, and added considerably to the strategic and diplomatic burdens stemming from the U.S. presence.

A compromise between total reversion and the continuation of complete American jurisdiction seems urgent to those who believe that the current official Japanese acquiescence in the *status quo* is only the uneasy calm before an impending nationalistic storm. The stakes are very high; for the fate of Okinawa affects as well the retention of the Japanese security treaty after 1970 and the nuclear protection of Japan. A firm stand on Okinawa might require greater U.S. concessions elsewhere to preserve a viable security pact. But on the other hand, concessions on Okinawa might help strengthen the treaty arrangement politically after 1970—at a high direct military cost.

One possibility is to return authority to Japan in some categories of Okinawan politics, but with the United States retaining jurisdiction over the military base areas. A gradual transfer of controls could be scheduled to go into effect over a period of years; or provision could be made for retention of American military authority for a considerable term, perhaps fifteen years, long enough to permit a gradual phase-out and the development of substitute arrangements.

The military analysts look askance at a phase-out arrangement at this time, since they see no adequate replacements for the advantages the base confers. They also oppose partial transfers of control, holding that American needs are so broad as to make separate territorial jurisdictions on such a small island unfeasible. Moreover, the Japanese public might not be satisfied with a half-way grant of civilian authority and might use such concessions to intensify demands for full jurisdictional control over the bases.

Inevitably, the nuclear aspect of the problem will come increasingly to the fore. As the Chinese acquire a nuclear capability, Peking will use nuclear blackmail against Japan to press for the removal of nuclear weapons, and American authority in general, from Okinawa. Greater Japanese authority might merely increase Tokyo's vulnerability to such pressure. Logically then, a settlement of the Okinawan question should be part of a broader American-Japanese agreement on the roles of the two powers regarding the use of nuclear weapons in the protection of the home islands. It might also be geared to other considerations vital to the Japanese, particularly trade with the United States and diplomatic relations with Peking.

Still another consideration is the interrelationship between changes in the U.S. presence on Okinawa and in Korea. Any weakening of the U.S. military posture in Korea, combined with a dilution of jurisdiction on Okinawa, would measurably enhance Japan's importance. The price for a larger Japanese defense effort—which would further increase Tokyo's power—and a favorable diplomatic-security orientation might rise sharply, despite (or perhaps because of) the uneasiness that would pervade the home islands in the wake of these partial American withdrawals. Whether Japan became "tougher" or "more paternal" in its bargaining with Seoul, new Japanese power might arouse South Korean fears of a renewal of Tokyo's domination as their price for security. The assurance of an American presence, therefore, seems an essential condition for a sustained diplomatic rapprochement between Seoul and Tokyo, let alone any defense agreement in the more distant future. (Here both military and diplomatic planners in the United States, although employing disparate approaches, reach a common conclusion.)

What Force Deployment in Asia?

The history of American security arrangements in Asia, despite the over-all successes, gives evidence of many vulnerable points: the abrasive SOFA issue, the repercussions of future changes in force composition, the thorny matter of base negotiations, and charges of infringements on sovereignty. Asia's rising nationalism—often directly encouraged by the United States—and China's mounting power jeopardize the existing U.S. security structures. Clearly, broad-scale contingency planning for alternate force deployments and installations is necessary if the United States is to continue to play an effective role in Asia.

Since its dependence on a few key bases breeds tension and strained relations with host governments, the United States would benefit from an adequate fall-back position in case such facilities became unavailable. Australia is one likely site, and in a deteriorating situation Canberra would probably favor an American presence with its air and naval links to Asia. Even so, without facilities nearer the South Asian mainland, the U.S. position would resemble that of the dark days of 1942, when the Japanese controlled all strategic installations. Costs in money and time would rise sharply, while still leaving a diminished capacity for action in Asia. The ability of the United States to take quick action at the start of the Korean War stemmed from the location of four divisions and air units with supply and support facilities in Japan. Though these forces were ill trained for such unanticipated use, their availability was just as important in producing a collective reaction as were the presence of a U.N. Commission in Korea to identify the aggressor and the Soviet absence from the Security Council. And the United States was able to sustain this war because it had a protected line of supply and staging areas across the Pacific that in some respects provided better access to the theater of combat than the Chinese enjoyed, despite their shorter lines of communication.

Even the introduction of new technological developments—particularly the ability to pre-position equipment and supplies and make rapid "big lift" air movements across the ocean—would not reduce the diplomatic or military value of a substantial base network. The proposal previously mentioned that would entail a base structure around the Chinese periphery, with existing gaps filled by strengthening the Indian Ocean area,[9] presupposes the capability of such rapid force deployments. These, in turn, would depend on systematic and large-scale pre-positioning of supplies, expanded staging facilities, an augmented trained reserve in the United States, and steadily increasing airlift facilities. As an experiment, three vessels laden with supplies are now in place in the Philippines.[10] Although this approach may permit some reduction in the size of forces, nevertheless, in order to screen the deployment of the new units, adequate American combat troops would have to be present in this area. And their bases would have to be kept at top effectiveness, with the pre-positioned equipment securely protected. Moreover, if reliance on pre-positioned equipment is increased, it must be properly maintained and replaced regularly with expensive up-to-date models.

Clearly, reliance on technological advances will be no panacea for the base problem, since the overseas components in the U.S. military system would be more important than ever before under an arrangement that depended so heavily on crisis deployments. The bases would be prime military targets, requiring considerable protection. The host state would come under tremendous pressure, both internal and external, to "avoid involvement" by denying access to America. Such *démarches* would come in time of greatest tension, with much American power still distant. Without a strong American presence to begin with, an opponent could easily contrive or play upon a crisis of confidence between Washington and its ally. An assured and speedy reaction might count far more than the magnitude of the response, and the requirements of such a capability— in effective forward bases, transport facilities, diplomatic clearance —would appear as formidable as ever. As the United States became more dependent on such bases, moreover, the price sought by the host country in aid, support of national policies, and control of American use might rise proportionately.

Another proposal to minimize the frictions surrounding the use of bases is that the United States rely solely on bilateral arrangements and avoid the complexities of a regional system. Each base would then be devoted to local concerns only, with American help unfettered by other alliance considerations. The main links in the pattern could be a series of separate east-west lines between these forward bases and American forces in the central Pacific or even in the continental United States. Such arrangements would sharply reduce Asian concern over the interbase American deployments that may involve an ally in a crisis against its will.

Technically, such an arrangement might have made better sense a decade ago, when it was actually easier to move forces from America to Southeast Asia than from Japan. Today, America's highly developed facilities across the Pacific make interbase movements far more efficient than total dependence on trans-Pacific connections. To have a system of two or three compartmentalized sectors in Asia that have no interregional military connections might seriously compromise the ability of the United States to sustain and coordinate operations. Diplomatically, such renewed bilateralism would further isolate and fragment the area, reinforcing its dangerous and powerful tendency to privatization of security matters.

In dealing with the base problem, we must consider a critical dilemma concerning the nature of the personnel and facilities involved. Many military experts argue that forces and bases developed to meet a conventional threat would also help a state to cope with guerrilla operations. Unfortunately, the Vietnamese experience demonstrates otherwise. American concern with a Korean-type assault by the powerful North Vietnamese army led it to develop a conventional force in the late 1950s. But when the primary threat took the form of guerrilla warfare, neither the Vietnamese army nor its American instructors could adapt to the new situation.

rapidly enough. However, though the security attitudes of the Ngo Dinh Diem regime both immobilized the army and reduced its willingness to risk casualties, President Diem did insist, against American advice, on expending scarce resources to create provincial forces and local militia—essential though insufficient ingredients for counterinsurgency. During the grueling years (1960–1964) of combat directed primarily against the Viet Cong, prior to the arrival in force of North Vietnamese regulars, both the Vietnamese and American officers displayed greater adherence to counterinsurgency in doctrine than in practice.

It is possible, nonetheless, that a mixed training program, combining conventional and guerrilla principles, can bring moderately good results in both categories. The Philippine army showed a high capacity to shift its tactics in fighting the Huk guerrillas in the early 1950s and proved better at this task than the Constabulary, the supposed specialists in antiguerrilla combat. Without a conventional establishment of some sort, an exposed mainland state would be extremely vulnerable to military pressure on its frontiers. Moreover, its relations with the United States could come under considerable strain. First, a posture of utter dependence on the United States might cause a grave crisis of self-respect, frequently leading to anti-American stands in other matters. Second, such dependence might well encourage unrealistic foreign policy attitudes that ignore security problems or minimize their importance. Confronted by an aggressor, the government of such a state, despite American commitments, might feel utterly helpless. It would undoubtedly adopt a policy of complete indifference to the security needs of others.

The complex variety and level of factors that must be reconciled in security planning necessitate the exploration of still another approach—the seaborne nuclear deterrent force. It would certainly obviate some of the problems caused by the physical presence of U.S. personnel and bases. Moreover, it might lead to a more broadly based security structure if Washington would agree to some allied participation in control over a portion of this force. Such a fleet would be fully mobile, able to operate without restrictions, and have the capacity for rapid shifts between theaters as well as within a region.

Popular pressure in Japan against pro-American conservative Cabinets, Filipino-American tensions, and Korean fears of Japanese domination might all be somewhat reduced. Nor would the basic American posture depend on the stability of specific regimes or the consistency of certain leaders. The capacity of a friendly regime to control hostile political elements would become less critical and perhaps, as a consequence, more attainable. The need and motivation to destroy the effectiveness of American bases in a crisis would also be sharply reduced. The possibility of Japanese security forces doing battle with rioting students or left-wing unionists at American installations during a grave international crisis dramatizes the dangers inherent in the present arrangement, both for the U.S. security posture and for the stability of Japan's democracy.

Heavy reliance on a self-contained, seaborne nuclear force, however, means taking a very restricted as well as a very long view. The weapons would undoubtedly pose a countercity and even a counterforce threat to a new and vulnerable Chinese nuclear-missile force. However, since the likelihood is that theories of deterrence have not yet had the practical impact on Asian affairs that they enjoy in Europe and America, this force might have only qualified success in psychologically reinforcing allied capitals against Chinese nuclear threats.

While developing and exploiting nuclear power, China will undoubtedly channel its diplomatic efforts into other approaches. It would probably respond to an American emphasis on specialized nuclear forces by putting an even higher premium on a variety of lower and more subtle uses of force. Existing installations today, for all the trouble they entail, enable the United States to confront a wide range of threats; they also provide the option of raising military counterpressures fairly quickly in proportion to the force mustered by the enemy. Without staging and support facilities to supply and reinforce elements originally committed, the U.S. defense system would lack staying power and might confront the United States with the cruel choice of withdrawal or intensive reliance on nuclear weapons. On the other hand, reliance on unseen nuclear forces, whose use will remain subject to an American veto, can only intensify suspicions about America's ultimate intentions. At the very least, Asians will conclude that the United States has abandoned existing installations as militarily untenable.

Admittedly, the same critics might also condemn the retention of such bases as magnets that will attract Communists attacks. Still, our allies would experience genuine fear following an American withdrawal. They would be sorely tempted to view this shift as a careful but firm step toward disengagement, especially since the

United States would be evacuating the only installations exposed to Chinese power—that is, as long as China lacks a long-range weapons delivery system. And the very removal of a forward position, according to this line of Asian reasoning, would in itself reduce the strategic importance of Far Eastern territory in American eyes. To complete this circular argument, Asians would view a pullback as proof that U.S. interests across the Pacific had fallen below that marginal level required for a response against aggression.

In the end, Asians, feeling more vulnerable and frightened, would become less reasonable in their security relations with the United States, demand clearer evidence of American firmness, and certainly, see more instances of American "recklessness" in the confrontation with China. The resultant instability of the entire security system—under this heavy diplomatic pressure—might well outweigh the benefits expected from this shift in the U.S. defense posture. A "forward strategy" of some sort, as in Germany, appears essential if all the vital elements in the alliance system are to be sustained.

Although the base network and the presence of U.S. personnel appear to be invariable components of the security arrangements, the defense accords themselves demonstrate great flexibility. Not only can different types of relationships evolve, but even within a treaty connection, a wide variety of understandings and obligations are feasible. Some states permit the stationing of forces, with a variety of conditions attached, whereas others will accept no forces at all. Some agree to cooperate in ventures beyond their homeland, whereas others, like Japan and Pakistan, for different reasons, refuse. American concern with a state's security can fluctuate with developments. The degree of cooperation possible between allies can also undergo broad and precipitous changes without necessarily destroying the basic relationship.

The case of India, on the other hand, illustrates that much can be accomplished in security affairs by having a wide array of instrumentalities at hand when, for various reasons, a formal treaty is undesirable. Executive agreements, informal negotiations with neutralists, military-assistance programs, staff talks in time of crisis, temporary deployment of fighter aircraft for defensive training, and fleet visits are some possibilities. Judicious use of unilateral political concessions can often assuage public opinion in an Asian state and so reduce political obstacles to such arrangments. Even connections of lesser substance might help. In its 1955–56 border crisis with Communist China, Burma placed tacit reliance on Thailand and the latter's SEATO link.

The ambivalence of the neutrals, although frustrating to policy-makers, holds out hope of turning military assistance to diplomatic advantage. Both the United States and the Soviet Union have been quick to recognize that in Asia tremendous political importance is attached to the defense of capital cities and other major metropolitan areas against potential air raids. These targets may be near the bottom of a military planner's priority list, but the memory of the Second World War, especially Japan's experience, has made urban security a vital psychological factor in Asian foreign policies. Therefore, a small military investment in deterring attack on cities can yield large diplomatic dividends. Consequently, although India's anxiety over the defense of New Delhi and Calcutta in 1962, during the Chinese attack, seemed to outsiders totally disproportionate to the threat, both Russia and the West responded. In the aftermath of the crisis, American and Commonwealth aircraft made brief reassuring appearances to assuage these fears. Subsequently, while forces for ground defense became perhaps the most important component of Western assistance, the Indians continued to seek modern fighter craft for security against air attack and extracted a promise of MIG's from the Soviet Union.

Following the American bombing of the Tonkin Gulf naval installations in 1964, the Chinese rushed a MIG squadron in North Vietnam to defend the strategic Hanoi area, and the Soviets sent MIG and antiaircraft-missile assistance the following year. The dispatch of Soviet antiaircraft missiles to protect Indonesian cities and the capital of Afghanistan, is further evidence that both Russia and the host country acknowledge this fear. It is generally difficult to evaluate the direct dividends of such aid. But after honoring a Thai request for allocation of a few fighter craft to protect Bangkok, the United States found it had far less difficulty in reaching agreements on the establishment of bases, deployment of aircraft, and cooperation in the Indochinese conflicts.

Although one cannot overlook the opportunities that lie outside a formal pact, treaties remain the most solid and durable foundation yet devised for security arrangements in Asia. Perhaps the mix of alliances with other approaches today will best suit our interests. However, the Indian and Malaysian efforts to gain American material help and support against aggressors—without making reciprocal commitments—indicate that flexible attitudes can also cause serious difficulties. For the foreseeable future, the treaty system continues to be the backbone of U.S. security policy in the Far East, and the other arrangements draw strength from its very existence and from the installations, bases, forces, and commitments that sustain it.

Confidence in America, improved relations among American allies in Asia, maintenance of a wide variety of options to deter or check aggression—in short, those elements needed to keep the alliance system alive—all depend on an American presence, where desired, that makes its imprint on the day-to-day security problems of the allied lands. The grave handicaps accompanying an American front-line position will remain and at times become even more trouble-some. But to the extent that Asian security rests on an American guarantee, there remains a strong need for a military presence, comprising both conventional and nuclear strength.

PART III

The Communist Threat in Asia

CHAPTER ELEVEN

Asian and Western Views

In any discussion of the threat that Asian Communist states pose to their neighbors, and to international stability in general, we encounter fundamental differences of opinion, not only among U.S. allies, but within the United States as well. A majority of the American public may endorse the basic outlook of the government: that Peking presents a threat to the regional and global balance, that it must be stopped by measures short of pre-emptive American military action, and that a future accommodation is desirable.[1] Still, many critics at home and abroad strongly challenge these views. One minority of Americans argues heatedly that it is best to have a showdown with such an implacable foe—since it is unlikely to change its fanatically militant perspective—while it is weak and at odds with its Soviet ally. Others take the opposite view: that it is the United States itself which is interfering most menacingly in the affairs of a proud civilization that has suffered more than a century of foreign depredations and that is now trying to command its own destiny.

In addition to its home-grown critics, official Washington policy meets considerable opposition, some of it severe, from many other governments. Each major power evidences its disagreement on specific points by adopting measures that Washington considers inimical to the security of all concerned—despite the fact that even the Russians have declared Peking a danger to world peace. In 1957, when the Russians launched Sputniks I and II and announced other missile advances, Peking proclaimed a bellicose ideology, depreciating the risk of war, and exhorted Moscow to prosecute the world revolution more energetically.[2] But the Soviet Union, evidently considering its own power less formidable than Peking did, would not go to the extremes proposed by Mao and his colleagues and

175

instead intensified its stress on peaceful coexistence. Moscow broadened this policy in the late 1950s with doctrinal innovations clearly departing from the belief in inevitable war. When the Russian economic aid and promises of assistance in modern weapons technology seemed only to spur the Chinese to greater militancy, Moscow began the disengagement that led to an open split within five years. Ironically, it is the United States and the Soviet Union which are more emphatic than any other major states in their view that China poses a direct, if not immediate, threat to world peace.

Apart from the two rival superpowers, the states of Asia and Europe are far from united in their views of China. Some see no threat at all; others agree that a danger exists but focus on different aspects of the problem; still others accept the American interpretation of danger but proceed with policies that to Washington seem to augment China's power. During 1961–65, it became increasingly apparent that Indonesia and Pakistan—facing more immediate dangers and opportunities—were moving away from their ambivalent attitudes of the past and, in operational terms at least, were rejecting the American view of Peking as a menace. Sukarno may sincerely have considered imperialism—whether in the original Dutch form, in its later alleged British incarnation of encirclement, or even in a "neo-colonial" American version—a real and continuing threat to the survival of his self-styled radical regime. His fears, revolving around the existence of Western bases used in the past to help rebellions against Jakarta, were heightened by the absence of ideologically sympathetic neighbors. Since Sukarno's loss of power, Indonesia's policy toward China has changed sharply. But although Pakistan may see China as a future danger, it does not allow this contingency to interefere with its pursuit of specific national interests against India, for which it seeks Peking's assistance. Cambodia, on the other hand, may be adopting a friendly attitude toward Peking because it considers Chinese hegemony inevitable. Given his immediate and overriding fear of conquest by North Vietnam, Prince Sihanouk may seek an international guarantee of neutralization—or, failing that, Chinese protection against depredations by Hanoi.[3]

Japan and India both regard China as a threat to their national security. Yet the Japanese are torn by emotions and material interests that make a hard line most difficult to follow. Apart from a strong neutralist, anti-American sentiment, a desire to expiate earlier crimes against China, and a wish to re-establish a close relationship with the historic neighbor, there is a feeling in Tokyo that Asians can best solve their own problems. To many Japanese, the direct, clear-cut American attitude, as applied in the Vietnamese situation, seems not sufficiently nuanced to cope with complex realities.[4] On the material side, many Japanese want to participate in what they believe must someday become a great market for their consumer industries, as well as for more sophisticated industrial products, finished goods, capital equipment, and technical expertise. Large-scale trade, especially when lubricated by long-term credits, increases China's stability and enhances its power without necessarily reducing its militancy. Yet the Japanese are already embarked on a course of improving commercial and cultural relations that only a recurrence of Peking's obtuse pressure tactics is likely to curtail.[5]

For its part, India now clearly recognizes the Chinese national (though not ideological) threat. Nonetheless, New Delhi has adhered to its essentially isolationist position in security policy. Though it participates in external peace-keeping operations as a member of the International Control Commission, which is charged with policing the 1962 Geneva Accords on Indochina, it refuses to involve itself in the area's defense, let alone a joint security accord with Pakistan. Yet India takes offense when any other state follows a China policy of its own, based on an equally narrow national interpretation of interests, with results that India considers harmful to itself. While far more sympathetic to the basic American posture since the Chinese invasion of 1962, India still maintains that the ideological confrontation does not present a direct security problem, continues to favor recognition of China by others, and supports Peking's admission to the U.N.

Thailand represents still a third Asian stance that shares our view of China's potential threat but espouses a different policy orientation. Thailand has long favored the support of right-wing regimes in Indochina and continually opposed American criticism of South Vietnam's Diem. It also disagreed with specific Washington policies: "temporizing" with Prince Sihanouk of Cambodia, acquiescence in the neutralization of Laos, and resistance to the reassertion of rightist control there. On broader security issues, Bangkok feels that the United States must act alone to deter nuclear blackmail and meet threats to the security of other lands. Consequently, Thailand concentrates on defense problems from its own national perspective, emphasizing its special interests and apprehensions and adjusting its commitments accordingly.

The English-speaking Commonwealth states likewise have individual—often quite disparate—approaches toward China. The Australians recognize the existence of a grave danger yet are wary of too heavy a reliance on a military posture. Besides, the Australians were very much absorbed in the threat from Jakarta during the early 1960s. They, like Japan, desire to expand their trade with China, and wheat exports to Peking have become a major feature of Canberra's foreign economic policy.[6] The government regards its nonrecognition of Peking as a concession to the United States rather than a reasonable act of security policy. Even so, its pro-American stand has stimulated several thrusts by the opposition party, aimed at weakening the Menzies and Holt administrations.

Canada, on the other hand, has adhered to the general British and Commonwealth position of extending recognition as well as continuing as large a wheat trade as possible. As the Western representative of the International Control Commission in Indochina, Canada can serve as a channel for diplomatic contacts with both Hanoi and Peking. Before North Vietnam banned ICC posts on its borders and in port cities, Canada was a valuable interpreter of events in that country.

Britain has also followed the trade-recognition-U.N. course in its China policy, though its refusal to recognize Peking's claim to Taiwan has kept the two at the chargé d'affaires rather than the ambassadorial level of representation. The British hold that China is more concerned with its internal problems, especially in economic development, than with foreign adventures. This attitude has brought sharp rejoinders from both New Delhi and Washington. On the other hand, under both Conservative and Labour cabinets, London has supported American policy in Vietnam. Concern with Malaysian security has probably strengthened this orientation in both Britain and Australia.

France has gone further than any other ally in opposing the American view. From the premise that no peace in Southeast Asia is possible without Chinese participation, the French proceed to infer that Peking must eventually become the dominant force in Indochina and perhaps in adjacent lands. They favored the neutralization of the Indochina successor states, with Vietnam unified or in separate segments, depending on the diplomatic possibilities.[7] Their position seems to include acceptance of indigenous Communists in the various regimes, the exclusion of the United States as a major factor, and a stronger French cultural and economic position within the broader framework of Chinese hegemony. These ambitions may explain France's assertion that the Viet Cong effort is a popularly supported national war,[8] their pressure on Souvanna Phouma in 1964 to make concessions to the Pathet Lao (which he rejected as unnecessary and dangerous), and their increased trade and other economic connections with North Vietnam.

Beyond genuine policy differences over Vietnam and a desire to re-establish some French interests there, Paris may have viewed its shift to an anti-American Southeast Asian policy in 1963 as a means of drawing closer to China. The restoration in 1964 of diplomatic relations with Peking (broken during the Indochina War) climaxed this policy. But the rapprochement remains limited in effect, and it has not deflected China from its set policies or opened a new and fruitful channel for American-Chinese exchanges. Nor have the French been able to learn much about Chinese affairs from their new embassy in Peking.

To Mao, the French affair was but another step in the long effort at splitting the "capitalist" world, separating the underdeveloped from the industrialized lands, and isolating the United States from all other states. France represents the most extreme "contradiction" in this enemy camp,[9] and its cordiality was extremely welcomed, for China itself faces severe problems of potential isolation, with its chosen policy of implacable hostility to America, scornful independence of the Soviet Union, and antagonism to India.

An American View

To Washington, hopes of reaching an accommodation with Peking appear far-fetched at present and depend for the future on a resolute effort to prevent Peking from increasing its power and successfully promoting the Maoist revolutionary movement in Asia, Africa, and Latin America. The United States must recognize that the inevitable refusal of many nations to accept this appraisal will limit its freedom of action. Still, it will undoubtedly treat its own partial isolation as an even greater challenge to stand firm; otherwise, China would have no need to come to terms with anyone.

Washington has a deep appreciation of China's ability to project its power abroad in many ways with great skill and determination. China can pursue its global objectives in three separate realms: the Communist states and parties in non-Communist lands, the nationalists (radical or otherwise) in the non-Western world, and a "new third force" of industrial states that are not superpowers. China's material assets—its great size and resources, strategic location, and enormous population—are bolstered by ideological militance, the ability to identify with the underdeveloped world and its frustrations, ruthless development policies, shrewd displays of power, a tested doctrine of guerrilla violence, powerful Chinese national sentiment, hostility to the outside world, and historic self-confidence as a center of civilization and suzerain protector of semi-independent neighbors.

In their relations with the "bourgeois" governments of underdeveloped states, as distinguished from the "true" revolutionary elements in these societies, the Chinese have stressed self-reliance but also pledged substantial economic aid, totaling somewhat more than $3 billion by 1965. Though two-thirds of this sum has gone to Communist states, even $1 billion judiciously used could have provided a major diplomatic boost elsewhere. Most of this aid had not been delivered by 1966, but we must recognize that China made these extensive offers during the period of its gravest economic crises. A much more ambitious foreign aid program will probably be formulated once the country's development gathers momentum. It is already a formidable undertaking in terms of the percentage of per capita income. Peking has used trade and will continue to use it as an instrument of foreign policy: to seek political concessions, to compel states to change specific policies, and to foster splits in the enemy camp.[10]

The split in the Communist camp, according to policy makers in Washington, has only stiffened China's militancy. Especially during the Khrushchev era, the Russians stressed the primacy of economics—i.e., that the people's well-being should be an immediate central goal of Communist regimes—and viewed gradual development as the surest route for communizing other lands. Peking emphasized the primacy of politics. This has come to mean stress on developing the power of the state, especially its military and industrial capacities, and the use of its resources to foster violent revolution abroad. At home, this approach requires exhortation rather than incentives to increase production, constant purification of cadres and masses, and the continued mobilization of wealth for the purposes of the state.[11] The great cultural revolutionary movement of 1966 appeared to Western observers to be a further extension—in extreme and ludicrous form—of this messianic and utopian vision. To justify such sacrifices, Peking must posit an implacable enemy who must be destroyed before he destroys communism; there is no place in this context for a triumph through coexistence.

Military force thus plays several crucial roles in China: on the national frontiers, in regional and world diplomacy, and in revolutionary politics. Military power is maintained in a condition of readiness, even if this absorbs more than 10 per cent of China's GNP, to safeguard the state against ever-threatening aggressors, to protect and strengthen its hold on border areas, to cow neighboring states into recognizing Chinese supremacy, and to compel them to recognize the high price involved in challenging Peking's wishes. China today seeks self-sufficiency in raw materials (especially oil), an industrial potential to maintain a modern war machine, reliable foreign trade relations, and continued technological growth. These bases for industrial modernization also comprise the essential elements to sustain both the armed forces and national power in general.

Of great importance to Peking is its ability to use its vaunted regional supremacy as a multipurpose instrument of foreign policy. China has developed a high degree of sophistication in the types of threats it can mount, the mix of devices employed, the timing of operations, and the choice of targets. As Washington sees it, China will exert different degrees of pressure at separate points along its frontier at any one time, and will vary its efforts against any one neighbor over a period of years.

Strength Through Weakness

One of the most baffling aspects of China in the past decade has been that its power has shown constant growth despite internal developments that signaled grave and unexpected weaknesses. Manifestations of resentment against an oppressive regime, inefficient and corrupt cadres, failures in economic planning, especially in agriculture, dissension in the military leadership, and even a purge of the heretofore united party leadership all marked the decade after 1956. At that time, with the wars on China's borders settled, attention centered on China's effort to industrialize. In the peaceful "race for modernization," China set out to prove the superiority of its totalitarian system, particularly in comparison with democratic but sluggish India. Through a combination of superior administration, greater capacity to mobilize, ability to direct investments more efficiently and massively, and capacity to energize and tax the peasantry, China expected to launch the country on a gigantic program of growth that would win over the underdeveloped world. Today this aspiration seems beyond Peking's reach despite impressive industrial achievements (for which the Russians deserve far more credit than the Chinese acknowledge). Peking's massive failures in the 1958 Great Leap Forward and later plans stemmed from over-all economic imbalance, which provided the modern sector with a temporarily excess capacity. Also, the inefficient administration and inadequate plant management hampered fully productive operation of the large number of new enterprises. Nevertheless, the country established a foundation for large-scale industrial growth. Coal production rose from 130 million to 220 million tons during the period 1957–64. For the same period steel output grew from about 5 million to over 9 million tons, while electric power went from 19 billion kilowatt hours to 35 billion. These estimates fall considerably below the more grandiose hopes (and figures) generated in Peking in the early 1960s.[12] They indicate that the Chinese may now move forward more slowly than they had hoped, but that they can realistically expect to have a self-sufficient industrial base during the 1970s. Even their conservative and realistic plans of the mid-1950s projected an economy comparable with that of the advanced industrial states by the last decade of this century.[13]

In agriculture, there can be no question that the years 1958–63 must be termed disastrous. Agriculture suffered such a setback that not until 1964 did the country regain its 1957 record annual production of 185–190 million tons of grain. There was one year when grain production fell below 160 million tons.[14] Even with the 200-million-ton mark in range, a 100-million rise in population since 1957 prolonged the need to import grain at a great cost in precious foreign exchange. Moreover, despite alleged slackening of the concentration on heavy industry in recent years, the government has not made a major shift in its investment resources in the direction of agriculture.[15] Instead, it has repeatedly warned the peasantry not to count on large-scale help to improve production. Because of the leadership's passion for doctrinal purity, it refuses to consider adopting incentives as an alternative approach to stimulate agriculture. It did retreat from the experiment of the communes to the twenty-family group as the producing unit, and it allows peasants some private production for market. But these have been most grudging concessions that are continually being whittled down.

Ideologically, the communes continue to receive fulsome praise as the proper ultimate form of organization. And the government is constantly on the alert against any substantial profit-making by the peasants, for fear that this will lead indirectly to a return of "corrupt" capitalistic tendencies.

Agricultural shortages, in turn, generate enormous difficulties for the cadres in the countryside. Under the near-famine conditions that followed the Great Leap Forward, there was at least one instance of banditry and rebellion in Honan Province in 1961, with lesser party officials and militia personnel taking an active role.[16] A different type of resistance had begun in the Spring of 1957, when the university students had responded to Mao's call "to let a hundred flowers bloom" by expressing such antagonism to communism as practiced in China that the entire experiment in liberalization was arrested abruptly in mid-1957. After 1962, with rigid controls over political expression very much in force, the regime launched an even tougher campaign of "socialist education" to keep the cadres, industrial workers, and ultimately the peasantry in line. Today, harsh discipline and rectification campaigns for the party, and extreme doctrinaire ideologies for the peasantry—with economic deprivation as a consequence—still dominate the Chinese scene.

Similarly paradoxical have been the effects of the great conflict with Moscow, which, predictably, dealt very harmful blows to the material and doctrinal bases of China's revolutionary posture. Given the country's tremendous dependence on Soviet help for industrial and nuclear weapons development, the timing of the split (beginning in 1958–60) seems to have been singular. Though Peking has frequently complained of Moscow's failure to extend sufficient help to a fraternal state, the Khrushchev government actually accelerated its industrial assistance, equaling in 1959–60 the substantial amounts allocated over the previous five years.[17]

While it is difficult for us to conceive that such a political or economic record can exert considerable attraction in underdeveloped states, we must recognize that it does. Though stress on the value of the big push, centralized planning, structural overhaul of the economy, and total government control is viewed skeptically by Western economists, and though an empirical survey of the progress of the states of Asia does not suggest that authoritarian or totalitarian regimes are essential for economic growth, these theories remain plausible to many Asians. Despite China's generally lackluster record, the supposed causal link between authoritarian planning and rapid economic development still seems logical to many Asian leaders. It has undoubtedly helped China to cushion the impact of its own economic and political failures on its image abroad.

Furthermore, the Chinese won a valuable offer of help in modern nuclear technology in October 1957, following a period of Soviet difficulties over de-Stalinization, uprisings in Eastern Europe, and ideological modifications in basic policy toward the neutrals and the West. Chinese assistance and Moscow-Peking compromises regarding points of disagreement must have accompanied this important weapons agreement. By the start of 1958, the Chinese army looked forward to the rapid development of an atomic bomb and missile delivery capacity, additional modern weapons, and new combat tactics and doctrines based on Russian experiences.[18] Later developments indicate that substantial help was apparently received, until June 1959 when the Soviets terminated the 1957 agreement on nuclear assistance. They withdrew all military technicians the following year. Yet even in 1958, the Chinese continued to voice their traditional faith in "man over matériel," in vast formations of militia, in the overriding importance of guerrilla-warfare doctrine for all wars, and in the error of relying excessively on foreign help or expert opinion.

The loss of Soviet aid proved very costly to the program of military modernization and may have triggered the opposition of the army's chief, Marshal P'eng Teh-huai, to the course adopted.[19] His ouster in 1959 reflected a still broader problem, the division between the professionals and the party on general military policy. In the following years, the party asserted its complete dominance and compelled officers to perform manual work to symbolize their commitment to pure egalitarian communism. The government compensated for this by undertaking a strenuous program of military modernization and keeping the armed forces well fed during the worst days of the food shortage; and it apparently made sufficient concessions in combat doctrine and personnel control to enable an effective officer corps to continue to function.[20]

Still the over-all effects of the split with Moscow, broadened in 1958–59 by the Taiwan crisis and later by Soviet support for India, must have seriously damaged the quality of the army's equipment and leadership at a time when the country was becoming diplomatically isolated and entering upon very hard times in all economic sectors. Its humiliating defeat in 1958 at the hands of the Nationalist air force disclosed Peking's weakness in modern combat potential. Inability to give modern equipment to North Vietnam on a large scale, at least to the extent of pre-empting a Russian contribution, or to join the war when sustained bombing assaults began in 1965, illustrated the acuteness of the problems this gap presented for Chinese policy-makers.

Apart from the economic and military fields, Peking also suffered many setbacks in a third category—diplomacy. It often found itself nearly isolated in the struggle for support among foreign Communists and neutrals because of its stress on violence, condemned even by the Russians. China's show of power in the Himalayas, first in suppressing Tibet and then in defeating India, definitely ratified Peking's reputation as a major force in world affairs. It also had the complementary effect of reducing India's prestige and sharply curtailing New Delhi's influence in neutralist councils. Nevertheless, China's policy of near-genocide in Tibet led to condemnations in the United Nations and by a non-Communist international body of jurists, with membership from neutralist as well as Western states.[21] The brutality in Tibet was bound to have long-range repercussions on the Chinese image, leaving a residue of antagonism that could not be eradicated by Peking's claim that it had merely destroyed a feudal order.

Similarly, the blow against India, despite all its short-term benefits to Peking, sharply diminished China's capacity to exert leadership over the underdeveloped world. The resort to violence, the unwillingness to compromise on terms proposed by the six neutralists who met at Colombo, and the antagonism aroused in several key neutralist lands proved important setbacks for a state that seeks to rest its power ultimately on the underdeveloped world. The alienation of India itself was an event of great significance, and it found reflection in the decline in importance of Krishna Menon and those like him whose neutralism embraces a strong anti-Western bias. The self-proclaimed "true neutralists," especially India, Yugoslavia, and the United Arab Republic, can be expected to oppose major Chinese efforts to swing the Afro-Asian world to a militant anti-Western, anti-Soviet course, or to win backing for a repudiation of peaceful coexistence.

China's refusal to sign the limited test-ban accord of 1963 opened it to Moscow's charge that it opposed peace—an accusation made more widely credible because of Peking's earlier expression of a willingness to risk nuclear conflict, its stress on the inevitability of war with America, and its doctrinal refusal to acknowledge that capitalism could live peacefully with other systems. With more than 100 states signing the 1963 pact, China did not win many over to its argument that the accord was a mere tool of Western aggression or a plot to maintain great-power hegemony. Though China's own nuclear detonation in October 1964 enhanced its power and formidability, it did not evoke widespread diplomatic support. In Europe, only its ally, Albania, and Rumania, eager to demonstrate its independence, responded favorably. In general, the great Sino-Soviet schism has been accompanied by Chinese alienation from Communist Europe. In Asia, North Vietnam and North Korea welcomed China's nuclear test, but of the nonaligned lands, only Cambodia and Indonesia joined them in laudatory comments. Pakistan did express its "satisfaction" and, along with Ceylon, argued that the explosion increased the need for Peking's representation at the United Nations. Some African states, especially Algeria, hailed the test of this "peace bomb." But the over-all reaction was dismay and a renewal of efforts, begun so tentatively in 1963, to control atomic power.

Frequently, this formidable list of miscarriages is underplayed in analyzing Chinese policy. More significant, however, than Peking's vulnerability and the frailty of its self-styled infallible leaders, has been its remarkable ability to keep in the forefront of regional affairs despite these deficiencies—in contrast, for example, to the modest role that Japan has chosen for itself.

Even more impressive than China's regional dominance has been its phenomenal ability to augment its influence on the world balance of power. An explanation of Chinese successes in this sphere requires detailed examination of Chinese policy. Two preliminary observations are in order. First, China's grave internal problems have been tempered by the fact that all its neighbors have also encountered severe difficulties. None except Japan demonstrates striking economic progress, though some states—notably Pakistan and Malaysia—show steady advances. Firm domestic political stability has eluded them all, including Japan, despite the durability of its post-1945 system. With others suffering greater setbacks, China could muster greater strength—particularly in the military realm—than anyone else.

In this situation, mutual hostilities undermined China's more prudent and moderate neighbors while Peking had the advantage of determined political leadership, fanatical devotion to a cause, clearly defined strategic ambitions, and consistent control of the initiative. Peking could even afford to defy international opinion; for example, the unfavorable world reaction to its atomic test did not deter China from preparing further detonations. Beyond this, on specific issues like relations with Japan or the terms of its representation at the United Nations, its stand became more inflexible with the passage of time. We must conclude that we live in an era of bellicose Chinese initiatives that will persist for some time despite internal weaknesses, ideological splits, loss of a vital alliance, and military inferiority.

What havoc China might wreak under more favorable circumstances staggers the imagination because of the scope of its ambitions: to replace Russia as the leader of a unified and resolute world Communist movement; to isolate Washington and Moscow from their allies and from one another; to dictate the terms and control the timing of its separate confrontations with these superpowers; to encourage revolutionary movements among the sovereign states of Africa, Latin America, and Asia while posing as their friend; and to exploit its own economic hardships or failures as a means of identifying itself more closely with the underdeveloped world, at the expense of other powers.

Ideology and the Role of Violence

To Mao and his colleagues, ideology is a way of life. Though the ideology may at times be merely an elaborate doctrinal rationalization of practical necessities, it nevertheless does provide the basic inspiration and grand design for both modernizing China and reshaping the world. Their ideology gives China's rulers philosophical assurance that they possess a clear view of reality and an unerring understanding of the world's political processes.[22]

With their messianic vision and sublime self-confidence, they see themselves operating in a setting of constant and ubiquitous tension and struggle that provide the dynamics of all change. Change, in their view, can only occur through historical discontinuities or revolutionary assaults against the existing order. Adopting the classical Marxist doctrine of antagonism and elevating it to the ultimate truth, they conclude that only violence can effect the final transition to the glorious new order, with the leadership determining—scientifically and accurately—whether any given moment is the proper occasion to strike or to exercise patience.

In Peking's foreign propaganda, the doctrine of revolutionary violence held the leading place at the very start, in 1949–50. It was adduced to corroborate Mao's claim to originality, which later became an important aspect in the struggle with Moscow for leadership of the world movement.[23] Though Lenin had used the peasants as an auxiliary to the proletarian spearhead, it was Mao who made the countryside the main base of rebellion. Moreover, military action by regular forces operating as guerrillas formed the prime component of the Chinese revolution. With the Communists drawing strength from the grass roots by paying careful attention to peasant needs and desires, they could rely on regional reserves and, at the third level, the local militia forces as back-up forces for the regulars. In this way, the doctrine knit rebellious action into a coherent political-military effort and gave the flexibility and staying power needed for survival against superior forces. When the Viet Cong developed a similar arrangement of forces in the mid-1960s, the Chinese could cite their own struggle as they stressed to the Vietnamese the importance of constant pressure on the enemy, patience, and the acceptance of setbacks in a protracted war of attrition—all reflecting an experience radically different from the Bolshevik seizure of power at the top of the political pyramid.[24]

During 1951–55, the Chinese had toned down their claims to a superior understanding of the revolutionary process in the underdeveloped world, and even refrained from commenting on rebellions begun in 1948 in India and Southeast Asia under Soviet auspices that had proved unsuccessful. Stalin's prestige, the desire for an alliance, and valuable Soviet assistance may have dictated a more moderate approach until the mid-1950s.[25] But after 1956, following the failure of the so-called contest of economic emulation, these major themes re-emerged—with emphasis on violence, a Red Army based on the peasantry, and systematic consolidation of power in the countryside by guerrilla forces.

On this foundation, the Chinese termed wars of national liberation the highest form of the class struggle and the indispensable medium of Communist triumph. Mao developed his theories further by reinterpreting class warfare to fit the international scene, with the impoverished nations assuming the proletariat's role and the industrial states equivalent to the indigenous capitalist rulers.[26] The Soviet stress on peaceful coexistence as the highest form of the class struggle,[27] and Moscow's caution even in supporting just wars of liberation revealed a growing and ultimately unbridgeable split.[28]

Despite the Soviets' acceptance of just wars in compromise agreements in 1957 and 1960,[29] they feared that guerrilla wars would escalate dangerously. In the twilight realm between internal and foreign affairs—as in the Quemoy and Matsu crisis in 1958—the Russians acknowledged the justness of China's cause, but Premier Khrushchev argued against interfering in this "internal" affair and, more broadly, opposed "the conquest of any . . . territory" as contrary to Marxism-Leninism.[30] Worse still—if this were possible, since the absorption of Nationalist-held territories is Peking's chief immediate national goal—Moscow labeled itself neutral in the 1959 Sino-Indian skirmishes. This was unheard of in confrontations between a Communist state and another power. Within a year, the Russians were warning that those who stressed violence might be likened to Hitler, who used the term socialist to camouflage his demonic behavior. Shortly thereafter, the Chinese responded with their famous broadside of April 1960 which launched the intra-bloc polemics frontally, though not yet involving open denunciation of the Russians.[31]

According to Chinese doctrine, all wars of liberation must receive encouragement, with Soviet power employed as a threat to keep the capitalists at bay. In fact, the West should be subjected to continual confrontations, and Moscow should issue warnings of nuclear retaliation whenever the imperialists try to thwart the expansion of communism. To do otherwise, Peking argued, or to negotiate with the West, would mean yielding to nuclear blackmail. Should the imperialists nonetheless intervene militarily, a firm Soviet posture would further weaken the foe by heightening the political awareness of the revolutionaries—giving them a kind of international proletarian class consciousness—and by intensifying global tensions.[32] Should the Communist camp timidly fail to support wars of liberation, it would merely invite capitalist-sponsored counterrevolutions. The Chinese also rejected Soviet arguments that limited wars were impossible to contain and would escalate to total war.[33] Moscow may have intended this argument to deter the West from engaging in counterrevolution, but Peking saw it as evidence that Russia would avoid involvement even in revolutionary struggles. Not until 1964 did Soviet strategists modify their earlier stand.[34]

In developing the theme that wars of national liberation represent the highest form of the class struggle, the Chinese drew heavily on the military doctrines of Mao. This had significant political, psychological, and propaganda ramifications, especially in the struggle with Moscow for leadership of the revolutionary movement.

Though the principles of combat had great value in themselves, the Chinese consistently anchored them in a political context. They repeatedly underlined the protracted nature of guerrilla warfare and emphasized a broad spectrum of nonmilitary devices, ranging from internal political action to international diplomacy. Thus war, despite its importance, remains only one of several policy instruments and its use depends on decisions reached from a very broad perspective.[35] A political struggle can erupt into violence at any time; even periods of peace do not really reflect quietude, since struggle is always with us, whether in a political, economic or psychological context.

Mao's doctrine on war continually stressed man's superiority over matériel, an attitude that took firm hold and was to an extent vindicated during the long civil war, the campaigns against Japan, and after. Though the Chinese attitude was reminiscent of the undaunted self-confidence of Japanese troops against superior American forces in the closing years of the Second World War, Peking could substantiate its case by citing its own real triumph, the Viet Minh victory over the French, the success of Castro against the better-armed Batista regime, and the growing power of the Viet Cong. Indonesia's victory over the Dutch and Algeria's independence gave evidence that political success could reward determined rebels even in the face of military defeats. Doctrinal belief in the triumph of "the people over force" finds expression in the Chinese response to every major crisis.[36]

In the years to come, when China's industrial production expands and when it has a military base more consistent with its ambitions, there will probably be sharp changes in Chinese attitudes. No doubt, the Chinese will become less scornful of material power, less inclined to exaggerate what the human spirit can do. However, we may also find that a stronger China may continue to believe that force should be closely coupled with diplomacy, and that Chinese national power should be freely used to champion the cause of communism throughout the world.

For the present, however, China has usually coupled its bellicose doctrinal declarations with prudent behavior. To a considerable extent, defensive concerns have been the determinant in Chinese policy-making. In short, one can argue that Chinese actions today have been inspired mainly by anxiety over foreign assaults, although this is not incompatible with a desire to pursue a more ambitious program after establishing a stronger power base.

Defensive Security Considerations

Most Chinese programs have defensive and offensive connotations simultaneously. In part, this stems from the broad scope of their objectives, which range from internal security and border issues to the communization of the world. Many observers, however, maintain with considerable vigor and some validity that China today is primarily defense-oriented and will be absorbed in the staggering task of internal development for many years to come. Government officials as well as important analysts in Britain and France hold this view and, therefore, conclude that China today does not pose a major national or ideological threat to its neighbors. According to this interpretation, the Communists seek first to maintain their authority within the country and to restore central control over their border regions. The removal of American power from adjacent areas becomes another major purpose, seen as a defensive move to reduce threats to the regime.[37] The menacing tone of Chinese statements may, it is argued, merely reflect the leadership's awareness of its weak power position; the fact that the Chinese act far more prudently than they talk further buttresses this opinion.[38]

Many analysts who do not subscribe to the defensive interpretation agree that Peking appraises its own power quite realistically and analyzes the risks most carefully in choosing courses of action. As has been noted, since the suppression of Tibet in 1959, the Indians have not thought that China is internally oriented. New Delhi now looks upon the Peking regime as expansionist and aggressive but in the conventional nation-state context.

Americans who consider the Chinese "outer-oriented" ascribe far more ambitious motives to Peking. Recognizing that China's border policies have specific delimited goals and acknowledging the importance of regional balance, they nevertheless believe that the main problem remains the international ideological movement in whose service Peking has harnessed and augmented the power of its territorial state. In fact, Americans are excessively prone to think that all China's actions are directed toward the achievement of the regime's ideological aspirations.

American officials and analysts recognize that internal security, primarily the function of the militia, has received considerable emphasis in China. The militia is designed for the dual role of defending the country from foreign invasion and of preventing domestic uprisings, and its successes and failures reveal much about the regime's capabilities. In the mid-1950s, the militia served not only as a force for sustaining internal order but also as an instrument for the regime's indoctrination of the people—shifting popular loyalties away from their traditional private and local perspectives toward the body politic as a whole and the government ideological programs. However, in the trying days of the Great Leap Forward, the militia proved unreliable. Membership fell sharply from its pre-1959 peak of more than 200 million as the institution fell into almost total disuse. In the 1960s, with internal order restored and the regime confident of its control, to the extent of resuming rectification and "teaching socialism" campaigns, the militia seemed to be growing again.[39] Though precise numbers are very difficult to ascertain, it probably amounts now to about one-tenth its peak size and is composed chiefly of a hard core rather than the less selective membership of the original militia. The regime continues to combine the militia's internal security functions with its use for indoctrination—to foster hard work without adequate material incentives and to sustain militancy in foreign policy.[40]

Domestic security also entails protecting the homeland against foreign military incursions and guarding against possible military assault by the Nationalists on Taiwan. For the most part, military threats in the past decade seem to have been confined to unsuccessful guerrilla operations—from Burma in the 1950s, and by seaborne Kuomintang Special Forces in 1963—and more fruitful air reconnaissance by the United States and the Nationalists. Though the Kuomintang poses an important challenge as a legitimate rival claimant to rule China, Nationalist military operations have not been very successful, and the Taipei government's capacity to launch future assaults appears very doubtful.[41] Still, the regime on Taiwan remains a major security problem in Peking's eyes.

In part because of China's efforts to create an image of great-power invincibility, few people realize that it has faced intractable problems in its border areas. The mainland's determination to assert its rule over Taiwan as a Chinese territory, as well as for political and military security, makes the fate of that island the foremost political issue in the area. With the tension heightened by the growing American military presence in the Far East, new political-military crises can be expected, reminiscent either of Peking's abortive assaults of 1955 and 1958 or of its invasion fears of 1962.[42]

The main difficulty in the southern area was the Tibetan situation.

Peking successfully extended its control over western Tibet in 1950 and sustained its power there in the difficult decade that followed. However, access to western Tibet was perilous. The only route traversed the length of Tibet and was exposed to mountain and snow slides, as well as guerrilla depredations. Facing tribal uprisings, especially by the indigenous, warlike Khamba in eastern Tibet, and acknowledging that violence was widespread, the Chinese in 1959 asserted their authority by force, compelling the Dalai Lama to flee to India.

To make its control over the western portion secure, Peking had apparently determined by the mid-1950s to construct a road starting in the west and running southward. Careful investigation probably led the Chinese to conclude that the only route that would serve the purpose led through the Aksai Chin, a high plateau in the Himalayas, which would have to cross territory claimed by India under old British treaty demarcation lines.[43] The Indians did not discover the Chinese presence until 1956 and did not inform the public of this until 1959. As border clashes occurred over the next three years, the Chinese presented stronger and more sharply defined territorial claims to the Indian northeast, as well as to the disputed northwest frontier regions. Essentially, the Chinese offered to accept an approximate version of the Indian line in the east for concessions that would secure its Aksai Chin route in the west.[44] India refused, advanced its patrols beyond the line of Chinese penetration, and engaged in several fire fights.

After a considerable number of warnings, the Chinese attacked, first in the west and then, with spectacular results, in the east during the fall of 1962. After overrunning the entire North East Frontier Agency and reaching the Brahmaputra River, the Chinese withdrew completely from the entire eastern sector without waiting for political concessions in the west. However, they would agree to a formal settlement only on their own terms, which were designed to safeguard their position in the Aksai Chin. The diplomatic stalemate persisted despite an offer by six neutralist nations to foster a compromise, and India continued to express its anxiety regarding the massing of Chinese power along its northern frontier.[45]

The Chinese for their part, reached territorial and diplomatic accords with Burma (1960) and Pakistan (1963), in part to keep India isolated.[46] But, the Chinese were unable to muster a neutralist initiative that would support their terms for settlement or exert pressure on India in that direction. Moreover, the accord with

Burma did not eliminate a source of irritation to Peking. After its defeat by the Communists, the Kuomintang took advantage of the rugged frontier terrain and Rangoon's weak control to use the territory as a sanctuary for its irregulars conducting raids in China. These activities fell to an insignificant level in the early 1950s, but they could not be entirely eliminated even after the signing of the pact.[47]

The long Russian frontier poses new difficulties for the Chinese. The arrangements made with Stalin in 1950 apparently rankled severely, judging by the fact that his successors agreed to yield the privileged economic positions he had won from Mao in Sinkiang and Manchuria.[48] However, this effort by Khrushchev to deal more sympathetically with the Chinese, by extending greater economic aid as well as relinquishing concessions, proved of little avail in averting the great split. In its wake, frontier problems re-emerged more vigorously than ever.

In the early 1960s, the flight of various Moslem ethnic groups from Sinkiang to the Soviet Union led Peking to close Russian consulates in Sinkiang and then, as a reprisal, in the rest of China. The Chinese claimed that the Russians were trying to undermine the security of the region. The government in recent years has made special efforts to indoctrinate the inhabitants of frontier areas with loyalty to Peking and has warned them not to succumb to blandishments from Moscow. Other border confrontations of differing types have occurred, with small clashes reported along the river-boundary areas in the north, where disputes center upon small bits of territory, river islands, and the like. When Khrushchev taunted Peking about permitting imperialist holdings to remain in Hong Kong and Macao, the Chinese responded with broad references to all the unequal treaties imposed on China in the past. On more than one occasion, they have referred to costly diplomatic accords of the nineteenth century, including three pacts under which Russia acquired substantial portions of Manchuria and territory in the extreme western area.[49] However, the Chinese are unlikely to use these border issues as a device for expansionist action aganist Russia because of their military inferiority, the difficulty of access, and the smaller, less-developed Chinese populations in the disputed area. Still, tensions along the extensive Sino-Soviet frontier can grow as relations between the two powers worsen.

Dominance in Eastern and Southern Asia

China's desire for predominance in the eastern half of Asia provides the medium-range basis for the American decision to confront its power. More immediately, of course, control over Taiwan is the irreducible Chinese demand on the United States and colors all current disputes. In the long run, China's global revolutionary objectives would menace American interests very directly. But the power for sustained Chinese operations at this advanced level must rest upon regional predominance. Peking sees the American presence as its chief obstacle and, therefore, has adopted as a major objective its removal in all embodiments. Hence, along with American bases and military-assistance programs, other U.S. efforts ranging from economic aid to cultural links and even diplomatic influences are Chinese targets. Once again, this may appear as merely a defensive security aspiration. But elimination of all alliances, neutralization of the area, and even the partial reduction of other American means of access would mark a signal Chinese victory [50] and would set the stage for the expansion of Communist power associated with Peking.

A sustained effort to cripple the power of Japan and India complements China's basic hostility to the United States. China considers it urgent to block any further security coalitions, especially involving either of these two powers, which thus far have avoided regional groupings.[51] In fact, a tightening of political relations among any of China's neighbors, even a grouping that had an exclusively regionalist or neutralist coloration, would arouse its concern. Such cohesion might reduce Peking's influence, which can flourish best if the region remains diplomatically fragmented.

For all its weaknesses, India remains a major obstacle to Chinese ambitions. Its size, its potential capacity to render defense assistance to its neighbors, its role as an ideological competitor, its friendly relations with other anti-Chinese neutralists, and its satisfactory diplomatic and aid relations with both Washington and Moscow keep it in the forefront of Asian security politics. A key to Chinese aspirations in India is the leftist Communist party that split off from the Moscow-oriented parent group. Support of China by elements of this group, advocacy of militant tactics in the countryside, and possible creation of a "Yenan" military base would provide clear clues to China's influences. Since it broke away in 1963, the leftists have demonstrated electoral strength, and enjoy popular support in those Indian states that are traditional Communist strongholds.[52] This leftist faction, though not formally pro-Chinese, poses a threat to the pro-Russian wing and could seriously jeopardize Congress party domination in the event of economic dislocations, failure of reform policy, and communal strife.

Japan, however, remains the greater problem for China potentially, despite its lack of military strength-in-being. Though there is no national support for a strong anti-Chinese foreign policy, and the country still agonizes over its sins toward China in the past, Japan's modern economy poses a twofold challenge to Peking. Japan can offer considerable assistance—in technical aid, finance capital, and trade—to developing states and can also provide a clear and attractive alternative to the Chinese route to modernization. To fulfill Chinese regional and world ambitions, Peking must muffle the impact of the Japanese model and prevent Japan from becoming a formidable military power. If possible, it must someday bring this neighbor under Chinese political control, thereby shifting the balance of power in Asia dramatically and perhaps decisively. Development of fairly simple and low-yield nuclear warheads plus a modest short-range missile capacity could fill a major role in this endeavor by posing a direct and serious military threat to Japan. The Chinese need not overplay their hand by issuing dire warnings of destruction, but they could use their nuclear capability as a backdrop to demands, in a crisis, that Japan dissociate itself from an American link that might involve the home islands in a dangerous war. Such efforts have been made repeatedly in past moments of tension without success, but they would have far greater weight if backed by nuclear threats.[53] The fact that in the case of Berlin, Moscow was unable to use this strategy successfully against Western Europe will hardly deter Peking, since it will assume that it is more skillful and that Japan can be detached from the American connection far more easily than could the Europeans. The latter, after all, share the same culture as the United States and draw strength from participation in a highly structured multilateral alliance.

The past record may not bear out Chinese confidence in their high diplomatic skills. We need only recall the attempt to compel Japan to make political concessions on the recognition question in 1958 as the price for a trade agreement that Peking, in its euphoria over the Great Leap Forward, thought more vital to Japan than to China.[54] Economic reality prevailed, and the Chinese found themselves thwarted in this diplomatic gambit. They also suffered considerably from the fall-off in trade. Nonetheless, in 1964, despite their evident need for long-term credit as well as straightforward trade accords, they took a very firm line against Japan on a number of political issues, including Japan's domestic politics, its efforts at a Korean accord, its opposition to Chinese atomic testing, and its alliance with America. The Chinese may still count on Japan's deep desire for trade, the appeal of Asian solidarity, leftist support in Tokyo, and their growing military reputation to win them some concessions in the near future, especially in economic matters, even without the capacity to extract them forcefully. Peking undoubtedly expects to do even better on this score once it has secured its industrial and commercial base and its missile technology.

In Southeast Asia the undoubted Chinese desire for predominance does not necessarily entail direct control or, for the present, even complete communization. China might derive more advantage from a situation in which most states in that region remained independent and non-Communist but with all outside influences but China's excluded. Nor would China treat a political *status quo* in Southeast Asia as anything more than a temporary expedient on the way to communization. The difficulty, from an American security perspective, would lie in the fact that Peking would exploit such a development as proof to distant continents of the inevitable triumph of its ideological cause.

China's historical experience, particularly in the Ming Dynasty, demonstrated the strategic importance of Southeast Asia in opening a route to the more important areas of the world beyond, where today Peking is bent on pursuing its ideological goals. Some Chinese control over this rich region is absolutely vital if China is to use it as a power base from which to broaden and strengthen its contacts with other states of Asia and with Africa.

Moreover, Peking would derive enormous advantage from utilizing Southeast Asia as a showcase of its benevolent wish to live in peace with small neighbors. China would try to prove that it can bestow protection and sponsorship, enabling these lands to live in harmony with one another, as sovereign entities, while adopting progressive social and economic programs. Thus the states of the region would be captives, bolstering China's security while enabling Peking to enhance its regional power, assuage fears elsewhere in the underdeveloped world, and sustain social revolutionary development along national lines. To a certain extent, Cambodia is already following this pattern, though it does far less in terms of social change than it claims. Peking would like to bring others, starting with neutralists, such as Burma and Ceylon,[55] into similar relationships. It could then display a benign countenance, while making certain that any doubters or opponents remained fully aware of the power and pressure it held in ready reserve. The region, cleared of "imperialists" and rendered a zone of peace and progress, would give Peking a geographically provident and politically disarming platform from which to extend its direct influence across the Indian Ocean, mainly to the East African coast, and perhaps also to the Southwest Asian mainland. In recent years, Chinese political activity and economic aid programs have pointed in these directions.

The Underdeveloped World

In promoting their claims as a regional and world power, the Chinese make highly effective use of ideology—communism, anti-colonialism, doctrines of modernization, and, to some extent, racism. They have taken on the West, the Russians, and formidable neutralist opponents on these fronts all at the same time. For they know that if they can become the political leaders of the underdeveloped world, they can not only reach the status of a global power most quickly and efficiently but will also be in an extremely favorable position to advance the revolutionary cause.[56]

Their policy does have a major internal contradiction in that it rests on winning over sovereign states at the formal diplomatic level while supporting revolutionary Communist efforts to overthrow regimes from within. For the intermediate time span, China also follows a third track—maintaining close relations with anti-Western radical neutralist states that lack strong Communist movements, without trying to subvert them.

At the Communist revolutionary level, Peking tries to win over as many parties as possible to the Chinese view, urging them to develop their strength patiently and prepare for violent revolution, more or less on the lines of the Chinese experience. The Chinese argue that their doctrines can be applied directly to situations in quite different lands, and consequently only the local Communists devoted to the Chinese interpretation of Marxism can emerge as the true leaders of the cause. Hence indigenous parties become pivotal targets for infiltration efforts by the Chinese and their supporters.[57]

Though the Chinese carefully avoid extending firm commitments to foreign Communist parties, they encourage them to shake off Soviet influence and follow the course of military revolution—often as a shortcut to power. Generally, the Chinese adopt an ambivalent, opportunistic attitude that enables them to promote violent change and render support where possible, but at no risk to themselves or to their reputation for sober realism. To validate their sponsorship of wars of national liberation, they backed the Algerian rebels at no cost, though they offered to dispatch volunteers. The Russians were hedging on this situation, in order to improve their relations with De Gaulle at a time when the general was moving toward a policy of independence from Washington. Later, the Chinese encouraged violent operations against the Portuguese colonies in Africa and against white rule in South Africa and Rhodesia. They have sent arms, money, and inflammatory propaganda and encouraged radicals in Congo-Brazzaville and Tropical and East Africa to seize power and implement revolutionary doctrine.[58] Peking has also supported the Palestinian Liberation Army, with some arms and money, as a means of keeping on good terms with radical Arab states and sustaining a high level of tension in the Middle East.

Often at the same time as they are urging revolution, visiting Chinese leaders will advise patience and emphasize the great sacrifices and time required to "build socialism through self-reliance." They preach that generations may have to pass before a revolution will reach fruition. While fostering the establishment of Communist movements, Peking is as aware as Moscow that a minimal level of civilization is needed before the party of the faithful can emerge. Chinese emissaries warn that opportunism and rashness breed great danger, and that China may be unable to bail out its allies, Communist or otherwise, if they run into trouble.

It is difficult to judge the degree of success in Chinese efforts because, as in the case of Latin America, several years of apparent dormancy can lead to a sudden upsurge of support for Peking. The first half of the decade brought some triumphs on that continent and considerable progress in Africa as well, with all the gains following the temporary consolidation of Chinese influence in the parties of East Asian states.[59] However, their supporters did not win out against pro-Russian factions.[60] Moreover, the bitter polemic with Moscow has alienated many left-leaning non-Communists. And by carrying revolutionary actions and objectives too far, the Chinese have aroused the antagonism of several sympathetic regimes, including Burundi and Kenya, and even, in early 1966, Castro's Cuba. The violent internal upheavals against pro-Chinese leaders, such as Ben Bella, Sukarno, and Nkrumah, in 1965–66 proved major setbacks for Peking's aspirations, but their long-range view supposedly leads them to anticipate and endure such vicissitudes.

Chinese relations with friendly governments are most complex. Peking treats the more radical ones in a straightforward manner, as second-best but acceptable substitutes for the true believers. The less radical nations are targets for subversion. Embassy channels, aid missions, and cultural exchange programs are all used to build clandestine Communist organizations in these lands. Meanwhile, Peking operates through formal diplomatic means to separate these states from the West. Agents set up and develop Communist parties where there are none and infiltrate existing parties to win them over to the Chinese side. This has occurred in many Asian states whose governments, though aware of these dangerous activities, have not seen fit to diminish their contacts with Peking. This situation obtained in a small land like Nepal as well as in a large state, like Indonesia, which had the largest Communist party of any non-Communist nation.[61]

On the other hand, when an advanced regime, like Nasser's, opposes China's basic policy and suppresses local Communists, Peking may try to maintain friendly diplomatic links, seek political freedom for extremists, and compete with Moscow for the allegiance of leftist organizations. The Chinese adjust their activity to suit the policies and degree of advancement of the host state, and whatever the nature of the local revolutionary movements, the ultimate Chinese purpose remains to fashion Communist parties in these lands as close to its own ideological image as possible.

The posture of China toward the underdeveloped world illustrates the fundamental component of China's stand in general: it depends to a large and quite dangerous extent on Peking's gamble that it can calculate, and often control, the policies and responses of other countries. Actually, it has both overestimated and underestimated the dangers facing it in recent wars and has, consequently, espoused policies of excessive caution or excessive boldness. As we have seen, in 1962 it seriously overrated the Nationalist readiness to attack in Fukien, and American willingness to support this move. Though an error on the side of caution, it still represents a grievous misreading of American intentions. The opposite apparently happened in the Himalayan episode, which the Chinese undertook when they thought India would receive no effective support. The rapid and vigorous Anglo-American response must have surprised them as much as the Russians' decision to stand by their Indian commitments. (Both these incidents are in sharp contrast to China's realistic assessment of the dangers run by North Korea in launching its invasion of 1950.) When a state that advocates an activist revolutionary policy and that depends primarily, and so confidently, on its own diplomatic skill and evaluations to keep down the risks makes persistent mistakes at so fundamental a level, there is cause for extreme uneasiness throughout the world.

Similarly, our failure to recognize the extent of Chinese misconceptions, should it prove greater than we realize, could be as damaging to our security as the failure to respect the extent of Peking's strength, skill, and patience. Peking's image of the United States is very simplistic—a caricature of a monopolistic, imperialistic, war-oriented, cold-blooded, yet lazy aggressor. One may justly ask how, against this background, Peking can discern the nuances in American policy, or the conflicting motivations that animate disputes in Washington over the proper course to adopt. Rational differences within the United States over objectives and tactics are difficult for Peking to comprehend. Even harder to understand are the emotional and nonrational aspects that underlie many of our commitments, and these probably do not enter into Chinese calculations concerning the policies of any Western state. An intense American feeling about Japan or the Philippines might escape China's ken altogether, thus depriving it of a most important clue to American response patterns. After all, it was a crucial factor in our diplomacy with Japan in 1941, when the fate of China itself hung in the balance.

Finally, it is hard for us to comprehend how the Chinese could really believe that one country can be (1) a cruel imperialist, so aggressive that war is inevitable, and (2) a sated tiger, unwilling to respond to challenges to its interests in distant lands because it finds the effort too bothersome. This construct is open to so many different uses by its creators that it is of little operational value. If it is but a national fable, what do the Chinese really believe about us? And can they avoid coming to believe in a fable that they repeat in all public discussions over a period of years?

CHAPTER TWELVE

Force in Chinese Diplomacy

In our attempt to assess the proportions of China's threat, our problem is compounded by a time factor. It is our assumption that there will be marked differences between China's short-range and long-range situations. But both now and in the future, the primary concern is how China will use its mounting stocks of conventional and nuclear weaponry and of industrial and agricultural products, as well as its swelling population. The special concern, of course, is what impact China's vast resources will have on the balance in Asia.

Since violence is embedded in the heart of Chinese revolutionary ideology, and political considerations dominate its employment, China's military doctrine and actions must be closely integrated with its foreign policy. Temporary or transitional weaknesses may, however, act as a brake on China's ambitions for the present.

Caution in International Affairs

Perhaps it is the time factor that explains why China's international behavior exhibits contradictory facets: extreme caution in its operations and prudence in its calculations, along with highly risky, provocative acts. Which is the real China?

Proponents of the view that the Chinese remain basically cautious attribute this course to Peking's recognition of its weaknesses, especially vis-à-vis American power. Further, this argument holds, the Chinese carefully evaluate all manifestations of U.S. power in the Far East, for their overriding aim is to avert a direct bilateral confrontation with the United States.

China's own observations reveal close attention to American statements over the past decade regarding the disposition of powerful U.S. combat forces in the area and the dispatch of particular kinds of arms, such as air-defense missiles to Taiwan in 1957 and later to Japan.[1] The Chinese responded vigorously to the stationing of strategic aircraft and Polaris submarines in the Pacific. The presence of modern American jet fighters and their transfer to indigenous Asian forces are of special importance to the Chinese, since this type of force is most likely to become engaged in combat, as in the Quemoy-Matsu incident of 1958. And the Chinese displayed full awareness of America's military presence and buildup in the area at that time. American maneuvers and joint operations with various SEATO states also have an impact on Peking's policies.

Two indications of Chinese fears of American power came in 1962, when Peking concluded that the Nationalists were about to mount an effort against Fukien Province, and late in 1965 when Peking warned that the danger of war was mounting. What it dreaded most in the first instance was the expected American support behind this anticipated Nationalist invasion. A more continuous, less dramatic worry has been the hostile air incursions.[2] Here the Chinese have restricted themselves to enumerating alleged incidents—by mid-1966 the total of "serious incidents" had passed 400—and uttering dire warnings and verbal assaults, in part to assuage their own feelings at minimal risk.

Moreover, China has on occasion limited its own combat engagements. The air and artillery actions against Quemoy remained carefully circumscribed in 1958. Thereafter, the Communists fell back on alternate-day bombing to symbolize their hostility with a literally token display of force. In the same year as the Fukien invasion scare, America's backing of India in the Himalayan incident was probably one factor in leading to China's caution with further military operations. The Chinese withdrawal from the Assam Plain also reflected a keen understanding of the diplomatic limitations on the use of force. Any sustained occupation of Indian territory, besides keeping China embroiled militarily under highly favorable conditions, would have exposed Peking to the irrefutable charge of overt, conventional aggression. This would have seriously contravened Peking's doctrinal arguments regarding the process of world revolution—which certainly does not depend on alien armies openly crossing the frontiers of target states.

Before launching an attack, the Chinese issue many warnings and repeat calls for negotiation (usually on their own terms). In 1950, many carefully worded statements—the most important being sent through Indian channels—stressed the dangers of Chinese intervention should the Americans cross into North Korea.[3] Similarly, from 1959 onward, the Chinese repeatedly warned the Indians of possible reprisals for alleged border violations, and became even more emphatic in mid-1962. They also intensified their efforts at that time to extract a favorable diplomatic settlement from New Delhi.[4] In 1965, after the Americans began the limited bombings of North Vietnam, Peking warned that it would respond if Washington stepped up its "aggression" by invading the North.[5] Presumably, other actions that could endanger the survival of the Hanoi regime, such as strategic attacks on its population centers, would also bring a Chinese response. While not signifying a willingness to compromise over vital issues, this behavior pattern at least indicates that the Chinese do not consider the unexpected use of force, without due warning, a normal instrument of foreign policy. (The situation in the Taiwan Strait might be an exception.)

Even the crisis in North Vietnam has demonstrated China's caution. When we look beyond the ominous warnings to the United States and the scornful denunciation of Moscow for failing to support Hanoi, we find only sober and measured Chinese responses.[6] North Vietnam long opposed the Sino-Soviet split and did everything it could to straddle the fence and reunite the feuding parties. Only in 1962–63, when Hanoi became deeply involved in the war to the South and could not gain Russian backing, did it side with Peking. Even then, it did not cut its lines to Moscow completely, thereby keeping the way open to closer relations after the fall of Khrushchev. For its part, Peking was slow to respond to Hanoi's efforts to associate it with even the protection of North Vietnam, let alone with effective opposition to American operations in the South. China apparently agreed to supply light field arms, anti-aircraft guns, and jet aircraft to Hanoi in 1963–64, but it became only gradually and partially committed to Hanoi's war objectives. With their ally under assault, the Chinese stand ready to assist its survival, but they do not appear prepared to risk an American confrontation directly in order to assure that Hanoi will collect its "Geneva inheritance." [7]

Since Peking has not made an unequivocal commitment to a Communist neighbor, North Vietnam, it is far from clear why Prince Sihanouk has constantly averred that Cambodia depends on Chinese protection to maintain its sovereign independence. The Chinese welcomed Sihanouk's statements, along with his anti-

American version of neutralism. This important diplomatic break-through enabled China to trumpet the Cambodian "model" as a pro-totype for the states of Southeast Asia and the underdeveloped world as a whole. Yet in contrast to its propaganda backing, Peking has avoided making any formal guarantee of the defense and security of Cambodia against aggression by its neighbors, acting on their own or in collusion with America. China did support Cam-bodia's call for a fourteen-nation conference to guarantee its neu-trality, at least until the spring of 1965. Then, realizing that such a meeting might serve as a convenient channel for American-Soviet efforts to settle the Vietnamese conflict, Peking denounced the proposal. China's policy on this point may well have perturbed the Cambodians and made them question the value of their heavy dependence on Peking.

Tendencies toward Imprudence

Although the proponents of the "school of caution" can make a formidable case in the area of external relations, they must acknowl-edge that the record in domestic affairs is another matter entirely. China's agricultural policy during the 1950s certainly has not been a model of consistency, prudence, or realism. The rapid changes in form—from private ownership to cooperative, collective, and then commune—were departures from the leaders' own carefully thought-out doctrines and policies.[8] The utterly unrealistic targets, poor coordination with other sectors of the economy, and the cha-otic state of administrative controls and authority all point to an astounding lack of caution in a most vital matter. The Cultural Revolution further drives this point home with renewed emphasis. Therefore, in assessing the conduct of foreign affairs, we may well consider whether political leaders whose fanaticism and self-certainty lead them to behave so rashly in one sector of public affairs will not follow a similar pattern in other fields.

The intense revolutionary impulse and *élan*, the conviction that Peking's interpretation of Marxism holds the exclusive key to all social truths, and an overwhelmingly optimistic "will to succeed in a hurry" all cut across the traditional stress on patience, acceptance of defeat, and the like. To what extent is this ambivalence displayed in foreign affairs?[9] We have already noted contradictory positions taken toward revolution and communization in the relatively primitive lands of Africa, though admittedly even an activist policy there does not entail great risk. Let us now look at graver security issues raised by Chinese recklessness.

Chinese entry into the Korean War may have been necessary to protect a vital interest—the survival of a fellow Communist state; but the continued effort in the South, to drive the Americans into the sea, constituted a dangerous extension of objectives. Much like the Russians in their counteroffensive of 1920 during the border conflict with Poland, the Chinese may have been carried away by revolutionary fervor in Korea. Beyond this, to continue the war for two years after a stalemate had developed on the battlefield was both dangerous and unrewarding since any escalation would have been certain to damage China,[10] without any assurance of effective Russian support.

In 1964, the Chinese undertook a commitment to go to the defense of North Vietnam should its integrity as a state be threatened. They did so at a time when, according to the Chinese themselves, the Soviet nuclear umbrella had become highly suspect and unreliable—at a time that their own leaders have called the most dangerous years, with nuclear weapons in the offing but not yet in hand. Moreover, Peking refused to compromise with Khrushchev's successors even to reduce grave Chinese vulnerability to nuclear attack and rejected all appeals for compromise in Vietnam itself. On the contrary, the Chinese treated the war as an excellent opportunity to validate their doctrine, to further revolutionary causes through violence, and reverse the mild Soviet-American drift toward *détente*. Though the rewards of success would admittedly be great, the dangers were terrible to contemplate. Military escalation could mean the destruction of North Vietnam, and/or a Chinese involvement under highly unfavorable conditions, with the Russians not intervening unless China's own survival was threatened. After having conducted vigorous anti-Soviet policy since 1960, the Chinese could have scant assurance of Soviet support even in that eventuality.

If, and this is far less evident, the Chinese do not care whether the war expands since this development would bring about a desired confrontation of the superpowers, the likely devastation in China would seem to an outsider an extremely high price to pay. It is also possible that the Chinese insistence on blocking a settlement may drive the Americans and the Russians, out of fear of an escalating war, to come to terms despite themselves. If the Chinese see these risks but believe this policy can maximize their gains and still allow them to retreat before the price gets too high, they are presuming that their ability to predict and control events and reactions is well-nigh perfect. This would be an extremely serious error in judgment. The war in Vietnam has become a highly dangerous business and Chinese opposition to a settlement reflects a boldness that certainly borders on rashness, if only because Peking is gambling with the fate of an ally whose survival, it has repeatedly declared, is a vital Chinese interest for national and ideological reasons.

In fact, the entire Chinese doctrine of brinkmanship, combining internal (and pseudo-internal) wars with nuclear blackmail (using the Soviet bomb), reflects what the Russians have characterized as exceeding recklessness. For Peking could be correct nine out of ten times and still provoke profound repercussions because of that one miscalculation. Nor can China be sure that all parties will retreat from the brink whenever Peking wishes, especially if other powers have lost out in previous showdowns and fear that the Chinese will reapply pressure when conditions again become advantageous.

The over-all record of Chinese-Russian relations does not support the image of a cautious regime in Peking. It is true that the Russians refused to use their nuclear power to support Peking's aggressive, if "just," claim to Taiwan in 1958. But they nevertheless committed themselves, at some risk, to defend the mainland regime against attack based on Taiwan. Though this position did deprive China of support regarding an absolutely vital interest, it does not validate Peking's polemical statement that Russian protection had proved to be a sham. The United States regarded Khrushchev's letters of September 7 and 19, 1958, to Eisenhower declaring Soviet defensive support for Peking as a very real commitment.[11] But it is somewhat unreasonable to expect a state to tie its very security to specific national objectives of another. After all, this was one aspect of Germany's erroneous diplomacy that issued in war in 1914. Nor does Peking operate in this manner strictly in the interests of international Communist solidarity, as its policy toward North Vietnam demonstrates.

In any event, if Russian support is so unreliable that China can protect itself only by developing its own nuclear weapons, then Peking has been living dangerously in risking war with America. Perhaps the Chinese really believe that the United States is a "sated tiger," vicious but too "lazy" to attack. If this is their conviction, then they may be correct in their predictions of how the United States will probably behave (that is, not attack) but wrong regarding the reasons (satiation and laziness) underlying this conclusion. This hardly constitutes the proper basis for a careful policy based on realistic calculations. Or the Chinese may really believe that Moscow will defend them and see clearly that Russian demurrals occur only when it is a question of supporting a dangerous offensive operation. If this is so, the Chinese are running great risks, gratuitously, which may almost have cost them their defense treaty toward the end of the Khrushchev era in 1964—all before they developed their own bomb, in the face of allegedly rapacious American aggressors, and while supporting a most provocative policy in Vietnam without the support of any other major power.

Lastly, can anyone argue with assurance that the record—of Chinese efforts to utilize Russian atomic power to win low-cost victories in diplomacy and guerrilla wars—indicates that China will use its nuclear power cautiously, or even wait until it has an arsenal to support the risky policy it has so ardently advocated? If reports about Premier Kosygin's February 1965 trip to Asia are correct, the Chinese apparently reiterated more forcefully than ever that war with America was inevitable, a point the Russians tried to use to advantage in Hanoi in advocating caution.[12] If the Chinese really do believe this, it puts an enormous strain on any other power's attitude and policy of caution. Even if this position serves only as an argument in debate, it still poisons the atmosphere and reduces the margin for error on all sides by another important degree.[13]

Perhaps rashness and opportunism are always with us, and perhaps the Chinese have theirs under better control than most. If this is the case, and it may well be, they are excellent dissimulators. Yet such intensive reliance on the doctrine of violence, vigorous advocacy of this doctrine, and, I believe, adoption of rash policies in moments of crisis puts China's reputation for caution in a less reassuring light.[14] For them, their vaunted caution is no more than a tactical feature in a strategic posture that is most dangerous and messianic. Nor will caution necessarily win out in each crucial instance. If compounded by miscalculations, especially on the part of leaders who believe that they can do no wrong, a single bold move may have the most deadly consequences.

Conditions of Military Action

Although the Chinese are clearly committed ideologically to heavy reliance on force, they recognize that at present, they are comparatively weak when measured against the superpowers. They have, therefore, developed a complex formulation of ways in which to use force in the pursuit of their objectives, probably devoting greater attention to this subject than have any of their rivals.

The Chinese generally decide to resort to force when they believe that the likelihood or level of Western response is fairly low.[15] Despite their inevitable miscalculations, the Chinese have enjoyed moderate successes without suffering undue consequences. Their entire Tibetan and Himalayan operations, as well as the attacks on the offshore islands, were executed without major counterblows, and even the Korean War did not bring a direct assault against China. It is only when we look at Western responses in terms of help to the beleaguered defendant, rather than in terms of threats against Peking directly, that the results appear less uniformly favorable. The assaults above the 17th parallel in Vietnam since 1965 mark the first time that the United States has attacked a state not universally condemned for overt aggression. Even here, however, the Chinese may be partially correct, in their estimate that the United States will not invade North Vietnam.

A second major political condition desired by the Chinese for their military operations is freedom from Russian control. This is somewhat ironic, since the Russians deserve considerable credit for the relative impunity with which the Chinese carried on their past ventures. Nonetheless, the Chinese have worked hard to maintain close relations with North Korea and North Vietnam, and to exclude major Soviet influence from these two countries.

A fundamental contradiction in the Chinese approach has been revealed by the North Vietnamese situation. Here the Chinese encouraged an intensified struggle and tried to prevent effective Russian involvement. But in its need for protection, Hanoi had to turn to Russia for help. For doctrinal reasons and because of intra-bloc requirements, the Soviet Union agreed to commit itself to Hanoi's policy. China could then do little but argue that Moscow would not really offer assistance or might use its position to betray the cause—i.e., insist on fostering a settlement, as in the Cuban crisis.[16] And in fact, the net effect of the expanded war in Vietnam was to increase the Soviet role and, theoretically, enhance its ability to press Hanoi for a moderate stance.

Implicit in these Chinese attitudes toward Russia and the West is a third condition the Chinese seek in their military ventures: control over their extent and outcome. Peking desires complete freedom to start an action, full power to decide its territorial range and combat intensity, and a firm grasp over the objectives underlying the operation. This approach is best suited to limited actions, though as the Korean case demonstrated, even the Chinese run the danger of being compelled to extend their objectives. The offshore islands and Himalayan campaigns afford better illustrations of controlled operations conducted to Chinese specifications. Quemoy and Matsu are highly vulnerable to military pressure, lack intrinsic strategic importance, and their defense evokes no political support abroad. Peking, therefore, has a start-and-stop level well suited to its requirements. However, if it seeks to dominate the course of events, it must severely limit its operations, and concentrate on political benefits that can flow from repeated crises over territory or issues for which the Western commitment is doubtful or unpopular. Both the Indian and Quemoy campaigns met these operational criteria—limited objectives, careful probing, and restricted engagements—and netted some political gains.

As we have noted, China incurred some costs in these campaigns —a disclosure of its air weakness over the Taiwan Strait and a new reputation as aggressor in some parts of the underdeveloped world. In addition, Peking may not always be able to maintain its more conservative guidelines. The momentum of a war, the importance of the objectives, and the desire to intensify the struggle for general doctrinal reasons could reduce its flexibility. Or, the United States might respond more vigorously than anticipated, making it impossible for the Chinese to maintain the limits desired. An increased American involvement might, in fact, induce Peking to change its mind and favor an expanded war, perhaps to embroil Moscow and Washington in a new confrontation.

Purposes of Military Action

The specific purposes for which the Chinese will use force are as important to understand as the conditions under which they wish to operate. The value of military power as a lever in global political strategy must change with the situation or with a realignment of objectives. Before the break with Moscow, China used force and the threat of force to keep the Cold War at a high pitch in an effort to block any *détente* between the superpowers, and to keep Moscow bound closely to China. With the open split, force can serve to improve China's position against the Soviet Union within the Communist world either by driving the Russians closer to the West or by inducing them to compete for support within the bloc by moving closer to the Chinese ideological position. On the whole, however, assuming that the Soviet Union stands by its premise that peaceful coexistence is possible, a Chinese campaign for greater militancy should compel Moscow to adopt a more moderate stance in dealing with both Communist and Western powers. Even in Vietnam, the Russians could take an anti-American position, yet seek a compromise solution and strengthen their ties with other Western states.

It is possible, though far from certain, that by the judicious use of force, China can still block further improvement in Soviet-American relations. The two superpowers, nevertheless, can make progress in weapons control, settlement of their U.N. disputes, and other compromises with only marginal Chinese interference. If the Soviet Union remains interested in ultimate control over nuclear weapons, then the Chinese will find it increasingly difficult to thwart Soviet-American accords or to swing Russia back into line as a sponsor of bloc unity on Chinese ideological terms. Yet the pull of Soviet loyalty to the Communist ideological cause and the need for some essential minimal understanding with the West constitute a conflict of Russian interests that Peking will try to exploit to the hilt.[17]

A second major role of force is to demonstrate China's regional superiority, especially until it overcomes its nuclear inadequacy. The Chinese have an asset that is heightened by skillful use of power—the realization by all concerned that Chinese strength will continue to rise rapidly relative to its neighbors' and, perhaps, even in comparison with the armed might that outside powers actually deploy in Asia. Displays of Chinese strength that generate fear and respect validate this projection of future power and, at the same time, inflate China's current position above its real worth. Specifically, Chinese power could keep Asian neutralists in line and intimidate other Asian states into following a neutralist course, particularly during a Sino-American confrontation. China can also invoke its armed might in a wide range of situations to deter an opponent from acting against any state China supports. For instance, in return for strong diplomatic backing, China might offer to defend Cambodia or North Vietnam, or it might have encouraged Indonesian efforts against Malaysia. If successful, this approach affords maximum political advantage at minimum cost. Even when deterrent threats fail and the Chinese have to give ground, they unflaggingly resume the same pose at the next opportunity and try again.

The establishment of an aura of dominance in the Afro-Asian world provides a third great incentive for the Chinese to challenge Western power on a limited scale. At the same time, Peking tries to maintain a benign attitude toward lands with which it is not in conflict, while castigating any Asian opponent as an imperialist stooge. Nonetheless, since the United States has become deeply committed in Asia, any Chinese threat to undertake serious military efforts involves the possibility of a significant American response. Thus, the diplomatic isolation of the United States and reduction of the American commitment comprise both a fourth purpose in the use of force and a major condition for it. Some analysts, in fact, maintain that China seems to use its military power primarily to upset and undercut the United States in Asia, with the actual issues relegated to secondary importance.

This approach would place policy toward the United States at the center of Chinese considerations. Apparently, the Chinese assume that, though operationally sluggish, the United States retains a desire to smash China while it is still vulnerable. Peking's key effort would, therefore, be to keep the United States off balance in a general strategic sense, as well as to reduce American mobility and effectiveness in the crisis at hand.[18] Further, these actions, taking advantage of U.S. "sluggishness," and reflecting China's aptitude for low-level or guerrilla conflict, would enable Peking to make significant political gains while serving notice that any nation that tangles with China runs the risk of a sharp clash and a severe mauling. Peking might prefer a series of incidents at a level low enough to avoid provoking a response, yet effective enough to make the next incident easier to launch. If the United States should decide to intervene, China could retreat, jettisoning its "paper tiger" harangues and inveighing against the Americans as nuclear-crazed imperialists seeking a wider war.

It may be going too far, however, to put the United States at the center of Chinese motivations. Many of China's military activities can be explained by direct and immediate Chinese requirements that have little to do with thwarting the United States. Peking will use force, that is, when absolutely necessary to protect vital, jeopardized interests.

It seems more valid, therefore, to adopt a compromise interpretation: that particular situations determine when force will be used, but that additional calculations, including the effects on Washington and other capitals, help decide the timing and extent of operations undertaken. Where one places the emphasis—whether on the immediate issue or on the strategic impact on Washington—crucially influences any analysis of the likelihood of violence and long-term prospects for negotiations. For, if the immediate issues provide but a carefully controlled pretext, then a certain number of conflicts must take place in time, no matter what conditions obtain.

Importance of Specific Interests

If Peking's military calculations derive first from urgent national requirements and only secondarily from a desire to control American behavior patterns, then Chinese estimates of American responses retain their central importance only in relation to the requirements of the immediate military situation. Generally, then, before proceeding with planned operations, the Chinese may have to be convinced that the United States will not respond. This expectation that there will be no U.S. response, plus the desire to secure the access road to Tibet, may be a more accurate explanation of the Indian conflict of 1962 than viewing it as a start-stop border war to keep the United States off balance. Conversely, fear of American reprisals may have kept China from entering the Vietnamese war when the bombings began in February 1965—especially since the survival of North Vietnam was not at stake.

In short, the Chinese probably act to attain specific objectives. Where these are not absolutely vital, their original decision and scope of operations depend on their estimate of American responses. Where vital interest is at stake, as in Korea, the Chinese will run the risk of war with the United States, regardless of whether the Russian nuclear umbrella is available. The Chinese will fight (1) to attain and secure what they consider to be the country's proper boundaries, (2) to protect the survival of a fellow Asian Communist state, (3) to avert a humiliating public defeat, if there is no other way out, and (4) to counter a substantial assault on the homeland. Other objectives, though important, are secondary to these. Military action still provides Peking with opportunities to undermine the Russian and U.S. positions and keep the less developed states diplomatically fragmented and in constant dread of Chinese power. But these very important benefits are often derived from policies rooted in more urgent considerations.

Opportunism plays its role as well, for instance, in China's support for the autonomous Viet Minh rebellion against the French around 1950, and perhaps opportunism once removed can explain Peking's support for the Viet Cong in a war directed and primarily sustained from Hanoi. But even such secondary involvement, however prudent, can enmesh the Chinese in a major confrontation. Since a successful war can justify the Chinese interpretation of history, it can take on an importance not originally inherent in the conflict. Chinese support of North Vietnam thus involves great risks, as one might expect from a policy that combines opportunism with strong ideological motivation but does not offer control over events. Much of the initiative, in the final analysis, lies in Washington and, to some extent, in Hanoi.

For its part, Washington has the task of keeping its military pressure on North Vietnam at an optimum level—sufficient to prove the Russians right in maintaining that America is not a paper tiger and leaving the Chinese in a bad light for not responding. On the other hand, Washington has to avoid that degree of severity that would compel the Chinese to act or would drive the Russians to full-fledged support of Hanoi. The Quemoy-Matsu imbroglio illustrates how careful use of American power can ward off a threat and intensify the Sino-Soviet split. Finding the proper mixture in the Vietnamese situation has proved more difficult because what might suffice to drive the wedge deeper between Peking and Moscow might not deflect Hanoi from its course.[19]

Scope of Military Activities

China's vital interests, as reflected in the zone of operations for its own armed forces, include the protection not only of the homeland but also of its neighbors North Korea and North Vietnam against enemy attacks. Peking's 1961 treaty with North Korea provides for military defense and joint military coordination. To maintain a balance, Pyongyang concluded a similar agreement with Moscow. But North Korean policy and actions during 1963–64 indicated a close synchronization with the Chinese and reliance on them for security.

After all, it was China that came to the rescue in 1950 after first expressing grave doubts about the military venture that June. Ideologically, North Korea adhered close to the Peking line in the great dispute with Moscow—particularly in denouncing India, condemning Yugoslav revisionism, and accusing Russia of betraying Cuba in 1962.[20] However, the Korean leaders echoed the Soviet call for peaceful coexistence during the Kosygin visit in early 1965. Though they refused to attend the March conference of international parties sponsored by Moscow and boycotted by Peking, new promises of Soviet aid swung them back to a less hostile position later that year. Peking's adamant demand that all Communists support the Chinese line, plus increased Russian assistance, drove Pyongyang to assert its independence of both "dogmatists" and "revisionists" in August 1966.

North Vietnam has also enjoyed closer military ties with China in recent years. Under the terms of the Geneva settlement of 1954, it cannot join an alliance and so is formally unaligned, as is South Vietnam. Both Vietnamese states undertook substantial armament programs in the late 1950s, and as the conflict intensified, Hanoi increased its military dependence upon Peking. Peking, in turn, stepped up its involvement during the Tonkin Gulf incident of August 1964, sending a squadron of MIG planes to North Vietnam. It is not known whether the pilots were Chinese or Chinese-trained North Vietnamese. Whichever the pilots were, a move like this requires many months of preparation and presumably was agreed to long in advance, though the timetable might have been telescoped because of the danger of escalation that summer. In the years that followed, the Chinese gave considerable help in arms, technological personnel, and matériel to sustain the North Vietnamese war effort.

The Korean War and, to a far more limited extent, the Vietnamese crisis thus proved exceptions to the general rule that China had avoided any military involvement beyond its own frontiers. Significantly, both cases have had very serious consequences for global diplomacy. Yet the Chinese have not indicated a desire to station their own forces in foreign lands. They withdrew their military units from North Korea in the late 1950s and did not send any combat formations into North Vietnam even after the American bombings began. Peking seeks primarily to use its known resolve to deter attacks that would require Chinese armies to cross the frontier. Of course, during several revolutionary crises, Peking has publicized its offers to dispatch volunteers to distant lands—among them, Cuba and Algeria—but these were demonstrations of moral rather than material support.[21] However, it is not difficult to imagine a somewhat different international situation, in which China has an effective nuclear armory and the Taiwan problem no longer exists, that would allow Peking to take bigger risks. It might try to project its power abroad with greater frequency, and other states would certainly attach greater significance to such efforts than in the past.

At present, the Chinese do not express an interest in using force to gain control of Taiwan, Hong Kong, or Macao. Probably in the expectation of regaining at least part of these lands through diplomatic negotiation in the near future, they argue that force should not be employed for this purpose. Though the European colonies bring material gains to China today, especially in trade and finance, Peking might not allow this anomalous situation to continue if the political cost of attack were not so steep.[22] There is little appeal to the idea of fighting over Taiwan, as long as this involves the prospect of widespread destruction and high military risk. Nor is China likely to resort to nuclear weapons; even the threat of such an attack is difficult to envision, for it would imply a willingness to use these most destructive devices against fellow Chinese. This constraint might not apply, however, if the United States established a strategic weapons base on the island.

In all likelihood, then, Peking would not launch any major attack on Taiwan, even of a conventional sort, unless it anticipated rapid capitulation of the garrison, perhaps after a major political-psychological victory. Any assault would also require local air and naval superiority in the Taiwan Strait, and this kind of power Peking essentially lacks. This same lack today sharply curtails China's ability to affect the course of Japanese policy, or even to present a serious threat to India, notwithstanding the fantastic success of the 1962 operation. However, we must not denigrate China's great achievement during that campaign in constructing roads and moving supplies and forces at a pace that was truly remarkable, given the problems of distance, terrain, and weather.

The sizable Chinese army remains a potent factor in its own right, because of its massiveness and its reputation for discipline and quality. It has been alleged that the war with India depleted the country's military resources markedly, but the scope of this effort appears to have been exaggerated.[23] In all likelihood, no more than

30,000 troops were involved in the campaign that brought Chinese power to the Brahmaputra River, and they apparently operated at very low cost in supplies and equipment. China's forte is its capacity to place powerful forces on many sectors of its frontier at the same time.

These formations do not have to be very numerous or formidable in size for China to gain local superiority on several scattered points simultaneously. As long as the various engagements remained small in scope, China could take on several indigenous opponents simultaneously, because they are comparatively so weak. However, the Chinese would still seek to avoid multiple operations in the future because they might drag on or expand, taxing Peking's power excessively, or drive a number of isolated states to work together and so increase China's diplomatic problems. War on several fronts, in Peking's eyes, could invite American intervention, a thrust from Taiwan, or both. But these very real difficulties should not lead us to conclude that Peking could not operate on several fronts effectively, if it had to.[24] It also retains the capacity to launch a massive conventional attack at a place and time of its own choosing to eliminate or reduce a pressing danger, without stripping itself of the ability to act on other fronts.

In recent years, Peking has made resourceful use of ambiguous military actions with a shrewd mix of combat operations. Along with subversion, infiltration, and low-level war by proxy (Laos and Vietnam) come verbal threats that vary in targets and intensity over the years but are usually directed against America's allies.[25] Sustained propaganda pressure against the Nationalists has been supplemented in recent years by a campaign of invective against India that functions at only a slightly lower key. Varying types of coercion, geared to the particular situation, also reflect flexibility; we have already noted the repeated and sporadic artillery shelling on the offshore islands, the brief thrust against India, and the pressure of a restricted occupation on the Burmese border. Any of these military actions can also serve as a backdrop, though not originally so planned, to get results elsewhere—e.g., Thailand, Cambodia, and Pakistan. In this regard, American reactions become very important considerations, not only in the foreign policies of the target state but also in neighboring lands. And this concern is not restricted by any means to those states with which Washington has treaty commitments.

The Taiwan Military Front

Peking can justify the use of force against the offshore islands as part of a civil war that does not violate international law. Since both Chinese parties claim to be the true government, neither would deny that this is a problem of internal jurisdiction. Hence, Peking can argue that others cannot, in justice, turn this conflict into an international confrontation. With the United States almost isolated diplomatically in its commitment to defend Taiwan, Peking can sustain a psychological offensive with feelers for negotiation, combined with rumors of interest on the part of some Nationalist officials, that could erode America's confidence in Nationalist staying power. Similarly, Peking can use any instance of apparent American interest in accommodation, or of retreat on any other front, to undermine the Kuomintang leadership's confidence in its essential ally.[26]

In this kind of approach, an image of the mainlander's military capacity as overpowering and irreversible would play a crucial role. Peking's development of modern nuclear and missile technology, plus a display of self-sufficiency in more advanced conventional arms, will have a major impact on the Nationalists. It is at this stage that appeals to national pride, calls for unity, and offers of amnesty and a fruitful role in Chinese public life might sap the will-to-persist on Taiwan and make it highly vulnerable to a Communist military move.

As we have seen, any achievement that further cements Peking's power at home increases the vulnerability of the Nationalists' fragile diplomatic-military defense system.[27] Peking's ability to survive the Russian split, prevent a recurrence of famine, develop new weapons, improve its trade with Japan and Western Europe, and regain some momentum in its economic development could contribute to undermining Nationalist self-confidence and sense of security.

Peking has repeatedly stated its total rejection of the "two-Chinas" solution. It considers a separate Taiwanese state under Nationalist rule totally unacceptable. It maintains that it would not permit its entry into the United Nations to hinge upon an additional seat for an independent Taiwanese China, either under the Nationalists or under Taiwanese self-government. In fact, Peking has categorically stated that it will have nothing to do with the United Nations except on its own terms.

The Kuomintang, meanwhile, claims jurisdiction over all China and treats Taiwan as one province in its political scheme of things. The Nationalists view the island as a base for their eventual return to the mainland, and like the Communists, they refuse to recognize the two-China concept. For acceptance of this solution would vitiate their justification for control over Taiwan and would inexorably lead to Taiwanese self-determination, fear of which has led the regime to curtail political freedom thus far. Though the African states might rally behind a campaign in the United Nations to keep Taiwan out of Peking's hands—which is America's basic interest—they would do so only on the grounds of self-determination. This the Kuomintang cannot accept. Its position is that it has not held out all these difficult years at great odds just to preserve America's minimal security interests, or to apply to its detriment great principles of international politics espoused in distant lands.

Both Chinese contestants will find their dilemma regarding the island more acute as the rest of the world takes greater note of this and related developments. Since Peking attaches crucial significance to the Taiwan problem, for reasons of international prestige as well as national security, it will undoubtedly direct much of its military energies toward developing the matériel necessary to mount an attack. It must give high priority to better-quality aircraft and air-defense equipment for use in future Strait operations. At the very least, the mainlanders would have to dominate the air over the offshore islands and part of the Strait, if not over Taiwan. The 1958 air battles in the Strait demonstrated the tactical superiority of the Nationalist air force, and Peking has avoided even limited engagements of that type since then, because it still cannot match its opponent.

However, the mainland forces have many more pilots, a well-developed infrastructure system, and a wider, more secure deployment. With their narrow territorial base, the Nationalists are far more vulnerable. Also, they cannot afford many losses since they have too few pilots per plane.[28] At present, their forces, numbering in the hundreds of thousands, depend increasingly on Taiwanese for technically skilled personnel, as well as sheer manpower. As the mainlanders improve the quality of their aircraft, the United States will find it increasingly necessary to train and equip the Nationalists with the most advanced fighter planes. Even so, the Communists may feel free to undertake a new test of strength over the Strait when they reach parity, for the political benefits from such an encounter may make a stalemate worthwhile. This could well bring U.S. carrier planes into action and perhaps provoke assaults from other American aircraft stationed at nearby land bases. Miscalculations on both sides in such a situation could heighten the danger of sudden escalation.

Peking's effectiveness would also depend in part on its capability, not necessarily to control the sea lanes or launch an invasion over 100 miles of water, but to subject the American presence to costly risks. It may well be within Peking's capacity in the near future to develop both the light surface craft and very short-range tactical submarines to threaten American warships and disrupt patrols, and to cut Nationalist supply lines to Quemoy and Matsu.[29] This might well be a serious blow to Taiwan's security, strategically and psychologically. Again, however, such seemingly controlled risks could lead to stronger American responses than anticipated, and so to a rising spiral of confrontations and tensions.[30]

The air and naval power required to sustain attacks on the offshore islands would be nowhere nearly as formidable as that required for assault against Taiwan itself. The offshore islands also represent the weakest spot in America's entire Far Eastern diplomatic stance, and the kind of limited operation necessary to capture them maximizes the mainlanders' military strength vis-à-vis the United States. If a large-scale assault were launched, it would be possible to deal the defenders a crippling blow. If the Nationalists continue to place one-third of their forces so close to the mainland, the attacks might well provide a spectacular triumph.[31] Peking may hope, by a success on Quemoy and Matsu, to thwart any movement for a separate Taiwanese state, shatter Nationalist morale, and induce other powers to put pressure on Washington to liquidate this dangerous stalemate on Communist terms.

The offshore-Taiwan complex of problems thus is potentially as dangerous a trigger for a large confrontation as the Vietnamese situation. For a victory by the mainlanders would shake the morale and military power of the Kuomintang so deeply as to jeopardize its hold on Taiwan. On the other hand, this possibility might enable the Nationalists to exert great pressure on the United States to become deeply involved on their behalf at the coast of China itself. Any escalation means at the very least a strike at nearby Chinese tactical air bases.

Japan's Pivotal Position

Perhaps an even greater thorn in China's flesh—potentially if not at present—is Japan. In many ways, its position vis-à-vis China is precisely the reverse of Taiwan's, though both the Nationalists and the Japanese are old enemies of the mainlanders. Certainly, Japan poses a greater obstacle to China's rise to power than the beleaguered Nationalist regime on Taiwan.

Still, for the moment, though a rival and a target, Japan is not subjected to the intensely hostile treatment that Peking reserves for the United States, India, or, in a different context, the Soviet Union. In part, this stems from Peking's desire not to add any more antagonists to this formidable list. In Japan, moreover, the Chinese still seek to win converts. They count on the great appeal of neutralization, the deep sense of guilt and affinity, and the economic advantage of close ties with China.

Finally, Western Europe and Japan are now the only two sources available for the trade-on-credit, capital assistance, technical aid, and industrial equipment required to help sustain China's economic growth, with all that that implies for the nation's power and ambitions. As we have seen, after years of dismal commercial relations, China and Japan have experienced a modest growth in trade, with the figures doubling from 1962 to 1963 and again from 1964 ($300 million) to 1966 ($600 million).

Nonetheless, it is highly unlikely that the rates of increase will continue to grow at this pace. For one thing, the Chinese will be unable to pay for much more, even with generous credits. Japan is hardly likely to accept a position of supplicant creditor, in which it must grant further concessions in order to win assurances of debt repayment. Nor is it likely to become so dependent on the Chinese markets as to give Peking political leverage over the course of its foreign and security policies. Tokyo has had too much experience with Communist China on this score and is too heavily dependent on its profitable relations elsewhere to run such risks.

Despite the prospect of better economic ties with Japan, the long-range potential for major rivalry between Tokyo and Peking persists. It cannot abate until China actually gains an ascendancy or resigns itself to more modest ambitions in Asia. Even with superior power in nuclear affairs, China would still have to cope with Japan's attractiveness as a model for economic development, as an alternate candidate for Asian leadership, and as a source of material aid for neighboring states. Should military inferiority drive Tokyo closer to the United States or in quest of its own atomic capacity under the umbrella of American power, the Chinese may find that their policies have turned a confused neighbor into a serious, potentially menacing rival.

All such eventualities are years away, but the possibility is there and will remain as long as Tokyo adheres to its American alliance. Relations with Taiwan may worsen as trade with Peking expands, but Japan will not in the foreseeable future break relations with Taiwan—i.e., grant Peking recognition on mainland terms. In fact, it will try to make amends to the Nationalists with a more friendly commercial policy, exemplified by the $150-million loan in 1964. Whether aid will ever extend to the military sphere remains an open and at present highly doubtful point, but Japan's powerful inclination to stay inside its present shell may alter sharply if China menaces it, however indirectly, after acquiring nuclear delivery systems.[32]

The Chinese atomic test of October 1964 disturbed the Japanese considerably and led to strong protests against further testing.[33] China is quite willing to pay the price of endangering its prestige in Japan, however. Until the past few years, the Japanese leftist parties had remained generally united on the bomb issue, directing their attacks primarily against the United States. The Soviet resumption of testing in 1961, following a three-year unofficial moratorium, had been dismaying, but Moscow's support of the test ban brought it back into agreement with Washington and enabled a large segment of the Japanese left to feel that its anti-bomb policy had been vindicated. This caused a rift in leftist ranks, in which, until then, there had been close collaboration between the main Socialist party (and its supporting federation of unions, SOHYO) and the Communists.[34] For they all favored the neutralization of Japan, the ending of the American alliance, and a dismantling of nuclear power.

However, with the Russian-Chinese split and the dispute over testing, the pro-Chinese faction won control of the Japanese Communist party in 1963 and committed it to the argument that though it is acceptable for Communist states to test, it is immoral for the Western powers to do so. In 1963, the left Socialist party and union leaders, while adhering to their anti-American position, walked out of a conference called to demonstrate against the American bomb but supporting Chinese nuclear weaponry.[35] As these differences intensified, the pro-Russian minority in the Communist party broke away. The split came at an inopportune time—just as the party was gaining some strength, climbing from 1.1 million votes in 1960 to 1.4 million in 1963.[36] Unlike a similar faction in India, the pro-Soviet group in Japan may stand a chance of holding its ground since it has some popular members and is in harmony with the public's general opposition to testing. In fact, the allegedly pro-Peking leadership of the Japanese Communist Party found Peking's strident demands for all-out support so repugnant that, like North Korea, it declared itself "independent" of foreign influences in the summer of 1966. Reversing completely the position of a few years earlier, the Socialists inherited the party with the pro-Peking label.

Yet, in examining the future course of Japanese policy, we may discover ample grounds for Chinese optimism. Peking has the great advantages of momentum and moral righteousness, and the Japanese are still uncertain about their commitment to their own security, let alone to the American alliance. Moreover, the current alignment of forces in Japan's body politic and the way it is structured make the country highly vulnerable to pressures toward a neutralist position. The determined anti-American policy of the Socialists in the wake of the Vietnamese conflict after 1964 gave added weight to this trend. However, China's past use of the trade question, its clumsy interventions in Japanese politics (now in internal Japanese Communist party affairs), the impact of the testing crisis, and the painfully increasing clarity of the security dilemma raise doubts about Peking's capacity to turn the situation to its strategic advantage.

If anything, the growth in Chinese military power may lead Japan to try to respond in kind. Tokyo can hope to match Peking in overall strength, since China's level is within the range of its capabilities, in contrast to the awesome magnitude of Soviet power. Such a development would create serious problems for the United States, although ultimately the advantages might far outweigh the difficulties.

There has not yet been a public commitment by the Japanese government to any significant increase in military strength, and the level of defense expenditures has been rising very slowly.[37] The military establishment, called the self-defense forces, was set at a modest level by the five-year defense plan of 1962: 180,000 men in the ground force, a 143,600-ton navy, and 1,036 aircraft.[38] In addition, the country is developing sophisticated modern equipment outside the nuclear field. But many Japanese analysts, and other intellectuals long hostile to a revival of militarism, have reluctantly concluded that the lack of autonomous military power has been a formidable obstacle to their government's widely supported objective of winning a respected voice in international councils.

Thus, Japan can, and probably will, shift in national security policy significantly, without adopting either the radical Socialist position—termination of the present defense arrangements—or a strong conservative stand for nuclear armament and a revival of the old military virtues. The middle course would demand creation over the next decade of a much stronger conventional defense force, endowed with an increasing capacity to project its power beyond the home islands.[39]

Until now, the issue of alignment has been linked to the question of Japan's own military strength in a curious way, with many neutralists arguing against both the alliance and the possession of armed power. However, the argument is currently being heard that lack of arms makes it impossible for Japan to follow a neutral course that would allow it to keep even a semblance of independence. Although those advocating greater national power do not imply that they desire to end the American security connection at this juncture, the logical connection of these two policies will become increasingly evident once the powerful association of pacifism with neutralism starts to weaken. For the moment, however, some advocates of greater military power for Japan hold that the American alliance should be extended until at least 1980, so as to match the time-span of the Sino-Soviet treaty of 1950.[40]

We should, nonetheless, beware of assuming that a stronger Japan, even one with greater interest in regional security affairs, would simply reinforce existing security patterns. Clearly, questions of levels of conventional strength, alignment, nuclear power, and territorial range of responsibility are coming to the fore in Tokyo. The answers are hardly likely to follow a preconceived path or fall into a pattern that an outside observer would consider "consistent."

In any event, a confrontation of some sort between an economically strong Japan and the militarily powerful Chinese can readily take place over the next generation, with the capacity of each state to reduce the other's respective lead playing a major, if not determining, role. The fate of American security policy in the Pacific may be influenced more by the course of future Japanese-Chinese diplomatic relations than by any other development within the Far East.

CHAPTER THIRTEEN

Threat from Hanoi:
A Study in Confrontation
and Escalation

The Democratic Republic of Vietnam (D.R.V.) may be a "little dragon," but it breathes fire in its own right. It provides the driving force behind the Viet Cong effort in South Vietnam and sustains the Pathet Lao across the border in eastern Laos. Beyond their own significance, Hanoi's policies—and the problems they raise for the rest of Indochina—have illuminated and intensified the great dilemmas confronting the major powers in Asia.

The D.R.V. has been a testing ground for the depth and durability of the rift between Moscow and Peking. Its role in South Vietnam produced an American-Soviet diplomatic freeze and put the compatibility between the Communist doctrines of peaceful coexistence and wars of national liberation to a severe test. In addition, the struggle for South Vietnam has vividly illustrated the broad range of America's capability to project its power abroad, as well as the cruel limitations inherent in a war against insurgency, especially when conducted in support of a politically weak, administratively ineffectual regime. Finally, the terrifying problems of escalation have become all too real as the war has unfolded, complicating the already dangerous Sino-American confrontation.

Hanoi's policy in the struggle is determined by two critical points: what Hanoi hopes to gain from the war in the South and what relationship Hanoi maintains with China and Russia. These questions, in turn, are direct outgrowths of Indochinese history.

One fact of life in the Indochinese Peninsula has been the domination of China, beginning around the second century B.C. and reas-

225

serting itself intermittently to our own times. At the end of the Second World War, Chiang Kai-shek's troops occupied Indochina briefly, but they withdrew, prodded by the French and other allies —and by local hostility. The extent of current Chinese influence defies precise definition, but Hanoi and Peking are each aware that outright domination would revive age-old resentments among the Vietnamese.

A second fact of history in East Asia is the movement of peoples southward. Under pressure of such advances by the Chinese, the Vietnamese of the North have pressed inexorably toward the rice-rich areas of the Mekong Delta. Indochina's geopolitical history was not blessed with any Bismarck to exert strong national control from a capital city. Vietnam itself was divided for several centuries into Northern and Southern kingdoms until the end of the eighteenth century. The Vietnamese considered Laos and Cambodia subject regions, from which their sovereigns exacted tribute as early as the sixteenth century. However, a strong sense of independent identity developed in these lands, and conflicts between the proud Khmers of Cambodia, earlier inhabitants of the region, and the Vietnamese were frequent occurrences.

The concept that the Indochinese Peninsula was an entity, rather than a group of discrete small states, found expression in 1930, when the Indochinese Communist Party was founded by a small group led by Ho Chi Minh. When the ICP re-emerged early in 1951 with headquarters in northern Vietnam, Cambodia and Laos were no longer members. Their omission was considered a temporary measure, and a Vietnamese Communist party directive in November of that year stated that "when conditions permit . . . , the three revolutionary parties of Vietnam, Cambodia and Laos will be reunited to form a single party." [1]

As the country is now divided, North Vietnam is perennially plagued by excess mouths to feed. Hanoi undoubtedly hoped to resolve this problem after winning independence from France by reuniting the country under the Geneva accords and so gaining control over the rice-surplus areas of the Mekong Delta. When the Diem regime refused to participate in this process in 1956 or even enter into economic relations with the North, the problem of unification involved major economic as well as ideological and nationalistic considerations for Hanoi. It is in this context that we must view the war in the South and the roles played in it by the two superpowers, the two Vietnamese regimes, and Peking.

Relations with China and Russia

D.R.V. leadership has remained remarkably stable for more than twenty years, since the days of the war against France and through its first decade of rule. However, reports of splits and antagonistic cliques, based on personality and policy differences, have persisted for several years. Almost from the start of the Sino-Soviet split, a major issue for Hanoi was whether to take sides or to straddle and try to end it. Hanoi desperately sought to have the dispute terminated without committing itself to either party, but individuals did lean to one side or the other almost from the outset. Upon gaining independence, Hanoi followed the Chinese line both in ideology and in policy, though in 1954 this did not imply hostility toward Moscow. One form of this emulation was the intensive agricultural collectivization on the Chinese model around 1955, which resulted in disastrous decreases in food production. Yet Hanoi never went beyond the relatively loose level of organization that China itself had favored at that time, and to which it returned by 1961 after the shattering experience with communes.

Hanoi also followed the Chinese pattern of industrialization, which at the time was modeled on the Russian approach, stressing heavy industry and aiming at a high growth rate. In 1957 the D.R.V. even imitated the Chinese "hundred flowers" campaign and, like its large neighbor, summarily suppressed the displays of popular unrest and antagonism to the regime evoked by the campaign. However, the North Vietnamese were pragmatic enough to see in the harsh restraints required on both agricultural and urban fronts —to sustain collectivization and halt agitation—a warning not to follow Peking in its next endeavors.[2] Hanoi did not copy the communes or the excesses of the Great Leap Forward, but its devotion to dogma blocked moves toward a more rational and more productive use of land. Hanoi restricted private plots on collectives to 5 per cent of the land, despite the fact that these areas provided 30 to 40 per cent of agricultural income in 1961 and approached 50 per cent in 1962.[3] During 1958–60, its domestic program, ideological line, and foreign policy carefully took a middle course between the Soviet and Chinese positions, which were drifting further apart. A substantial Soviet aid program undertaken at the time contributed to Hanoi's decision.

Despite significant differences among the D.R.V. leaders over whether to support Peking or Moscow, when the split broke into the open, the government held to its middle course and pressed both great powers to settle their argument. Hanoi believed that the confrontation weakened the revolutionary movement, harmed the D.R.V.'s national interests, and could pose a dangerous dilemma if the two giants insisted that it take sides. The combination of Soviet aid, Chinese failures, and nationalist opposition to control from Peking strengthened the argument for neutrality in the dispute.

In maintaining this equilibrium during the trying years 1958–62, Hanoi evaded taking a stand on many issues, such as the efficacy of communes, China's pressure tactics against the offshore islands, Russian policy in Cuba, and the Sino-Indian struggle. North Vietnam even followed a cautious policy regarding Laos, though it had a vital interest in that little kingdom for two reasons: to protect guerrilla access routes to South Vietnam and, eventually, to re-establish a united Indochina under D.R.V. rule. In 1961, when the Russians and Chinese agreed to negotiate with the West to settle the Laos question, the North Vietnamese went along, agreeing to the cease-fire agreement of 1962. It probably thought that with D.R.V. forces in position inside the eastern frontier of Laos, it could always defend its interest there.

Escalating War in the South

The crucial factor in Hanoi's bloc diplomacy became the struggle for South Vietnam, to which it had committed itself by 1959 and which absorbed an increasing proportion of its scarce resources every year thereafter.[4] After the elections promised for 1956 were blocked by the Saigon government, the 80,000-odd South Vietnamese combatants who had gone north in 1954 after the independence war against the French were organized for a clandestine return below the 17th parallel. Though technically the war began as a struggle between Southerners, Hanoi regrouped, retrained, and re-equipped the former southern Viet Minh troops, organized and directed their deployment to the South, and sustained them in combat. Between 1959 and 1961, the infiltrators, now known as the Viet Cong, built their bases, terrorized selected areas in the countryside, and prepared the political groundwork for the next stage of the war.[5]

The next stage of intensified hostilities is, unhappily, all too well known. Although the North did not immediately dispatch regular army forces, it continued to control and direct the effort, providing the guidance, cadres, reinforcements, and instructions needed to sustain the war. Hanoi also supplied the vitally needed skilled technicians, propagandists, and the administrators to conduct both the civil and military aspects of the operation.[6] As the war on the ground escalated, the American effort increased. Air bases were built and mounting numbers of troops were deployed to protect these bases and support the counterinsurgency operation. At the end of 1964, regular North Vietnamese troops were noted in the South for the first time. With the start of American combat air missions in February 1965, the war extended to all of Vietnam. From then on all four regular forces—American, North Vietnamese, South Vietnamese, and Viet Cong expanded their forces in the South as rapidly as they could.[7]

Ideological, diplomatic, and material support from China became vital to Hanoi in the early 1960s, as the war intensified and the strain of supporting it increased; for the D.R.V. had made little progress in the industrial and agricultural development of what is basically a poor country.

However, Ho Chi Minh remained a popular leader, and the regime, with its powerful internal-security apparatus, was never in any danger despite the atmosphere of mounting instability and uncertainty, accentuated by the bombings that began in 1965. Though these attacks may have intensified patriotic solidarity, they may also have increased public disaffection with the regime's adventurous foreign policy. Victory became vitally important to the D.R.V., not only to enhance national unity and further the Communist cause, but—more immediately—to compensate for the costs of the struggle with the economic benefits that control of the South would bring.

If ideological rigidity harmed North Vietnam's effort at "nation-building" by leading it to unsound economic policy and a costly military venture, adherence to doctrine helped sustain the military campaign at the tactical level in the South. Until the appearance of the American ground forces, the Viet Cong's organizational methods, combat operations, and relations with the populace followed now classic guerrilla principles. However, Viet Cong combat strategy and deployment of forces did not rest on purely military considerations. Rather than make their major effort in the rugged areas of the northern provinces, where they could use the havens of North Vietnam and Laos, the guerrillas concentrated their operations in Central Vietnam, the area around Saigon, and especially in the populous Mekong Delta to the south. The difficult terrain and the existence of strong Communist bases since before 1954 gave this deployment some military plausibility, and the inadequacies of the South Vietnamese army and the Diem regime enabled the Viet Cong to dominate many parts of these regions.[8] In 1965, however, apparently responding to American pressure, they moved most of their forces to less exposed areas.

The Political Struggle

Until 1963, Hanoi did not give the highest priority to a massive effort in the South. It recognized that an adequate cadre, absolutely essential to its plan, could be developed only gradually. Accordingly, the Viet Cong propaganda program was carefully modulated. It identified the struggle as primarily political, called for the neutralization of South Vietnam, and demanded its "liberation" from its American "occupiers" and their "puppets" in Saigon. A National Liberation Front (NLF), formed in 1960, allegedly had non-Communist membership, but no important Southern leaders ever joined it.[9] It was, in fact, a political arm of the Viet Cong. The NLF had little success in gaining diplomatic recognition or support abroad and did not even set up offices in Moscow until 1965, and then on a basis short of formal recognition. As the war intensified, it did not become a respectable cover group within the country nor did it prove a satisfactory basis for a pro-Communist government, in part because Hanoi did not want to see an independence-oriented movement to emerge in the South.

The NLF advocated a zone of neutrality devoid of American influence, embracing South Vietnam, Laos, and Cambodia, and demanded the formation of a coalition government in South Vietnam incorporating all parties. Assuming America's departure and the demoralization of non-Communist forces in the country, this device would have enabled the Viet Cong to gain full control almost immediately. The Communists were careful to avoid proposing coalition, including the NLF, under an enforced military stalemate—a different proposition altogether. Because the Communists lack urban backing and could not be certain of rural support without coercion, this latter arrangement, if kept within a nonviolent political framework, might lead to a nationalist, non-Communist electoral triumph.[10]

In July 1963, Hanoi made a cease-fire offer along NLF terms, indicating that the two were working in close collaboration with the ultimate purpose of unifying Vietnam, but Hanoi stressed that neutralization applied only to the South. In part, this effort was a propaganda response to an unfavorable finding by the International Control Commission which held in 1962, by a 2-1 vote, that D.R.V. was guilty of aggression. The NLF also played a role in North Vietnam's larger plans for all Indochina. As a front regime for Hanoi in the South, it could serve as a model for the establishment of subservient regimes in Laos and Cambodia. These could later serve as way stations to a reunified Indochinese state under control of the Communist party of North Vietnam. Until 1967 Hanoi has generally followed a hard line toward Cambodia, adamantly refusing to settle conflicting border claims.[11] This stance, important in itself, may also be an indicator of the D.R.V.'s unwillingness to stabilize the situation in Indochina on any other terms than Vietnamese Communist hegemony.

The Diplomacy of Intensified Struggle

In mid-1963, when the political crisis came to a head in Saigon, Hanoi abruptly abandoned its caution, up to then complemented by Peking's care to avoid an overt commitment in the war. The rise of Buddhist political activism, its confrontation with the Diem regime, and the series of coups triggered by the fall of Diem in November 1963 offered Hanoi a great opportunity for new military initiatives. China, too, adopted a harsher tone toward South Vietnam, favoring the "just" struggle there, and backing the D.R.V. call for an Asian Buddhist conference against religious oppression in South Vietnam. The crisis thus moved to a higher pitch on all fronts—the political contest in Saigon, the guerrilla campaign, and the American confrontation with Hanoi and Peking. At the time, the Chinese probably agreed to support a large military effort, although guarding themselves from direct exposure to a confrontation. This assistance, though modest by superpower standards, did give Hanoi a better air defense posture by 1964 and a greater capacity to sustain guerrilla operations in the South. As succeeding regimes in Saigon demonstrated their desperate political weakness, the NLF pressed for a coalition government on its own terms and the neutrality of South Vietnam.

In conjunction with its deepening involvement in the military struggle, Hanoi swung closer to China in its foreign policy during 1963, while at the same time keeping its channels to Moscow open in case of future need. China's head of state, Liu Shao-ch'i, visited Hanoi that May, and during the rest of the year, North Vietnam expressed a series of views at odds with the Russian position. It rejected "the primacy of economics," and though continuing to give lip service to the concept of peaceful coexistence, it did not object when Liu, while in North Vietnam, delivered a blistering attack on this basic Russian doctrine.[12] Hanoi backed the Chinese on major points of disagreement with Moscow: the justice of Peking's claim to Taiwan, and its right to employ all means in this cause, and the denunciation of the United States as an imperialist warlike aggressor.

In 1964, Hanoi went further by denying that those who backed "wars of liberation" were guilty of adventurism or risking major war, as Premier Khrushchev had argued. Continuing along the Chinese course, Hanoi justified strategic offensives and denounced a purely defensive posture as a compromise with imperialism and an abandonment of the revolution. The D.R.V. denounced the test-ban treaty of 1963, backed Peking's proposals on total nuclear disarmament, blasted away at Yugoslav revisionism, and accused India of harboring imperialist designs. Until this time, Hanoi had moved cautiously on all these delicate issues out of deference to the Soviet Union. In accelerating the war against the weakened Saigon regime, the Viet Cong held, or could assert temporary control over, about half of South Vietnam. It was at this juncture that the Americans responded by assuming a direct combat role in the war and thus, ironically, drove Hanoi closer to the Russians.

It is difficult to determine whether Hanoi or Peking was the prime motivating force behind the D.R.V.'s greater emphasis on violence in 1963. The Chinese probably encouraged such a stance, which would have been very attractive to Hanoi as long as it would bring victory in sight at a moderate risk—a risk that would be further reduced by Chinese help. However, North Vietnam probably made its own decision. Hanoi is an autonomous policy-making center over which the Chinese exercise considerable influence but not control. Peking could offer only limited aid and would not extend a blanket guarantee of protection against all consequences.[13] This is not to say that China did not strongly desire an intensified Vietnamese effort. Such a campaign, if successful, would justify its view of the proper way to communize the underdeveloped world and would strike a telling blow against the doctrine of peaceful coexistence. And it would be an even more effective blow if Moscow extended support to Hanoi, for in that case, the hated American-Russian *détente* would collapse. If, on the other hand, Russia failed to assist a "fraternal" state, it would lose ground in the struggle with Peking for the loyalty of Communist parties all over the world. Finally, even if the Viet Cong failed, Peking believed that the escalation of hostilities would sharpen the "class struggle," heighten international tensions generally, and deepen existing contradictions so that the long-range cause of world revolution would be advanced.

When in 1963 Hanoi abandoned its earlier caution concerning the war in the South, it probably did not fear this would embroil it in dangerous dependence upon Peking. Hanoi never rejected Moscow completely, for the Russians could serve as a counterweight to excessive Chinese influence and as a valuable emergency source of military backing.[14] After the fall of Khrushchev, in October 1964, North Vietnam actually received Russian promises of material support, even before the American attacks began, without altering its own course to any significant degree.

The D.R.V. thus benefited from the Sino-Soviet dispute, by getting both powers to compete for its support and assistance without yielding control of policy to them. In fact, with both Moscow and Peking participating, it became less likely than ever that either one would gain a dominant position in Hanoi. Peking seemingly held a lead, because it had sustained North Vietnam in the early stages after Hanoi's decision to intensify the struggle—a decision that greatly complicated matters for Moscow. China's verbal support intensified during 1964, with repeated affirmations that it would consider an attack on North Vietnam as an attack on itself. Asserting that the two states were as close as lips and teeth, China declared it would "absolutely not stand idly by" if North Vietnam were endangered. Moreover, China entered the strongest objections when the D.R.V. considered accepting further Soviet aid. Peking, resenting any resurgence of Soviet influence in an Asian Communist state, charged that Moscow would use the power it acquired through an extensive aid program to compel a D.R.V. capitulation, along the lines of the 1962 Cuban-missile fiasco.[15] But China could not prevent Hanoi from making a new arrangement for Soviet aid with Khrushchev's successors.

Despite Peking's failure to block the re-entry of Russian influence, it need not have feared any flagging in Hanoi's determination, even in the face of Soviet pressure for moderation. North Vietnam did modify its attitude somewhat in 1965, supporting peaceful coexistence and favoring a conference to guarantee Cambodian neutrality.[16] But neither Hanoi nor Moscow would press this latter point in the face of Chinese opposition. On the whole, Hanoi received Soviet aid without slackening its vigorous and intensive prosecution of the war.

The Russian dilemma intensified in 1965 when, probably to Moscow's great surprise, the United States escalated the war. One effect of the U.S. bombings was to highlight the contradiction that the Kremlin had tried to ignore between its support of peaceful coexistence and of wars of national liberation. Moscow could only profess continued adherence to the two positions and grimly warn Washington that further escalation would bring dire consequences. Ideological conviction of the "justness" of the Viet Cong's struggle and fear of retreating in the face of Peking's denunciations impelled the Russians to continue supporting Hanoi. However, they did their best to minimize their involvement and keep the conflict from deepening.[17]

Ironically, the "parallel" support of North Vietnam seems to have exacerbated relations between Moscow and Peking. Since each great power adheres to its original view regarding the role of force in the revolutionary process and the practical dangers of any confrontation with the United States, the Vietnamese War provides a crucial testing ground for the validity of these views and intimately involves the political fortunes and security interests of the two great Communist powers.[17]

This situation is doubly ironic because the beneficiary, North Vietnam, has steadfastly sought to heal the rift, fearing it would destroy the international Communist movement and undermine its own security. Though Hanoi's policies have deepened the split, this apparently has enhanced rather than harmed its immediate security position. Hanoi's own motivations remain highly specific—to gain its rightful heritage, all of Vietnam.[18] Hanoi has traditionally been slow to take a stand on ideological or theoretical issues. It publicly endorsed Chinese views only in return for support that it considered absolutely vital for the more vigorous prosecution of the war; and even then, it was quite willing to shift course or reverse itself in part to win Soviet backing.

In short, to receive help, Hanoi did not have to make any significant change in its essential policy of nonalignment in the Sino-Soviet conflict. It adopted neither the doctrinal extremes of Peking nor the Soviet preference for moderation. The Russians probably failed to anticipate an American combat role in Vietnam when they offered Hanoi assistance,[19] and then they could not avoid extending further help—in air defense, petroleum, transportation, industrial aid. But Hanoi, too, has had to pay a high price, bearing the full weight of the American air offensive while its two sponsors stayed out of the war. China has not intervened despite its many warnings to Washington, and Moscow has kept its aid in the defensive category, conducting its own supporting effort in a low-key, nonprovocative manner.

The Tonkin Gulf Incidents

The naval incidents in the Gulf of Tonkin during the summer of 1964 cast some light on Hanoi's initiatives and determination as it copes with the tangled ramifications of the Sino-Soviet split and increasing American intervention in the South. The affair is also noteworthy as an instance of an early stage in military and political escalation of a war.[20]

This first action took place on August 2, 1964, when D.R.V. patrol and motor torpedo boats unsuccessfully assaulted an American destroyer in daylight and then, despite a warning from Washington, repeated the effort two nights later. In the wake of these encounters, the United States retaliated with air assaults against the boats and their shore bases, and a D.R.V. squadron of MIGs moved from their training bases in China into North Vietnam. President Johnson took this opportunity to have the Congress authorize him to use armed force in defense of any member or protocol state of the SEATO treaty system.[21] For all their threats, the Chinese limited their actions to massive popular demonstrations against the United States.

How do we explain this bizarre incident? On ideological grounds, Hanoi is convinced of the justice of its military action in South Vietnam in order to unify the country and put it on a progressive path.[22] It denies its opponents a moral right to respond because they are imperialist aggressors or reactionary stooges who have no will of their own, but act only on the orders of the United States. They cite the Diem era, the repeated coups, and the rise and fall of military leaders, and the heavy American political influence as substantiation for their argument.

Retaliatory South Vietnamese guerrilla efforts or naval coastal raids, frequently reported by Hanoi in 1964, appeared to the North as acts of blatant American intervention. Hanoi placed ultimate responsibility on the United States even after it had identified the attack vessels as South Vietnamese vessels to avoid the danger of escalation. With the war going well, Hanoi seemingly had a stake in freezing American operations at existing levels, short of direct combat action.

Much of China's diplomacy and declaratory policy seemed pointed toward blocking assaults against North Vietnam. Hanoi and Peking conducted global propaganda campaigns to deter Washington, depicting Americans as "war maniacs" who had to be restrained by the people of the world. Proposals for a neutralist way-station government in Saigon under an NLF-coalition regime also seemed to offer a good way to move toward full Communist control without giving Washington an opportunity to intervene. Further, the powerful North Vietnamese army had remained formally out of war at that time, and the threat of its use could also help deter direct American action. Finally, Hanoi had gone to great lengths to gain Chinese backing and had inflated Peking's commitments to keep the Americans from escalating the war.

Yet the Tonkin naval engagement could have precipitated a substantial American escalation, especially if the torpedo assault had succeeded. Even in failure, it gave Washington an excellent excuse to attack the North if it so chose. The Congressional authorization established the legislative framework and atmospheric conditioning for the escalation that later occurred. The North Vietnamese foray thus contravened a fundamental strategy of military diplomacy that the Asian Communist powers had espoused. The Chinese may have pressed Hanoi to take such action, but it is hard to see how they could make a convincing case without committing themselves to the war. It seems equally probable that Hanoi itself determined to act. It was very sensitive to any naval presence, especially since it had suffered some Southern naval raids just prior to the appearance of the American destroyer on patrol, and the situation may have been misinterpreted by the North Vietnamese. However, there was no mistaking the import of the solemn American warning of retaliation that followed the August 2 attack. The renewed assault of August 4 must, therefore, have been conscious policy, chosen deliberately and not in the heat of battle.[23] Yet while undertaking this open attack against an American vessel on the high seas, Hanoi itself was unprepared either for military defense or diplomatic and propaganda action. Its confused statements of August stand in sharp contrast to its polished performance following another, uncertain naval incident a month later.

Perhaps the D.R.V. acted in the hope that a successful torpedo attack would have made the United States halt its gradually but steadily mounting military effort. It may have felt harassed by air strikes in Laos, air reconnaissance over its own territory, and increasing talk in Washington about escalation. A naval triumph might have enabled the North Vietnamese to close the Gulf. Having made the United States look ridiculous, Hanoi could then have mobilized the International Control Commission or some other international forum to head off an American retaliation. North Vietnam may also have judged that it ran little risk if it did not succeed. Like the Chinese, Hanoi may have overestimated the general danger of an American threat while underestimating the chances of its materializing in a particular situation. Similarly, the measured and restricted nature of the American response may have led Hanoi to conclude that Washington would not resort to bombings on a broad scale. Miscalculations of the opponent's intentions and determination have plagued all parties in this particular confrontation.

It is probable that on the specific question of the unity of Vietnam, the D.R.V. has a lower boiling point than China, even though Peking's ideology and global strategy may be considerably more extreme. And it is possible that emotionalism—righteous belief in the cause, serious concern over the strain of the war effort—played a part in Hanoi's ill-prepared and risky response.[24]

The Question of Escalation

Since the United States response of August 1964 remained limited to shore installations, boats, and related oil-storage facilities, both the question of escalation in the strategic sense and the question of American motivation remained unanswered during 1964. One reason for the American reaction was the need to stabilize a deteriorating political situation in Saigon, and in this regard, the bombings proved to be of some, though limited, value. Military action against the North could have little constructive effect as long as Southern leadership could not come to terms with new nationalist movements in the country or reduce the distrust that major interest groups felt toward the government and one another.[25] For example, morale rose and then sank rapidly following the Gulf of Tonkin incident, and the existing Saigon government remained as unpopular as ever.

The sustained bombings of 1965 did have useful effects. First, they helped bolster the succession of regimes in Saigon until they attained a broader degree of support, or at least acceptance, among the populace. Saigon thus gained time in which to put its house in order, and face the country's grave internal political difficulties.[26] But there was also a high political price. The increased confidence in the American commitment, now extended to carrying a large burden of the war, gave South Vietnamese interest groups more leeway to compete with one another in an unrealistic atmosphere of indifference to the Communist danger. Entrenched elements could feel free to go on thwarting proposals for land reform and economic development. The nation's elite could preserve the country's highly stratified social system and continue to restrict real educational, job, and political opportunities to a small upper class. And the powerful generals in Saigon, arbiters of the political scene, could insist on a no-compromise war effort, without undertaking the fundamental military reforms or administrative improvements essential to enable the South Vietnamese army to execute its major role effectively. Thus, a realistic accounting of the escalation's political consequences in the South must list important costs as well as benefits. Even assuming that the benefits outweigh the costs politically, we must still look to military and diplomatic considerations for the major justification of the February 1965 decision to bomb North Vietnam.

The hope was to punish North Vietnam with moderate but not fatal attacks, and demonstrate to Hanoi and to would-be "indirect aggressors" that their homelands would no longer be sanctuaries.[27] In a more limited military sense, the attacks were intended to make the war more difficult to conduct, especially in supplying the forces below the 17th parallel. Most important, the attacks were designed to make Hanoi adopt a more reasonable bargaining position—by raising the cost of the war, demonstrating America's will to persist, and showing that the North's Communist allies would not join in the struggle.

The danger lay in the possibility of a double failure, that North Vietnam might absorb this degree of punishment without quitting and that one or both of the large Communist powers might make a drastic response. These developments, in turn, could have led to a still higher escalation, launched by frustrated Americans or by the Communist states seeking to retaliate. As events unfolded, Moscow and Peking did not widen the conflict, but Hanoi continued the war with renewed determination and a more rigid position on negotiations.[28]

The main American hope lay in the Moscow-Hanoi side of the Communist triangle. Washington carefully assured the Russians of its limited intentions—to preserve the South and to remove all military bases after the war—in the hope that the Soviet's desire for peace, intensified by China's intransigence, would lead them to press the D.R.V. to settle the war. Russia denounced the United States, gave more aid to the D.R.V., sought to rally neutralist support, and warned that it would help Hanoi protect its national interests. But apparently it was too worried about Chinese bellicosity to go further.[29] The Chinese equivocated, standing firmly against a negotiated settlement but reiterating that they would go to war against America only if attacked.[30] In a similar vein, the Chinese army's Chief of staff, General Lo Jui-ch'ing, pledged aid "to the limits of our capabilities," and offered "to send men to fight" if requested.[31]

To a degree, then, the moderate American escalation succeeded. Fear of provoking further escalation may have helped deter the Chinese from entering the war, or the North Vietnamese army from making a large-scale attack on the South. But NVA forces had already moved into the Laos-South Vietnamese border area, and they continued to arrive in modest increments as American ground forces poured into South Vietnam. Though this type of D.R.V. response avoided a clear-cut confrontation over escalation, it left the United States with the difficult decision—of whether to threaten North Vietnam with strategic bombing if it continued to reinforce the Viet Cong with its regulars. The air attacks on the Hanoi-Haiphong oil facilities in 1966 were a partial response to the growing D.R.V. military presence in the South. The United States hoped that its graded and controlled reply would still fall far short of provoking significant Chinese or Soviet responses.

The underlying great-power confrontation was but one difficult consequence of the new American commitment. Escalation may have stabilized the conflict, preventing an otherwise imminent defeat. But it did not turn the war around. The infiltration continued, the Viet Cong force remained formidable, and the outcome remained an open question. Could America compel the attacker to withdraw by denying him victory and punishing him moderately, while sustaining a wobbly but dogged administration in Saigon? Could it escalate further without leading the D.R.V. to extensive counteraction in Laos, as well as South Vietnam?

If a large-scale war ensues and the D.R.V. seems near defeat, the Chinese may feel obliged to give backing on the ground. Vietnam, because of its location, may not be as strategically essential to Chinese security as Korea, but the survival of a Communist state remains a vital interest to Peking. Though there would be formidable logistical problems in sustaining a war effort there, the Chinese have demonstrated their capacity to operate over difficult terrain.[32] China itself, moreover, might not have to bear the major part of the burden. North Vietnam has an impressive army in being, in contrast to the shattered North Korean force of September 1950, and the Communists still have a considerable body of troops in South Vietnam. Chinese intervention, of course, would raise the possibility of American attack against China itself.

The road to a solution in Vietnam remained long and grim as the war intensified and opened new dangers of further escalation. The Communist powers all remained committed to a Viet Cong victory, and the struggle raged on many fronts—in guerrilla war, aerial assaults on the North, internal Saigonese politics, and world diplomacy. The chances of compromise seemed remote. The Viet Cong lacked the political capacity to survive as a party or faction in Saigon without retaining autonomous military power. The South Vietnamese regime, fearful of its capacity to survive, would not accept a coalition on such terms. Even if it did, North Vietnam would be unwilling to withdraw its support and abandon its loyal forces in the South. To Saigon, moreover, even a Northern withdrawal would seem temporary, with Hanoi again awaiting its chance to return in force.

Given this deep-rooted hostility and mistrust, it is difficult to see how Washington can get the North to accept and the South to believe in any compromise arrangement whose objective is to keep the two states permanently divided. America's offer of massive economic aid to the Southeast Asian region is its way of making mutual concessions more acceptable.[33] Its suggestion that Moscow participate in this new donors' club reflects the hope that the Soviet Union will decide that the mounting dangers make it advisable to accept a compromise in the interests of stability. But this hope seems as unrealistic as most of the previous hopes the West has entertained toward Indochina since 1945. In terms of duration and violence, Vietnam remains the most intractable problem of the postwar era.

A settlement that left South Vietnam neutralized but independent is consistent with American policy objectives and might suit the Russians, who found such a formula tolerable in Laos. It would remove American bases from Indochina, keep Saigon from entering alliances, and strengthen Soviet relations with the neutralist powers. It would also demonstrate at moderate cost that America was not a paper tiger, that wars of national liberation might escalate dangerously, that peaceful coexistence—not warfare—was the highest form of the class struggle. But North Vietnam would have to yield a cherished ambition while the chance of victory remained. How the Soviet Union would deal with an "aggressive" America, induce Hanoi to quit, and resolve its dilemma of trying to lead a world revolution while keeping peace, remains beyond the grasp of most analysts.[34] As in the case of policy toward India, developments are pushing the Russians toward a choice between an intensification of the Cold War and accommodation with the West. But the Russian leadership does not seem to have the stomach for this type of brinkmanship within the Communist movement any more than it desires a strategic confrontation with the United States. "Internal contradictions" appear to be the one thing all the protagonists in this confrontation have in common, and in plenty.

The Communists in Laos

North Vietnam has had a vital interest in Laos from the moment both states gained their freedom in 1954. At that time, the Pathet Lao retained control of two border provinces with D.R.V. help, and used North Vietnam as a haven when it was endangered by a rightwing coup a few years later. In 1960, a neutralist-rightist split gave the Pathet Lao a great opportunity to seek a dominant role. During 1961, Soviet diplomacy backed the neutralists, and Russian air-borne supplies sustained them materially and psychologically, while the United States proved unwilling to undertake a substantial military venture under such difficult strategic and diplomatic circumstances.

This American restraint seemed to bode well for the Pathet Lao, especially when the rightists proved unable to stabilize the situation. The United States decided to seek an accommodation with the Soviet Union, and the June 1961 Kennedy-Khrushchev meeting in Vienna produced an understanding.[35] A year-long conference followed that led to the neutralization agreement of 1962. Many criticized this settlement as a sellout to the Communists, but in fact the Pathet Lao position deteriorated after that date.[36]

The key lay in the split between the neutralists and the Pathet Lao. Prince Souvanna Phouma emerged as an authentic neutral, determined to control the government and not serve merely as a front man for the exercise of power by the Communists. As a result, military friction arose with the Pathet Lao, and the Russians ended their logistical support to the disunited coalition. Though this appeared to weaken the neutralists also, the Russians were in effect disengaging from an operation that had extended material help to the Communists, who dominated the regions in which the two forces were interspersed. Diplomatically, the Soviets continued to support the neutrality of Laos and Souvanna's regime. They did not even protest vigorously when this renowned neutralist agreed to allow American military air operations against Communist units that were attacking his forces.[37]

These assaults stemmed from a Pathet Lao decision to try to destroy the military base of the neutralist regime. Late in 1962, when they saw that coalition had failed to lead to Communist control over the country, the Communists ejected neutralist forces from the areas granted to them as a gesture of alliance during 1961–62. This drove the right wing and the neutralists into working alignment until, by 1963–64, they were actually cooperating in fairly complex military operations against the new common enemy.[38] Though dual threats of Communist assaults and coups by the rightists continued to plague Souvanna's regime, strong American support again enabled Vientiane to withstand both in 1964–65. The new coalition cleared the Pathet Lao from parts of the western section of Laos but lacked the strength to regain complete control of the Plain of Jars. The two sides faced each other in various parts of the country without a clear-cut geographic front.

A major factor in the situation is the role of North Vietnam, which has stationed several battalions in Laos, mainly along the Vietnamese frontier. These forces undertook two related missions: protection of the vital Lao infiltration routes to South Vietnam, and preservation of the Pathet Lao army and the territory under Lao Communist control. Whenever government offensives gain any momentum against local Communists, D.R.V. military elements apparently step in and quickly redress the military balance.[39]

Thus a delicate equilibrium prevails in Laos. The opposing sides are well matched, though the neutralist-rightist coalition holds a numerical advantage over the Pathet Lao. The indigenous forces enjoy the support of outside powers who became involved to protect frontier regions of great importance to their interests.[40] Just as Hanoi must control the Vietnamese border, so Washington insists on protecting the western Thai frontier along the Mekong and the southern border with Cambodia. Any Communist advance to these positions becomes a cause of grave concern. We should recall the sudden disptach of American marines and allied air power to Thailand in the spring of 1962 when the Pathet Lao reached the Mekong in the northwest region at Nam Tha, in the last great crisis before the neutralization settlement. The new American base system in Thailand and air operations in Laos reflect a determination to preserve the non-Communist Lao regime that at least equals Hanoi's commitment to sustain its political and territorial interests there.[41]

This precarious situation, in a sense, is another hostage to the war in Vietnam. The little war in Laos can escalate and become internationalized if the conflict in Vietnam should assume broader proportions. Ironically, the situation in Laos, so discouraging just a few years earlier, became a relatively bright spot in 1963, in contrast to the deteriorating situation in Vietnam. Rather than undermining the security of South Vietnam, Laos itself now stands to suffer from any spillover of the crisis in that land. Any increase in American pressure on North Vietnam can find Hanoi choosing to expand its position in Laos as one means of retaliation. To deter such a move, American and Thai forces must be prepared to establish control over the strategically most important segments of that little kingdom. In short, any major escalation to the east may lead to territorial extension of the war, at least to Laos and perhaps to Thailand's frontier areas, as well.

PART IV

The Nuclear Factor

CHAPTER FOURTEEN

China as a Nuclear Power

The achievement of national stability and regional balance in Asia has been sorely hindered by ancient suspicion and enmities in intra-regional relations. In the past few decades, the rise of communism has complicated and bedeviled progress further. For some states, this meant that instead of concentrating their resources on nation-building, they had to devote scarce manpower and money to fighting indigenous subversion or overt aggression. For others, this meant that while in a premature stage of national development, they were put under pressure to choose whether to join or not to join a Western alliance. And if they opted for neutralism, their relations with both rival sides frequently encountered serious difficulties.

When the Chinese Communists became strong enough to invade India's Himalayan territories, all Asia, and indeed the world, had cause for worry. Two years later, when they joined the nuclear club, the security situation in Asia changed even more drastically.

At present, China's successes are more impressive as indicators of its ambitions and determination than of actual military power. The Chinese explosion of a nuclear device at Lop Nor, Sinkiang, in October 1964 did not really alter the world nuclear equation quantitatively; and it will be several years before Peking can develop bombs for aircraft delivery, and even longer before it can produce a significant system of long-distance missiles with warheads. However, we should not discount the Chinese achievement too greatly, for although India and Japan and many European states can follow suit if they wish, it is the Chinese who have demonstrated the requisite will and capacity.

Though China's breakthrough will not add appreciably to its power for some time to come, we must attempt to calculate how China is likely to act when it attains effective nuclear power. In these chapters, therefore, we shall have to leave the comparatively firm ground of historical analysis and venture onto more speculative terrain. The fact that our analysis will have to rest upon forecasts and judgments about future possibilities and probabilities puts it in the standard tradition of security planning. All efforts at policy-making in the fields of foreign affairs and national security must rest to an inordinate degree upon contingency considerations and estimates about the relative likelihood of different developments.

In beginning our analysis of China as a nuclear power, we must observe that it is pointless to maintain—as many did after the Soviet explosion of 1949—that possession of a single bomb has only marginal significance. China's nuclear power is of central importance for Asian regional security and diplomatic affairs. Nevertheless, we need not anticipate that China will exhibit dramatic changes at once. The bomb is unlikely to change the traditional Chinese use of force and diplomacy as mutually reinforcing weapons; it need not diminish Chinese caution confronting American power. But we must also keep in mind Peking's past record of switching suddenly from prudent to quite risky acts. Moreover, China's leaders have demonstrated a deep-seated desire to speed up the processes of history at least as often as they have displayed their vaunted patience. In short, we ought to build on our current analyses rather than add to our burdens by positing a major shift in Peking's outlook.

If the effects of the bomb on Chinese foreign policy constitute one area of analysis, they provide a second in terms of the world political scene: the diplomatic costs and benefits of continued Chinese testing and weapons production, the fate of the test-ban treaty, and the problem of proliferation. Will wars become more or less likely, and will lower-level conflicts increase in number under the umbrella of a Sino-American nuclear confrontation? Given China's intransigent and at times contradictory attitude toward the United States, will Peking pursue its objectives more intensely, on the assumption that its new power has neutralized Washington? Or will it presume that America is now more willing to retaliate with nuclear weapons?

China's Technical Capacity

Making an accurate assessment of China's capacity in the nuclear and missile fields is extremely difficult because of the regime's secrecy and because of the rapid changes inevitable over the next decade. During the regime's first fifteen years, there has been persistent underestimation in America and elsewhere of China's technical and industrial capacity in both the civilian and the military spheres. Almost at the start, Peking surprised the United States with an ability to field a competent force in Korea, despite primitive communication facilities, untrained field officers, and the need to weld former Kuomintang elements with Communist units. The atomic explosions of October 16, 1964, May 14, 1965, and May 9, 1966, and the nuclear missile shot of October 27, 1966, provide a later example—this time of technological surprise. Among other achievements is its ability to down U-2 aircraft relatively consistently, indicating the existence of effective defense aircraft, ground-to-air missiles, and radar installations. The Chinese may also be developing sophisticated fighter aircraft based on Russian models. They have demonstrated skill in producing light battlefield equipment and small coastal naval vessels. The more complex engines of war still appear beyond their capacity—especially long-range submarines, bombers, and missiles. But it is precisely in these categories that it is most dangerous to assume that they will not make rapid progress.

We must always keep in mind the narrow base of China's technological achievements as revealed by its need to buy Soviet and British long-range transport planes and by its general dependence on foreign experts and capital equipment for sustained growth. But China's technical capacity nevertheless has the breadth and depth to make considerable strides in the modern weapons field, as long as it is willing to pay the economic price.[1] China may not be able to advance on a broad front today, but it has the capacity to move forward in one chosen sector, by devoting a disproportionate share of its industrial capacity, limited expert manpower, and foreign-exchange resources to the effort.

This is precisely what China has done in the nuclear weapons field. It was surmised after the first test that only Russian help had made such an explosion possible, and that this aid, though it spanned only 1957–59, had saved the Chinese many years and considerable expense. Developments since October 1964, however, point to a considerable domestic effort built upon the original Soviet assistance.

China's ability to produce the uranium-235 used in the first two tests indicates a competence that surprised foreign analysts, for the other four nuclear powers all began their experiments with plutonium, which is less expensive and more easily obtained. Since experts agree that plutonium is a more efficient material to start with, the use of U-235 in both experiments suggests that China did not have the plutonium available at the time.

The plants for producing nuclear fuel are of Soviet origin, and Peking remains heavily dependent on this legacy of Soviet technological assistance. At present, China has two fissionable material plants: a reactor at Paotow and a U-235 gaseous diffusion plant that covers about eight acres in the Lanchow area. In addition, there are reportedly four research reactors: a small one for enriched uranium near Peking, built with Russian help, and, according to Japanese sources, three others in Mukden, Chungkiang, and Sian.[2] With a probable capability to produce plutonium, even if it has not done so as yet, as well as weapons-grade U-235, China seems to have the basis for manufacturing a considerable range of nuclear weapons.

However, two facts will most certainly delay China's attainment of nuclear parity: supporting a weapons test program is a very difficult and expensive proposition; and the same is true of the effort to develop a modern weapons-delivery system. China's first test involved a bomb of about 20 kilotons; the range of the second bomb tested was approximately twice that strength, and the third involved thermonuclear material. China will be able to test a hydrogen device in the next few years, with weapons production following shortly thereafter. Thus in the near future, China will be able to produce some moderate-size atomic bombs,[3] which its TU-4 planes can carry. When medium- and intermediate-range missiles are available, Peking will also probably have the required warheads for them[4] and will have the capacity to pursue the development of long-range delivery systems and compatible warheads. In this connection, Secretary McNamara, in an apparent reference to China, cited "the possibility in the 1970s of a small nuclear attack on the United States by a nation possessing only a primitive nuclear force."[5]

China still lacks the fully developed industrial system that is usually considered a prerequisite for nuclear power. Even the French, with their more strongly based economy, have had considerably more difficulty with advanced weapons development, and their expenditures of time and money have consistently outrun expectations.[6] However, the Chinese have the plants and funds to sustain a costly long-term effort. They can provide most of the raw material and technology on their own. The supplementary portion that must come from imports constitutes only a small percentage of the entire program and China's foreign exchange can provide the necessary funds for these purchases when these materials are available.[7]

Manpower is a critical category. According to rough estimates, the research and development aspects of the nuclear weapons program require about 1,500 highly skilled people, with an equal number needed to put the operation into full production. But it is believed that the Chinese can provide and effectively use the required personnel. Chinese scientists trained at the Joint Research Institute at Dubna, U.S.S.R., alone totaled 950 by 1965.[8] Though the weapons program absorbs a large number of skilled people needed in other sectors of the economy, there are compensating advantages: the improved general technical competence of the individuals involved and advances in the country's knowledge of nuclear industrial process. China appears willing to bear the costs now demanded and hopes to expand the educational base over the next generation to overcome shortages of skilled personnel.

In the 1970s, then, Peking expects to have manpower sufficient, in quantity and quality, to sustain a program of steady development.[9] Over the next decade, Peking hopes to produce 2 million—perhaps 3 million college graduates—all better trained than in the past—with 40 per cent specializing in engineering and sciences.[10]

Peking will presumably continue primary emphasis on heavy industry, with highest priority going to the nuclear weapons program. If it concentrates on fission bombs in the submegaton range, it can acquire a small stockpile by 1968. Production of warheads for missiles will take longer, although development of prototypes in all categories is undoubtedly being pushed at top speeds. If it takes five or more years to develop large-yield weapons to fit on missiles, it is possible that Chinese long-range missilery will keep pace with the development of warheads.

Peking has been working on missiles since 1958; at that time, the Russians reported that the Chinese were studying Soviet techniques in order to launch their own satellite.[11] Chinese scientists who have left the mainland since then have reported that work was continuing on rockets and computers for missile guidance systems. They identified important scientists whose knowledge of missilery American experts respect. It is believed that Chien Hsueh-shen, who worked on American rockets before returning to China in 1955, heads the entire missile program.

The ill-effects that beset China's nuclear program when the Soviets withdrew in 1959 have also been felt in its missile efforts as well. While exact dates are difficult to project, it seems probable that the Chinese will have an operational medium-range device before 1970. The nuclear missile test of October 22, 1966, represented China's first public announcement regarding this delivery system. Though Britain and France both found longer-range weapons expensive, the Chinese may also keep open their capacity to produce intermediate and intercontinental missiles, as well.

However, since the Soviet Union already possesses this capability, China need not feel as exposed to "capitalist aggression" as Moscow considered itself to be in the late 1940s. Consequently, despite the Communist split, Peking may not have an absolute immediate requirement for long-range weapons, and so may move more slowly in this category. In any case, submarines could bring the American Pacific islands and even the West Coast of this continent under a missile threat at less cost, perhaps sooner than would be possible in a long-range missile program.[12]

Secretary McNamara evidently thinks that a Chinese missile threat in the 1970s is a real enough possibility for the United States to consider the development of an antimissile system costing about $8 to $10 billion.[13] Since the Chinese strategic threat would not be great, a partially developed antimissile capacity might well afford protection for a decade or two. But the United States must also keep in mind that a shorter-range missile capacity is very attractive to China. With no major, well-armed, indigenous opponent to confront Peking around its periphery, Peking could pose a major threat in this region with a relatively modest program of shorter-range missiles, attainable quickly and at tolerable cost.

Benefits and Drawbacks

For an imposing variety of reasons, Communist China had a powerful craving for nuclear power. Its motives and objectives resembled those of the French but also went much further in intention and aspiration. Besides the elements it had in common with France —nationalism and the desire to be master of its own fate—China added the diplomatic and territorial aspirations of a have-not state, one that desired to shed once and for all a heritage of exploitation. China's tragic historical experience gained greater poignancy when contrasted with the idealized Confucian heritage of the Middle Kingdom as the center of civilized life, graciously leading and protecting its neighbors while guiding them toward higher levels of culture. In this context, it is not surprising that the Chinese would cite an advanced nuclear capacity as a qualification for status as a "super state," which alone could "lead the world and . . . control and direct" other states.[14]

China also hoped to gain prestige in Asia as the first state in the area to equal the great technical advances of the West. Peking has long disparaged the considerable achievements of its great rival, Japan, and claimed dominance in the race for modernity. Development of nuclear power would strengthen this claim and lay the groundwork for Chinese physical dominance over Japan and all Eastern Asia. Elsewhere in Asia and Africa, Peking hoped to establish its position as an uncontested leader—the first underdeveloped state to attain nuclear power.[15] Beyond demonstrating a technical achievement that could inspire others (to follow China's leadership, not make their own bombs), this success in matching the crowning military achievement of the Western world would vividly symbolize the end of the industrial states' monopoly on prestige and power. In fact, for the first time in the modern era, the very continuity of the industrial world could be directly threatened by one of its former victims.

It is only logical for the Chinese, with their strategy of war and violence, to regard nuclear weapons as a key instrument for the expansion of communism. Mao's exultant claim in 1957 that the east wind was prevailing over the west wind expressed this attitude. Russia had then developed intercontinental missile and hydrogen warheads, and had promised to assist China "in new technology for national defense."[16] Though the Chinese did not necessarily desire to trigger a nuclear war and compel the Russians to launch such a conflict, they clearly had hoped for a more aggressive use of the weapon as an instrument of diplomacy and as a shield for waging just wars of national liberation. Rancor against Moscow built up as Peking realized that the Russians desired to control all nuclear weapons in the Communist bloc and to determine all policies associated with their use—in a manner that the Chinese found incorrect and cowardly.[17] Possession of nuclear weapons would thus liberate Peking from two great shadows—the threat of "blackmail" from the bloodthirsty Americans [18] and dependence for security on the unreliable Russians.

The role of the Soviet Union in Peking's nuclear quest should not be underestimated. We should recall that in 1958, the year after Sputnik appeared, the commanding general of the Chinese air force called his country's prospective acquisition of atomic weapons and rockets "a probable turning point" in the world Communist movement.[19] Five years later, in 1963, Marshal Ch'en Yi made his famous comment that the Chinese would do without trousers if necessary in order to acquire nuclear weapons.[20]

Peking fully realized the diplomatic costs involved in testing and did its best to minimize these by taking the unusual step of preparing the world, especially the underdeveloped states, for the first detonation. Though it may have been planned for the fifteenth anniversary of the founding of the regime, out of deference to the Cairo conference of nonaligned nations then in session, the Chinese seem to have postponed their explosion two weeks.[21] The Chinese also aver, as have the Russians on many occasions, that they will never be the first to use nuclear weapons. Rather, they stress the need for weapons to deter attacks against the homeland and to thwart imperialist aggression elsewhere in the world.[22] If China attempts to use its nuclear power to pursue its foreign policy objectives more vigorously, this effort may be compromised by the American reaction. For the Chinese by themselves will be as vulnerable as ever to an American assault. Though Peking will undoubtedly remain as alert to American capabilities as in the past, tensions between the two powers might reach new heights. Through bolder actions, China might well trigger the American response that it had hoped to deter by acquiring nuclear weapons.[23]

For China and its neighbors, China's role as the first Asian nuclear power creates a variety of other problems. This achievement may win Peking some support among fellow Communist parties and regimes, as well as some neutralist backing. Only India among the nonaligned countries expressed open disapproval. But as long as substantial American-backed resistance to China persists, other neutrals, such as Burma and Ceylon, may withdraw into deep isolation rather than endorse the Chinese position. Rangoon thus far has demonstrated steadfast adherence to the test-ban treaty, thereby politely rejecting China's call for support. Also, it is of great significance that New Delhi and Tokyo are in the forefront of Peking's critics,[24] for these are the two powers with the greatest capacity for and interest in developing their own nuclear strength. Hence they will be driven to a choice of developing their own weapons (i.e., proliferation and all its dangers) or relying on outside powers to protect them against Peking's efforts to take diplomatic and military advantage of its nuclear superiority over them. Chinese threats, denunciation of America as unreliable, and offers of nonaggression treaties may thus only backfire.

If prestige in Asia, capacity to conduct an independent foreign policy, and leadership in the underdeveloped world require sovereign control of nuclear weapons—as the Chinese repeatedly emphasize—then any proof that Peking offers to validate this position will generate powerful, nationalistic urgings to emulate such "leadership." Policy goals, expansionist ambitions, and fear of China could make proliferation almost irresistible. After all, demands for control over nuclear plans and decisions persist even in Europe, where the United States has a massive nuclear presence and, since 1962 at least, has shared much of its technical knowledge and strategic planning with its NATO allies. It is possible that Asian states —despite the earlier aversion of many for nuclear weapons—will react similarly once the Chinese arsenal grows.

Despite these drawbacks, the Chinese anticipate great advantages for themselves on the world diplomatic stage. With nuclear power assuring them of great-power status, the Chinese will seek to assert their full equality with the West, Japan, and the Soviet Union, while at the same time trying to maintain a position as protector and leader in the underdeveloped camp. China may seek to advertise its new eminence by increased intransigence on points at issue with the great powers. It will certainly argue that possession of nuclear weapons proves once and for all that Peking alone is the voice of China. Beyond precluding a Nationalist return to the mainland, Peking will insist that neither the Kuomintang nor Taiwanese separatists be allowed any representation in the United Nations.[25] As the only Chinese delegation at the U.N., it could wear down the number of states still recognizing the Taipei regime until only the United States and its "lackeys" remained. The Chinese would consider it a major gain if Washington should take the unlikely course of retaliating against the U.N. for admitting Peking. For this action would disrupt a body that the Chinese consider a tool of the existing international order.[26] Even as matters now stand, the United Nations is weakened by the bitter annual struggles over the admission of Peking.

In the long run, China undoubtedly hopes to use its nuclear capability to enlarge its role in the councils of world affairs, affect the global balance of power, and influence major political decisions. China looks upon its part in the 1954 Geneva settlement and its intervention in Eastern Europe of 1956–57 as rudimentary examples of future possibilities. It may still hope to gain a major voice in Soviet foreign policy-making and nuclear strategy. Above all, Peking may try to use its new power to block a further Soviet-American *détente* and to end whatever cooperation the two powers may have achieved.

A most obvious entree is in disarmament affairs—a field in which all other powers have long recognized that there can be no stable accord without Peking.[27] The Chinese can utilize any role granted them in this arena to pursue other foreign policy goals and, if they enter serious negotiations, to adapt to their own interests the terms and objectives of a settlement. It is conceivable, for example, that taking advantage of the global desire for disarmament, China could achieve a compromise that would make its conventional strength appear the dominant power factor in Eastern Asia without depriving China or its allies of the capacity to sustain revolutionary momentum in the underdeveloped world.

In a sense, nuclear power may add disproportionately to Chinese weight in world affairs. In the eyes of many, China already looms as the greatest threat to world peace; to them, "the bomb" will seem to augment its menace tremendously.[28] The image of China unafraid of nuclear war, actively supporting "internal" wars that in fact cross frontiers, may combine with fears of a "yellow peril now come true" in a merger of sophisticated diplomatic analysis with crude racial apprehensions. The result may be a global antagonism that could intensify any international instability.

China's broad objectives and bold tactics might draw strength and encouragement from such a turn of events, and all concerned, Peking included, might be led to overestimate Chinese power.[29] As it is, many Western officials and writers seem to give the Chinese at least partial credit for almost every violent revolutionary act anywhere, further fortifying the image of China as a global threat. The atomic weapon may intensify such reactions and increase Chinese leverage in world affairs. In the end, such misapprehensions could contribute to military miscalculations and lead to consequences magnified far beyond those of China's pre-atomic policies.

Familiar Goals, Intensive Quests

We dare not underestimate the global diplomatic aspects of Chinese nuclear power or the danger of war resulting from a more militant policy in Peking. Asian foreign affairs in the near future will probably seem to flow in the traditional channels, but because of greater Chinese confidence, the confrontations will be harsher and the crises more dangerous. Imperceptibly, differences with the past will become ones of kind rather than degree, despite the deceptive familiarity of the setting.

The most immediate impact will undoubtedly be felt on the defensive and offensive goals noted earlier: internal security and the stability of the regime, prevention of invasion and deterrence of aggression, ruin of the Nationalists, firm control of the border areas and reshaping of the frontier regions, the exclusion of non-Asian power from its periphery, and establishment of Chinese hegemony. Internal security remains important, essentially as a function of domestic power and prestige, which may not be as high as the regime had hoped. In China proper, uprisings and effective opposition do not appear to be in the offing, but the depth of popular commitment to the regime remains far below desired levels. Superpower status would not only make rebellion even less likely but would generate nationalistic pride in the government as well as the state.

Possession of nuclear weapons, Peking believes, will do much to prevent the deeply feared invasion of the mainland. The reality of Peking's anxiety on this score was demonstrated by its panicky behavior during the invasion scare of 1962, its fear of American support for such an effort by Taiwan, and its repeated assertions of Soviet unreliability. Now combining with the belief that nuclear power protects the homeland is the related view that the possibility of a successful Nationalist assault is diminishing rapidly.

The recent disparagement of the threat from Taiwan comes opportunely. For its part, the Kuomintang—after denying for years that the monolithic Moscow-Peking bloc could ever divide—has come to believe that the rift gives it hope of confronting an isolated Peking regime under advantageous psychological and diplomatic conditions. Nonetheless, the Nationalists must recognize that they can rally little popular support on the mainland against such a militarily powerful regime and that their ability to sustain diplomatic support abroad, always a wasting asset, will continue to dissipate. The desire of others to talk to the real power-holders, at the United Nations or disarmament conferences, will grow stronger yearly. In fact, Peking's intransigence may make these states even more eager to end the competing-Chinas anomaly, if past reactions to the mainlanders' hard line are any guide.

China may believe, with good cause, that nuclear power will enhance its grip on distant border regions. Certainly Peking will now feel more secure against pressure, threats or incursions by the Russians, or other countries on its frontiers. And its capacity to retaliate against such moves is likewise enhanced. Beyond this, Peking might seek to dominate its small neighbors more assertively, using a nuclear shield to frighten off opponents like India and to guarantee exclusion of the distant and presumably disinterested Americans. China could, for example, try to make Nepal more subservient in both its domestic and foreign affairs. Or it might pursue a relatively new objective: creation of an initially independent federation of small territories now generally considered in the Indian sphere of influence, with a view to their gravitating into the Chinese sphere. In addition to Nepal, this would include Bhutan and Sikkim (two protectorates now under Indian control in foreign policy), the North East Frontier Agency, and perhaps other parts of India as well.[30] Though establishment of such a federation would constitute an act of aggression against India, the Chinese could stress the sovereign and allegedly more viable nature of such an entity, the absence of territorial acquisition by China, and possibly a tacit acceptance by Pakistan. Peking could display moderation and encourage neutralists to act as brokers in seeking a "compromise" between Indian claims and the possibility of more dire Chinese demands. The growth of Chinese influence in such a so-called buffer zone, along with the diminution of Indian power, would mark a major step on Peking's road to regional hegemony.

The region's inaccessibility, possible Pakistani support for Chinese claims, the lack of adequate allied bases, and an accompanying propaganda barrage could combine to keep the United States out of the play.[31] In this instance, nuclear weapons would add to the demonstrable difficulties that must accompany any American intervention. To the neutralists, the atomic strength of the antagonists may increase the risks of taking sides, thereby reinforcing the rejection of collective defense they manifested during the 1962 invasion of India.

Even partial attainment of these goals would do much to further China's ambition to clear the region of hostile powers, along with their installations and influence. Only with the removal of the United States from the area could China assert its hegemony and eventually reoccupy Taiwan. Any success, even along the obscure Himalayan frontier, would bolster the Chinese argument that Americans are unreliable supporters of those who oppose Peking. The difficult terrain, the dangerous complications of the Indian-Pakistani quarrel, and the absence of direct American interests might encourage a nuclear-armed China to be confident that the United States would stay out.

Though the Chinese may well be extremely cautious in the physical use of nuclear power—as distinguished from their often rash actions in conventional operations—they will almost certainly try to make full use of the great psychological impact these weapons can create. The tension and dangers flowing from this policy will not be any less because they are directed at familiar goals. In the border case just cited, by encouraging the belief that the United States is reluctant to take risks for marginal interests, Peking may compel Washington to accept its challenge and so raise the stakes of each new challenge. Meanwhile, anticipating this, Peking could point out to each of its neighbors beforehand that their cities, and especially the American bases on their soil, would become targets for Chinese counteraction should the United States strike against China or its allies. Hence, in the nuclear era, the danger of China's use of the "opening wedge" approach against the American presence grows, especially when the target area is politically weak.

Pressure on Allies and Neutrals

The American-Asian alliance system, fragile and fragmented to begin with, will more than ever be a prime object of Chinese pressure, as will the bases that support it. Even the self-defense efforts of the indigenous powers that provide important supplementary strength can be placed in a provocative light by the new nuclear power. Of course, Chinese allegations of the grave danger posed by American bases appear to contradict the Chinese contention that the United States lacks sufficient interest and resolve to run the risk of a nuclear war. But there is no evidence that this inconsistency would daunt Peking from using both arguments in the same crisis.

Perhaps the Chinese need not wait until they can threaten the United States before making their bomb an effective instrument of nuclear diplomacy. The concept that the United States, a distant third party, could deter a dangerous, nuclear-armed state from threatening its neighbors is not easily grasped or believed in Asia, however self-evident and "natural" this notion may be in the Western world. After all, nuclear force in place is a new phenomenon in the Far East, and reliance on what to Asian states may be abstract theories of deterrence may seem very foolhardy in such new and unnerving circumstances. The argument that China would not use the weapon against fellow Asians may be valid [32] but, again, not very reassuring against a concrete threat, subtly invoked. Under these circumstances, physical protection in the form of the most modern antiballistic-missile facilities around the major cities of all our allies may become mandatory for the maintenance of our alliance system.

Again reverting to the obverse of its argument, Peking could play up the extensiveness of American control over the course of events and the dangers this portends for others. It could stress the practical loss of sovereign authority among Asian states as their power positions decline relative to the U.S. and Chinese positions. Compounding the problem would be the specter—readily enhanced and exploited by China—of alleged American inadequacy and impetuosity, mounting desperation, ignorance of Asia, and willingness to escalate without regard for the loss of Asian lives. And Peking could certainly play up the greater possibility of accidental war.

The cases of Taiwan and Vietnam could be cited to illustrate these arguments. In both instances, U.S. policy has gained little diplomatic support and in the larger Asian states has encountered widespread popular hostility. In the future, Peking will increasingly try to exploit such situations to separate America from its Asian allies. Japan's fear of becoming involved with China in a confrontation over Quemoy and Matsu in 1958 left a lasting mark on the nation's thinking, and two years later, when the security treaty with America was revised, Japan refused to agree to American troop deployments from the home islands without its permission. With nuclear weapons, China will try to make the danger to Japan even more pointed. Of course, Peking may take a tougher line in all its relations with Japan—from trade and aid to internal Japanese politics—and this approach may backfire. Whether China uses the carrot or the stick, or both, its new strength will be directed toward the dissolution of the American alliance structure in the Pacific.

However vulnerable alliance relationships may be, they do carry some security value, and the strenuousness of Peking's efforts to break these ties give a clue to their importance. Consequently, with its nuclear strength, China may exert even greater pressure on neutrals than on allies. For all their vaunted freedom from involvement in the Cold War, the neutrals stand unprotected in a highly vulnerable position. As in the past, they may continue to draw tacit encouragement from an American presence. They may urge, more explicitly than before the Chinese detonations, that American power remain visible in their region and even ask Washington for unilateral guarantees. India has sought such a commitment, but from the Soviets as well.[33] Such an undertaking from the two greatest powers might be acceptable to Ceylon. Burma, however, desires to adhere to an isolationist policy that does not irritate China in any way, and it is even less likely that Cambodia would respond favorably. In any event, before such a dual guarantee could be issued, there would have to be a major, almost revolutionary shift, in the center of gravity of Soviet foreign policy, and there is no evidence of such a shift in the offing.

In fact, judging from the neutrals' behavior over the past few years, we cannot even be certain that they would be inclined to move closer to the American protective mantle, however informally. The drift of Pnompenh (and pre-coup Jakarta) toward Peking, the deep neutralism of Burma and Ceylon, and the strong misgivings about too close an American tie (coupled with a vital interest in maintaining good relations with Moscow) in New Delhi all provide grounds for doubt. Perhaps the neutrals would hope to derive no more than unsolicited and unrequested benefits from an American presence. Under such circumstances, there is every likelihood that, like Cambodia, they would persist in following foreign policies that would intensify Washington's problems in maintaining a forward position of strength. Our relations with India may have improved but the net total effect of developments on the Indian subcontinent, in terms of their impact on the American security position, is far from reassuring.

However, China's modest short-term nuclear capacity and its optimistic estimation of diplomatic trends may diminish the relevance of nuclear weapons in South Asia. Of all the mainland states in that region, only Thailand remains effectively anchored in the American alliance system. The small neutrals remain unaligned, India refuses to modify its neutralism or develop a close military rapport with America, and Pakistan is drifting rapidly away from SEATO. China, therefore, may be able to satisfy its immediate policy needs without using overt threats, and still maintain a global image as a benign friend and protector who leaves its neighbors alone. Moreover, the crisis in Vietnam served to deter China from a deeper involvement in India, since this would carry the risk of active confrontation in two major sectors at the same time. But China can also use the war against Saigon as a device for bringing Thailand under pressure and justify such behavior in the propaganda forum of world diplomacy. Peking has already argued that all of Southeast Asia comprises a single campaign, one that involves as well the countries which allow American air power to use their soil.[34] With nuclear power at its disposal, Peking can put even greater menace in this assertion.

By 1970, nuclear power will be a reality that can threaten these lands and serve as a solid backdrop to Chinese power. It will intensify the already potent awareness of China's great strength and proximity in an area long ridden with fears of an American withdrawal. Regardless of whether specific policies or operational tactics seem to place the nuclear factor in the background, China's new weapon will seriously compound the problems confronting a region suffering from a basically unstable power pattern.

Increasing Global Tensions

Finally, nuclear power may reinforce the great Chinese desire to speed revolutions in the world and attain leadership of the underdeveloped states. If the Chinese really believe that a Communist nuclear capacity, properly exploited, can cause a decisive shift in the world balance, then they may well apply the tactics that they were urging the Russians to follow after the launching of the first Sputnik. At the very least, we should not assume that they were then cynically trying to exploit Russian strength to their own benefit, with only Moscow bearing the risks. Nor should we conclude that they will become extremely cautious once they have been through the experience of testing and understanding nuclear power. The United States may have to thwart the Chinese in grave world crises before they settle into a pattern of tolerable relationships with other states. These confrontations may make previous American-Soviet standoffs, such as the U-2 flights and the Cuban missile crisis, appear tame in comparison—in both danger and complexity. They will have new explosive elements: the intensity of the Chinese effort, the uncertain role of the Soviet Union, the imbalances between American and Chinese power, the large number of states involved, and possible changes in American attitudes if the crises prove to be as numerous as Chinese doctrine implies.

The Chinese may overvalue their acquisition of nuclear power in the belief that a qualitative improvement in their own position more than compensates for the opponent's quantitative superiority. That is, possession of similar weapons, even in inferior numbers, may appear to Peking as the beginning of a great opportunity. After all, this is similar to what happened in China after 1945, when the Communists acquired Japanese field pieces and so could confront the Nationalists for the first time with conventional instead of guerrilla power. Despite numerical inferiority, the Communists in 1945 concluded that they had gained the upper hand, due to better discipline, ideological superiority, tactical competence, support by the peasantry, and the political weakness of the opposition. They might not judge today that the power balance has shifted so decisively in the purely military sense, but the Chinese may again inject a considerable political-ideological factor into the equation. Given their isolation from the world, their limited understanding of political processes in many other lands, and the single-cause approach to the behavior of others, they may not find it farfetched to conclude that the tide has again turned—this time on a global scale.

The Chinese may also seize upon every possible bit of evidence to prove to themselves that the American position is deteriorating in a manner comparable to that of the Nationalists in 1947–48. And there will always be some important developments—successful revolutionary acts of violence, difficulties in America's relations with underdeveloped lands, instability or even a partial breakup in Washington's alliances with other industrial states, failure by Moscow and Washington to sustain efforts at a *détente*—to convince the Chinese that their time has come, or that their policies are speeding its arrival.

Relations with the Soviet Union

Though it may be safe to assume that China would never be so rash as to trigger an American-Russian nuclear war deliberately, the Chinese might play, or threaten to play, the catalyst, abstaining only in return for specific concessions by Moscow. China could work directly to heighten American-Russian tensions by forcing Moscow to decide whether to support Peking at various levels of an American-Chinese confrontation, or by sustaining a "war of liberation" that would compel Russia to support acts of increasing violence lest it lose ground in the Communist movement. Peking has come very close to thrusting this course on Russia in Vietnam.

With nuclear weapons, moreover, the Chinese will undoubtedly intensify their already great pressures on the Soviet Union to accept their views. Unification of the bloc on Peking's terms remains a prime objective, as Chou En-lai made painfully clear in his visit to Moscow after the fall of Khrushchev.[35] An end to any American-Russian *rapprochement* and termination of the nuclear test-ban agreement, in particular, loomed as possibilities at that time. The Americans were considerably relieved by Moscow's statements that the new regime stood by the 1963 treaty. Earlier declarations had not dealt with this point, and it seems to have been a crucial issue in the Russian-Chinese negotiations that autumn. The Chinese may hope that their own tests will bring an additional bonus, by inducing the United States to disavow the treaty and thereby break a link between the two great protagonists that Peking is striving to eliminate.

Regardless of how the Russians respond or wish to respond, China's ability to invoke the image of the Russian presence becomes a major issue for American actions in Southeast Asia and elsewhere. To the extent that a nuclear arsenal encourages Chinese initiatives, the frequency and intensity of Soviet-American crises may rise markedly.

If China provokes a confrontation, and the Soviets react cautiously, Peking will taunt its erstwhile ally with failing the cause. The Russians may calculate that damage to their prestige will be prohibitive if they refuse to stand firm or to support the Chinese in threats of escalation designed to keep the Americans at bay. Moscow may, therefore, respond with partial or vague commitments, but these may nevertheless enmesh Russia in a serious confrontation with Washington. The decision of the Brezhnev-Kosygin administration to stand by North Vietnam in February 1965, thereby reversing Khrushchev's effort at deliberate withdrawal, seems to indicate a commitment to halfway measures. Nonetheless, that decision could entail serious risks. Further, China may feel that its own rising military capacity will permit it to use the many opportunities that are emerging in the underdeveloped world to maneuver Washington and Moscow into conflict.

It will be extremely difficult for Russian diplomacy to keep lines open to the United States, simultaneously support revolutionary movements that China can manipulate or intensify, and still prevent the increasingly confident Chinese from getting out of hand. However successful Russia has been in the past in maintaining this balancing act—and its achievements have generally been underestimated in

Washington and Peking—its task will be greatly complicated in the future.

In fact, the Chinese can take heart from their success thus far in pressuring the Communist bloc, and a good part of the nonaligned world as well, into viewing the United States as an imperialist menace and in watering down the bloc's commitments to peaceful co-existence. Even that "arch-splitter" Khrushchev did his best to reach some compromise with Peking, going so far as to denounce Yugoslav revisionism on several occasions between 1957 and 1961. In these years, Russians also denounced India occasionally as an imperialist lackey and frequently described the United States as the malevolent leader of the imperialist camp. There seem to have been powerful elements inside the Soviet Union that were doctrinally opposed to a break with China during this period—even if that meant making unpalatable compromises. Support for North Vietnam after the fall of Khrushchev bears witness to the resurgent strength of ideological motivation in Soviet foreign policy, and a self-imposed obligation on Moscow's part to back Hanoi's quest for victory underlined the potential dangers involved in such a course.

What Moscow considers Chinese obduracy and extremism finally led the Russians to oppose Peking's view of world politics, but not before Chinese views had made a considerable impact. Today it is possible that the Chinese believe that they possess the additional leverage to swing the Russians back into line. Peking may reason that successful revolutions abroad, proving that America is a "paper tiger" afraid to confront even a weak but determined nuclear power, might lead to a favorable shift in the internal Soviet political balance.[36]

Of course, the Chinese may miscalculate and produce the reverse effect. They have miscalculated about Russian behavior before, notably when they expected latent support for them to manifest itself in the Kremlin after Khrushchev's fall. Having failed to bring Russia into line before 1964 because Russia viewed Mao's policies as too dangerous, Peking may find Moscow even more cautious precisely because China can now invoke the cutting edge of nuclear power. As a result, the Chinese may not attain a major objective—to participate in the dialogue between the superpowers and have a direct impact upon the central balance of world power. But they may adhere to their basic approach nonetheless: to isolate and alienate the United States rather than follow the discourse-compromise-competition line that the Russians advocate.

The role of ideology in both Chinese and Russian policy remains crucial—however different their interpretations may be. A policy of graded threats, when a nation has a vulnerable first-strike force, creates serious problems for the international system. The probability of a miscalculation increases when the nuclear force serves a revolutionary foreign policy and is considered by its possessors a vital political instrument to bring about an avidly sought turning point in history. There is every likelihood that if the Chinese take advantage of their many opportunities to engage in "just" struggles or support wars by proxy in their immediate environs or elsewhere in the underdeveloped world, they may find themselves in a nuclear diplomatic and perhaps military involvement.[37] Though Peking has largely succeeded in enmeshing others in conflicts while avoiding direct involvement itself (consider China's aversion to deploying its own force abroad and its denunciations of Russian "adventurism" in 1962), we must recall that the Soviet Union before the Cuban missile crisis was similarly considered too prudent and too concerned with the security of its nuclear weapons to put them in distant lands.[38] Moreover, China's grandiose offers to send volunteers to distant lands (e.g., Algeria), although without practical significance, may well reflect the wish to be able to do so—a wish that may be fulfilled in the future.

Prospects for Increased Chinese Intervention

If one identifying mark of a superpower is the capacity to intervene well beyond national frontiers, China may decide to become more active even in distant wars of liberation, as its military strength increases. Western incompetence to cope with these conflicts may serve as an additional spur to action. China has already been involved in a number of nearby conflicts. Korea, Taiwan, and India witnessed direct Chinese participation at varying levels of intensity, and Vietnam has drawn several declarations designed to deter American action. The dire warnings to Washington in December 1964 against bombing Hanoi's supply routes in Laos indicate how ready Peking is to threaten reprisals even against relatively slight escalations.[39] It can be argued that, the Korean War apart, these examples reveal either carefully limited Chinese actions or verbal threats that Peking did not carry out. Nevertheless, this attitude makes for a highly volatile situation.

In the first place, the Chinese know now that their mere words failed to stop the Americans in Vietnam. The more frequently the United States finds that Peking's warnings have no teeth, the more it will discount their credibility and intensify American military operations around the Chinese periphery. In rejoinder, as China expands its nuclear arsenal, it may find itself driven to make threats and to carry them out at some point, lest its diplomatic and doctrinal positions come under suspicion abroad, in friendly as well as hostile capitals. To retreat to caution as one's power grows would be to copy Moscow and to acknowledge the correctness of the Soviet position. We have noted that Chinese pressure causes Russia to demonstrate, albeit in a low key, its support for just revolutionary wars. Similarly, China's ideological commitments and increases in its own power may compel Peking to become more deeply involved in the area and degree of confrontation than its leaders consider necessary or desirable.

Further, there is little validity in the argument that staying out of a proxy war is a brilliant maneuver that involves, and thus weakens, the Americans while allowing the interested neutral state to reap benefits at low cost. During the Korean War, many analysts credited the Russians with a success on this score. Yet it is not a triumph, a demonstration of strength, or a relative power benefit. It is, instead, an indication of weakness, one that allows an opponent to engage in a struggle as he chooses while depriving the nonbelligerent state of equivalent leeway.

The Chinese resent bitterly the lack of power that checks their freedom to take sustained major diplomatic and military actions beyond their frontier. Whereas in Laos in the early 1960s, China worked through two allies—the Democratic Republic of Vietnam and a proxy once removed, the Pathet Lao—the United States and the Soviet Union were able to intervene at will, diplomatically and with substantial military aid. In the future, Peking may refuse to stay out of proxy struggles or make nonintervention contingent upon a similar stance by other powers.

It would be misleading to use the term "noninvolvement" to characterize Chinese use of nuclear power to deter American intervention, even in areas nearest to their homeland. In such a case, China would be committing its strength to produce a radical change in the pattern of the area's diplomacy. Also, if China as a nuclear power will no longer tolerate lopsided interventions in "its" region, then the buffer role played by proxies will be sharply cut. Future confrontations could then pit Washington and Peking against one another more frequently and swiftly. If at the same time the Chinese extend their sponsorship to guerrilla wars, in Thailand and the Philippines in particular, this will further increase the danger that such encounters will involve the nuclear component, at least in the realm of diplomacy of bargaining and threats.

It is unwise to conclude that the chances of nuclear confrontations are likely to remain small because American-Chinese clashes would invariably begin at the lowest levels of conflict. It is precisely the link between these extremes of the spectrum of violence that is so dangerous. Although there are gradations between the two, offering many opportunities to halt an escalation, the alleged value of the low-key operation—"securely" distant from the other extreme—attracts the Chinese toward a policy of violence and opens the possibility of rapid escalation. As the Korean and Vietnamese wars have shown, pressures for extending combat snowball far beyond anyone's expectations. To complete this vicious circle, possession of a nuclear capacity may induce, perhaps psychologically impel, the Chinese to foster these low-grade activities even more than in the past. And unless the political opponent is toppled rapidly, even a genuinely internal conflict has a propensity to escalate as it reaches a military climax.

The Specter of a U.S. Attack

The question of an American nuclear attack against China inevitably arises in any discussion of a Sino-American confrontation. In Chinese minds, such an attack is far more than theoretical; it is a cause for real and continuing fear. Conditioned by their Maoist history of mistreatment by Western imperialists with no regard for Asian life, many Chinese leaders genuinely fear a pre-emptive U.S. nuclear attack—the old pattern recurring in a contemporary manifestation. The fact that the American government has never threatened to launch a war with nuclear weapons will carry little weight in Peking. In recent years, we have seen that even the threat of a land invasion by Nationalist troops, backed by America, has caused widespread alarm in Peking. If this was the reaction provoked by a non-nuclear threat, it is easy to imagine what impact the specter of nuclear bombing must produce.

Those in America who advocate a nuclear attack confine their discussions to military targets, envisioning a preventive strike directed against Chinese nuclear plants and installations. However, the

Chinese anticipate that, if an attack does occur, America will launch a strategic assault on their major urban-industrial centers, wreaking mass destruction in an attempt to destroy the regime, and perhaps the state as well.[40] Hence, as in so many other matters in the bitter relations between Washington and Peking, the same words have significantly different meanings. We should also note that the American government has in no way indicated that it is seriously considering a selective preventive assault, let alone the broad attack for which the Chinese leaders repeatedly warn their people to prepare.

The first major statement published in China to deal with this fear appeared in May 1965 in an article by General Lo Jui-ch'ing.[41] Significantly, it faithfully reflected the thoughts and attitudes developed by the regime's leaders, as expressed in the secret documents obtained by the United States in 1961. It is likely that the surfacing of the problem of nuclear war had to await a demonstration that China also possessed a nuclear capacity, presumably because this would make the threat of attack on the homeland somewhat less likely.

Lo tried to impress upon the Chinese people two themes that seem, if not incompatible, at least difficult to reconcile. First, he sought to alert them to the dangers inherent in nuclear war, emphasizing that such a conflict was not beyond the realm of probability. However, he then cushioned his revelation of this problem with references to old dogmas that perhaps still reassure Chinese leadership —such as the claim that men will prevail over matériel. He also followed tradition by downgrading the importance of nuclear weapons.[42] Enumerating the different types of war that might occur, Lo acknowledged that nuclear conflict would cause great destruction and require tremendous sacrifices, but as a good Maoist, he argued that "it will also educate the people," and that "people and not things are the fundamental factors determining the outcome of wars." Finally, Lo discounted the contention that people cannot defend themselves against such weapons by citing China's allegedly effective preparations for defense against nuclear attack during the Korean War and recalling the capacity of various creatures to survive the Bikini test explosions in the 1950s.[43]

Lo further held that wars would continue to follow conventional lines despite the use of modern weapons. He invoked the traditional argument that China would triumph even against a nuclear aggressor by employing an "active defense." It would trade space for time and prepare for counterattacks, somewhat along the lines of the Soviet strategy of 1941–45, and concentrate on destroying the enemy's forces rather than seeking to hold territory. Victory, he maintained, was still dependent primarily upon infantry forces rather than upon new weapons; victory stemmed from "close integration of the armed forces and the civilian masses" in the proper political preparation and in determination for war.[44]

The implied context is clear—an American nuclear attack directed primarily against the Chinese people, in a situation in which Peking could not expect deterrent protection or wartime aid from the Soviet Union. The analysis is rudimentary for it does not demonstrate how a state can fashion a victory under such unfavorable circumstances. Still, this essay could be interpreted as an early transitional step toward a more rational appraisal of nuclear warfare—in which the "paper tiger" theme dominates but is now fused with a call for realism. If this trend toward a more sober estimate takes shape, Lo's essay will appear retrospectively as a landmark. But we cannot now anticipate such a development, especially in light of the secret papers, which disclose that the leadership accepted this sombre appraisal of potential destruction many years earlier without swerving from its chosen course.[45]

The Chinese have repeatedly indicated their awareness that their ideological and policy approaches mean risking repeated confrontations with American nuclear power under conditions highly disadvantageous to themselves. General Lo's statement, coming at a time when the Vietnamese War entered a phase of serious escalation, may have been timed in part to warn the people that such a danger was on the horizon. The realistic strand of argument may eventually attain a more central role, but at present it is merely one of several instruments of existing policy, and at this point it cannot be said to have had a serious deflective impact. In fact, public confirmation of policies and beliefs long adhered to by the leaders may portend a more vigorous application of the traditional line.

The Danger of Violence

In summation, we can observe that lower-level wars may loom as more frequent possibilities than in the past—especially if China tries to use nuclear weapons to establish a hegemonial position in the region. Further, Peking's tendency to miscalculate American motives and intentions may become magnified in a nuclear context. With a vulnerable first-strike force-in-being, such errors could have the gravest consequences.

In addition, the other Asian states may assume that China's development of nuclear power has somewhat inhibited America's will-to-respond. The target states could reason from this that Peking could use its great conventional power more freely than in the past, either as a threat or in actual operations, without provoking an immediate American counterblow. China's new weapons, and the possibility of Russian intervention in the event of an American stategic strike, may lead American allies to conclude that the United States will become increasingly cautious about invoking its strategic power in response to aggression.

Thus in Asian eyes, the Chinese may appear more prone to rely on force, while the United States may seem to be drifting toward a position of greater caution. This seemingly higher threshold of American responses would in turn discourage U.S. allies and give further impetus for Chinese actions. Since contrary to these expectations, the threshold for American counteractions in reality may well become lower (i.e., because of the nuclear element, the United States might be quicker to respond to threats and acts of violence), miscalculations leading to conflict could increase considerably.

Meanwhile, the Chinese will seek to exploit both contradictory aspects of the situation. They will do their utmost to sustain an image of an incident-prone, desperate America, longing to use nuclear weapons and drag its allies into catastrophic war. At the same time, they will claim that their own new power has shriveled America's will to stand by its alliance commitments. All this may place the United States in an unenviable position: of feeling obliged to "overrespond" to low-level threats with conventional means in order to demonstrate first that the threshold has not risen, and second that this country is capable of conducting restrained but firm military actions. Washington will probably encounter even greater difficulty than before in mustering widespread diplomatic support for any such series of small-scale operations, especially in light of a mounting danger that these might lead to nuclear war.

Even in China's prenuclear days, America had trouble getting European and Asian backing at the points of greatest vulnerability and tension—Taiwan and Vietnam. In the Korean War, U.N. members provided only spotty military support, and the Asian states pressed for a compromise instead of a victory. In 1962, the Indians could rally very little help outside the English-speaking world, and their problem in winning additional diplomatic backing in the future will increase as Chinese power rises. These diplomatic weaknesses of divided opponents may encourage China further and so make a credible deterrent all the more essential. Therefore, grim confrontations among nuclear states seem in the offing in Asia. The question is whether the setting and tactics will be such as to allow for some resolution before the level of violence rises dramatically.

At a minimum, the Chinese will use their military power more vigorously than ever to maintain their national security, reshape border arrangements, and support their allies. They will also assist uprisings abroad, especially in Eastern Asia. The diplomatic and psychological pressure on Taiwan will undoubtedly intensify. As in the past, Peking will try to keep its operations at a low level and of a type that it can terminate when it wishes—but this will become increasingly difficult to achieve. To obtain maximum propaganda value from their new weapons, the Chinese hope to keep their warnings at a general or vague level, though, as we noted earlier, they may be driven to specific threats and so force the risk of having to respond or back down. They would, for example, prefer to issue a broad warning that American bases made the host countries targets, and point up the greater Chinese capacity to survive a nuclear war. While conveying an image of formidable military strength, and asserting its own disdain for nuclear threats, China would also adopt the pose of a reasonable power that favors broad disarmament and seeks only the exclusion of foreign elements from Asian soil.

However, we cannot discount the possibility that even the propaganda line may change as Peking's power increases. If China thinks that specific threats could bring greater rewards, it may take a bolder tack. It may conclude that the potential gain may be worth the possible loss in prestige that a setback would cause, and that a later triumph would more than offset this bad effect. From 1963 onward, in the Laos, Vietnamese and Kashmiri conflicts, Peking demonstrated a willingness to make specific threats and to brazen out its failure to carry them out by making further threats when new opportunities arose. Nor did the Pathet Lao, North Vietnamese, or Pakistanis respond with recriminations; instead, they expressed gratitude for whatever support the Chinese did render.

As Chinese power grows and American concern to thwart it becomes more immediate and comprehensive, the number of so-called ambiguous issues will diminish rapidly. One unexpected consequence of China's nuclear capacity, therefore, may be an American unwillingness to let modest Chinese politico-military success, territorial or political, take place without offering some response. As a result, tension will increase, and so make it increasingly difficult to keep operations at a low level of violence. The Chinese will continue to try to direct at least some military actions toward areas in which America seems to have little direct interest. Hoping to create uncertainty of sufficient scope to hamper an effective American response, they will then cite this instance of ineffectuality to undermine Washington's prestige in more vital sectors. However, if nuclear weapons make such gambits more likely, they also increase the likelihood of an American response. The net effect is not pleasant to contemplate: the continual eruption of low-level acts of violence that could entangle the major powers in nuclear confrontations.

CHAPTER FIFTEEN

Proliferation, Arms Control, and the Future Balance in Asia

Since our analysis indicates that the growth of Chinese nuclear power will make American policy more hazardous and complicated in Asia, we must determine what the likelihood is of further proliferation of nuclear power in Asia and what the prospects are for arms control. Judgments on these points are the most critical estimates the United States must make in seeking to maintain a stable balance of power in the region in the future.

To gain a better appreciation of the pressing considerations likely to shape Chinese attitudes toward nuclear power, we shall use a two-dimensional approach, viewing China's position along with that of a Western state which, in the nuclear realm, is in a situation analagous to China—namely, France.

France and China: A Comparison

For all their differences, the French and Chinese positions on nuclear weapons have many points in common. Both have steadfastly opposed the doctrines and policies of arms control as proposed by their nuclear predecessors. Both might consider their own nuclear weapons as triggers for the nuclear arsenal of the two superpowers, though their ultimate political objectives differ widely. Again for essentially different reasons, each seeks to prevent an American-Soviet *détente* at present. And both have strained their major alliances to the utmost, without actually breaking them.[1]

These similarities and dissimilarities fall into four major groups: attitude toward arms control, influence on a great ally's policy, revision of alliance arrangements, and assertions of national autonomy.

The central Chinese position on nuclear disarmament was stated in the summer of 1963 in response to the test-ban-treaty proposal drafted by the nuclear powers. Peking denounced the pact as a fraud, because it sought to prevent "all Socialist countries except the Soviet Union" from acquiring nuclear weapons, while permitting the have powers to conduct underground tests and build stockpiles. Also, Peking charged, it failed to ban the use of nuclear weapons and permitted the signatories to abrogate the accord at will. Much like the French, China viewed the accord as an unequal treaty that simply perpetuated the hegemony of the nuclear powers.[2] As a precondition of its adherence to the test-ban treaty,[3] France had repeatedly demanded that the other major powers agree to ban delivery systems, cease all production of nuclear weapons, and destroy all nuclear stockpiles.

Peking's proposal of August 31, 1963, paralleled the French terms. It called for a conference of the heads of every state to ban all use, production, testing, research, and transfer of nuclear weapons and to destroy all nuclear stockpiles and delivery systems.[4] As preliminary steps, the Chinese insisted on removal of all bases (non-nuclear as well as nuclear) and all nuclear weapons from foreign soil; creation of a nuclear-weapon-free zone in "the Asian and Pacific regions"; prohibition of export or import of nuclear weapons or data concerning them; and termination of all tests, including those conducted underground. The Chinese also demanded signed promises not to use nuclear weapons in war.

In general, the Chinese were much closer to the French than to the Russian position, though a decade earlier Peking had supported Russian disarmament offers, including test-ban proposals and nuclear-free zones. In fact, Chou En-lai had endorsed the American-Russian-British moratorium on atmospheric tests that went into effect in 1958. The Chinese did not reverse themselves until August 1962, when the Russians expressed interest in the American draft for a limited test-ban treaty.[5]

In October 1964, with their first test completed, the Chinese reiterated their demand for the "complete prohibition and thorough destruction of nuclear weapons" as the price of halting their own test program.[6] Significantly, Peking now introduced important reservations to its earlier sweeping proposals, rejecting destruction of nuclear delivery systems.[7] In 1965, it also dropped its earlier support of nuclear-free zones. This stand reflected China's calculation that possession of some weapons gave it greater security than it could achieve through broad arms-limitation arrangements. Some analysts believe that we will also hear less of the "no first use" arguments as China's arsenal grows, although Peking's ideological line asserts that one cannot expand socialism through nuclear military initiatives. Further, China may have insisted on protecting its delivery systems, as distinct from weapons, from any international control because it still had not reached an adequate level of development to provide a basis for rapid future progress in this category. In this respect, it differed from France.

The United States believes that the Chinese seek to reduce its advantage in advanced weaponry without making equivalent concessions in conventional power. In other words, it holds that Peking views arms negotiation as a possible route to change the balance of power.[8] However, it is precisely because this may be the effect of total nuclear disarmament that Washington finds the French views so incomprehensible. America considers that French conditions for adherence to the test-ban agreement require the West to make a frightful security sacrifice at the alter of sovereign equality. Both France and China seem to have "illogical" aspects in their demands and may not always base their calculations on straightforward power considerations.

In a most practical sense, despite their fervent ideological hatred of the West and their belief that general and complete disarmament —the only valid kind, according to Peking—can come about only after the fall of capitalism, the Chinese are on record as willing to consider nuclear weapons (even specific aspects of such armament) as a special case. Like France, however, China will bargain vigorously from its own perspective of values and interests.

One of the issues in the forefront of both French and Chinese thinking is the leverage nuclear weapons offer for influencing the superpowers and affecting their policies and strategic plans. Nevertheless, there is a fundamental disparity in aspiration between Peking and Paris and, therefore, in the reason that they seek such influence. Like America, France accepts the present alignment of world power and the sovereign-state system through which it operates. Though having the same basic view of interstate politics and similar hopes for the future, these two allies have conflicting opinions about what can advance the common interest in our age. In particular, they disagree in theory (if less so in practice) about the degree of autonomy states should enjoy. Superficially, one can say much the same about Sino-Soviet relations. But there are quantitative and qualitative dissimilarities between the French and Chinese terms of the equation—China's greater strength compared to France and its more intense antagonism toward its ally (fed by commitment of each to reshape the world). It is probably these differences in the proportions of the equation that make it much more difficult for Moscow and Peking than for the two Atlantic powers to coordinate strategic policies.

Though the French have developed a nuclear force that could set off a strategic war, they have no desire to overturn the present order or use American power for aggressive intent. Still, a danger remains, and the United States cannot exercise it simply by announcing that it will never allow the French *force de frappe* to serve as a trigger for American nuclear forces. The French may assume that the Russians can never be certain of this separation, regardless of what we say, and might therefore see in any French atomic action a need to respond with a maximum effort.[9] Since the French would employ nuclear weapons only under grave duress in the first place, it is difficult to envision such a crisis in which France would be so diplomatically isolated that America would not step in with protective action. Following this line of reasoning, the French may well conclude that the Americans will harmonize their diplomatic and strategic efforts with French interests so as to avoid such crises.

Similarly, the Chinese could conceivably involve the Soviets in a nuclear confrontation with the U.S. despite the latter's numerical advantage over both states in secure strategic weapons. If the Chinese manage to entangle the Russians in a hostile relationship with Washington, the comparison with the French example might be uncomfortably close. With China increasingly engaged in crises at the "war of national liberation" level, and endeavoring to prove the efficacy of their new weapons in blackmail diplomacy, the Russians may be impelled on a much more dangerous anti-American course than they intended to follow.[10] In this instance, Washington would be the uncertain party, especially regarding Moscow's stand in any conflict between Russian ideological commitments and national interests.

The new nuclear powers may also seek a greater role in developing concepts for the employment of strategic weapons. In this respect, the French may enjoy greater success than the Chinese, who will probably find the Russians too suspicious and hostile to modify their plans according to Chinese desires. French power has already been instrumental in getting Washington to share its target planning and knowledge about weapons effects with its NATO allies. In addition, France's possession of an independent nuclear force eases European worry that the American concept of a "pause" before nuclear escalation might invite Soviet conventional attack or the collateral apprehension that the United States and the Soviet Union will escalate gradually, with strikes first restricted to one another's allies.

If the French are to achieve their desired influence on American strategy, they will have to make a stronger commitment to the alliance than they have recently shown. But such a commitment is not necessarily incompatible with having an independent force, as later French governments may demonstrate. In any event, such coordination is within the realm of the possible for Paris; for Peking, it would require a staggering change in ideological orientation and in relations with the Soviet Union.

On the other hand, both France and China seem determined to revise regional alliances to suit their own aspirations, rather than compromise with the superpowers. The French feel that they still need the NATO security ties but not the international-organization aspects of the alliance. They imply that the alliance, too, would be expendable if France could only guarantee its own security. Within this restriction, France seems determined to dismantle as much of the alliance structure as possible and reorganize continental Europe around itself as the major protective power. Clearly, an independent, effective nuclear force plays a crucial role in this aspiration. President de Gaulle has repeatedly stated his preference for an organization of sovereign European national states, somehow "confederated" to coordinate policies on non-nuclear matters and with sufficient cohesion to function as an important bloc in world politics.[11] The French would not seek to dominate but would certainly wish to guide the others and keep them dependent upon France's nuclear force. By "setting Europe free" of America, France would use the reconstituted alliance as a source of its own power and prestige. At the same time, France would not share "sovereign control" or use of nuclear weapons with others, especially West Germany. Meanwhile, the French would keep a line out to the United States, so as to be able to invoke its power in case the admittedly weaker European order encountered excessive pressure from the Soviet Union. Herein, of course, lies the weakness, for what European state would wish to trade a close American tie for an uncertain French link whose benefits, apart from an all-European membership, are so doubtful?

The French pattern exhibits many similarities to China's in the hopes and practices of its alliance policies and in potential achievements and weaknesses, as well. For different reasons, the Chinese have allowed their alliance system with Russia to wither. Yet they also hope, though apparently with less confidence, to fall back on it for protection when they run into trouble. A residual Soviet obligation might survive even a complete disintegration of the formal alliance, to judge from repeated affirmations of socialist unity made in both capitals amid the most severe mutual recrimination.

Like France, China seeks regional supremacy; but unlike France, with its emphasis on national sovereignty, China also seeks to foster or impose a militant ideology near and far by means of wars conducted by indigenous Communist parties. Nonetheless, for the present, the Chinese seem to be seeking a looser regional hegemony that would allow a considerable degree of national sovereignty and political autonomy under Peking's guidance and protection. This tactic of tolerance appears essential at present to the propagation of the revolutionary cause.

The Chinese sought to weld together a bloc of their own, consisting of North Korea, North (or all) Vietnam, Cambodia, the Japanese Communist party, left-wing Indian Communists, and perhaps Burma and Pakistan. This effort suffered serious reverses when the leftist coup in Indonesia failed in 1965. China's dogmatic position in 1966 drove both North Korea and the Japanese Communist party to assert their independence and neutrality in the Sino-Soviet dispute. Nonetheless, Peking's potential for leadership, demonstrated earlier in the 1960s, remains formidable and with more flexible policies may again reassert itself under favorable conditions. Even while Western power remains in the area, the Chinese may seek to exercise a light-handed suzerainty and move toward a unified approach in questions of security, cultural affairs, and perhaps a politico-economic development. Structurally, this stage of development bears some resemblance to France's aspirations for its European grouping. In both cases, the possession of nuclear weapons can be advanced as a major reason for leadership. Though this approach opens the way for other regional powers to justify their entering the nuclear club, both China and France have stated that such emulation is "unnecessary." [12]

Finally, nuclear weapons underline and strengthen national autonomy and seemingly make the pursuit of state interests easier. Self-defense remains a primary sovereign responsibility. However quixotic this may seem in light of massive American and Soviet power, the French and Chinese are convinced that possession of some nuclear strength affords a state its only true opportunity to protect itself.[13]

This does not mean that Paris or Peking actually believes that either America or Russia seeks to absorb the rest of the world, or could do so in the face of the other's opposition. However, it is always possible that the two superpowers would at some time agree to respect each other's exclusive spheres of influence, and there are lesser and more realistic levels of cooperation, at which a superpower *détente* could seriously diminish the freedom of action of third parties.

With nuclear weapons, states can at least try to plan their own strategic defense and might also become successful in averting direct threats and diplomatic pressure against their homeland. They could also try to keep clear of superpower problems and confrontations and block the spread of nuclear war to their soil over issues irrelevant to their interests. Thus they could promise neutrality in these and lesser crises in return for being left alone, using the "nuisance" value of their force as an instrument of persuasion.

France's main security argument is that it feels a reasonable uncertainty regarding the permanence of American protection against Russian threats. How, the Gaullist French ask, can anyone depend on a foreign power indefinitely in this world of sovereign states? Even in the most stable nations, new administrations with differing political orientations can win office. Underlying this view is the fear that the Soviet Union's great capacity to strike at the United States makes the American commitment to a nuclear defense of Europe less dependable.

The Chinese take an even less optimistic view of the Russian commitment than do the French of ours. Ignoring Soviet counterarguments that the Chinese mainland has never been seriously threatened and that the Soviet Union is committed to defend China only against aggression, Peking argues that Moscow has failed to fulfill its pledges twice in the past, in connection with Quemoy in 1958 and with India in 1962. Even when Russia offered nuclear assistance this posed other problems in Sino-Soviet relations. On September 6, 1963, when Peking detailed the story of the nuclear agreement and its abrogation, it stated that in 1958 the Russians had "put forward unreasonable demands designed to bring China under Soviet military control. These unreasonable demands were rightly and firmly rejected by the Chinese government." [14]

Both the French and Chinese advance contradictory arguments about superpower behavior in times of crisis. While being concerned that a Russian threat or assault might not evoke an American response, Paris also avers, as in the Berlin confrontations of 1958–61, that the Russians do not really constitute a menace, mainly because of America's strategic superiority.[15] Hence the French opposed negotiations in the face of Soviet demands and looked on America's willingness to bargain on lesser points, while bolstering the allied conventional posture, as indications of weakness. Washington's interest in diplomatic "movement" and its refusal to gamble everything on the nuclear deterrent reinforced the French conclusion that a national nuclear force was needed.

The Chinese attitude toward Russia is analogous. On the one hand, China calls America a paper tiger and repeatedly exhorts the Russians to take the United States to the brink and extort concessions under the threat of nuclear warfare. On the other hand, Peking calls the United States a menace that repeatedly uses nuclear blackmail for diplomatic gains and counterrevolutionary purposes. Though the purposes differ sharply from the French case, China's argument is remarkably similar in shape. (1) Russia did not and will not support Peking against a very real American nuclear threat, and so China needs its own weapons. (2) Since Russia has the advantage (the prevailing east wind), it should stand firm on its demands and face the enemy down with nuclear power.[16] However, neither Paris and Peking envisages a need for nuclear war since one can always modify a particular stand if firmness does not produce the desired results.

In this connection, both China and France have a high stake in perpetuating the Cold War, albeit for different reasons. The Chinese cannot conceive of a meaningful and orderly relationship with non-Communist nations, particularly the United States, on a long-term basis. Committed to revolutionary violence and warfare, Peking would view a superpower *détente* as further proof of Soviet revisionism and a serious blow to its hopes to reunite the bloc on its own ideological terms. The French, essentially traditional and nationalistic, enjoy the freedom for diplomatic movement afforded them by a continual American-Russian confrontation. As an autonomous force, Paris can deal with both superpowers and even try to ingratiate itself with the neutralist world. More important, an agreement on Europe—particularly with regard to Germany and nuclear weapons dispositions—would undermine the entire effort to set up a regional zone under French leadership.[17] However, despite these similarities in diplomatic tactics, and immediate policy interests, basic ideological differences evidently preclude any systematic co-operation between France and China.

Possession of nuclear weapons also gives a state an important voice in any international agreements concerning the disposition of such arms. Future accords on arms control will increasingly require the participation of France and China as their power grows. Their influence over other pacts, especially within alliances, may also grow. Here as in other matters, the open and developed Western alliance structure gives France a great opportunity to affect events. French opposition to the multilateral force carried considerable weight, in good part because Paris had independent nuclear power. By contrast, defense relationships among the major Communist powers were more rudimentary and suspicion-laden even before the great rift, thereby minimizing Chinese influence in questions of alliance security policy. Further, a structured allied control of nuclear weapons is far less likely in Communist Asia than in Western or Eastern Europe. Still, with a nuclear force, China can certainly have a major impact upon any multilateral arrangements the Soviets may later seek in the Far East, perhaps in response to American steps in this direction with Japan and others.

The French may also win an even larger voice in American planning. On several occasions, the United States has shown a willingness to go beyond sharing information and combined targeting, offering its allies a greater role in general strategic planning in exchange for a commitment that their national forces will operate under agreed plans. In 1965, Secretary MacNamara proposed the creation of a special defense directorate of representative NATO states. The French rejected this and similar plans providing "integration" without control over American decisions on when to employ nuclear weapons. During 1966, France disengaged itself from all integrated military aspects of NATO; and while continuing to consider itself in the alliance, it declared that only "unprovoked aggression," as determined by France, would make the pact operative for Paris. It would be a signal achievement if the French should succeed in inducing the United States to accept partial allied controls in these spheres, even if France had to surrender some of its freedom in decision-making. The implications of American efforts to cope with the demands of its nuclear-armed ally may not be lost on the Chinese. Any cooperation between China and Russia, however, can occur only in the setting of a Sino-Soviet *rapprochement*, which now appears as unlikely as the split seemed a decade ago.

Proliferation: Pro and Con

American policy has made a major objective of nonproliferation in the belief that widespread possession of nuclear weapons would seriously damage the security and stability of the world political order. With France and China now nuclear powers, we must consider anew whether the quest for and acquisition of nuclear weapons by Japan, India, Pakistan, Indonesia, and/or Australia would comprise a net loss to American interests in the area. If this is the case, there is a further question: What price would the United States have to pay—especially in diplomatic friction and extended security obligations—to block proliferation, and would the benefits be worth the cost, especially if the effort was made without Soviet cooperation? Should fear of the consequences of proliferation prove exaggerated, or the price appear too high, Washington may decide not to make the broad concessions necessary to keep the nuclear *status quo*. This issue is basic to security policy in the region as a whole and to other major American goals that at first glance do not seem related to the question of nuclear power.

From an American perspective, the arguments against proliferation in Asia stem from the more general Nth-country problem. As President John F. Kennedy noted:

The reason why we keep moving and working on this question, taking up a good deal of energy and effort, is because personally I am haunted by the feeling that by 1970, unless we are successful, there may be ten nuclear powers instead of four, and by 1975, fifteen or twenty. . . . I regard this as the greatest possible danger and hazard.[18]

Should the major Asian and Pacific states all acquire nuclear weapons, a very large number of disputes could quickly reach a highly critical stage. The United States would soon be enmeshed in many issues that did not involve American security interests apart from the nuclear factor. It takes very little imagination to envision the dangers confronting the protagonists and the need for great-power intervention (not necessarily with ameliorating effects) in case of a confrontation between Pakistan and India, if these countries should acquire nuclear weapons. The role of a re-emergent Japan in world affairs, already freighted with major uncertainties, would also become more problematical if Tokyo possessed modern weapons. Other Pacific allies and Britain, with important security commitments in the Far East, would be gravely concerned about this potential threat from Tokyo, even if Japan lacked a sizable naval force.

The larger states of the area, most of them well-developed cultural and national entities, are comparable to European states in having the political and administrative capacity to maintain at least a rudimentary nuclear force. On the other hand, their relative lack of experience, their deep mutual animosities, and the absence of regional organizations able to control conflicts all provide numerous opportunities and ample motivation for recourse to violence. In this sense, the area resembles the Europe of a few generations ago rather than of the present. With the added complication of the Communist threat to this tense and unstable political system, we may well conclude that widespread possession of nuclear weapons could make Eastern Asia the most dangerous place on the globe.

If any one of these states acquires nuclear weapons, it is quite possible that at least one other will make a matching effort. Only the most ironclad foreign commitments could keep a state from seeking to match a rival's entry into the club. Consequently, if the United States cannot hold the line at the present number, we may witness a jump of two or three.

From the vantage point of its own security interests, therefore, the United States may have strong reasons to oppose proliferation. Still, it should evaluate the merits of the case presented by an Asian state and consider the problem from that vantage point, as well. An American decision to oppose the spread of nuclear weapons is going to demand great diplomatic skill—in compromises, concessions, and argumentation. Advocates of such a policy must repeatedly reappraise their assumption that the security advantages of nonproliferation outweigh the costs of opposing it. And there is no prospect that the burdens will be eased by any greater Soviet-American cooperation than in the French or Chinese instances.

How, for example, would Washington respond to a diplomat of a friendly Asian state who asked why his nation should not produce a weapon if it is capable of doing so? He might argue, along French lines, that no state in a sovereign-state system can count on the protection of another for an indefinite period of time. He might add that the United States is distant and not as irrevocably committed to

Asian as to European security. Washington might reply that the Sino-American confrontation seems to be the most deep-rooted and durable "given" in the present pattern of international relations. Stressing its willingness to defend Europe against a strong Russian menace, the United States would declare an equal willingness to defend Asia against a more immediate but—to it—less directly dangerous Chinese opponent.

But the Asian might still not be satisfied. He might point out that certain doubts about U.S. reliability persist in Europe. Why is uncertainty no less reasonable in Asia, where a lesser danger to America is balanced by a less direct security stake? And though Asia represents a lesser American interest, China presents a more likely source of diplomatic nuclear initiatives than do the more cautious "Westernized" Russians. Nor can anyone hypothesize with certainty that the Soviet Union will stay out of a major Washington-Peking dispute. The American counterargument would rest on the resolve to defend the Asian states and on the likelihood that the Soviet Union would restrict its intervention, if any, to China provided that Soviet territory was left alone. This line of reasoning might not carry conviction as to the reliability of the United States in a future crisis.

The United States also might find direct security disadvantages in opposing proliferation. Of the five states in question, four can be classified as "friendly." Only Indonesia's political leaders were "hostile neutrals," and even this was no longer the case by 1967. In Asia, as throughout the world generally, the states with a capacity to produce their own nuclear arms have security interests more in accord with Washington's than with Moscow's or Peking's. If they actually possessed arms, one over-all regional effect might be a strengthening of national defense capabilities against aggression in general and Communist threats in particular. Moreover, all are on or near the borders of China and Russia, making whatever danger might emerge more immediate for Moscow and Peking.

Of course, interstate rivalries might well be heightened. If India developed nuclear weapons, Pakistan would be intensely upset over such a qualitative change in India's military power. Still, it might be satisfied with a close nuclear-weapons relationship with the United States, backed by a treaty guarantee, as the price for stabilizing the security system of South Asia. Further, China might be less prone to threaten nuclear war if it faced neighbors sufficiently armed and determined to protect themselves. Certainly the fear of such wars starting through American involvement, and over interests of little direct concern to a particular Asian ally, would be sharply reduced. On the other hand, disputes between China and any one of these states would have a greater likelihood than before of involving nuclear power, thereby frightening the others.

The possibility of proliferation in Asia raises the matter of obligations under the test-ban treaty. Adherents to the 1963 pact have pledged not to test, and the United States has agreed not to help any other states in efforts to test under water, on the surface of the earth, or in the atmosphere.[19] Though legally it could give away weapons, it would be no more likely to do so in Asia than in Europe. Nor would it be likely to assist these lands in underground tests, whose cost would be almost prohibitively high for Asian nations. However, the treaty may be renounced unilaterally if a signatory judges that changing conditions have impaired its security. Moscow and Washington might not consider French and Chinese efforts sufficient to warrant such action. But others might judge that a determined Chinese program gave them the legal right to abrogate their commitment.

Neutrals and allies alike would hardly be dissuaded from a nuclear quest by the argument that a costly investment in special weapons would mean a weakening of their conventional forces. They could readily retort that without a nuclear force, their conventional forces are merely a nominal weapon disguising their real impotence before the nuclear powers. Conversely, they might demand of the United States and others greater financial assistance in the conventional or nuclear field, or both, on the grounds that a well-rounded defense program would enhance the security of all opponents of China.

Over the long run, the United States might find that proliferation among its Asian friends and allies would make harmonious relations with them easier to maintain. The short haul might be somewhat rocky, as these lands (e.g., Pakistan, should it insist on matching India) struck out on their own foreign-policy course even more vigorously or perhaps used their new strength unwisely in dealing with their neighbors. But eventually, if this analysis is correct and it becomes apparent that China poses a common threat to all, these states might find the stakes high enough to warrant their mutual cooperation in a multilateral containment effort backed by American power.

The darker side of the argument, however, is still formidable.

Anyone who hopes for greater cooperation among Asian states, and counts on nuclear weapons to help this process along, is taking a major gamble. The fragmentation of policy, mutual hostility, and isolationist attitudes toward the problems of others might actually intensify when Asian states realize that one of their number could involve them all in a nuclear confrontation with the powerful Chinese. It is not totally unlikely that in consequence of proliferation, the Chinese might be able to face one Asian opponent at a time even more easily than in the past.

All major policy lines entail serious problems. Proliferation would open a Pandora's box of dangers in which new nuclear powers could threaten their neighbors and induce rivals to join in the arms race as additional nuclear powers. The regional alliance approach, however attractive as a concept, does not seem realistic for the near future—at least as a way of enabling both India and Japan to possess nuclear power and yet do so under controls that would allay the security fears of their non-Communist neighbors. Nonproliferation would raise serious security difficulties for the have-not states and create tremendous pressures on the nations that can quickly produce nuclear devices. If the United States alone undertook to guarantee the security of all lands against nuclear threat, the commitment could involve America deeply in every security crisis of the region, regardless of whether its own interests were at stake. It may be more feasible to limit assurances simply to its allies, though this would still extend the obligations in some instances and place a tremendous burden on fragile alliances such as the Pakistan-SEATO connection.

We must recognize that Peking has held the strategic-diplomatic initiative in Asia since 1949, and there is no reason to expect it to follow a less forceful line in dealing with its neighbors in a period of nuclear plenty. To sustain the balance, under conditions of proliferation as well as nonproliferation, the United States will find it necessary to "earmark" a portion of its nuclear forces—if only for reasons of public relations—as available for Chinese targets, above and beyond those elements assigned to deter the Soviet Union.

Although this discussion of proliferation points to no clear-cut policy, it may help to determine what decision to make in a particular situation. Moreover, the United States should at least be aware of the costs involved in espousing nonproliferation as well as in acquiescing to *ad hoc* proliferation.

Alternatives to Proliferation

Japan and India can match China in nuclear power if they should try to do so at an early date. But an air of complacency frequently accompanies this assertion, as if the gap between potential and reality is not truly significant.[20] Yet the question of will grows in importance with the passage of time as the effort necessary to catch China becomes more formidable.

There are several reasons why Japan and India might seek nuclear weapons after allowing several years to pass. China's actual possession of such weapons will have a greater impact than had been anticipated in neighboring states before 1964. An increasing role for China in the world arena, aided by exaggeration of its actual power and accompanied by the subtle use of nuclear blackmail against its neighbors, would provide a major inducement for New Delhi and Tokyo to reconsider their position. As the Chinese lead grows, the downgrading of the significance of even a small arsenal of nuclear weapons—widespread before the 1964 test—may appear to have been a serious error.

At this point, if the United States is determined to avoid proliferation, it will find itself compelled to undertake extensive long-term commitments to sustain the region's basic security. Washington must also be prepared to have its degree of firmness repeatedly tested by friend and foe alike, and it must be willing to reiterate endlessly its resolve to stand by its solemn obligations. At the simplest level, the American responsibility might take the form already suggested: a unilateral guarantee to all allies against nuclear threats from any source. This might be extended, under special circumstances and under controlled conditions, to specific neutral states. In any case, the United States must also have a credible position regarding its willingness to use nuclear weapons in a crisis. This is an extremely delicate issue, since too ready a posture will help the Chinese in their effort to picture the United States as eager to kill Asian masses. At the same time, unless there is some assertiveness, an image of American vacillation will be conveyed. Washington is also liable to encounter contradictory pressures in a specific case: the state directly threatened may call for a vigorous American declaratory policy and perhaps threats or even actions of a preventive nature, whereas the other guaranteed states may urge a more cautious approach, lest they, too, become involved in a major showdown.

Beyond guarantees, the United States might offer some joint control of weapons stationed on Asian soil, with provision for prior consultation and for a dual veto along the lines employed in the missile arrangements with Britain, Italy, and Turkey during 1958–63. Or there might be a combined sea-going force on bilateral and multilateral lines, using surface missile ships, aircraft carriers, or submarines, or any combination of these.

Apart from the establishment of joint nuclear forces by the United States and major Asian states, the other approach that offers the greatest promise of security without proliferation is the achievement of arms control along with joint nuclear defense arrangements. These two approaches may be at least partially incompatible, as the Soviets have argued in opposing a multilateral force involving German participation. The Western powers have maintained that it is possible to proceed along both tracks simultaneously. Also, China's refusal to sign the test-ban treaty diminishes the thrust of its diplomatic campaign against joint nuclear defense arrangements.

As long as China refuses to participate in existing agreements or negotiations, India and Japan can hardly hope to find security in any additional arms-control accords that Washington and Moscow accept. Yet the non-nuclear powers have all pursued this approach, and with greater vigor since the Chinese tests. In fact, since the Chinese demonstrated their possession of the bomb, important non-nuclear powers have called on the United States and the U.S.S.R. to take bolder disarmament steps to limit their own freedom.

Chinese participation has not been made an immediate condition of this bargaining process which centers on winning substantial American-Soviet cooperation. Even if China holds out, as is likely, new instruments of arms control may still be devised and applied.[21] Going beyond earlier U.N. Assembly appeals for an end to all testing, a ban against stationing nuclear-armed forces abroad, and a promise of no-first-use in warfare,[22] the possibilities now include controls over, or a halt to, the production of nuclear weapons, control over fissionable materials, a freeze on the development and production of delivery systems, a ban against proliferation, and the establishment of nuclear-free zones.[23] These are not as sweeping as China's disarmament program, since they do not call for leveling out all differences between nuclear and non-nuclear powers. Rather, such arrangements would put a halt to the widening of the gap between the have and have-not states, and perhaps limit the use of nuclear weapons as an instrument of diplomacy. China and France have consistently opposed legislation of this sort because it would legalize and guarantee the advantageous position of the original nuclear powers.

Soviet acceptance of the limitations desired by the non-nuclear powers would be an important new factor contributing to global stability. Above all, it would mean that the Soviets are willing to follow an anti-Chinese line even at the height of the Vietnamese crisis, thereby indicating the high priority they attach to a treaty against proliferation. Yet, if China continued to hold out, some type of Soviet as well as American guarantees would be needed to prevent the non-nuclear powers from developing their own weapons. Otherwise, the security gap would increase dangerously as Chinese nuclear power grew. Upon successful completion of a comprehensive nonproliferation accord, the non-nuclear states might proceed with a major effort to induce Peking to adhere to the settlement. They might even go so far as to agree to special if limited exceptions in China's favor in order to persuade Peking to accept some compromise on arms control.[24]

China may not yield in its insistence on a total leveling of differences in the nuclear power of nations and might prove even more intransigent in negotiating controls over conventional forces, which it considers the backbone of its security.[25] It is possible but unlikely that unified pressure from the underdeveloped world, adequate compromise terms, and the threat of proliferation might move the Chinese to sign a nuclear-arms accord.[26] However, as Chou En-lai has pointed out, China would first insist that the question of its recognition and the even thornier problem of Taiwan be settled on its terms.

New Orientations in the Status Quo and Beyond

In considering the alternatives to proliferation, we must again emphasize that without nuclear weapons, India and the major allies of the United States will depend heavily on American nuclear protection. Yet it is questionable whether the fragile alliances in this region or a tacit understanding with India can sustain the heavy burden of a nuclear defense accord.[27] The difficulties that NATO has faced in recent years, and the knowledge that alliances in general are not immutable, cast additional doubt on the efficacy of these vehicles to bear the awesome responsibility of nuclear security.

For example, the Asian alliances have been seriously harmed by disputes over policy toward third parties; notably, the American link with Pakistan was weakened because of U.S. military aid to India. States dependent on American nuclear protection might find their leverage to block or work against American initiatives severely reduced. It is also conceivable that shifts in the domestic power balance in Japan or Australia could produce sharp changes in the style of the alliance relationships or even imperil the survival of a nuclear security pact, though it might be of fundamental importance to the nation's security.[28]

For a state with modest resources, the commitment not to develop nuclear weapons is extremely serious, especially if a potentially dangerous neighbor has begun to make progress in that field. In such a situation, the have-not state's deep dependence on foreign support becomes painfully obvious. Neutrals would probably feel even less certain than an American ally of gaining nuclear protection as China acquires a nearly insuperable nuclear lead.[29] Prime Minister Shastri opposed proliferation in his public statements during 1965, as did Mrs. Gandhi the following year. However, we should recall that, in discussing Indian weapons policy in the event that China developed nuclear warheads as well as bombs and then perfected a missile system, Shastri stated, "We will certainly consider as to what we have to do because . . . the integrity and sovereignty of the country and its preservation is utmost in our mind." [30]

As a prerequisite for an Asian nation to decide not to produce nuclear weapons, the United States will have to extend broad, credible, and permanent security guarantees. Failing this, to refrain from seeking one's own weapon means putting one's fate in China's hands, or so it will appear to the leaders of the large Asian states.[31] America's moral obligation in this regard will rise in proportion to its efforts to dissuade these states from producing their own weapons. A firm understanding between Washington and its allies might allow reassurance to neutrals such as India that, even without a formal tie, defensive support would be forthcoming against a nuclear threat in a time of crisis. But such an arrangement must appear an extremely shaky basis for the security policy of a state that has already experienced Chinese incursions.

It would always be possible for the United States to undertake unilateral commitments to help avert the spread of nuclear weapons.[32] But in the absence of support by the other nuclear powers, Washington might consider it unwise to adopt sweeping obligations, such as guaranteeing to protect all Peking's neighbors from Chinese nuclear-diplomatic pressure. America might keep its own obligations in line with its power and, at the same time, enhance the prestige of its alliances by limiting such unequivocal promises to its treaty partners. This could have unfortunate consequences, including an unbalanced movement in the tangled diplomacy of the subcontinent. For example, the United States might find itself protecting Pakistan against neutral India as well as China, but refusing to support New Delhi against a Communist threat. On the other hand, if it limits its nuclear support still further—along the lines of the SEATO understandings—to Communist threats, it would be putting a restrictive gloss on the Japanese, Philippine, and ANZUS pacts. Presumably, the United States would not then have to respond if Australia and the Philippines sought help to counter a threat from a nuclear-armed Indonesia. Clearly, if defense accords are to substitute for proliferation, the United States must broaden, rather than narrow, existing alliances to afford protection against a nuclear threat from any source.

We should not assume that an ally will find it "normal" to concentrate on building his conventional strength and allow the United States to provide the nuclear power. Uneasiness over total dependence on the American tie, the judgment that only a national nuclear force can sustain certain substantial interests, and the loss of a general capacity to negotiate on a wide range of issues may lead various states to balk at such a division of labor on a permanent basis.[33] Some states may give new weight to considerations of status.

Pakistan and Indonesia have already displayed interest in acquiring nuclear weapons for reasons that could be described as diffusely nationalistic, as well as for specific foreign-policy objectives. It is essentially an accident that Japan and India, two vulnerable states that can rapidly produce nuclear weapons, are at present only moderately concerned with physical power as a source of international prestige. But how long can the United States count on a pacifist or idealistic rejection of "the bomb" to influence policymakers in Tokyo and New Delhi? Can it expect these two to continue to deny themselves recourse to nuclear weapons? Might the United States benefit in the long run from a change in their attitude, since their present orientation results in a passivity and self-isolation that is considered inappropriate for the security interests of the entire area? A fundamental change in attitude—i.e., a rise of nationalism, stronger defense policies, and a greater focus on regional security interests—combined with the quest for nuclear military power might make their contribution to the area's defense considerably more significant over the coming years than is anticipated.

At the same time, such a basic reorientation could generate new and important security problems for their non-Communist neighbors. As in Europe, where the foremost question is how to manage West German power, Japan and India could maximize their contributions if they channeled their efforts into a regional system that established and controlled collective-defense arrangements. Yet the European experience demonstrates that even a well-structured multistate system can breed serious uncertainties. In Asia, the relative weakness of the other lands, the lack of regionalist feelings, and the fear of New Delhi or Tokyo could well preclude the establishment of a regional structure able to contain their power, even if the United States agreed to participate. In fact, China might exploit the fear of rising Japanese or Indian power to disrupt the present strained defense ties and might extend its influence in non-Communist lands to a far greater degree than Russia did in Western Europe by playing on fear of Germany.

Japan, like West Germany, poses a special problem with regard to nuclear weapons because of its role in Axis aggression. In some ways, the potential danger from Japan is more serious, because unlike Germany, its strength is not reduced by political division, and Japan's neighbors have not taken steps to integrate it politically and militarily into their camp. In Europe, moreover, there is a strong, multinational alliance structure comprising several strong democracies that can reinforce their ideological allies in West Germany and help them respond to any threat from a nationalistic right wing.

Nonetheless, Japan can muster strong arguments in favor of its seeking nuclear weapons. For one thing, it is a less powerful state than West Germany, does not have its formidable historical record as a great military force, and lacks inflammatory nationalist issues comparable to the German desire for unity and quest for the lost eastern territories. Japan, furthermore, lacking a large naval force and having to reckon with an American fleet in the area, could not present as direct a threat to its former victims as West Germany could in Europe. Still, Tokyo's neighbors would deeply fear the possible consequences of Japan's obtaining an independent nuclear force. Such a development could come to pass only at the price of profound changes in the entire American Pacific alliance system.

India, of course, is in a different category since it has been the primary Asian target of Chinese military actions and threats. New Delhi can justly fear that China will seize upon the first opportunity to humiliate India with an adroit use of nuclear power in the service of territorial or political demands, or as a backdrop for low-level acts of violence. The rise of Indian nationalist feeling, apparent in the 1962 war and reflected in the bitter comments on the first Chinese nuclear test two years later,[34] reached a new pitch with the "stalemate victory" of the seventeen-day war with Pakistan, in 1965. Yet it is precisely the convergence of this new and persistent nationalism with the acquisition of nuclear weapons that would have such a profound and frightening impact on Pakistan. During those seventeen days, as Pakistan accused India of aggressive intent and desperately sought to invoke American and/or Chinese protection (what other nation could even think of such unlikely "co-protectors"?), and as India stood firm on Kashmir and warned America not to be duped again by an ally then allegedly showing its true pro-Peking colors, both the stability of the subcontinent and American security interests there stood in peril. With a nuclear-armed India, the consequences for the subcontinental triangle might well be explosive.

Bilateral Arrangements: Japan and Australia

Even with some progress toward a nonproliferation treaty, the United States will still have to consider extending nuclear guarantees to its allies and creating joint nuclear forces of some sort. Given the political fragmentation of the area, a multilateral arrangement on a regional basis appears beyond reach in the near future, just as it has been for the better organized Europeans. If the United States is to proceed in an individual, bilateral fashion, the most crucial component will be its policy toward Japan. Japan is the Asian state with the greatest capacity to produce modern weapons; it is also physically the most exposed state, with numerous cities vulnerable to Chinese thermonuclear threats. Japan alone has suffered from nuclear warfare and might, therefore, be even more sensitive than other states to carefully manipulated nuclear blackmail. Tokyo's problem is compounded by the strong popular revulsion against acquiring such weapons, again because of the country's horrible experience.[35] Yet if Japan lacks a deterrent when Peking gains the capacity to attack the home islands, the consequences might be politically disastrous.

As China moves steadily along the path to nuclear power, Japan might threaten to match it with a graded series of responses—either by itself or in conjunction with Washington—in weapons production, stationing, and control. It is possible that inept diplomacy on Peking's part will drive Japan into some type of nuclear alliance with the United States, just as Soviet policy in the early 1950s left the three Western allies with no alternative but to bring West Germany into NATO and eventually into the alliance's nuclear defense system. At this point, Japan could offer to halt its nuclear involvement if China did the same.[36] However a protracted process might be too difficult for the Japanese government to sustain—given the hostile domestic response it would arouse—in a contest of wills with the implacable Chinese. In fact, in view of China's global ambitions and belief that the United States is its primary enemy, Peking would hardly agree to quit the race merely to keep a neighboring rival from joining the club. For this would consign China to the lesser category of a regional power, and at this level, it would find itself balanced and blocked by Japan.

Would Japan be willing to avoid any participation in nuclear armament? Would it settle for a nuclear-free zone that allowed China to develop nuclear weapons but prevented their effective deployment against the home islands? Such a solution seems ruled out because of the improbability of such a sweeping Chinese concession and of obtaining the requisite Soviet participation, if not a Soviet guarantee. From the American viewpoint, a treaty that removed all nuclear weapons from the area around Japan while leaving the two great Communist states in possession of such arms would undermine Japan's security and diplomatic position.[37] If it did come to pass, the pact would require a counterconcession that America would have the right to remain in or return to the area of Japanese home waters if the situation so required. Tensions between Washington and Tokyo could mount rapidly under such conditions. The American nuclear withdrawal might be interpreted as a sign of weakness, casting doubt upon its return in case of future Japanese need. Similarly, Washington might consider that a defenseless Japan would lack the capacity to call for this help in a crisis.

Because of strong foreign and domestic antagonism to Tokyo's acquisition of nuclear weapons, Peking can readily reject Japanese proposals that would restrict Chinese nuclear power. Yet it would be dangerous for the United States to let Japan's nuclear status drift too long. Illogical as it might seem to us, Japan's vulnerability, combined with repeated Washington-Peking crises in distant lands, might lead it to a groundswell of neutralism against foreign entanglements and move to abrogate the defense treaty after 1970.

Assuming Japan's desire to sustain the alliance,[38] a substantial and organized political effort behind this desire, and a wish to reach some accord with Washington on nuclear affairs, the Tokyo government might find that a naval bilateral nuclear force (BLF) best suits Japan's needs. For all its defects in European eyes, the proposed multilateral force (MLF) had certain advantages. Being based at sea, it would not have presented a nearby land target for enemy missiles. It provided strategic weapons for the theater that the United States could not withdraw unilaterally, as it could with SAC planes. Washington retained a veto on its of force; though this offended the French, the other European powers approved of this control because it guaranteed that another signatory could not trigger the force.[39] In a BLF arrangement, a double veto could satisfy both partners and relieve the fears of others that Japan would gain a strategic force of its own. Also being sea-based, the BLF would give Japan some nuclear security by guaranteeing the presence of atomic weapons that would not act as a magnet for retaliatory or pre-emptive strikes on Japanese soil. The accord could also provide restrictions on the operations of this force so as to protect Japan against involvement in distant conflicts.

Thus a joint combat element would be earmarked for Japanese security, as a deterrent pointed directly at China. Combined planning, an equal Japanese voice in the deployment of this sizable force, and a dual veto could simultaneously enhance Japanese responsibility and the credibility of the American guarantee. The chief question for Japan is whether any force not wholly under sovereign control can be sufficiently reliable. Evidently the Japanese feel, as do most Europeans, that Washington is a reliable ally. They, too, have rejected the Gaullist notion that one can depend only on sovereign national power in an age of nuclear weapons. In addition, unlike France, Japan lacks the domestic political and diplomatic freedom to carry off a program of its own. If the threat of Chinese nuclear power is real, the bilateral solution offers Japan some control over a nuclear force without incurring the antagonism at home and abroad that a quest for nuclear sovereignty would arouse.

Australia poses fewer problems in that it does not represent a potential threat to its neighbors, is less vulnerable to Chinese power than are the other states, and can count on British as well as American nuclear support. Whereas Britain would be most uneasy at the prospect of any rise in Japanese nuclear power, even of a BLF with American controls, it might be willing to station its nuclear aircraft in Australia or establish a combined force with the Australians if the need arose. However, the major source of support again would be the United States. As we have noted, if the Chinese were to develop an intermediate-range-missile capacity, Australia might see some deterrent value in the stationing of American strategic power in its vast realm.[40] It might be either a bomber or a missile force, or some combination of the two. But the difficulties encountered in Australia in setting up the Exmouth communications center should warn us that political storms could brew during negotiations for such an arrangement. Like Japan prior to the mid-1960s, Australia might find American strategic naval power in the Pacific reassuring, without desiring any combat forces on its own soil. It might favor sharing operational responsibilities in a nuclear sea force with Washington and London in both the Pacific and Indian Oceans.

A far more ambitious approach than either bilateral force would be an MLF with the United States, Japan, and Australia at its core, and perhaps including other interested Pacific allies. Such an arrangement would be extremely difficult to achieve, though its great diplomatic value would make the effort worthwhile. It would blunt the image fostered by China of a "militaristic" Japan allegedly possessing nuclear weapons under a BLF arrangement. And it would help to counter the lack of cohesion among the allies, each of which considers its own problems in isolation from the others, and almost exclusively in terms of its relationship with the United States. Yet it is this pervasive fragmentation that makes an MLF so unlikely from the outset. It is, on the whole, unwise to expect that the increased dangers associated with nuclear weapons will resolve difficulties and antagonisms that have persisted in the face of what America has long considered an overwhelming common danger.

Great-Power Guarantees for the Indian Subcontinent

Most difficult of all is the problem of the subcontinent, where the Indian-Pakistani hostility makes any move in the direction of nuclear weapons by one power appear a direct threat to the other.

Rather than serve as a force for conciliation, this new element now presents a grave danger. Its appearance on the subcontinent might cause untold diplomatic hardships; yet its absence might make India feel that it is drifting into an intolerable security position. How can this dilemma be resolved short of having both India and Pakistan acquire their own nuclear weapons and engage in a dangerous contest that might involve China and other powers?

One possible solution, again, is a unilateral American guarantee,[41] but such a commitment would encounter several problems. For example, the danger might be ambiguous, with India pleading for support against a particular Chinese threat that the United States did not think serious enough to warrant action. There could also be significant differences over the proper response even if both parties agreed that some response was necessary—with India perhaps calling for pre-emptive threats or operations and Washington considering such steps as precipitate. Or there might be uncertainty as to which is the aggressor, as the Indian-Pakistani border war of 1965 demonstrated. In a hypothetical similar clash in the future, Pakistan might invoke Chinese nuclear protection, leading India to invoke the American guarantee against both opponents. Finally, India might calculate that it is paying too high a price for such uncertain support, especially if it feels itself pressured by the superpowers to concede on the Kashmir issue, or if it concludes that a settlement on Kashmir has become a *quid pro quo* for nuclear protection.

Even from the American perspective, a straightforward guarantee to India would pose difficulties. It would require specific assurances of some sort to gain credence. But this would further extend American obligations and commitments, in all likelihood without compensating defense arrangements to reduce the strain of the additional undertaking. The two most crucial requirements are an Indian *rapprochement* with Pakistan and an agreement on prepositioning the strength that Washington considers essential to deter or ward off a blow. Otherwise, this enormous strategic burden would obligate the United States to operate at a very high level on the scale of violence, with minimal opportunities to employ the diplomatic and military tactics of deterrence and gradual escalation. Under present arrangements, Washington would have to operate from an unfavorable "distant containment" posture that relies upon bases and vessels in the Indian Ocean.

In the wake of additional American demonstrations of support for its greatest enemy, Pakistan would drift closer to China. It does not feel itself threatened by Peking and complains that, by offering help to India, the United States would dilute the value of the Chinese threat as a lever for prying a favorable Kashmiri settlement from India. The argument that America's offer of protection would deter New Delhi from producing its own weapons would have little effect on Pakistani sentiments.

If India, in turn, concluded that some specific accords, however "informal or technical," are required to make the guarantee durable and reliable, it too would face grave problems. For such arrangements would fly squarely in the face of the entire concept of nonalignment, which comprises India's very birthright and the *raison d'être* of its foreign policy. So deep is this basic outlook held by the Indian polity, so contemptuous has New Delhi been of all who "joined the Cold War," and so important is nonalignment as a badge of sovereign independence and anticolonialism that any step away from this position would seem a desperate act of last resort. Furthermore, despite New Delhi's fall as a leader of the underdeveloped world in recent years, it still hopes to recoup lost ground. This would be rendered extremely difficult for a huge state that had to depend upon Washington for protection against a fellow Asian nation.

Finally, a unilateral American tie would seriously strain Indian relations with the Soviet Union. Indian neutrality is much more than the cornerstone of Moscow's policy toward the subcontinent. As the largest and most important neutral state in the world, India is the prime exemplar of what the Soviets consider the proper emerging nation—especially in its political orientation, which Moscow anticipates will ultimately be amenable to Soviet-style communism. Today, Soviet military aid and a continuation of the Moscow-Peking split are both crucial factors in India's security planning.[42] The United States might extend a formal nuclear guarantee without provoking a confrontation with Moscow, but follow-up arrangements would appear as "alignment" for India and so constitute a setback for the Soviet Union. On the other hand, should the Soviet Union stop favoring India with material aid and benevolent diplomatic support, India might be inclined to seek a meaningful American guarantee with supporting arrangements. It is, therefore, possible that New Delhi will keep the American option open, if only to maintain some pressure on the Soviet Union to continue on a pro-Indian course.[43]

If a unilateral American commitment, especially one with teeth in it, seems beyond the realm of practical diplomacy today, there is the possibility of the joint Soviet-American guarantee that India has officially sought.[44] This seemingly attractive solution would be extremely difficult to implement. In the first place, it would further widen the Sino-Soviet split and end Moscow's fading hopes of re-unifying the bloc under some compromise arrangement. Such would probably be the case even if the guarantee took a general form, so as to avoid provoking the Chinese by singling out India for protection. For such a sweeping undertaking of the superpowers, especially if tied to further arms-control accords, would have the same significance to the Chinese as the test-ban treaty. It would clearly imply a superpower *détente*, repudiation of the Chinese view of world revolution, and a firm commitment to isolate Peking diplomatically from both the industrial and underdeveloped worlds. Even without the burdensome Vietnamese crisis and its long-run effects, it is doubtful whether Khrushchev's successors are prepared to take such a dramatic step, however, attractive it may appear to New Delhi.

Washington and Moscow might extend a less significant offer, in the form of separate but parallel assurances to India. This might generate fewer political and ideological difficulties, but it would still harm Soviet-Chinese relations markedly. One might also imagine a Communist uprising in India being suppressed by New Delhi's armed forces while Peking tried to support its co-believers with material support (if near the Chinese border) or by military threats, nuclear or otherwise. It is difficult to envisage an effective Soviet guarantee of Indian security in such circumstances without a dra-matic change in Moscow's diplomatic and ideological position oc-curring beforehand. Thus far the Russians have flatly refused to make an outright unilateral commitment, though professing a strong desire to maintain close relations with New Delhi.

In January 1966, Premier Kosygin merely proposed—in connec-tion with a nonproliferation treaty—that the nuclear powers prom-ise not to use nuclear weapons against have-not states. However, should China still refuse to become a party to this arms-control agreement while India accepted a have-not status in the absence of a guarantee, New Delhi might even be worse off than before. In view of the Soviet refusal to extend any kind of guarantee of protection against attack, both Washington and New Delhi found the Kosygin proposal inadequate.

For the United States, even a tacit arrangement with Moscow to protect India would have the disadvantage of alienating Pakistan and perhaps driving it closer to China than would a unilateral American assurance to the entire subcontinent. Moreover, the problem of implementing a two-power guarantee, even if the Soviets were receptive, might cause concern in New Delhi.[45] The Russians might offer assurances in the least precise manner possible, in the form of a diplomatic guarantee that lacked specific military undertakings.[46] In this way, they could hope to reap political benefits without undue costs. But how would such a deterrent fare in a crisis—would it be credible enough to give the Chinese pause? And even if the Russian offer were specific, would India need the concurrence of both guarantors to make their commitments effective? If so, this arrangement might seem very palatable diplomatically and have the appearance of a valid undertaking. Yet in the actual moment of crisis, it could prove far less reliable than a simple American undertaking.

A British Guarantee

One way out of the dilemma is a British guarantee. With a nuclear force more formidable than all but the superpowers, Britain has indicated on several occasions its awareness of the need to stand by its Commonwealth obligations. It helped three East African states confronted with mutiny in January 1964. It took forceful action to defend Malaysia against Indonesia. More directly, the Labour government realized when it took office in 1964 that it would have to retain at least one wing of V-bombers under national control for the protection of India. It thereupon modified its earlier offer to internationalize its nuclear arms under NATO and so strengthened Britain's credibility as an independent guarantor.[47] With the development of the Polaris capability under the 1962 Nassau agreement, Britain could have a wide-ranging effective deterrent force during the 1970s, as well. Presumably the United States would waive any restrictions implied in that agreement on the sovereign use of the Polaris force to protect India against China. Moreover, British arms could threaten China without being subjected to a serious counterdanger in turn, until Peking developed an ICBM that could reach Europe—probably not until late in the 1970s.

In this way, without totally endangering its neutrality, India could fall back on the "traditional" Commonwealth protection. Neither Washington nor Moscow need become unduly embroiled with their errant Asian allies, and Britain could take pride in using its expensive force in a constructive manner.

However, the negative aspects of this proposal also appear formidable. While not as blatant an involvement in the Cold War as an American guarantee (especially if the British guarantee had Russian blessings), such a move on India's part would demonstrate that it was not and would not become China's equal. It would be most difficult for India to live down dependence on its old imperial ruler for protection.[48] Whatever diplomatic benefits India derived from self-restraint in testing would be more than wiped out by the grievous loss in prestige signified by this arrangement.

For Britain, the costs in Commonwealth and subcontinental diplomacy would be even higher. Pakistan would turn its ire against London, probably without coming closer to Washington, which it would suspect of sponsoring or sustaining this arrangement. In recent years, British-Pakistani relations have been good, and London does not want to come down squarely on the side of either of the two states of the subcontinent, for fear of alienating the other. Such a choice could disrupt the Commonwealth and deprive Britain of its already limited capacity to advocate a compromise settlement in Kashmir. Britain's slowness to support American proposals to aid India after 1962 reflects this caution. After the first sum of $60 million from all Commonwealth sources, London concluded that further substantial installments would inflame Pakistan to such an extent that, on balance, they would do the subcontinent more harm than good. Britain's military aid programs to India, though substantial, have been colored by that concern ever since. In other words, the Pakistani problem would persist even if the Anglo-American powers shared the burden of responsibility.

In addition, the sheer cost of sustaining this commitment over a long period of years must be appalling to a government now confronted by an excess of military responsibilities—for strategic defense of the homeland, the Army of the Rhine, and conventional and guerrilla confrontations east of Suez. As a concrete example, Britain may require both a Polaris force to serve general security needs and a V-bomber command to protect India. This would add considerably to the burden of the defense budget, especially if both forces require modernization in a few years and costly replacement over the long haul. By 1980, a possible Chinese capacity to threaten Britain with missiles would raise serious questions about the credibility of a British deterrent.

Furthermore, although a British guarantee might stop proliferation in India, Britain's ability and will to affect this issue would simply underline the value of an independent national nuclear force. For it gives Britain freedom of choice in an important matter and generally allows the Western states greater diplomatic flexibility. This issue casts grave doubts on Britain's ability to pool its nuclear sovereignty in a common European arrangement, unless such a collective body proves willing to engage in nuclear diplomacy on distant continents.

Under present conditions, India could make an arrangement with Britain directly. Yet as the Pakistanis have observed, this guarantee would require American support to have any durability. As at Nassau, the United States would in effect be sponsoring further British developments—technically and financially—in the nuclear field. Both English-speaking powers might then feel more impelled than ever to hedge their offers to integrate national nuclear forces.

India as a Nuclear Power

Although the British route appears the most realistic and attractive among the "outside guarantee" approaches, nevertheless, for the reasons just indicated, India probably could not accept this arrangement without great misgivings, even assuming a continued willingness by the other non-nuclear states to stay out of the nuclear club. Should a satisfactory arms-control agreement prove unattainable, India would probably feel impelled to produce nuclear weapons for a number of motives: its fear of and antagonism to China as a neighboring national state, its own great size and capacity, its aspirations as a force in world diplomacy, the inevitable power comparison with China, and its desire to preserve true neutrality.

Since India, at least at the outset, is Asia's only neutral with the capacity to develop nuclear armament, it could rationalize its endeavor as a means of reasserting neutralist influence in international affairs generally, as well as in specific arms control negotiations. But India too has obstacles to overcome if it is to develop its own weapons. First there is the intense repugnance felt by Indians toward testing, the weapons themselves, and their use in war. It would be very painful for New Delhi to bear the onus of breaking the nonproliferation barrier and providing, by its example, the marginal incentive and favorable conditions for others—not the least, Japan—to follow.[49] In seeking a compromise between these considerations and national security needs, India might accept a temporary foreign guarantee, pending final efforts to gain permanent protection (superpower guarantees combined with serious arms-control pacts). In the interim, the country might proceed with all steps preliminary to producing a weapon. Preparing its public opinion for the development, India could then, if necessary, acquire its own weapons—hopefully by the time China develops a delivery system—with the guarantee phasing out at the proper time.

Any Indian quest for its own weapons will create major budgetary strains on a country that has encountered great difficulty in strengthening and rearming its conventional forces ever since the 1962 invasion.[50] British, French, and Chinese experience demonstrate that initial estimates of the cost and time involved are invariably overoptimistic.[51] Over the long term, there are also the formidable expenses of maintenance and modernization.

In addition, an Indian capability will drive Pakistan to great extremes—in seeking its own weapons, stationing foreign nuclear weapons on its soil, or making some joint arrangement with a foreign power, even China—if it fails to gain satisfaction from the United States. The increased tension between the two states will make it more difficult than ever for Washington and London to extend other forms of military assistance to both. Pakistan employed American tanks in the Rann of Cutch in the spring of 1965, and both sides made important use of American military equipment in the summer war later that year. In a nuclear situation, it is hard to see how any power could put confidence in a pledge that military aid would be used only against a Communist aggressor. If India should get a nuclear force, therefore, the United States might have to make major concessions to Pakistan or run the risk that Peking would gain an ally. Thus for New Delhi, the price may be a nuclear force across the border, a deeper Pakistani tie with Washington, or a dangerous Pakistani alignment (possibly with nuclear aspects) with Peking.

Yet what is India to do? It could rely on conventional aid from London, Washington, and Moscow—and the diplomatic significance this help conveys—up to a point. It might temporize for a while and then decide that ultimate security lies in its own nuclear force. The suggestion has been made that India is now developing nuclear devices but is refraining from testing immediately.[52] After a few years, in the absence of an arms accord and some control over

Chinese nuclear power, India could then swing into a testing and production program with little loss of time.[53] Meanwhile, this policy could increase the pressure on the present nuclear powers to reach an accord, or at least induce the original three to provide the guarantees required to make India's own contribution to proliferation unnecessary. To repeat, this would comprise a momentous departure in Soviet diplomacy away from "bloc unity" and amount to a resurgence of the Moscow-Washington *détente*. India cannot count on this happening, and may feel compelled to develop a modest tactical nuclear deterrent with a capacity to strike at China. But if it is to prepare its own nuclear force, it must also take significant steps to terminate the Pakistani dispute on generous terms. In fact, any state (e.g., Britain) that helps India in the diplomatic arena or in acquiring weapons might make such a settlement an important—if not controlling—condition of assistance. As matters now stand, India's foreign policy comprises objectives—Kashmir, nonalignment, security against China, and opposition to nuclear weapons—whose pursuit involves greater tensions. Merely to sustain this program, let alone make adjustments that New Delhi deems necessary for its security, will require a radical reordering of priorities, modifications of beliefs, and sacrifices of some goals.

Concluding Observations

A discussion of proliferation in Asia as a path to nuclear security against China must necessarily be inconclusive. Unquestionably, proliferation presents serious dangers and problems. But it appears unwise for the United States to expend enormous diplomatic efforts, without significant cooperation by other nuclear powers, in resisting the emergence of additional national forces. It might even prove skillful enough to use the problem of proliferation to further American policy objectives, including arms control. Perhaps the possibility of new national nuclear forces, combined with an improved American security position in Asia, will induce the Chinese to compromises on this and other issues. Or the nuclear question might enable the United States to reduce the fragmentation and isolation of its alliances, perhaps even providing a rationale for a bond between New Delhi and Tokyo. American policies should be as consistent as possible with the cultivation of these developments, even if their prospects do not appear very promising at present.

Today, the best hope for preserving the security of China's neighbors without proliferation probably rests in a series of bilateral accords that would give U.S. allies unequivocal guarantees and afford them a greater role in developing joint nuclear policy. But from the outset the United States should candidly recognize and evaluate the costs and difficulties inherent in such an undertaking. It must expect to be drawn into a variety of crises and find its reliability constantly questioned by allies who may be quite wobbly in their own determination to hold fast against Chinese probes. Many pressures among non-Communist states will continue, putting a great strain on U.S. diplomacy, especially when two antagonists both enjoy American nuclear guarantees. An ally may well believe that its abstention from nuclear weapons should command a special price—such as support for foreign policy goals that the ally considers vital but that the United States has no interest in sponsoring. Moreover, nuclear proliferation may occur in any event if India decides that this is the only path to its security, since it will not terminate its nonalignment or make major concessions to Pakistan.

If the United States does make bilateral accords, each ally will want to share control over any portion of the American nuclear force with which it is directly involved. As in the European theater, such arrangements would be acceptable as long as the United States also had a substantial strategic force under its own control in the area. The equivalent of SAC forces in station in Europe in the late 1950s would be a sizeable Polaris contingent in the Pacific and Indian Oceans. The combination of tied and unassigned American nuclear forces would ensure the availability of adequate power along all the compartments of the Asian defense perimeter in time of crisis.

Under this arrangement, each Asian participant might see little value in any bilateral accords in the area, apart from the one in which it is involved. However, focusing on the particular threats to its own homeland, a given state may find its crucial margin of safety in (1) the general American presence in the region, (2) the fact that forces are specifically allocated under the bilateral pact, and (3) the knowledge that its government has a voice in the deployment and use of a portion of these forces.

The United States would then remain the major security prop in the region, probably more so than ever. The danger of fragmentation would continue high because a state with a bilateral accord that its leaders considered reliable would hardly wish to become involved in the dangerous security crises of other states—especially when it refused to do so before China became a nuclear power. Hence, the more general American security perspective and American political strategy in dealing with China become more important than ever.

PART V

Patterns and Problems
for American Security Policy
in Asia

CHAPTER SIXTEEN

Allies, Neutrals, and
American Security Policy

Although China's introduction of the nuclear factor into the Asian situation is a hard and irrevocable fact, its repercussions remain highly speculative. Whether the United States should (or, in fact, can) control the proliferation of nuclear power in Asia, whether other nuclear powers will support U.S. initiatives on arms control or advance conflicting alternatives, what diplomatic arrangements will best secure the non-Communist nations against a nuclear China's pressures—all these critical questions are posed by the nuclear factor. Yet satisfactory solutions have eluded us since China unveiled its nuclear potential in 1964.

Because of its past and present involvements and its abundant resources, America will continue to be a pivotal power in the nuclear Asia. But in light of this new factor in Asia, the United States must contemplate a number of preparatory moves to strengthen the American base system, especially forward positions and installations. Since its allies may fear that modifications desired by Washington stem from weakness, such proposals may increase the sense of insecurity the bomb has already engendered. However sound the technical reasons for revising the base structure, the United States will find it essential to demonstrate in other ways a high and continuing capacity to protect these states if it is to benefit from such shifts in its military posture. Similarly, the nature of the American conventional posture acquires great significance. Does it need augmentation in the area around China, or would the United States be able to reduce its extended conventional forces, since the new Chinese capacity would, ironically, make it easier and more credible to rely on a nuclear retaliatory threat? But all such questions, of course,

311

depend on realistic evaluations of China's competence as a nuclear power.

Whatever changes are made in its security policies—as a result of the nuclear factor or of changes in regional or world relationships—clearly the United States will have a broad and sustained military commitment for the foreseeable future. The substantive policies the United States adopts in future crises and the changes it makes in force deployment are of the utmost importance, as are the clarity and persuasiveness of its explanations, the timing of military actions, the political arrangements that accompany them, and the extent to which they are integrated with long-range diplomatic expectations. The degree of support that the United States extends to its alliances will be closely observed, since these arrangements have been under considerable strain from their inception. The key considerations here remain as interdependent and potentially contradictory as in past years. American efforts against Chinese hegemony must remain credible.[1] Yet each ally also wants American policies to entail as little risk to itself as possible. American willingness to hold fast and yet operate prudently under mounting Chinese pressure will require great self-control in domestic politics.[2] In this vital field, the major Asian allies could make a significant contribution by supporting more active defense policies, but they have thus far made little attempt to convince the American public that its burdens are being shared by Asian nations themselves. For example, the Asians do not appreciate the degree to which their isolationist attitudes strengthen the extremists who hold parallel views in the United States. And allies whose very security rests on U.S. bases and installations, also essential for an adequate American military policy, treat these facilities as bargaining counters.

Moreover, there is no reason to assume that the United States will enjoy greater leeway than in the past in changing its base systems or radically altering the size, mix and location of its forces. The problems that existed before 1964 will be compounded many times by the injection of nuclear considerations. Since there will be a higher premium on demonstrating an American ability to perceive threats from an Asian vantage point, political considerations will impinge on straightforward military analyses more heavily than ever before. As a result, the United States may often be compelled to allocate precious military resources for low-priority objectives, such as providing extensive and costly defense arrangements to protect major

Asian population centers as China develops a short- and medium-range missile capability.

In some military calculations, an increase in the conventional capability of the United States in the Far East might represent an inefficient deflection of strength for purely political purposes. Combat elements on station might in addition require expensive preparations to assure the availability of reserve components, transport mobility, pre-positioned supplies, adequate staging and operations bases, and diplomatic clearances. Even a prudent, conventional commitment can lead to further difficulties, despite the fact that it would stem from an Asian desire to avoid the dilemma of a holocaust-or-surrender confrontation. American policy will have to combine proofs of proportionate and effective response with assurances that these do not reflect a fear of nuclear commitment and involvement. As Chinese power grows, our European experience tells us, this balancing effort will tax our skills and strain the more rudimentary Asian alliance system.

If the United States should also decide to maintain a stronger nuclear presence and a more open emphasis on existing atomic forces, it would be departing from the low-key approach of the past that stemmed from a vivid awareness of how deeply Asians fear such weapons. The risks, as well as the advantages, this change of policy would involve must be recognized. For its own political protection, the United States should simultaneously encourage an airing of the contradictory attitudes held in allied lands regarding the role of nuclear weapons. If this is done well in advance of actual Chinese nuclear pressure, it can measurably reduce the impact of threats emanating from Peking. Serious Asian consideration of the value of proliferation would in itself indicate a widespread awareness of the need to rely to some extent on nuclear strength for defense. Further, Washington must constantly gear its actions to a primary political task and make it clear that the main threat comes from China, not the United States. Chinese propaganda has been very skillful in the past, and once Peking has nuclear weapons, it will undoubtedly present an even greater challenge to our intellectual resources.

Adjusting American Security Arrangements

As we have noted, the fact that America's security alliances constitute a somewhat disparate mosaic yields an unexpected dividend.

It affords us adaptability and flexibility. With this additive, the United States should be able to reshape its alliance policy to deal with an unprecedented Chinese nuclear threat. Nevertheless, we have also seen, considerable difficulties arise from any effort to alter the composition of forces, especially when missile forces are proposed as manpower substitutes—for example, in Thailand or South Korea —or when such weapons are introduced into a state like Japan, where the domestic political environment is hostile to them.

Along somewhat different lines, the United States will have to overcome stubborn obstacles if it is to provide India with an adequate air defense system when China's missile striking force becomes a reality. With or without a security treaty, for India to have effective on-the-ground protection, an elaborate network of installations [3] will be needed. This may mean that foreign troops will have to be stationed at key points, at least in the early uncertain years. Beyond this, nuclear antiballistic missiles and additional bases ready for occupation in emergencies may increase India's dependence on foreign power. Since a sweeping arrangement covering all these aspects probably lies beyond the diplomatic range of Washington and New Delhi, India may seek stopgap arrangements with all possible sources, including the Soviet Union. [4] If the present pattern of Russian aid is any guide, Moscow might provide India with a modest antimissile system to defend some major cities but not the massive defense net that India seeks. The limited—though substantial—degree of Russian aid may lead India to further American negotiations, which would then be more tangled than ever because of the security problems created by the attempt to commingle sophisticated weapons.

In the attempt to reduce allied fears for their physical security, the United States encounters in accute form the issue of where to draw the line in requests for help that are considered unwarranted. Should Washington, for example, commit itself to provide—by stationing or earmarking—a separate air defense system for each ally? This would mean pinning down a large number of combat units. Even contingent promises invite trouble, for disputes could easily arise over the seriousness of a particular emergency. An elaboration of the present arrangement seems the most logical solution: to place adequate forces in the theater with regional assignments, without tying them to a specific location or function but keeping them on call as needed. By means of negotiations for more specific arrangements, Washington could involve its allies in one another's air defense problems or operations. This might lead to an integration of some national air defense systems, or at least move states a step away from strategic isolationism, which would be intensified by any series of bilateral blanket defense commitments. In general, the United States can work closely with any willing ally in such matters as evaluating Chinese power and intentions, formulating joint defense strategy, and agreeing to major courses of related political actions. It could make the degree of shared security confidences and undertakings contingent upon progress in these broader areas of cooperation.

America must be wary of extending additional promises to respond to Chinese threats without providing matching capabilities. Moreover, an ally that receives assurances without assuming obligations might take U.S. aid for granted and use it as a shield for the pursuit of objectives harmful to U.S. security interests. Or an ally might harbor military estimates or ambitions that Washington would consider implausible or dangerous, as the South Koreans and Chinese Nationalists did in the mid-1950s. Washington could try to negate the impact of these views by imposing precise specifications on its commitment, but the result might be to damage relations with the ally in question or to inhibit flexibility and initiative in security policy.

The United States lacks a free hand to make its commitments as selective as it might wish because any withdrawal from an existing alliance obligation—especially once China can pose a nuclear threat —may appear as a cowardly betrayal. In many instances, the United States could have good cause for disengaging from security obligations. To cite a few hypothetical justifications we might claim: Saigon's unwillingness to set its political house in order, Pakistan's adoption of a radical pro-Peking policy, or Nationalist China's assuming a new and dangerous posture. Under certain circumstances, Washington probably could present disengagement in a favorable light to other lands. Still, counterarguments are inevitable, and they would undoubtedly be to the security detriment of all.

In the end, the fear and confusion generated by withdrawal would probably outweigh the advantage gained in teaching a lesson to a refractory ally. Peking might become more willing to gamble than before. Though little can be said for persevering in unwise or obsolescent alliances—especially as more important obligations grow more taxing—it may be best to allow such ties to atrophy gradually, function by function, as a natural consequence of specific developments, without principled statements of general intent or policy.

Disengagement of this type, combined with a steadfast refusal to undertake a blanket commitment to the entire region, is not intended and need not appear as a preliminary to an American withdrawal. If handled subtly, such a policy might enable Washington to establish even closer ties with certain allies, to which it might offer deeper commitments to protect their vital interests in return for specific concessions that enhance its capacity to act in defense of the region. The United States should be willing to discuss with individual neutralist states any mutually beneficial security relationship, on a temporary or long-term basis. On the other hand, a public American refusal to undertake a protective role without specific understandings could be as harmful as breaking an alliance for demonstration effect. Apart from appearing to be a clumsy effort to align neutrals on American terms, it would frighten the small vulnerable states such as Burma, Ceylon, and Cambodia without bringing compensating benefits.

Clearly, the problems of the pre-nuclear era in Asia remain, and will certainly intensify as China's power grows. The scope of American involvement, problems of composition and distribution of forces, the security fragmentation of the area, fragile alliances, conflicts of interest with out allies, Asians' fears for their physical security, and Asians' concern lest America do too much or too little highlight a list of issues that seemingly have an enduring life of their own.

Against this background, Peking will redouble its efforts to blame all confrontations on "Washington war maniacs" and to treat every American effort at conciliation as a sign of weakness and unreliability. For example, a Chinese analysis of American policy in the fall of 1964 referred to the August naval assaults in the Gulf of Tonkin as President Johnson's "greatest war adventures," which nonetheless failed "to ease his difficult situation." The fact that no further military ventures occurred soon after did not appear to the Chinese as a gesture for peace. Rather, as *Jen-min Jih-pao* noted, "the President again resorts to deceptive peace tactics, clear evidence that U.S. imperialism is in a helpless predicament."

In appraising security patterns and potentialities, we must proceed with the clear realization that there is no prospect for a regional mutual security organization. Of course, there have been a few tentative moves toward reviving regionalism, and the Association of Southeast Asian Nations has some security value because it includes

Singapore and Indonesia, as well as the Phillipines, Thailand and Malaysia. The Asian and Pacific Council, formed in 1966 with a membership that included states of both northeast and southeast Asia, should hold promise of development in the fields of political and economic cooperation but gave little indication of making much progress in security matters, especially because of Japan's desire to avoid involvement in cooperative efforts of this sort. The Manila Conference in October 1966 was another indication of the continent's emerging awareness that its nations must assume responsibility for some of their regional problems, but it was a meeting dominated by the United States. In the absence of a viable area-wide movement in Asia, the best United States option appears to lie in revising existing alliance structures to meet the problems of the future.

Consequently, we shall return now to our earlier scheme and again make a tour of Asia in an arc from the Western Pacific, through Southeast Asia, to the Indian subcontinent. But to accord with the realities of the 1960s and 1970s, rather than those of the 1950s, we shall occasionally depart from our previous itinerary.

The Western Pacific

Since Japan remains the major bastion of power in the Far West, the value of any U.S. approach depends heavily upon results in this critical sector. At present, our diplomatic security relations with Japan are considerably healthier than those with the countries in the Indian Ocean area. The basic Japanese alliance is intact and has not suffered erosion, as has the tie with Pakistan. Moreover, with an American military position on the home islands and security arrangements with nearby South Korea and Taiwan, Japan is within sight of a coherent security system for itself and the Western Pacific, even though the structure is politically fragmented. Apart from the political developments in Japan proper, existing problems center upon the weapons and base arrangements, the future of Okinawa, and Japan's role as a subregional power.

In our discussion of nuclear weapons we concluded that as a price for continuing the alliance, Japan may desire some nuclear weapons on call as security against possible Chinese nuclear blackmail. Yet Japan does not want to risk being drawn into distant conflicts against its will or to possess a force that might attract attacks or threats of attack. In the solution we discussed earlier—a possible BLF at sea, with Japanese participation but not control—there would remain the question of whether such vessels could use Japanese bases on a restricted or a more general basis. This type of question would provide a test, at the most elementary level, of whether Japan is willing to run any serious risks for its own national defense. The mild popular reaction to the issue of whether Polaris missiles should enter Japanese ports does not throw too much light on the prospects for this bolder undertaking, because these vessels did not carry nuclear warheads.[5] On the other hand, Japanese sailors would comprise a major component of the manpower in a BLF, and Japan would be engaged as part owner of strategic combat vehicles. Under such circumstances, the accomodation of nuclear-armed vessels in Japanese ports would represent a major shift by Japan toward a more active security policy. It would also be a step away from military isolationism since such a force, despite its limited political terms of reference, would have an impact throughout the Western Pacific.

If Japan is willing to go this far, could the United States then also negotiate reduced restrictions over American use of other bases in Japan for the movement of conventional forces? At present, the Japanese government takes refuge in the technicality that departing American combat elements move from Japan to Okinawa and holds that further deployment of these forces to combat zones is of no concern to Japan. But if Japan cannot in practice veto moves to a war zone, what controls actually exist?

The situation on Okinawa itself is an even greater problem. We have already discussed the issue of jurisdictional control and the difficulties the United States would encounter if it agreed to divide its prerogatives with Japan. Another element of pressure is added, of course, by the Chinese nuclear threat to this vulnerable and compact base. If the threat becomes a reality in a few years, the United States will be compelled to provide a credible deterrent in order to neutralize its political impact. If, indeed, Okinawa becomes too exposed to Chinese missiles to be relied on as heavily as in the past, the United States will have to begin systematically reducing its dependence on the island—before the pressure from China becomes manifest. If Tokyo agreed to somewhat greater use of the home islands as a base or transfer point for American conventional forces, creation of a BLF with liberal use of Japanese ports, and a long-term extension of the security treaty, the United States might find a return of jurisdiction over Okinawa an equitable trade-off in security terms. In negotiating the United States could arrange either to retain special military privileges there or have the same use of the island as it would under the more liberal arrangements here proposed for the home islands. All this might place Japan in a far more engaged position than it would like.[6] But if the leadership in Tokyo really wishes to meet the problem of nuclear security, it can reasonably contend that the BLF and the return of Okinawa represent substantial compensation for the country's greater involvement.[7]

In terms of American security costs, Okinawa may be irreplaceable, in that no modified access could serve as well. Yet the arrangement suggested here could be developed in carefully regulated phases [8] and made contingent upon less restricted use of bases in Japan proper. The alternative may be mounting Chinese threats against Okinawa, justified by Peking as a blow against the Western imperialists rather than against fellow Asians. The Japanese in turn might then direct their anguish and antagonism against their ally rather than against China. In view of the island's sensitive role, an early search for diplomatic and military substitutes is very much in order.

A final problem regarding this ally centers on the role it might play in subregional affairs. It is logical to envisage a grouping of states around Japan comprising South Korea, Taiwan, and the Philippines. Japan is strategically located at the center of this complex, has the capacity to afford protection, and could shoulder much of the cost of sustaining their economic development. Unfortunately, this attractive pattern of relationship does not seem attainable in the near future, and if they prove too eager to bring it to pass, American policy-makers may endanger whatever limited opportunities the future may provide.

For the present, the United States must contend with the antagonism still felt toward Japan in the Philippines and the residual hostility of the Koreans, reciprocated to a degree in Japanese public opinion.[9] Taiwan is in a somewhat different situation, since the indigenous population feels sympathetic toward its former rulers and perhaps would see in a diplomatic link with Tokyo an opportunity to escape association with either of the Chinese claimants to the island. However, this merely underlines the massive political obstacle—adamant opposition by both Nationalists and Communists to Taiwanese independence. With regard to this particular issue and regional leadership in general, Japan lacks the will and the military strength to take new initiatives in the face of great-power hostility. Before Japan can become an active force in security matters, it must overcome the specific difficulties that infect relations with its neighbors, develop military strength capable of being projected to these lands (which in itself would provoke a tremendous domestic political dispute), and resolve to face the diplomatic wrath and reprisals of Russia and Red China. In these unlikely circumstances, the United States would still face the task of convincing the former victims that Japanese power can be contained within such an alliance framework in such a way that the protection would not be as dangerous as the threat.[10]

The challenges to Japan and its neighbors are admittedly serious, and we must always be prepared for failure and the dangers that would follow in its wake. Still, the gravity of this situation does not match that of Southcentral Asia, where we see our only alliance in danger of disintegration, where we have no land or offshore military presence, and where the awful prospect of continued tension between India and Pakistan make the development of a subregional system out of the question for the indefinite future.

The Indian Ocean Area and Australia

Given such a difficult situation, the United States has found it expedient to fall back upon a military position in the Indian Ocean to backstop its security position in Southcentral Asia. Here, it is assisted by Britain which retains a military presence in the Indian Ocean area, and which in 1965 made a joint agreement with the United States to establish a fueling and communications center at Diego Garcia. Though this new undertaking brings a portion of America's strength to bear in the region, it does not provide the capacity to render early and effective assistance to India and Pakistan in case of aggression, let alone establish the presence that could deter an attack. Under these unfavorable circumstances, advocates of a substantial force-in-being in the Indian Ocean argue that it could provide a rally point for others in time of need and enable the United States to develop an effective security position even during a crisis.

Since its border war with China, India has muted its earlier opposition to an American military presence in the Indian Ocean. But precisely because an American presence might bolster India's position against China, Pakistan challenges any American deployment in this area and musters neutralist support against the U.S. plan. This is but one example of how Pakistan's anti-Indian campaign contributes measurably to the further fragmentation of the security system of the area south of China.

A defense posture based on the Indian Ocean suffers as well from the dangers of territorial overextension. With the scope of its assignment ranging from East Africa to Malaysia, a modest U.S. deployment may find itself too thinly spread, and evoke strong pressures for augmentation. And for the near future, it will lack the physical power and political assets required to provide the core of combat strength—especially in conventional arms—upon which to build a viable defense system.

We may be able to perceive the benefits and drawbacks of such an involvement more readily if we look at it from the perspective of an American-Commonwealth relationship. Australia's fear of a Soviet naval penetration of South Asian waters reached new heights when Indonesia seemed bound for the Communist camp, before the anti-leftist developments of 1965. Australia also dreads the extension of Chinese power to the shores of southern Asia.[11] During the early 1960s, Indonesia itself emerged as a threat when it obtained West New Guinea through a power play that jolted Australia considerably. More intent than ever to secure the periphery of the Asian mainland as the diplomatic and defense position of Malaysia and Singapore weakened, Australia naturally welcomed new force deployments in its environs.

The security system of this sector, resting on Australia and Indian Ocean island bases and using U.S.–U.K.–ANZ forces of moderate strength, must still have its ultimate form and purpose clarified. At present, the United States is directly involved through its communications bases at Exmouth in Australia and Diego Garcia and whatever naval strength it deploys in the Indian Ocean. It also has a major security position in Thailand,[12] and presumably these bases could legally be employed on behalf of Bangkok's SEATO allies, Australia and Pakistan. At present, this seems farfetched in light of Pakistan's near-neutralism, Australia's relative security, and the Thais' traditional reluctance to become engaged in the troubles of distant lands. Yet the American base systems in Japan and the Philippines have played major roles in their respective subregions in the past. A strong American position in Thailand might similarly play an important role in the future of a broad South Asian security system.

Britain, of course, remains very much engaged in Singapore and Malaysia, where it has bases, forces, and security commitments.[13]

However, the bases apparently have limited value, since both Asian states wish to restrict their use to security operations in their own territories.[14] In part, this reflects their attempt to maintain their credentials as neutrals, in the hope that they can persuade their fellow Afro-Asians to "overlook" their extensive security reliance on a former imperial power. At best, Malaysia and Singapore may continue the joint defense systems they projected before the collapse of their federation; but beyond this, the rule still seems to be fragmentation of security arrangements. If there had been any expectation that the Federation of Malaysia, as formed in 1963, would allow British bases there to serve the wider security needs of Southeast Asia, it faded after the ousting of Singapore in 1965.

London has decided to retain its security position east of Suez, but only for the present. Its commitments, however, appear uncertain at best, in view of Egyptian pressure against Britain's base in Aden, the unstable domestic political situation in southern Arabia, the breakup of Malaysia as originally conceived, and the great financial costs to Britain of this distant involvement.[15] The struggle to thwart Indonesia's confrontation required eleven British battalions and reinforced naval and air components. This operation accounted for the major part of British military expenses in Asia, which in turn absorbed one-quarter of Britain's entire defense budget in 1964. The United States places great value on having Britain maintain a presence in southern Asia—to share the defense burden and to prevent the complete political isolation of Washington in Asian defense.[16] Britain's importance to Singapore, its concern for the security of the Indian subcontinent, and its links to Australia remain the vital reasons for this involvement. These engagements have global significance: they provide the basis for France's contention that Britain is not primarily a European power and thus is ineligible for Common Market membership, and they add incentives for Britain to remain an independent nuclear power.

Australia may find the continued presence of Britain helpful in softening the traditionalist sentiment against overdependence on the United States in dealing with growing defense problems and obligations. These evolved from ANZAM in 1949, which coordinated planning with Britain and New Zealand for the defense of Britain's nearby territories, to include ANZUS and SEATO commitments over the next five years, and the acquisition of sovereign control over the Cocos and Christmas Islands in the Indian Ocean still later in the 1950s. Australia's defense efforts rose markedly during the following decade; the military budget of £200 million in 1962 doubled within the next three years. The army planned a rise from 22,700 men to 37,000, and the country adopted a conscription system in 1964. Troop deployments in Northern Australia and New Guinea were strengthened, as Australian troops engaged in combat in Borneo and now in Vietnam.

However reassuring the appearance of Western naval power in the Indian Ocean may be, Australia may also face conflicts of interest with its two great allies. For one thing, it was clear that neither London nor Washington desired to become embroiled in a major conflict with Indonesia,[17] despite a display of military firmness by Britain and political backing by Washington during the confrontation crisis of 1963–65.[18] It is, therefore, quite likely that Canberra will seek at least a stronger interpretation of the ANZUS accord in return for any further agreements to provide bases for America's nuclear deterrent.

Second, both Washington and London may have many security interests in the Indian Ocean outside the eastern section that involves Australia directly. These two powers may expend considerable energy protecting moderately representative governments in East Africa against subversion and rebellion, maintaining a security position in the Persian Gulf, and becoming engaged in the military problems that could emerge from Egyptian policy, Ethiopian-Somalian clashes, and the like. Australia's allies may become even more deeply embroiled in the delicate political decisions on when to intervene in domestic and international problems that seem constantly to beset the western part of the vast Indian Ocean region. To Canberra, this signifies possible dissipation of allied strength in distant lands and poses the threat that Australia may become entangled in areas from which it had disengaged in 1942 when Japan first menaced its security.[19]

Beyond these potential differences, an Anglo-American naval presence in the Indian Ocean raises questions regarding the role of nuclear power. The Exmouth facility will probably enable Polaris submarines to range the Indian Ocean in significant numbers with augmented effectiveness against both Chinese and Russian targets. Should Australia desire to participate in a nuclear defense program in the future, it might do so through combined naval operations or by means of joint control over bombers and missiles stationed on its own soil. However, unlike the case of Japan, in Australia these operations would not be directly responsive to what remains the nation's potentially most immediate problem—a threat from Indonesia that would not necessarily involve either a Communist regime or a nuclear factor.

Still, Australia will clearly benefit from a stronger Anglo-American presence (both nuclear and conventional) in the Indian Ocean. Canberra will (1) gain nuclear protection against possible Chinese threats, centering on Australia's role in the American strategic deterrent system through the Exmouth base; (2) be able to invoke assurances of support against Indonesia as needed; and (3) exploit Britain's role to satisfy its own traditionalists and reduce latent anti-Americanism. Australia may also provide additional resources—a land base or naval participation—to strengthen allied nuclear power should it judge this necessary for its own security, but it is likely to do this only in return for very binding security guarantees.

Small-Vulnerable States: Allies . . .

America's smaller allies in Asia are so scattered and face such divergent problems in the fields of security, domestic politics, and economic development that it is very difficult to generalize about them. Yet apart from the Philippines, they border on, or are extremely close to, the Asian Communist states and three of them (South Korea, Taiwan, and South Vietnam) are politically vulnerable as well, because in various ways they are partitioned. The fifth power, Thailand, grows more vulnerable as the might of the Communists increases in the Indochina area.

General anxiety lies close to the surface, save in the Philippines, about America's determination to retain a strong security position in Asia in the face of rising costs, combat losses, and even danger to itself. Theoretically, the large Asian powers have some capacity to preserve their security if the international environment should change markedly for the worse. The lesser powers, however, cannot fend for themselves; nor does the record of recent years justify reliance upon their larger non-Communist neighbors for effective aid against an aggressor. In a nonpejorative sense of the term, they are client allies of the United States.

All seek American protection against attack from any quarter and chafe under any limitations in the defense commitment, such as a stipulation that the United States will act only against the Communists. By 1965, this particular point had become an academic distinction in all our alliances except the one with Pakistan. Equally important, however, are differences between Washington and an ally in identifying and evaluating a particular threat. Since its own security is directly threatened, an ally is prone to take a more alarmist view than Washington—as the past behavior of Thailand, Nationalist China, and Laos demonstrates. Our Asian partners also become more quickly concerned with security problems in neighboring states and usually urge extensive American countermeasures at an early stage.

Finally, the small allies have proved highly sensitive to changes in American military and economic aid, redeployment of combat elements, and decisions to alter the mix of forces stationed on their soil. Interestingly, this also holds for the injection of additional defense components. The Seventh Fleet off Taiwan, two divisions in Korea, combat bases and weapons in the Philippines, and deployment of forces and use of air bases in Thailand all have encountered such local objections.[20] But the balance sheet has shown greater security benefits to these states in return for increased freedom of maneuver for American forces in the theater. Though a certain degree of dispersion and reduced flexibility in the use of American power is inevitable in such a situation, the United States has used these alliances to form a security chain of surprising cohesion and durability. These links will probably last as long as the United States maintains both a major military position in the area and allied confidence in its determination to defend them.

The smaller states have been blocked from developing more than a very rudimentary system of mutual security by important policy differences, large geographic distances, modest available power, and special national preoccupations. Nevertheless, the smaller allies, feeling their vulnerability more acutely, do make more of an effort to cooperate with one another than do the larger anti-Communist powers. Thailand sent a contingent to fight in Korea and has allowed its territory to become a key base in the wars in Laos and Vietnam. South Korea sent about 45,000 troops to South Vietnam by 1966, and the Philippines expressed its interest in a similar though lesser effort, by dispatching a 2,000-man engineer unit in 1966. Manila permitted America to use bases on Luzon for the Vietnamese War even though, since the United States did not formally place this operation under SEATO auspices, Manila was not technically obliged to do so.

Nationalist China also offered to participate in both Korea and Vietnam, but these proposals were not accepted, chiefly because of the Nationalists' lack of political attraction elsewhere, fears that Peking would gain the initiative to intervene at will in Vietnam for a strong propaganda position, and general concern that Nationalist participation would expand the conflict.[21] Like the other two partitioned states, Nationalist China has vital interests that center on national reunification on its own terms, but neither the United States nor any of its major allies wish to become involved in a struggle for this objective.

A related problem has been that these smaller allied states have engendered scant appeal or respect in the rest of Asia and of the underdeveloped world. The existence of dictatorships at one time or another in Seoul, Taipei, Saigon, and Bangkok also reduced support for these lands in the democratic states of the West, as well. The sluggish economic growth records of South Korea, South Vietnam, and the Philippines during the 1950s also cost them support. Even when progress along democratic lines or in economic development does occur, it evokes little enthusiasm elsewhere. For all its faults, the Philippines has conducted fair presidential elections, with an elected encumbent yet to gain a second victory. In the mid-1960s, following its military coup, Korea restored democratic government while Thailand became considerably less authoritarian after the death of Premier Sarit Thanarat in 1963. Yet these important matters receive scant attention from "world public opinion."

In economic affairs, Taiwan has had an outstanding growth rate, and Thailand, though less spectacular, has made consistent progress. South Korea, too, has made important strides in recent years, even before it began receiving help from Japan. Yet their refusal to espouse a socialist ideology or to follow a neutralist course consistently mars the image of these states in the underdeveloped world. Malaysia—as a limited ally of Britain—found itself in much the same difficulty, unable to win world support against aggression from Indonesia partly because the latter could claim to be a "socialist" neutralist fighting against "neocolonialism." The smaller allies of the United States have learned that neutralism and good relations with the rest of the underdeveloped world are of little value when one's security becomes endangered. They have the experience of India in 1962 very much in mind.

Nevertheless, they are somewhat isolated diplomatically from the main currents of the Afro-Asian world, a matter of some concern for their security as well as their more general political position. In this setting, their military vulnerability and heavy dependence on

America cannot fail to inject tension into their relationship with Washington. The Taipei anti-American riots and the government-inspired anti-American press campaign in Bangkok in 1957–58 [22] should remind us that difficulties have existed from the early years of the alliances.

The proximate causes of friction are many. There may be a major difference over policy, for example, U.S. refusal to support a Nationalist Chinese campaign against the mainland or to maintain a large military presence on the offshore islands. Differences over Laos' domestic and international course were a major source of concern in Bangkok, and U.S. support of Malaysia disturbed the Philippines during the Macapagal administration. Efforts to reduce economic aid to Seoul brought sharp nationalistic rejoinders backed with anti-American sentiments. Both the Philippines and South Korea have repeatedly placed great pressure on Washington for additional assistance of all sorts and made a particularly strong case for compensatory aid in return for military contributions in the Vietnamese War. In Manila, Seoul, and Taipei, the SOFA issue has at various times constituted another sore point.

Authoritarian regimes in states allied to the United States may readily fear American intervention in their domestic political affairs to reshape local politics in accordance with Washington's concept of what will enhance the region's security. The U.S. attitude toward the coup in Vietnam in 1963 and efforts to induce the military leaders in Seoul to restore democratic government after 1961 may give other lands cause for apprehension. At the other extreme, despite criticisms in neutralist states that authoritarian rulers in allied lands are merely American puppets, the United States has repeatedly found that it had a very limited capacity to influence these leaders on issues they considered vital. American respect for the domestic jurisdiction of indigenous regimes frequently enabled them to overcome their utter dependence on American protection in pursuing their objectives. Presidents Rhee of South Korea and Diem of South Vietnam usually adhered to their policy lines not only in domestic affairs, ignoring American efforts to foster reform, but in critical foreign and military matters as well, often in the face of strong American pressure. The same has been, and is, true of Nationalist Chinese President Chiang.

We must expect problems in U.S. relations with client-allies to continue as long as the security situation remains grave. Relations will be especially difficult when a regime's domestic political position is also very vulnerable. Generally, progress will be uneven at best in mitigating the difficulties of dealing with the smaller allies. The fields that seem to offer hope of more rapid results are the development of multilateral cooperation in security affairs and improvement in the international stature of those allies that possess good domestic records. With regard to the second point, for example, the United States could highlight and strengthen elements of ideological identity and similarity of political outlook and experiences among all democratic states of the area. These would be especially meaningful when they cut across neutralist-allied lines. Thus, conferences on party systems, joint evaluations of electoral processes, and meetings of interest groups could prove mutually profitable for Malaysia, India, Ceylon, the Philippines, South Korea, Singapore, and Japan. Economic success in one allied state could serve as a model for investigation by other lands, both allied and neutral.

The United States will have to continue to work patiently to induce its larger and smaller allies to work more closely with one another. It must recognize this as a long-term objective that can come to pass only through extensive American participation in Asian security affairs. Admittedly, this is very difficult to achieve even with a major commitment from Washington, especially since a deeper American involvement may lead these states to follow their own policy lines more vigorously than before. Much hinges on the way in which the United States goes about extending its military undertakings. In any event, a collective defense effort against China without a large American input seems out of the question.

. . . and a Neutral Cambodian Perspective

Though neutralist Indonesia and Ceylon enjoy the benefits of distance and water between them and the Asian Communist powers, Burma and Cambodia are at the very fringe of great-power confrontations. Burma has certain defensive advantages over Cambodia in size, difficulty of terrain, and political isolation from conflict. Nor is there any question of Burma's right to exist as a sovereign entity, free of claims to its territory and interference in its political affairs. Cambodia, however, fears that the Democratic Republic of Vietnam aspires to absorb it and re-create old Indochina—either under Hanoi's direct control, or through a federation of Communist regimes under the leadership of the North Vietnamese party. This central factor, in combination with Prince Sihanouk's flamboyant personality and Cambodia's historic difficulties with South Vietnam and Thailand, prevents Pnompenh from following the Burmese road to neutralist isolationism.[23]

Vietnam, North and South, remains Cambodia's prime source of difficulty. As long as Prince Sihanouk suspects that Hanoi has designs to take over all of Vietnam, he must believe that his country is in vital peril.

A D.R.V. victory in South Vietnam seemed likely after 1961 and convinced Sihanouk that a political link with Washington was worthless. Hence, he threw his diplomatic lot in with Peking, even breaking relations with the United States in May 1965, probably in the hope that China would treat Cambodia as a protégée and protect it against North Vietnam.[24] Nonetheless, pending the outcome of the struggle for Vietnam, Cambodia appeared determined to adhere to neutrality in the war. It also sought to preserve some balance in its position by accepting help from Peking without a large Chinese presence and in retaining a French tie, especially in military assistance. It tries, without success, to prevent Vietnamese belligerents from using its soil. The northeast portion of the country, as well as the Mekong and other waterways that flow from Cambodia to South Vietnam, have proved too difficult to deny to infiltrators.

Cambodia's troubles with Thailand are serious, but among the country's non-Communist neighbors, Saigon presents the most critical problem. Important minorities of Cambodians in Vietnam and of Vietnamese in Cambodia, problems of border trade, and recurrent clashes due to the war have generated a series of dangerous exchanges. Sihanouk cannot get South Vietnam to curtail unfriendly activities on its soil, including the harboring of political enemies, any more than he can induce North Vietnam to accept other demands, such as minority accords.

Cambodia can side with China and still hope for a stalemate in the Vietnamese struggle. Yet its pro-Chinese stance has frequently led to vitriolic propaganda campaigns that have poisoned domestic opinion against the United States and given rise to considerable diplomatic irritation. Pnompenh also emitted frequent criticisms of the U.S. aid program (terminated in November 1963) and consistently supported Chinese foreign policy positions, even before the break in relations with Washington.[25] Prince Sihanouk may feel that if his country's security situation becomes desperate and China does not come to the rescue, he can still turn to the United States. Perhaps to keep this possibility open, and because he is truly determined to follow a neutralist course, the Prince has not allowed his country to be turned into a Communist base.[26] He also maintains an effective security program against such subversion from within.

It has been difficult for the United States to strike a proper balance between retaliation and accommodation in response to Cambodian tactics. Prince Sihanouk's policies have been troublesome, but only marginally so. His quest for the neutralization of Laos, international guarantees of Cambodia's integrity, and a stronger ICC supervisory role over border areas can hardly be termed hostile to American interests. Cambodia is undoubtedly used by Vietnamese Communists, but not to the extent of becoming a significant factor in the war for Vietnam. That this infiltration can occur against Sihanouk's wishes demonstrates how vulnerable the country's strategic position has become. It also reflects Saigon's inability to control large portions of its own side of the border with Cambodia.

Washington could not accede to the numerous demands set forth by Cambodia before 1965. One could have made a case for concessions on the grounds that Cambodia did not aid the enemies, desired to remain neutral, and presented demands that involved little cost to American interests. For example, the Prince repeatedly called for apologies for hostile actions (including propaganda, support of subversives, and border attacks) allegedly perpetrated by the allies and the United States. But it was precisely the antagonism toward Sihanouk in South Vietnam and especially in Thailand that proved the major stumbling block to a policy of accommodation. As the U.S. security commitment in Southeast Asia grew, Washington found itself unable to follow a course that Bangkok considered psychologically demeaning and objectionable in substance.

We have seen how Thai-Cambodian relations, after a promising start in the mid-1950s, deteriorated when Pnompenh adopted its course of accommodation with China. Had the United States adopted a "soft" line toward Cambodia, Thailand might have concluded that Washington was weakening in its determination to sustain its alliance obligations. Saigon, in more immediate danger than Bangkok, would have been even more disconcerted by concessions to a hostile state, concessions that would have made the Vietnamese appear in the wrong, and so weakened their diplomatic position as well.

At the other extreme, once Sihanouk broke relations and the war in Vietnam intensified, the temptation grew to take military action against Cambodia. Both Bangkok and Saigon would undoubtedly support such a move enthusiastically. The possibilities include support of subversion, small-scale assaults, substantial retaliatory actions against hostile Vietnamese forces and a full-fledged occupation of the state.[27] The case against such action, however, is formidable. First, Cambodia unswervingly opposes use of its territory by belligerent forces, especially to advance the cause of its greatest menace, North Vietnam. Most impartial observers have concluded that the Vietnamese Communists have not established significant supply or reserve facilities on Cambodian territory. A major military thrust into Cambodia would, therefore, appear to the rest of the world as a desperate act born of frustration. It would substantiate Communist claims that the Americans are guilty of aggression throughout Indochina, and welcome any excuse to escalate the war.

Beyond this, Washington has an interest in the preservation of Cambodian integrity. Southeast Asia can hardly progress toward stability if the security of any state, even a "hostile neutral," is undermined. In a long-term view, Cambodia could easily swing back toward an impartial foreign policy should the United States stabilize the military situation in Indochina. Indeed, as America's military position improved during 1966, Sihanouk seemed to be changing his course in precisely this manner. Also, China might fail to assure Pnompenh's independence, not an unlikely possibility if Hanoi presses its claim vigorously. Sihanouk might then cooperate with Washington and Bangkok, should they still appear determined to carry on a vigorous defense effort, even if all Vietnam fell to the Communists. Thus, a strong conventional military posture and a tolerant policy toward this neutral state could form complementary aspects of American security policy in Southeast Asia.

The Indian Subcontinent

The outlook for the Indian subcontinent is far from optimistic, even given the establishment of a stable and substantial military presence in the Indian Ocean. The unfortunately extensive experience of Indian-Pakistani antagonism indicates that an Indian Ocean force or a similar arrangement would at best make a marginal contribution to the subcontinent's security. An oceanic force can hardly succeed in luring the two bitter rivals to cooperate in response to the pull of its nuclear guarantee. In its present mood, Pakistan has denounced the concept of a nuclear umbrella or unilateral guarantees, because like an Indian Ocean force, they would enhance India's security against China. With Pakistan antagonized and India aloof, if less hostile—though its dedicated neutralists still emit muffled criticisms—a Western military presence in the Indian Ocean may actually produce negative political results in its early years.

Another limitation of the deployment is that it would have restricted utility as an instrument of crisis diplomacy, save in the unlikely event of a fairly unambiguous nuclear threat from Peking, though one should not underrate the value of blunting this most dangerous of all challenges to Indian security. But without a base system, joint contingency planning, and advance preparations, the United States could hardly give extensive help to India at the onset of a serious attack, such as the two-front war now haunting the planners in New Delhi.[28]

Any near-permanent allocation of strategic might to this segment of the globe, however, would produce a greater impact if it came in conjunction with a multilateral guarantee to India upon New Delhi's signing a nonproliferation accord that China had rejected. Though this deployment would undoubtedly strain American-Pakistani relations, it need not lead to a rupture in the alliance, for the commitment to India would remain somewhat vague, and there would not be any American military presence on the subcontinent itself. Moreover, it is unlikely that Pakistan would entirely relinquish its military link with America as long as the dispute with India remains unsettled. And if Pakistan should go neutral, is it conceivable that no security benefits would derive from an improved relationship with a neutralist India that depends on the United States for military assistance and considerable economic help?

What guidelines can one propose for American relations with these two great rivals? There is some truth in the assertion that the American security position has deteriorated drastically, since the Pakistani alliance is badly frayed without any compensatory arrangement with India. Both states are almost totally isolationist regarding the security of all areas beyond their immediate frontiers. Along with the neutralism of Ceylon and Burma and the privatism of Malaysia and Singapore, the Pakistani-Indian rivalry comprises the final blow to whatever security system the British had hoped to keep alive in the region through Commonwealth ties.

From another vantage point, American interests may not yet be damaged beyond repair. For Pakistan has not gone over to the Chinese side and would probably not commit itself to Peking even in return for the limited military aid that China could provide.[29] The important American base at Peshawar remains, as does Pakistan's need for substantial U.S. economic help and military support. Nor does the more equivocal Soviet position on Kashmir, though a departure from its traditional pro-Indian stand, advance Pakistan's case on this front. Despite its apparent shift away from its completely pro-Indian policy of recent years, Moscow still probably feels unable to extend very much support to Pakistan for fear of driving India into the Western camp. Furthermore, direct American strategic support to India, though resented in Pakistan, will probably remain well out to sea and will be of uncertain diplomatic value because of Indian neutrality. It would not be the least of all ironies in Asian diplomacy for Indian foreign policy to play an essential role in averting an irrevocable Pakistan-American split, by preventing the military relationship between Washington and New Delhi from becoming too intimate.

If the situation remains one of diplomatic disarray, the United States might benefit from choosing sides between Pakistan and India rather than trying to maintain the strongest link possible with both parties at the same time, as it is now doing. The drawback of the current U.S. policy is that each improvement with one state is offset by a negative reaction in the rival camp. If a settlement with Pakistan can enable the United States to sustain security relations of a more durable and intimate type than could ever be hoped for with neutralist India, it would seem logical to investigate that possibility thoroughly. There is also the stark fact that Pakistan has more diplomatic leeway; it could move toward neutralism, thereby satisfying Russia, while keeping a close tie with China. Consequently, preventive American action to repair damages here can ward off harmful shifts in the regional alignment, whereas India is quite firmly set on a neutralist course the policy consequences of which are determined strictly according to New Delhi's interests, without the need to consider the wishes of an "entangling" ally.

Second, an extended American commitment along bilateral lines could give Pakistan unambiguous American assurances of support against aggression from all sources. Like the Rusk-Thant agreement of 1962, that promised direct American assistance in case of aggression, regardless of the response made by other allies, it could operate within the SEATO framework. Subcontinental diplomacy, in contrast to the Thai situation, must overcome an unhappy history of broken agreements. India and Pakistan used American aid against each other in violation of their solemn pledges, for each viewed the other as the aggressor in 1965. Pakistan felt especially betrayed by

Washington's failure to rally to an ally's cause. A broader defense commitment, especially if coupled with renewed military aid, would thus involve serious risks. It could enable Pakistan to launch new military ventures, as in 1965. However, firm warnings that aid would be terminated and the alliance ended might carry more weight if the connection were strengthened by a broader guarantee and provided the legal basis for continued large-scale economic and military aid.

However, the United States should keep its expectations modest, since the tie has never enjoyed a wide base of Pakistani public support, either in educated circles or among the mass of people. Nor did a government-inspired press campaign of virulent anti-Americanism during 1962–65 augur well for the future. It may be reassuring, however, to recall that neither the Thai people nor their government was particularly in favor of the SEATO connection in its early years. It was a sober appraisal of the threat to Thailand's survival and America's willingness to stand firm that led Bangkok to set aside its doubts and cooperate fully in the American defense effort on the Southeast Asian mainland.[30] Pakistan, however, will probably not follow such a course, since unlike Thailand, its identification of the main threat to its security does not coincide with the American view. Also, as a sizable power with aspirations of its own, Pakistan will probably continue to assert an independent foreign policy line.

What we must consider, then, is the value of retaining this alliance, recognizing that it can only have limited scope and that it must remain contingent upon the willingness of both parties to honor a burdensome array of restrictions. Still, a minimal alliance relationship that both parties will honor has great advantages over ties with a neutralist state. Our dealings with India have demonstrated how severely one party's commitment to neutrality can retard the evolution of meaningful security arrangements. For all their difficulties, alliances provide room for partners to maneuver, adjust, and expand their relationships, as our dealings with Thailand and Japan have demonstrated. If, within limits (excluding, for instance, a Pakistani attack on India), each party can display tolerance toward security policies vital to its partner but not to itself, the American-Pakistani alliance has a chance of surviving.

Its hard core remains Pakistan's deep-seated insecurity and long-term vulnerability, and the political-military value to the United States of having an ally in Central Asia in the gap between the Middle East and Thailand. Perhaps neither side can derive adequate satisfaction from an accord that substantially restricts its freedom of action in return for such limited benefits. And each may again find policies of its partner toward third parties seriously objectionable, if not counter to its own vital interests. Nonetheless, even if such difficulties re-emerge, the United States must determine precisely how it would be better off if it were free of the Pakistani tie.

Admittedly, India bulks larger on the global scene than Pakistan. However, it is difficult to see how a firm reiteration of the Pakistan alignment can do us much damage in India, provided Washington continues to assist New Delhi in its struggle for economic development and remain available as a nuclear guarantor. A blanket guarantee to Pakistan, per capita aid substantially above that offered to India, and acquiescence in Pakistan's effort to keep on good terms with China might overcome Pakistan's complaints against these pro-Indian policies. Of course, should the Indian domestic situation deteriorate, Washington would be compelled to follow a radically different policy. But with or without a reestablishment of close ties with Pakistan, the United States is unlikely to have a significant capacity to affect the course of Indian politics.

Basic American Military Posture

From this survey of American relations with allies and neutrals, it is clear that the United States cannot respond to the rise of Chinese nuclear power by cautiously withdrawing its advanced military deployments from Asia to more secure positions. If strategic plans, concentration of personnel, and base agreements should be arranged in this manner, the United States would be gratuitously applying to all other sectors the unfavorable situation that now prevails in the Indian Ocean area. Yet it has been reported that the highest American military authorities have considered a revision of America's Asian security position along such lines. They were said to favor reducing American personnel and equipment in fixed positions near China and increasing the capacity for rapid deployment by improved air- and sea-lift facilities.[31]

A broad-scale response of this type, undertaken unilaterally, would have just the dire results most feared in Washington. The Asian allies can hardly avoid the conclusion that the United States was restricting its diplomatic obligations and reducing military risks on a distant continent because of an increase in Chinese power. To an ally, Washington's promise to return when a crisis arises would seem very hollow after having removed U.S. forces essentially because of their increased vulnerability to attack. Even less convincing would be verbal encouragement to allies and neutrals to hold fast to their clearly exposed positions. Asian suspicions of the United States would reach new heights just as the need for intimate collaboration and great trust became paramount—to resist Chinese pressures to end all security links with America and to keep the bases open for our occupancy in time of duress.

The American position in Okinawa differs from other cases because of the unpopularity of the underlying political arrangements. Here alone, in the entire Western Pacific defense system, has the question of political self-determination been at odds with our security network. Should the military stronghold of Okinawa (500 miles offshore) and the political bastion of Taiwan prove untenable, then Guam (2000 miles from the Asian mainland) might provide a partial substitute at least for Okinawa.[32] Therefore, the political costs of a retreat from Okinawa would not be as high as a withdrawal from lands under allied jurisdiction, especially if special arrangements with Japan, noted earlier in this chapter, could be implemented. However, the problems facing Taiwan in the event of a U.S. withdrawal would become acute, even if the Peking regime did not threaten the island directly.

Nevertheless, it would be unreasonable for the United States to begin stationing combat forces on Taiwan, especially with nuclear components. For their military utility today would soon be seriously diminished by the greater vulnerability of the island in the future. Since there are no American combat forces ashore now, their continued absence would not be considered a retreat. Whatever advantages there may be in the introduction of troops at this time would be more than offset by the diplomatic rigidities in efforts to work toward a settlement of the two-Chinas question that would be consequent upon any addition to the deep interests already at stake in Taiwan. Moreover, the United States would expose itself to the possible loss, under duress, of another valuable military installation.

In sum, when the moment of truth comes, the United States may find it no more prudent to yield ground under nuclear pressure in Asia than it was in Europe after 1957. However if America is to adjust, it seems politic to consider disengaging from areas (like Okinawa) where its diplomatic position is already weak. Conversely, where diminution of American forces might mean serious decay in an alliance and in the security values it affords, the United States may find it necessary, though burdensome, to sustain and perhaps augment its combat posture.

In this context, American conventional power may well be more of a key to area stability after the Chinese acquire nuclear weapons than in the past. Since ability to counter low-level thrusts effectively and on the scene of their origin will be of the utmost importance —both to maintain regional stability and avert repeated escalations —the United States cannot meet the threat posed by Chinese nuclear weapons simply by enhancing its own nuclear strategic capacity in Asia.[33]

For the target state sees first and foremost a specific low-level threat to its security backed by Chinese nuclear power. America would not respond with nuclear threats immediately after Chinese pressure began. Hence, nuclear power alone will not deter such attacks nor appear an appropriate or credible instrument for bringing them to a halt. In fact, if by the 1970s, China has some ability to threaten the American continent, this may have a political impact in Asia far out of proportion to its military value.[34]

Yet there are major problems in maintaining or augmenting a major conventional force in the Far East. The expense will be great, since the United States will need a larger nuclear presence, as well. Moreover, despite persistent heavy deployments, the United States has never been willing to undertake a formal obligation to tie its relatively limited conventional power to this region. Nevertheless, with large contingents engaged in the Vietnamese war, in addition to the great forces on permanent station—the Seventh Fleet, the equivalent of almost three divisions, and major air force components—the extent of actual commitment goes beyond the image U.S. policy declarations have conveyed.

Perhaps the time has come to reshape American policy and its rationale to fit this extensive array of power, instead of minimizing the value, size, or durability of the Asian deployments. At the very least, American diplomacy in the years between such commitments, and especially in the critical months preceding the employment of such forces, should not suffer from the handicap that stems from the assumption by all parties concerned that the United States will probably not make such a commitment.

To sustain or augment American conventional force, however, requires further development of the staging and operational base system, more careful planning and pre-positioning of supplies, and closer coordination with allies. Inevitably, these bases and the allied governments will become targets of Chinese nuclear pressure. Though China might not assume such a menacing stance without good cause, it is precisely this point that makes American policy, to a certain extent, a hostage to the ally's interests and sensibilities. The ally might, for example, exert considerable pressure on Washington to adopt a more cautious policy, in order to avoid giving the Chinese good cause, even if the United States maintains a formidable and diversified military presence at hand. Or states that play key roles in this intricate base system may demand special protection as well as diplomatic support for their vital policy objectives. We must, therefore, recognize that the price of a security policy in Asia will rise as a logical consequence of the increase in Chinese power, and we must then determine whether we wish to pay this price.

For practical reasons, Peking may give priority to efforts within the region of the Far East and for a while repress its desires to make a global political impact with its nuclear might. Hence this middle range, between ability to affect the global great-power balance on the one hand and minimal preservation of Chinese national security on the other, may prove the main testing ground for the efficacy of China's new power. If this proves true, American-Chinese confrontations in Asia will be frequent and dangerous, and a conventional United States combat presence will be a prime diplomatic and military necessity.

In the late 1950s, the Russians tried to use what was only a regional nuclear force to induce changes in the European balance, particularly regarding Berlin and Germany as a whole. When the Chinese possess a regional nuclear force-in-being, they may try the same tactics, especially since the Asian states are more isolated and more easily frightened than those in Western Europe. The Chinese, convinced of their own moral and intellectual superiority, hold that even a small improvement in their material power position can open up great opportunities. Since conventional force can play a very important defensive role, it is unfortunate that the pivotal power of the Seventh Fleet cannot be demonstrated with a physical impact like that of the Seventh Army in Europe.

While China is fashioning its nuclear arsenal, there is much to be done, notably, the development of strategic concepts for the deployment of nuclear forces, and of the relation of their utility to that of conventional force. We must also explore the degree to which we can create a more viable alliance network in Asia, one capable of bearing the heavy burden of nuclear armament, enhancing the deterrent value of such weapons, and providing for their most rational deployment and use. Some of these tasks will be easier to accomplish if we set to work immediately. But we also need repeated reappraisals of our commitments, deployments, and installations, to see how closely we can harmonize our strategic views, treaty obligations, and political objectives.

Many other important American political interests in Asia will depend on the adequacy of our security policies and our actions in times of crisis, as well as on our ability to cope with China's furious propaganda and diplomatic initiatives. Even if there is no sudden qualitative change in the defense problems facing the United States, the persistence, intensification, and increased interdependence of military and political issues mean that a new era for security policy is opening in the Far East. It will take many years of experience in dealing with China as a nuclear power before the major nations can hope to adopt a common policy toward Peking. Meanwhile, the United States must devise a carefully thought-out national policy toward China, in which defense needs are coordinated with major political considerations so that the two aspects mutually reinforce one another. At the same time, the way must be opened for some accommodation with Peking. It is to these issues that we must now turn.

CHAPTER SEVENTEEN

United States Policy and China

An ever-deepening American involvement in Asia runs the danger that the local Asian states will feel proportionately less need to take unpalatable measures in their own defense. It also makes more apparent than ever that Washington is much more engaged in checking what it views as a serious threat from Peking than are any of the major states close to China—although according to the classic theory of the balance of power, these states should be more fearful and so more directly committed in their own defense. Yet for a series of reasons that later generations may consider bizarre, India, Japan, and the Soviet Union have not engaged in a concerted effort to halt the expansion of Chinese power in the traditional diplomatic-military sense. It is true that India views China as an enemy state and that Moscow seeks to thwart Chinese political and ideological influence within the Communist and underdeveloped worlds. But coordinated and high-priority efforts to check Chinese power, together or in conjunction with the United States, are lacking in all three capitals.

It is always dangerous for one party to argue that he is right and everyone else is wrong. Washington finds itself in this situation now. The United States government believes that China represents a clear and present danger and that the failure of the others to respond to this threat is incomprehensible inasmuch as they have a significant capacity to act. Others may agree that the Chinese wish to be as menacing as they sound, but they maintain that China is still so weak that for some time to come, words must serve as substitutes for achievements. Some are optimistic enough to contend that China adopts its current bellicose posture only because it has been outlawed, feels threatened by America, and is engaged in a fierce ideological struggle with the Soviet Union.

340

Admittedly, the actions of China's leaders differ markedly from their words, so there is room for considerable difference of opinion regarding their intentions, especially for the future. But since Peking has carried out the threats and promises that lie within its limited capabilities, even occasionally at serious risk, prudence requires us to take the Chinese at their word. Those who disparage the significance of official Chinese doctrine must explain unremitting efforts to inculcate it in their own cadres and people and to spread it abroad at great cost, splitting the Communist world and nullifying the military alliance with Russia in the process.

From this perspective, Washington considers an extensive American involvement to be appropriate policy and not an act of folly. American leaders maintain that they are holding a line until other states respond to the reality of the situation and participate more rationally in this effort. They would deny the charge of adventurism and overextension and reject the relevance of such historical examples as the ill-fated Athenian adventure in Sicily during the Peloponnesian War. For it is not conquest but the containment of the power of determined expansionist ideologues that motivates United States policy. If it avoids acting until the others are ready to join together and stand firm—if indeed they ever decide to take a stand —the United States will guarantee the foe a stronger position at the time of the inevitable confrontation.

All speculations about China must take account of the changing relationships among the great powers. The Sino-Soviet antagonism is very real and should benefit the United States in terms of the strategic balance of power. Yet in specific tactical situations, the two Communist opponents may vie with one another to demonstrate their ideological purity and their antagonism to the great capitalist foe. For both still seek to attain their major global objectives— nothing less than a restructuring of national political societies and a recasting of interstate relations. Western Europe remains a potential fourth power in this struggle, but today it is not so constituted.[1] It does not have any design for ordering this planet's affairs, or the political interest and capacity to impress its will on the shape of world events. Should it assume a global role, through the vehicle of political unification, Washington's supporting effort may come to seem ironic, especially if sharp divergences emerge between American and West European policies. The United States recognizes this risk but presumably feels that a strong Western ally would have a stabilizing effect on areas beyond the European continent and, on balance, enhance the security position of the non-Communist lands. A strong Europe could play a crucial role, for example, in fostering compromises between Washington and Moscow, in the face of persistent Chinese antagonism and diplomatic efforts to fragment the industrialized world. The power potential exists in Europe, but for the present, the great-power struggle remains triangular.

There is much validity to the argument that America's exertions may be delaying the decision of major Asian powers to face up to the realities of their situation. Moreover, a stalemate in the Sino-American confrontation enables third parties to sustain attitudes and policies detrimental to American security interests. Indians can continue criticizing America's reliance on force and its impairment of a neutralist doctrine for Asia. In Japan, America's involvement in foreign problems and resort to military action can still be attacked as violations of the country's security interests, instead of being welcomed as rational steps for the defense of the home islands. The Soviet Union can preserve its ideological hostility toward the United States and use every opportunity to weaken American interests, which it still treats as threats to its national security and political cause. Finally, specific American measures taken for security reasons may anger one of these powers and make it even less willing to cooperate with Washington or any other state to contain China.

Yet if the United States interprets Peking's policy correctly, its failure to respond now, at least with a moderate deployment of power, would create a situation all too often encountered in the past—in which none of the great powers acted against an evident central threat until the eleventh hour. The last time this occurred was during the 1930s, when the other Western powers, for reasons they could defend brilliantly and at great length all failed to cooperate to halt the rise of German power. This example is meant not to suggest that Chinese motives, ideology, or power position resembles that of the National Socialists, but to point up the inadequacy of arguing that a position must be right because everyone adopts it. But, however different the situations of China and Nazi Germany, the threat of a power imbalance remains in Asia today, as does China's ideological motivation to exploit it. China certainly is the dominant indigenous force in Asia, the state with the greatest military power there—Russia and America excepted—and the political entity with the highest degree of motivation and drive. Moreover, if the rate of growth of China and the other Asian states is projected over the next ten to twenty years, China's relative advantage may be similar to that of Germany over the rest of continental Europe at the start of the Second World War. Given Moscow's inability to oppose Peking openly, and assuming some Chinese success in building support among underdeveloped Communist and neutralist states, the power balance in Asia might become as precarious as it was in Europe in the years 1919–39, the last period when America stood on the sidelines. Unless there is an important American input, Asia may well undergo a holocaust or at the very least a massive security crisis with a very harmful outcome.

The United States may be skillful enough to employ some of the components of a sustained containment effort, inducing others, particularly the Soviet Union, to contribute to the stability of Eastern Asia. This may already be occurring within the framework of present American policy, though at a very slow pace, with each state operating strictly on its own terms and exclusively in accordance with its own interests. There is, for example, the extensive Soviet commitment to peace on the Indian subcontinent. In addition, India has concluded, however limited the policy consequences, that China poses a serious threat to its security. As a consequence, it may eventually produce its own atomic weapons or exact from the superpowers a more structured position on the question of nuclear guarantees. A mounting concern with nuclear security in Japan may facilitate the establishment of a workable long-term alliance relationship with Washington. In addition, the process of Japan's emergence as an acceptable neighbor continues, though in a slow and painful manner, especially in economic affairs. A significant economic assistance program, however closely tied to Tokyo's self-interest, would speed the developments of the smaller states on the Chinese perimeter and relieve Washington of sole responsibility for every difficult decision and inadequate result.[2] In addition, it would point up the vitality of an effective alternative to China as a socio-economic model for economic growth. But for a Japanese assistance program to be effective, the Asian security environment must be stable. Ultimately, therefore, we return to our initial premise: an upturn in the fortunes of the Asian nations requires a substantial American presence.

The American Response to the Chinese Threat

Though the Chinese challenge is both formidable and complex, requiring a painstaking examination of the full range of politics in developing a proper response, this study has centered its attentions on security considerations. It is recognized that other major considerations may prove more decisive in the long run, but it must also be understood that alliances, security force deployments, strategies of engagement, and the intensity of combat encounters are vital and immediate considerations in their own right. They could well exert crucial influence over the economic and political aspects of the struggle. The Communists in general rely heavily on force in all its forms, including veiled threats, to advance their own cause. To a large extent, Peking's position stems from its uncontested superiority in power relative to all other Asian states. Its impact diminishes with distance, but the effect on its neighbors is profound. In the Vietnamese War, for example, fear of China probably accounts for the refusal of several nations aiding the United States to publicize or at times so much as acknowledge their military cooperation.[3] Yet even in such favorable geographic conditions, China finds that there are limits to the role of overt force. To exert a decisive influence, China usually must have a strong and relatively pro-Chinese local Communist party in these neighboring lands. Other crucial political issues, such as the state's degree of national cohesion, also profoundly affect its ability to conduct an effective security policy.

Nuclear armament will provide a backdrop for whatever military pressures the Chinese may bring to bear. It will be the trump card to demonstrate that American security influence must inevitably fade from the area and give way to Chinese hegemony. To strengthen this image and for tactical advantages in a specific crisis, the Chinese might at some point simulate a bold threat against Japan or India, allegedly because of their American military links. This move might follow the lines of the Soviet pseudo-threat against Britain in the 1965 Suez crisis, which had a powerful impact in the Afro-Asian world. Similar pressures, if less overtly expressed, might also be applied against American military installations on Okinawa or Taiwan.

A significant American response must operate with several considerations in mind. First, the United States must recognize the complex nature of the Chinese threat and devise adequate security countermeasures in an uncongenial political and diplomatic environment. At the same time, it must continually strive to keep open a way to negotiate some kind of settlement. If Peking encounters expensive failures in its efforts to expand the Communist realm, as well as new problems of internal development, a new generation of Chinese leaders, lacking the militancy of the "founding fathers," may be impelled to seek a reasonable settlement. Mao's Cultural Revolution of 1966 and his use of middle school and university students as Red Guards may reflect a real fear on his part that the country is in danger of going "revisionist." His employment of the country's youth in a pseudo-revolutionary experience, as violent agitators, to further his utopian mission may comprise the major means available to him both to reverse the present trend and assure the "purity" of the next generation. Third, the United States must not feel apologetic or politically inadequate if its main effort for many years to come consists of security undertakings to thwart Peking's efforts. For in dealing with the Chinese Communists, the United States must recall that military considerations do not evoke the same negative connotations for them that they do in the democratic West. Rather, force and violence remain central to the entire Chinese concept of the course of history, political change, and the application of ideology to the analyses of government and society. Of course, America should be aware of excessive dependence on security actions, for in dealing with a dedicated totaliarian enemy, all aspects of public policy become interrelated combat fronts.

Conversely, Peking may seek to improve its relative power position by blunting Western efforts. This would be facilitated for the Chinese by the vulnerability of the United States as a Western power in Asia and by the comprehensiveness of the totally politicized Chinese effort. A partial listing of U.S. objectives gives an indication of their scope, which in turn offers China a wide choice of targets: alleviation of racial hostility, maintenance of economic growth in the West, moderation of nationalist militance and recalcitrance, and creation of strong regional and global international organizations. In repairing the damages that might ensue from a failure in these and related fields, this country might find itself forced to make an agonizing decision to go ahead, despite the knowledge that this would entail sacrificing some immediate security interest. For example, the United States may not be able to create an effective regional organization without surrendering some freedom of military action.

A related group of nonmilitary problems concerns the underdeveloped world more directly. It is crucial that the United States acquire a theoretical notion of how states develop, economically and politically. Doctrine and practice are both woefully inadequate at present, reflecting the great gaps in American understanding of this process. It would be unpardonable for so irrelevant an approach as neo-Marxism, using the vacuous concept of "neocolonialism," to continue to dominate the intellectual environment in which the analysis of development takes place—particularly since Western research has already brought forth so many meaningful insights.[4] Needless to say, a change in the basic emotional orientation of Asian intellectuals, reversing the current of generations of academic training, would be of paramount importance. Improved economic analysis can make the United States far more efficient in determining proper levels of aid and allocations for complex mutual commitments required of the industrial and underdeveloped lands. The relationship of the modernization process to political and institutional development opens still other areas for new theoretical approaches to mitigate the baleful and simplistic ideological heritage of the past, as well as to provide tools for seeking and evaluating new programs of national improvement. And it is conceivable that even a partially successful effort in these matters might eventually modify the Chinese political epistemology.

The Continuing Importance of Military Security

Though these are important considerations, the problem of physical security remains paramount. In terms of historical experience, the territorial expansion of communism has usually rested upon war, military power, and the use of force. Not only are Eastern Europe and North Korea in their present situation as a direct consequence of war, but to a large extent, the same is true of the indigenous triumphs in Russia, China, and Vietnam. Both Moscow and Peking are quick to resort to physical power when they think they have the edge or when other forms of "competition" with the enemy do not redound to their advantage.[5]

A second major reason for giving security matters primacy is that they play a central role in Communist theory. For analytical purposes, there is often a distinction made between the maintenance of internal order and the defense against foreign threats. Yet Communist doctrine recognizes that they closely affect one another and frequently merge.[6] Only a Westerner would place security and ideology at opposite ends of a spectrum of political issues. In Chinese writings, the emphasis on military power as the mainspring of revolutionary activity is so great that even Moscow has charged that it amounts to almost a caricature of the original doctrine.

However, all agree that political and military considerations become intertwined when there is an internal war in an underdeveloped state. And because these wars become major international issues, they quickly politicize the formal military aspects of international relations. The nightmarish example of Vietnam illustrates this point all too well. The strength of the Communists here has stemmed in large part from their use of political arguments with which they have turned an act of aggression into a cause that carries considerable moral plausibility in many capitals of the world. Hanoi has used the incredibly muddled terms of the Geneva accord of 1954 to win legitimacy for its cause; it has employed infiltration rather than direct aggression along North Korean lines, masking its own central role; and it has depended on Southerners to carry the burden of the war in accordance with highly competent military plans, devised by D.R.V. leaders. The political ineptness of the Saigon regime in administration, reform, arguing its case abroad, and winning the loyalty of its citizenry have strengthened Hanoi's hand immeasurably. These factors have had a major impact on military issues, such as the combat doctrines followed by each side, their fighting capabilities, and the ability of outside elements to help the favored side. The result is an intricate web of political and military considerations that has also demolished many of the boundaries between domestic and international affairs. In stressing the importance of security issues, therefore, we are not slighting the great significance of the political aspect. Rather, it must be realized that military skills play a major role, that the Communists are quick to use force in a favorable political setting, and that the outcome of armed conflicts has very "positive" political consequences.[7]

However, the United States may find it necessary to revise its military techniques in some situations. For example, in response to enemy guerrilla tactics, the United States might employ its conventional modern weapons in an intermittent and "unsystematic" manner. Sporadic and occasional air attacks on important enemy targets, rather than a systematic assault on its war-making capacity, could produce over-all optimum results in terms of strategic military effect, pressure on an enemy to negotiate, and maintenance of a strong diplomatic posture with allies and neutrals. In short, America must keep the vital aspects of its political military efforts to the fore, rather than try to attain results along one track at the expense of the other.

The threat from China will always present a mixture of political and military issues. The United States dares not make judgments on "purely" military grounds for fear of suffering political losses that would more than balance anticipated gains. Yet it should not begrudge efforts to study the military aspects of a problem or consider it simply a necessary evil to be handled so that America can free itself to proceed with the central issues of a social, political, economic or ideological nature. The military aspect is no less integral or important a part of the problem than these. Success or failure in any one of these aspects significantly affects the ability of this country to sustain its efforts in all other realms.

Avoiding a Frozen Security Posture

It is tempting and dangerous to assert that all existing security arrangements are vital to maintain the U.S. position. Admittedly, preservation of a system affords some stability, but it also involves the risk of viewing any change in the *status quo* as a loss in power and security. If Pakistan turned neutral and also settled its dispute with an India that remained neutral, the United States would lose an important military asset. But is it certain that the security of the subcontinent would be diminished, even if the settlement also brought a sharp rise in Russian prestige and influence there?

The conventional American security approach has been to work from whatever situation the United States finds, to anticipate the simultaneous pressures that can be applied against its strong points, and to devise an effective foreign-military policy in response. This has the advantages of official sanction and understanding, as well as of prudent reliance on an actual situation as a point of departure. The great requirement of the United States today is to retain the essential values of this orientation while becoming more receptive to changes in its security arrangements. This means more than recognizing that alterations in existing conditions could work for the benefit as well as to the harm of the United States. It implies an expectation that certain changes are inevitable and a recognition that others are more acceptable than a maintenance of the *status quo* at great cost. Frequently, by taking the initiative in negotiating modifications in existing security patterns, the United States can minimize their negative impact or forge new relationships that will enable an existing alliance to survive adversity. The 1960 revision of the Japanese treaty, for all the domestic furor it aroused, nevertheless exemplifies a diplomatic strategy that responded to a problem with foresight and initiative.

Washington also faces a problem of inflexibility in its method of coping with specific military pressures. The need to protect American security interests in Asia—the Indian subcontinent, Japan, an offshore line, and an ill-defined area on the mainland—necessitates a response to all serious Communist threats. But this general objective does not indicate the degree of military response required, the level of punishment that should be inflicted on the attacker, or whether he must be prevented from making even the smallest territorial gain. Again, the Vietnamese situation illustrates the problem and the choices. The United States could succeed in preventing the loss of any South Vietnamese territory and thereby demonstrate its determination to thwart the expansion of the Communist realm. Yet what if this should cause a rebirth of the "never again" school—one important consequence of the Korean War—which leads some military leaders to oppose more adamantly than before any large-scale engagements on the Asian mainland? [8] Should this view prevail, it will quickly find reflection in U.S. base arrangements and force deployments. As American allies learn of it, their confidence in the credibility of the United States and in the value of deterrent strategy may become seriously undermined. In short, a response that is less ambitious may have less harmful long-range consequences than a more sweeping effort the costs of which may later be judged to have been excessive.

From another perspective, should South Vietnam be preserved in war, only to fall a few years later because of political ineptitude? This country would be in the position of the surgeon whose operation was a success but whose patient died. It is difficult to believe that the United States could then expect to retain the confidence of its allies. If America undertakes to sustain grave combat losses, it must concurrently take effective steps to enable the regime to survive—despite cries of "intervention." Otherwise, however hopeless the political cause may have been from the start, American capacity to fight against future wars of liberation will be gravely damaged. A more modest military response and a deeper and more imaginative political intervention might better meet U.S. needs under the novel conditions that prevail in Indochina. The example is not the essence, however vital it appears at the moment of writing; rather, the main point is the need to realize that the most direct and forceful response to a particular threat does not always best meet the general threat to security interests. Quite possibly, a compromise settlement entailing some costs, when accompanied by adequate political measures in the target state and a satisfactory follow-up military policy, will do more to enhance American credibility in Asia than a major military effort to avert even a minor setback.

This leads once more to the question of how Communists read American intentions. The argument that they act in Asia somewhat irrationally and imprudently presupposes that they believe that Washington will be reluctant to balk their efforts in pursuit of certain major objectives. North Korea assumed that it could conquer the South. Peking has repeatedly acted along its frontiers without expecting a major American input, and North Vietnam moved against Saigon in the hope of a guerrilla victory without an effective military response. The Chinese image of Washington as a paper tiger reflects this assumption, as well as Peking's belief that the United States does not understand the proper relationship of force, in its various gradations, to effective ideological concepts and political organization. Furthermore, the Asian Communists, with their ideological blinders, are convinced that they represent popular will, and that any indigenous government linked to the United States must be a puppet that exploits its own people.

The problem is compounded, as noted earlier, by a consistent American underestimation of the Communists' willingness to take risks. Hanoi's rapidly increased participation in the ground war in South Vietnam following the intensification of American bombings of the North during 1965 is but a recent case in point. The general problem of mutual misunderstanding of intent may become crucial in the future, when Chinese threats are backed by nuclear weapons that give Peking superiority over its neighbors but leave it obviously inferior to the United States. If America undertakes commitments at the arduous low levels of confrontation—particularly against wars of national liberation—and develops effective policies to stabilize target states (reflecting mastery of politico-military techniques), all Asian lands, including the Communist lands, may become convinced of the credibility of American effort to neutralize China's nuclear power.

Problems in the Use of Force

China's attitude toward the United States, as has been remarked before, is ambivalent. In addition to jeering at America as a "paper tiger," Peking seems also genuinely to fear an American atomic attack before it has acquired an adequate nuclear deterrent. The fact that the U.S. government has issued no threat of this kind means little to Peking, with its views of America as a dangerous would-be aggressor that is also a sated paper tiger, unwilling to act when risk is involved.

Pre-emptive assaults have been advocated by a number of Americans, but even they do not envisage mass destruction. Rather, they propose an assault against Peking's nuclear power—specifically, its productive facilities and military installations. The case for such a strike rests on the fear that nuclear weapons are far more dangerous in Chinese than in other hands, and that this qualitative difference makes the possibility of nuclear warfare much more likely than in other conceivable circumstances. Early adoption and rapid execution of such a policy, according to its advocates, will have a greater chance of success, reduce the danger of escalation, and minimize the number of Chinese lives lost.

For their part, Chinese officials have said that a well-trained and disciplined populace can withstand such assaults and that the massive size of China would thwart a military invasion. Apparently Peking has neither faced up to the problem of nuclear attacks—especially limited to military targets—that are not coupled with an American ground invasion of continental China, nor seriously analyzed the purposes behind such attacks, save for the imputed assumption that Washington would hope to destroy the entire Communist order. A severe yet controlled attack, with more limited political purposes, might prove a far more realistic danger in the future.

The unprecedented assumption under the pre-emptive approach is that China is so dangerous it belongs in a category apart from all other sovereign states, which traditionally enjoy freedom in their choices of foreign policy and armaments. However, can it be concluded from China's past behavior that it would employ nuclear power at the first opportunity, thus compelling the United States to execute a preventive strike now, in a departure from all accepted norms of international behavior?

As evidence against such a categorical judgment, the fact can be adduced that, in its stress on revolution, Peking centers its emphasis on national forces enjoying close political ties with the indigenous population. China has not used its own potent conventional armies in open aggression to seize lands it acknowledges to be alien, even to advance a most cherished cause of Communist expansion. The case for prudence gains strength from the fact that for another generation China will have a significantly inferior nuclear combat capacity.

Further, the other industrially advanced states of the world now disagree with the United States on the matters of recognition of China and trade, and they do not share the appraisal of China as an immediate strategic threat. Given such divergent attitudes, it seems reasonable to assume that they would not support a preventive strike. Since the United States is the great power most hostile to Peking, a unilateral U.S. attack would add immeasurably to the burden of conducting American foreign and security policies in a post-strike period. The United States acted militarily without consulting others in the past, but these steps have been defensive in nature or designed to affect internal political developments in particular states. Also to some extent these moves were reversible, and they were notably more moderate than the move now under discussion.

At stake is the American ideological goal of an international legal system of sovereign states, to which it has paid allegiance for several generations as the proper way of ordering world politics. Underlying this commitment has been the sincere belief that these national entities could coexist, each kept intact by constructive nationalism. A rough balance of power, in the American view, protects the interplay of the international system, with rudimentary international mechanisms helping somewhat to cope with certain of the more difficult problems. If the United States shatters this belief system, it must provide an alternative basic approach that can win genuine support in this country and enable this country to sustain its cause in the long ideological war over the future shape of a world political order. The United States must also consider whether a preventive strike might fatally weaken the moral and humanistic controls now exercised over its own terrible power as it faces recurrent crises. The United States has always emphatically criticized Bolshevism for separating means from ends, holding that this great flaw in Leninism led to a moral corruption and a brutalization of the Soviet political environment.

Many formidable problems also arise on a more practical and prosaic level. Since the United States cannot assume an American-Soviet understanding for such an undertaking, it must recognize that such an attack or the threat of one might drive Moscow and Peking together, if only out of common fear of American power and the further uses to which it might be put. It is quite possible that the assault itself would provoke an immediate Soviet response, regardless of the state of the Russian-Chinese dispute at the time. The common bond of a Communist ideology might have greater attraction in such a moment of crisis, not simply for these two major powers but throughout the world, as adherents come to accept literally what was until then essentially a propaganda line about aggressive American imperialism. In the broader realm of world politics among allies as well as neutrals, the United States would be considered an aggressor who has again demonstrated a willingness to bomb Asians, even though China's means to implement a security threat were then far less significant than those at Russia's disposal for more than a decade.

Finally, our position regarding China itself would become most difficult, not merely because of the tidal wave of antagonism such as an assault would generate. Government-fostered hate-campaigns would have a meaningful content, and the popular antagonisms that the regime now tries to inculcate would become genuine. Any chances of inducing a reversal of such attitudes would well-nigh vanish, and any calculations about the eventual modification of Peking's harsh view of contemporary world political processes would be upset. More simply and immediately, how would the United States—and others, especially the Soviet Union—react to a Chinese effort to rebuild its destroyed establishments? This Peking could quite readily do, since it would be a matter of regaining previous levels of proved technical competence.

On balance, a preventive attack upon Chinese nuclear installations would entail moral dangers, an erosion of American ideology, high diplomatic costs, and a general deterioration of our long-range political position in the Cold War. These would more than balance any immediate benefits—and these may be largely illusory—that might accrue to such a strike.

Although political and moral considerations rule out a preemptive nuclear attack, a major American goal should be to convince China that the United States nevertheless has the will and the capacity to use force at the conventional or nuclear level in a limited and judicious manner, tied to specific and limited political security objectives. (How to convince ideologues in Peking that these are nonaggressive in purpose is another and infinitely more difficult matter.) Open discussions of the possible use of nuclear force, under controlled conditions, may become an essential ingredient of this policy. However, Washington might adopt a page from the Chinese book in making the threats subtle and indirect, keeping them in the background, while denying any desire or intent to resort to strategic assaults on Peking's military power. Interestingly, this is what the Chinese try to do with their nuclear power, even at this early stage—by making it seem more developed and effective than it is, and by employing it only as an indirect instrument of coercion. In contrast, Peking seeks to bring the threat of American military nuclear power constantly to the forefront. There is no reason why the United States cannot play the same game of keeping its own nuclear strength as a background factor, while clarifying the various ways in which it can be used as an instrument of policy apart from strategic retaliation.

A high expectation of violence exists in both Washington and Peking, however much each side may overstate its fears of the other for domestic or international political purposes. The result may be a dangerous lowering of the threshold of violence and of each side's proneness to react to threats. Thus, Peking may be far too ready to judge an American action as intent to commit aggression; the United States may think that any loss of territory to China or its allies has such dangerous implications that it must undertake vigorous counteractions everywhere, even under unfavorable circumstances; the Chinese, in turn, may overreact to these counterblows and speed the escalatory process. As the Chinese nuclear arsenal grows, this dangerous pattern may become even more pronounced. Each side begins to consider taking preventive military actions and tends to magnify the significance of these threats beyond their apparent value. The nuclear and conventional "gamesmanship" just discussed may intensify all these problems of miscalculation, excessive readiness to use force, and proneness toward escalation.

Despite these risks, the United States cannot back away from recognizing the great significance that armed might and its use plays in the Chinese scheme of things and how important it is to negate this impact. The United States must remain willing to resort to violence and yet manage to keep such moves under control under extremely difficult conditions. Credibility on both these points is a major asset, extremely hard to gain and to sustain in a crisis, particularly when combined with efforts to keep the door open for negotiations. For a comprehensive security policy must include a strategy for establishing meaningful diplomatic contact with Peking, seeking some understandings, if only at a low substantive level, and maintaining as many routes as possible for an eventual settlement of outstanding disputes and a normalization of relations.

On Negotiating with China

How does one even approach an effort to reduce the tensions between two states that appear so irrevocably hostile to one another? Any discussions of bargaining strategy, tactics to facilitate exchanges of views, and, especially, important substantive negotiations appear very unrealistic even to the sympathetic observer. In addition, the content and sequence of negotiations are so closely interrelated that it is almost impossible to strike an acceptable balance of mutual accommodation except in terms of an over-all settlement. Yet because of the existing enmity, it would be utterly impossible to insist that America must settle all outstanding issues in one grand accord if it is to settle anything. The United States, therefore, is reduced to the grim reality of hard bargaining on individual points.

Consequently, the negotiations risk coming a cropper on any one of a series of separate issues. And Peking will undoubtedly emulate the Russians by holding out for its maximum position as long as possible and require a considerable period of time for each issue. As in the Soviet case, delays and impasses may result in the loss of hard-won benefits and agreements that seemed within reach. The Soviets failed to reap the concessions offered over Berlin in 1959,[9] because Moscow refused to compromise at that time, and the allies then withdrew their offer. Equally striking are the years the Russians have wasted in pursuit of the control over nuclear weapons they seem so earnestly to desire. In Asia, with violence so near the surface, and the diplomatic leeway of the United States for negotiation so limited, failure to make demonstrable progress—especially when accompanied by the inevitable Chinese efforts to undermine the American position—may strengthen the advocates of intransigence on both sides. In addition to the dangers that would ensue on failure to reach a settlement, there would be added risks resulting from the efforts of both sides to increase their strength at the outset, in order to make their negotiating position credible with friend and foe alike.

Negotiations of any sort may well shake the confidence of America's allies. Efforts to break the Cold War freeze in Europe a decade ago aroused considerable apprehension in other Western capitals that Washington might sacrifice allied interests, diminish its security commitment, and generally work with the Russians to settle the affairs of others on a bilateral basis. Since the Asian allies feel even less certain about the United States than did the Europeans, they would be highly vulnerable to divisive tactics from Peking—combining threats and blandishments—which would accompany protracted negotiations with the United States.

The dual task of displaying both firmness and a willingness to negotiate, of satisfying both hostile Chinese and nervous allies regarding American intentions, will constitute a very heavy diplomatic burden. Complaints of bad faith from either side can be met only by skillful diplomatic tactics together with a convincing substantive position. A backdrop of available force and a capacity to persevere in a systematic way despite occasional setbacks are equally vital ingredients for successful negotiation with the Communist powers. These will be even more important in negotiating with China than with Russia because Sino-American antagonism is so profound, U.S. allies are uncertain and ambivalent, and the specific issues separating Washington and Peking are difficult to resolve. Lest the United States become too pessimistic, it should recall that America and Russia have also found certain issues, especially Germany and nuclear inspection, insoluble; yet they have made progress on lesser matters and have demonstrated the value, however limited, of a piecemeal approach.

Basic Policy Toward China

The long-range U.S. goal in Asia has been described as the creation of a balance of power. Simply put, this vital American security objective requires that Japan and the Indian subcontinent remain viable, non-Communist states, free of Chinese control and influence. Derived from this is the need to prevent Chinese power and influence from pervading the entire intermediate zone between these lands; though the vital zone of no return may be inexact, it is clear that a line, however ragged and flexible, must be maintained. The United States has ruled out a massive preventive war as morally repugnant. Such a conflict would also create tremendous political instability, the consequences of which Washington would be unable to cope with. Nuclear escalation would create insuperable obstacles for future efforts to create an international order, moderate the ideologies now generating their own firestorms in world politics, or enable the underdeveloped states to achieve and maintain a steady rate of progress toward modernization.

The dangers of war lie in miscalculation, China's encouragement of violence, escalation to overcome a stalemate, or the erosion of one side's combat position, and the attraction of pre-emptive action. The American purpose is to avoid a major war with China while applying unremitting pressure to thwart the ambitions of the original revolutionary leadership and so demonstrate to pragmatic Chinese party officials—old and young—that the chances of success are constantly diminishing. Finally, while carrying out this trying assignment in an admittedly difficult political setting, the United States must also consider how to deal with Peking in more positive terms and how to demonstrate, through form and substance, the credibility of its interest in accommodation.[10]

A quest for rational policy that seeks to satisfy minimal security and negotiating requirements must move along several uncharted courses simultaneously. Therefore, any concluding observations can hardly be made with so grandiose a term as "blueprint for the future." At best, they can only be tentative policy recommendations, separable for purposes of analysis, but whose time sequence and mutual relationship can be perceived only dimly at present. (1) There must be a review of the changes in American security policy that may occur both within the present framework and in a somewhat different setting than the U.S. seeks or finds imposed upon it in the immediate future. (2) Opening moves must be examined, both conciliatory and protective, to create a better environment for negotiation. (3) There must be a critical re-examination of the persistent failure of the United States to win meaningful cooperation from the other major powers. (4) The United States must list and appraise, at least in rough outline, the major issues in any serious negotiation between Washington and Peking. These points will not be considered comprehensively here; rather, the intention is to illustrate the type of analysis and policy line that may enable the United States to reach some form of coexistence with China sometime in the indefinite future.

We have noted that new short-term security requirements might include an important strategic force in Australia, a combined-purpose naval force in the Indian Ocean, and a stronger military position in Thailand. On the other hand, we recommended a diminished emphasis on holding fast in Okinawa and Taiwan. A mix of American atomic and conventional forces in South Korea, a more binding nuclear security arrangement with Japan, and a strengthened naval-air presence in the Pacific, with the Philippines retaining a key position, also seemed to be possible results of a sustained security effort. If possible, Malaysia should be brought under the shelter of this arc of deployments, by means of its Commonwealth connection. Extensive erosion of the non-Communist position in Indochina would add urgency to this last point.

In the difficult sphere of American relations with allies and neutrals, it must be made clear that treaty undertakings with allies bring greater benefits than more informal arrangements. At the same time, there should be an unequivocal recognition of the right of others to follow a neutralist course without suffering discriminatory treatment. However, this does not mean that the United States should obligate itself to extend a neutralist help in security affairs, via arms program or support in a crisis, on the same basis that it would back an ally. Economic aid presents a different problem, though here, too, it should be emphasized that allies have received more help per capita than neutrals. Washington should publicize this difference and, at the same time, stress that it is a marginal one. For the central criteria in deciding whether to aid a particular state should be the effectiveness of its economic development program (as related to its capacity to act) and the absence of gross incompatibilities with American foreign policy (but not the degree of positive support for those objectives).

Though Washington should encourage multilateral security accords in Southeast and Southcentral Asia, a more modest but urgent need is to induce antagonistic neighbors to settle their quarrels or at least mitigate their antagonisms. Thus far, the indifferent record of the United States in this respect does not augur well for the future and might perhaps lead it to confine its ambitions simply to the prevention of hostilities between non-Communist states. Even this will require a diplomacy of risk—with the possibility of offending at least one of the contesting parties. Of special importance for the area as a whole would be Japan's emergence as a major political and economic factor. Again, the best chance of success, though time is of the essence in the race against the growth of Chinese power, is to make haste slowly.

The United States must be realistic enough to recognize that indigenous subregional defense arrangements are unlikely to emerge today. If they existed, they would hardly do more than symbolize a will to unite against Chinese pressures. Given the weakness of the non-Communist states of Asia, such groupings would have profound political and psychological value, but in raw security terms, the area would still depend on American military commitments.

Any discussion of the intermediate future, assuming a somewhat altered political environment, entails an even higher degree of imprecision than consideration of current specific policy changes. The United States could hypothesize the emergence of a subregional group anywhere along the Chinese perimeter, signifying a stronger political-ideological stand on the part of the member states against pressures from Peking. But these governments might also follow a more independent line in important questions of diplomacy and security while continuing to depend on Washington for their military protection.

The United States might, to take another example, agree with the Communist powers and other states of the area to neutralize most of Southeast Asia. Such an arrangement could include Laos, Cambodia, Malaysia, Singapore, and South Vietnam without being incompatible with vital American interests, although some U.S. allies or opponents might not find this acceptable. America for its part might balk at the inclusion of Thailand without a balancing concession since it would consider Thai neutralization—assuming that the country desires the alliance and that its internal stability had not been eroded by a war of national liberation—a setback for the U.S. security position in southern Asia.

A third possibility, not necessarily incompatible with subregional alignments or neutralization clusters, would be a major extension of American security commitments, especially in nuclear guarantees. The status of arms-control efforts and the participation of other nuclear-armed states would be crucial variables in determining the form and significance of such arrangements.

Associated with the security issue is the further question: How to devise a situation in which Americans and Chinese would be willing and able to negotiate with one another in meaningful terms? If Washington succeeds in thwarting Peking's ambitions, it may become more intransigent than ever, yet no other policy offers any better hope at this time. The security measures considered throughout this book would, we hope, play a major role in maintaining a military stalemate, blocking subversion, and preventing China from overawing its neighbors. Equally important to the political containment of China are sustained efforts at reducing antagonisms among Asian states, and a reduction in the hostility toward the West that stems from the heritage of imperial rule, inferiority in wealth and economic development, fear of exploitation, and the agony of racial antagonism. Continued respect for indigenous nationalist movements and their terms of reference, plus a near-permanent economic assistance program in aid and trade would help in the quest for political stability and sustained economic growth.[11] The United States should not, however, be afraid to use its aid programs as levers to press for reforms and policies that benefit the development of recipient states.

Success in this endeavor would seriously diminish the effectiveness of China's staple propaganda charge that America is the archimperialist whose every action is motivated by rapacious exploitative designs. A substantial and durable program of intimate contacts in socio-economic affairs would help to prevent critical situations from deteriorating and above all blunt the threat of utter disaster when the inevitable setbacks occur in population control, food production, and industrial development. The Asian lands would gain reassurance that time does not necessarily favor only Peking and that the Chinese pattern of political development need not be adopted by the rest of the Afro-Asian world. Officials in these lands could therefore argue, with some persuasiveness in Peking's view, that the world is not so needful of and susceptible to revolution as the Chinese argue. However, China would still retain the respect of these lands as the revolutionary leader who stood up to the old imperialists and matched them in their strong card—power. Constant pressure for realism from Peking's neighbors, combined with some success in economic development and successful American-led efforts to check Communist wars of liberation, might eventually have a softening effect on Peking—especially if accompanied by evidence that the United States is not engaged in any effort to destroy the Chinese system.

In this context, the Vietnamese war gains in significance, not only as evidence of America's determination to stand against Communist expansion, but also as a test of its commitment not to seek the destruction of an existing Communist state. The American position toward North Vietnam, after several years of war, differs markedly from Washington's response to aggression in 1950, when it tried to eliminate the North Korean regime. The large commitment of conventional forces in South Vietnam has given Washington breathing time to avoid a major setback while it goes about the grim business of learning how to cope militarily with one of the most proficient current practitioners of wars of liberation.[12] Unfortunately, this fierce struggle has also tested, under the most unfavorable conditions imaginable, the capacity of an underdeveloped state to devise an effective political-administrative order. American failings in dealing with this problem reveal the inexperience of the United States and the inadequacy of a doctrine it had believed applicable to such situations.[13] While learning "on the job," the United States has also had to prepare a fallback position in case of defeat and demonstrate its willingness to hold fast in a host state—namely, Thailand—that presents a more favorable defensive setting.

In short, the iron test of Vietnam is to demonstrate American determination to block Communist expansion—even in the face of a severe setback. At the same time, if proof can be amassed that underdeveloped states can make real progress without turning to communism and that the Chinese approach to development is laden with theoretical and practical errors, the United States will maximize its chances of making the desired impression on the next group of Chinese leaders.

An additional and essential element in this containment policy is a valid manifestation of a desire to live in peace with China. By undertaking moderately conciliatory policies at a low-key tactical level over the next few years, the United States can give future leaders in Peking sufficient lead time to absorb this point. To this end, the United States might ease restrictions on trade or reduce the embargo on strategic items in effect since the Korean War. (These regulations, adhered to by American allies, apply to all European and Asian Communist powers but the provisions concerning Eastern Europe are much more lenient.) The United States can afford China greater access to foreign sources in humanitarian fields, such as technical and material medical assistance, and essential security operations can be conducted with scrupulous control to avoid provocative actions. In basic strategic policy, the United States can clearly point up its resolution to avoid massive nuclear threats against the mainland.

Admittedly, Peking can use these particular points, or any others geared to the same purpose, to "prove" American hypocrisy or loss of resolve; employing its particular double think, Peking can assert that firmness equals aggression, conciliation equals weakness. This is a risk worth taking in an effort to reach potential leaders still two stages removed from power. The proposals listed here are merely suggestive of the general approach. The content and timing of any effort to implement this program is the responsibility of those in charge of current foreign policy operations, but the basic decision to follow this course and the search for as many indicators as possible is a matter of high national policy.

The unpleasant fact remains that the United States seems locked into its present complex campaign without the support of any other major power, with the partial exception of Britain. This virtual policy of isolation signifies a major success for Peking, since Communist diplomacy consistently seeks to isolate the major opponent in the inevitable struggle, usually identified as the most powerful and active capitalist state. A less rigid American posture toward China might gain support for the tactical introductory approaches just discussed and bring about a greater degree of cooperation with other powers when interests focus on a long-range settlement. Some policy coordination, in conciliation and containment, will be essential in moving China toward a less dogmatic and utopian foreign policy outlook. Can the United States hold the line against China until the others rally to a moderate containment position? Will they move toward a firmer stand as this country adopts a more flexible approach toward negotiation?

Only the most optimistic analysts would give good odds on this, especially since responses will differ in individual states according to the specific issues at hand. A brief discussion of two issues, trade and nuclear arms, may throw some light on this difficult process. A restriction on China's capacity to trade might delay the growth of its power and hamper its maturation in certain fields. Yet in proposing such restrictions, the United States immediately encounters two major problems: the intense unwillingness of other powers to dovetail their foreign economic policies with American interests, and the hostility toward the outside world that such a program would generate in Peking.

However marginal, trade for cash or on credit does influence the growth of the Chinese economy and Peking's military power, and some transactions make a marked contribution to the degree of sophistication of China's industrial-technical plant. A steady supply of foreign capital, machinery, and technical expertise would allow China to allocate its own resources in a more productive and orderly manner. This would enable Peking to buy grain as needed to ward off or cushion food crises and even facilitate its own foreign aid program, which plays an important role in expanding Chinese influence abroad. Peking also seeks to use assistance programs to isolate these lands from the industrial powers and to develop subversive organizations.

But how is the United States to induce allies, let alone others, to abstain from profitable commercial relations when they already show every evidence of expanding trade with China despite American warnings that this policy jeopardizes the security of all non-Communist lands? Rationalizations or justifications are so numerous and ingenious when it comes to defending trade policies that only the strongest arguments can have any appeal. For example, states dealing with East Germany agree that trade strengthens the Pankow regime but justify their action with the argument that this helps eventual reunification since the two parts can never come together as long as one remains weak. Similarly, despite commitments of all sorts to the contrary, many states go on trading with the Republic of South Africa.

Does the arms-control issue provide a basis for a different trade policy? Other major powers concerned, except France, concur on the need to halt proliferation, though they still disagree on many crucial particulars.[14] Assuming the successful conclusion of agreements on some of the important points—nonproliferation by the have-nots, underground testing, international inspection of peaceful uses of nuclear power, no-transfer, and some type of guarantees against nuclear attack—and assuming eventual French adherence, China would be in an isolated position, opposing a major current of world politics upon which all other diverse camps are in agreement.

Could the United States then press for some coercive measures to induce China to come to terms, such as control of foreign trade? If it brought such a policy to fruition, would it work? What other concessions would the United States be obliged to make in the pursuit of this objective, as, for example, to win French support? Should this effort fail to persuade Peking to change its nuclear policy, would there be a residual benefit in having gotten the others, the underdeveloped states included, to work together on a common policy that underlined Chinese intransigence? Or would a setback here irreparably damage future efforts to hold China in check by means of multilateral diplomacy?

This leads logically to the argument that so crucial an issue as arms control cannot be dealt with—even if related to trade policy —apart from the many other major issues upon which Peking and Washington disagree.[15] In considering the central questions of high policy, America is looking far into the future and treating extremely difficult matters. The fate of such negotiations hinges essentially on preceding achievements or failures in restraining Chinese power, blunting its ideological offensive, strengthening its neighbors, demonstrating good will, and rallying some international pressure against Peking.

Still, an approach to the issues at stake has value, if only as a rough approximation of the task confronting us. Including some of the topics already considered, these are (1) the fate of Taiwan; (2) Peking's diplomatic recognition; (3) U.N. membership, and (4) a seat on the Security Council; (5) an arms-control agreement; (6) nonaggression agreements; (7) the disposition of American power and commitments on the periphery of China; (8) China's stress on force to further the Communist cause and (9) its interpretation of history and politics—especially the role of the United States; (10) trade between America and China; and (11) economic assistance from the world's wealthiest power to the world's most populous state.

To add to the difficulties, changes of perspective on some points may radically alter American views on other matters. On the most intractable problem, Taiwan, the stand of the United States derives essentially from its overall appreciation of the Chinese threat. Taiwan symbolizes U.S. determination to adhere to a political and geographic line of resistance; it also serves as a key element in the American security system. Peking has repeatedly demanded control of the island as a prerequisite for negotiating on other major problems. Discussions have foundered on this point since 1955, when the Communists refused to renounce the right to use force to regain the island. Still, if other issues need urgent attention in future years, and progress can be made on these points, how would both parties then treat the case of Taiwan? On the other hand, how would significant political changes on the island, such as the rise of Taiwanese particularism, affect the prospects of successful negotiation on other issues?

The specific negotiations made here on major problems are bound to suffer from their essentially American perspective and are liable to seem obsolete after only a short period of time. For the near future, advocacy of the "two Chinas" policy seems fruitless, because both Chinese parties oppose it so bitterly.[16] Even if this solution were implemented, given the present degree of Peking's hostility, the United States would pay a stiff security price for the agreement. But what about a decade from now—if developments in the right direction are systematically encouraged?

Each man has his own image of a compromise settlement, and I present mine more as an illustration than as a prescription for policy. It includes mainland China recognized and on the Security Council, Taiwan at least nominally independent, ideological retreat in Peking's fanatical antagonism to rival forms of politico-social organization, renunciation of the use of force by the protagonists, Peking's adherence to a nuclear-arms accord that makes important accommodations to its views on arms control, a thinning out of American military power in Asia, neutralization of certain areas near China, radical curtailment of support by the Communist states of subversion in other lands, and an American trade and assistance program to help Chinese economic growth.

A public discussion of how to move toward a compromise, and what its content should be, has merit even in the present discouraging setting. Obviously, such a debate can harm the security position of the United States by arousing concern among its allies and giving comfort to a most unreasonable foe. Yet open consideration of these points in some detail might enable the United States to clarify its own views, and perhaps demonstrate to others its sincerity of purpose. I am convinced that this effort is necessary and would be valuable even if it does not lead to a "normalization" of relations. It should be recalled that relations with the Soviet Union have still not become normal, however much they have improved, since the death of Stalin.

Rather, the justification for a national discussion is that the United States must think through, to the fullest extent possible, the issues, timing, and tactical approaches involved in an effort to reach an accommodation with China.[17] Those who place primary emphasis on the justness of China's indignant antagonism to the outside world will find it easier to adopt and adhere to a conciliatory position on the issues noted here, as well as on numerous additional points. Others, like myself, who hold that Mao and his colleagues are committed to deny the American system the right of survival, believe that only a lack of means prevents them from realizing their fantastic ambitions. For those of such a persuasion, the difficulty lies in taking steps to preserve a necessary security system while indicating to Peking a strong desire to conciliate. The task is made more difficult as the passage of time reduces compassion for the Chinese. The records of past sins committed by outside powers comes to have less relevance as the nightmare that confronts the United States today grows in intensity.

Yet the essentially deadly nature of other possible courses of action remains the major motivation for investigating approaches toward a conciliatory resolution of this crisis, however cautionary and hedged by security requirements these steps may have to be. It is a pity that China's leaders refuse to recognize that there has been, and still exists, warm admiration for China in this country. It is a tragedy beyond the capacity of words to describe that, in an era when the term "world politics" has finally become a reality, the bitter enmity between these former friends should threaten the planet's political and physical integrity.

Notes

Chapter 1

1. See John K. Fairbank, "Dilemma of American Far Eastern Policy," *Pacific Affairs*, vol. 36 (Winter 1963–64), p. 434.
2. See the U.N. publications *Economic Security for Asia and the Far East, 1962*, p. 179, and *Yearbook of National Income Statistics, 1962*, p. 311.

Chapter 2

1. For a typical presentation, see N. S. Khrushchev, "On Peaceful Coexistence," *Foreign Affairs*, vol. 38 (October 1959), pp. 1–18. Marshall Shulman argues that a limited and tactical policy of co-existence was already begun in the last years of the Stalin era. See his *Stalin's Foreign Policy Reappraised* (Cambridge: Harvard University Press, 1963).
2. Testimony of the general staff officers in Washington in 1951 make this abundantly clear. See *Military Situation in the Far East*. Hearings before the Armed Services Committee and Foreign Relations Committee, U.S. Senate, 82nd Congress, 1st session (Washington: Government Printing Office, 1952). See especially the testimony of General Omar Bradley, Chairman of the Joint Chiefs of Staff. See also General Omar Bradley, "U.S. Military Policy: 1950," *Combat Forces Journal*, vol. 1 (October 1950), p. 7.
3. It should also be noted that the Japanese unsuccessfully suggested an American alliance at the time the Open Door notes were first issued and then again in 1905, during the Taft-Katsura talks.
4. Robert J. C. Butow, *Tojo and the Coming of the War* (Princeton: Princeton University Press, 1961), Chapter 11.
5. See my "The Military View of American National Policy, 1904–1940," *American Historical Review*, vol. 66 (January 1961), pp. 370–376.
6. Toward the end the roles became reversed as Ambassador Grew argued vainly for a more flexible negotiating position. Cordell Hull, *The Memoirs of Cordell Hull* (New York: Macmillan, 1948), vol. II, pp. 1031 ff. Joseph S. Grew, *Turbulent Era* (Boston: Houghton Mifflin, 1952), vol. II, Chapter 35, esp. pp. 196 ff.
7. Plans to fortify Guam in order to protect the Philippines were put forward

367

in 1919. With the Washington Conference treaty of 1922, such proposals fell into abeyance until 1938, when appropriations were sought to develop this base. See "Strategy in the Pacific," Joint Board 325 S28e, December 18, 1919.

8. Stetson Conn, "Changing Concepts of National Defense in the United States, 1937–1947," *Military Affairs*, vol. 28 (Spring 1964), contrasts the Continental and hemispheric orientations that prevailed as late as 1940 (as noted in WPD 4250–1) with the broader interests expressed by the Joint Board estimate of September 11, 1941. In addition to aiding Britain and the Soviet Union, we were to resist Japanese expansion by all means short of war. The basic long-range objective, according to the Joint Board, was "the eventual establishment in Europe and Asia of a balance of power which will most nearly insure political stability in those regions and the future security of the United States; and, so far as practicable, the establishment of regimes favorable to economic and individual liberty." Pp. 1, 6.

9. See the overall survey on the first two years of the Pacific War published by the Department of the Army, Office of Military History. Louis Morton, *Strategy in the Pacific* (Washington: Government Printing Office, 1962), Chapter 26.

10. According to an undated memorandum from the State-War-Navy Co-ordinating Committee to the Joint Chiefs of Staff, "the State Department requests, as a matter of urgency, the views of the Joint Chiefs of Staff regarding the interest of the United States in military occupation of South Korea from the point of view of the military security of the United States." A reply by Secretary of Defense James Forrestal in a memorandum to the Secretary of State dated September 26, 1947, declared that

> The United States has little strategic interest in maintaining the present troops and bases in Korea. . . .
>
> In the event of hostilities in the Far East, our present forces in Korea would be a military liability and could not be maintained there without substantial reinforcement prior to the onset of hostilities.
>
> If . . . an enemy were able to establish and maintain strong air and naval bases in the Korean peninsula, he might be able to interfere with United States communications and operations. . . . Such interference would require an enemy to maintain substantial air and naval forces in that area where they would be subject to neutralization by air action. Neutralization by air action would be more feasible and less costly than large-scale ground operations.
>
> In light of the present severe shortage of military manpower, the corps of two divisions, totalling some 45,000 men now maintained in South Korea, could well be used elsewhere. The withdrawal of these forces from Korea would not impair the military positions of the Far East Command unless, in consequence, the Soviets established military strength in South Korea capable of mounting an assault against Japan.
>
> (*The New York Times*, November 3, 1952.)

11. Secretary Acheson defined the island line as part of our military perimeter. Other areas, Korea included, he viewed as part of the "commitments of the entire civilized world under the Charter of the United Nations." See

McGeorge Bundy, ed., *The Pattern of Responsibility* (Cambridge: Houghton Mifflin, 1952), pp. 199–200.
12. Dwight Eisenhower, *Mandate for Change* (New York: Doubleday, 1963), Chapter 7.
13. It can be argued that, at that time, we had no duty even under the U.N. Charter to protect the Nationalists, since they were engaged in a civil war in which the question of aggression did not arise.

Chapter 3

1. See, for example, "Moscow's Fateful Choice," *The Economist*, vol. 215 (June 19, 1965), p. 1369, which cites a Soviet party secretary, Mr. Demichev, who argued, "Some people are foisting a false choice on us—either to support the liberation struggles of the peoples, or to pursue the policy of peaceful coexistence. In reality such a dilemma does not exist."
2. The efforts made by America and Russia to maintain disarmament discussions and improve scientific contacts during July 1965 sat oddly with the warnings of direct Soviet action in response to any new American departures in the Vietnamese War. This juxtaposition of attitudes summed up the strain this agonizing war has imposed upon the efforts of the two superpowers to conduct a "moderate Cold War."
3. This was a major thrust in the arguments presented by Army planners in 1935 against involvement in a confrontation with Japan. See papers prepared by Colonel Walter Krueger, General Stanley Embick and Colonel Sherman Miles in "Military (including Naval) Situation in the Far East," Joint Board 305, Ser. 573.
4. G. R. Storry argues that, even apart from Communist territorial gains, Japan may respond to China's acquisition of nuclear power by ending its defensive tie with the United States. "Japan's Position as a World Power," *The World Today*, vol. 21 (May 1965), pp. 221–222. In the same issue, Alistair Buchan expresses great concern regarding India's capacity to handle its foreign problems, which he considers as presenting a greater danger to the state than its formidable domestic economic and political crises. He, too, finds the rise in Chinese power at the heart of the problem. "The Security of India," pp. 210–216.

Chapter 4

1. A variation on this view gained renewed currency during the summer of 1965 when Walter Lippmann argued in his newspaper columns that the United States should (a) limit its large-scale military effort in Vietnam to the key coastal port-population perimeters and (b) use this stance to negotiate a compromise settlement.
2. It has been argued that, with the Russians committed to peaceful coexistence, it is possible for the United States to drive the weaker Chinese state toward this posture by a policy of firmness. See John R. Thomas, "Sino-Soviet Relations after Khrushchev and Mao," *Orbis*, vol. 7 (October 1963), pp. 537–549. However, this still leaves unanswered the question of Soviet responses if American firmness takes the form of military action.

3. To an important extent, therefore, the types of strategic analyses that Americans undertook in the 1950s regarding potential Soviet power would not be applicable in early stages of this situation. The established potentials of our missile power and the great gap between American and Chinese strategic strength are the two greatest points of difference.

4. For the view that President Roosevelt had far less dramatic immediate purposes behind his "Quarantine speech," see Dorothy Borg, "Notes on Roosevelt's Quarantine Speech," *Political Science Quarterly*, vol. 72 (September 1957), pp. 405–433. More generally, see her *The United States and the Far Eastern Crisis of 1933–1938* (Cambridge: Harvard University Press, 1964).

5. In July 1964, the United States did gain OAS approval for action against Cuba, but only in response to Cuban initiatives to undermine other regimes. The Ninth Meeting of Consultation agreed to warn Cuba "that if it should persist in carrying out acts that possess characteristics of aggression and intervention against one or more member States of the Organization, the member States shall preserve their essential rights as sovereign States by the use of self-defense in either individual or collective form, which could go so far as resort to armed force, until such time as the Organ of Consultation takes measures to guarantee the peace and security of the hemisphere." The events of the following year concerning civil conflict in the Dominican Republic crystallized (a) the hostility the United States encountered when it intervened unilaterally in a domestic struggle with armed force and (b) the difficulty of getting the OAS to provide an inter-American force ready on a standby basis to act to preserve hemispheric security.

Chapter 5

1. T.I.A.S. 2491, signed September 8, 1951, in force April 28, 1952, expired with the treaty revision of 1960.

2. W. Macmahon Ball asserted that Australia was concentrating on security considerations at the expense of developing plans to draw closer to its Asian neighbors in political and economic affairs. "An Australian View of Southeast Asian Security," *Far Eastern Survey*, vol. 23 (November 1954), pp. 165–168. Norman D. Harper noted a growing tension between his country's worried security policy and its interest in warm political ties with neighboring states in "Australia and Southeast Asia," *Pacific Affairs*, vol. 28 (September 1955), pp. 203–220. W. F. Monk argued that New Zealand was neither building the power to secure itself nor reforming its policies to be more amenable to Asian interests in "New Zealand Faces North," *Pacific Affairs*, vol. 26 (September 1935), pp. 220–229.

3. In the 1949 NATO debates, Senators Tom Connally and Arthur Vandenberg, both strong supporters of the treaty, argued that it did not obligate us to go to war. However, the implication of an "ultimate commitment" was there—allowing the Congress to determine only if the aggression provided against had indeed occurred—and even these two senators agreed that we had a strong moral obligation to fight. See James Reston, *The New York Times*, February 15, 1949.

4. T.I.A.S. 2493, signed September 1, 1951, in force April 29, 1952.

5. T.I.A.S. 2529, signed August 30, 1951, in force August 27, 1952.
6. T.I.A.S. 4033, signed May 15, 1958, in force May 15, 1958.
7. T.I.A.S. 3097, signed October 1, 1953; in force November 19, 1954.
8. T.I.A.S. 3170, signed September 8, 1954; in force February 19, 1955.
9. T.I.A.S. 3178, signed December 2, 1954; in force, March 3, 1955. Article VI stipulated that the territories covered included Taiwan and the Pescadores, and island territories in the Western Pacific under American jurisdiction. It noted that other territories could be added, by mutual agreement.
10. It can be argued that the Nationalist bastion on Taiwan would have fallen had the Korean War not occurred. For in 1950, the United States was not committed to Taiwan's defense until the June 25 attack by North Korea induced President Truman, in effect, to protect the island by committing American naval power to block Communist assaults. The Nationalists had no serious capacity to threaten the mainland and so were not materially affected by the 1950 two-way interdiction. See Frank A. Kierman, *The Fluke That Saved Formosa* (Cambridge: M.I.T. Press, 1954).
11. *The Origin of the Differences Between the CPSU*, etc.
12. T.I.A.S. 4509, signed January 19, 1960, in force June 23, 1960.

Chapter 6

1. The draft peace treaties of 1947–48 concentrated on strengthening the Japanese economy while guarding against a revival of militarism. There had not yet been any stress on security for Japan against outside assault or any provision for American strategic and military interests. Within the State Department, the debate centered upon the degree to which Japanese society and the reformed political system could cope with full self-government. See Frederick S. Dunn, *Peacemaking and the Settlement with Japan* (Princeton: Princeton University Press, 1963), pp. 54–62.
2. Reports of these comments reached the United States over the weekend of February 12–13, 1949. Vigorous denials by all officials concerned, including Royall, followed in the next few days. The Secretary did note, however, that General MacArthur was refused the additional forces he had requested in light of the Communist victory in China.
3. For example, the Army's Vice Chief of Staff, General J. Lawton Collins, called for strengthening American forces in Japan on February 25, 1949.
4. The proposal that the United States guarantee Japanese security had originally been presented to the United States by the country's only Socialist Administration, the Katayama Cabinet of 1947–48. This, of course, did not take up the question of a separate peace. See Premier Yoshida's volume, *The Yoshida Memoirs* (Boston: Houghton Mifflin, 1962), p. 265.
5. See Dunn, *op. cit.*, pp. 92–94.
6. These polls are summarized in Douglas H. Mendel, Jr., *The Japanese People and Foreign Policy* (Berkeley: University of California Press, 1961), pp. 43, 69, 102.
7. In 1956, Japan had an army of 160,000 (in six divisions), a navy of 19,000 and an air force of 11,500.
8. Mendel, *op. cit.*, pp. 68, 69, 74, shows the trends during the middle years of the decade. In 1953, only 10 per cent believed that rearmament and im-

proving Japan's defense force would benefit Japan, as compared with 28 per cent who held that it would benefit both America and Japan and 39 per cent who felt that only America would benefit.

9. Mendel, *op. cit.*, pp. 102, 112, 139, for results of polls on these topics.

10. Leng Shao-chuan, "Japanese Attitudes toward Communist China," *Far Eastern Survey*, vol. 27 (June 1958), pp. 81–89. Also Mendel, *op. cit.*, pp. 43, 50–51, 237. See Part V, below, for a discussion of the Chinese recognition questions in the 1960s.

11. D. H. Mendel, "Behind the 1959 Japanese Elections," *Pacific Affairs*, vol. 32 (September 1959), pp. 298–307. In contrast to the 1955 and 1958 lower-house electoral pattern, in which the combined Socialist vote rose from 29.2 to 32.9 per cent, the 1959 upper-house election, admittedly less vital politically, nevertheless witnessed a reversal in their fortunes and a loss of 10 seats.

12. There was grave concern in 1960 that a serious gap had arisen between American and Japanese perspectives on social and political as well as foreign affairs. See the four Japanese comments in Robert A. Scalapino (intro.) "Japanese Intellectuals Discuss American-Japanese Relations," *Far Eastern Survey*, vol. 29 (October 1960), pp. 145–160. These views generally stressed military neutralism, commitment to democracy, and opposition to American foreign policy, and raised the disquieting issue that these three attitudes were closely related to one another. See also Edwin Reischauer, "The Broken Dialogue with Japan," *Foreign Affairs*, vol. 39 (October 1960), pp. 11–26.

13. U.N., Doc. 5/3079, August 7, 1953, pp. 4–5.

14. Eisenhower, *op. cit.*, pp. 180–181.

15. Eisenhower, *ibid.*, Chapter 19. The President noted that the Communist interest centered on Taiwan, and that the offshore islands were merely incidental to their larger plans to eliminate the Nationalist base of power.

16. Ironically, Secretary Dulles had included Quemoy and Matsu in a draft of the defense treaty, but President Eisenhower felt this specific obligation to be too binding and so removed it. John R. Beal, *John Foster Dulles* (New York: Harper, 1957), pp. 226–227.

17. Tang Tsou, in his "Mao's Limited War in the Taiwan Straits," *Orbis*, vol. 3 (October 1959), pp. 332–350, argues that Mao hoped to wean the Nationalists away from their American tie by this action.

18. T.I.A.S. 1775. For later modifications in base agreements, see T.I.A.S. 1963, 2406, 2739, 2835, and 2936.

Chapter 7

1. Sir Anthony Eden, *Full Circle* (Boston: Houghton Mifflin, 1960), Chapter 5.
2. Charles Lerche, "The United States, Great Britain, and SEATO: A Case Study in the Fait Accompli," *Journal of Politics*, vol. 18 (August 1956), pp. 459–478.
3. Eden, *op. cit.*, Chapter 5.
4. See Eisenhower, *op. cit.*, Chapter 14.
5. Eden, *op. cit.*, Chapter 6; Lerche, *loc. cit.*

6. See Coral Bell, for example, in *Survey of International Affairs, 1954* (London: Royal Institute of International Affairs, 1957), p. 290.
7. Brissenden, *loc. cit.,* p. 215.
8. *SEATO: The Second Year* (Bangkok, 1957).
9. See communiqué of the seventh Council meeting, in *Department of State Bulletin,* vol. 44 (April 17, 1961), pp. 549–550.
10. The United States acted under the bilateral Rusk-Thant agreement of March 6, 1962. American forces went to Thailand two months later.
11. The key American commitments were: (1) a promise of aid in a letter from President Eisenhower to President Ngo Dinh Diem on October 23, 1954 in return for Vietnamese efforts toward self-help and reform and (2) President Kennedy's promise of greater assistance to the Vietnamese defense effort on December 14, 1961.
12. T.I.A.S. 2434, signed October 17, 1950, under the Military Defense Assistance Act, beginning with 1951. This was continued under the Mutual Security Act.
13. "Voice of Free Thailand" broadcasts from across the Indochinese border and Peking's support of the "Independent Thailand Movement" in 1965 gave rise to fears that an assault would begin in earnest.
14. It was not until early 1966, in response to Senatorial resentment over the President's reliance on the pledges given by his predecessors and on a joint resolution of 1964 in the wake of the Gulf of Tonkin incident, that the Johnson Administration rested its Vietnamese effort on the SEATO commitment. Testimony of Secretary Rusk before the Senate Committee on Foreign Relations, February 25, 1966.

Chapter 8

1. George Patterson has argued this at some length. See his *Peking versus Delhi* (New York: Praeger, 1963).
2. T.I.A.S. 2967, May 19, 1954.
3. In fact, this pledge had already been given in December 1950. In an exchange of notes effecting an agreement on Mutual Defense Assistance, the American statement held that "the Department [of State] understands . . . that the items to be provided . . . are required by the government of Pakistan to maintain its internal security, its legitimate self-defense, or permit it to participate in the defense of the area of which it is a part; and that it will not undertake any act of aggression against another state." Pakistan accepted these terms in the note of November 29, 1950. T.I.A.S. 2165.
4. Article I of Agreement of Cooperation between the Government of the United States of America and the Government of Pakistan. T.I.A.S 4190.
5. President Ayub again made this offer early in 1960 while on a tour of East Pakistan. *Dawn,* January 25, 1960.
6. In a related matter, it is significant that in 1962, at the time they were placing missiles in Cuba, the Russians accepted a unilateral declaration from Tehran that Iran would not allow foreign bases on its soil, after having insisted for three years that this assurance take the form of a bilateral treaty agreement.

7. Mohammed Ayub Khan, "Pakistan Perspective," *Foreign Affairs*, vol. 38 (July 1960), unequivocally stressed his country's aligned posture, in an essay devoted essentially to domestic affairs. P. 555.

8. Later in 1961, reflecting on the experience of that spring, President Ayub called on America to bypass SEATO, which he considered too cumbersome a mechanism, and assume direct responsibility for the states of Indochina covered in the SEATO Protocol.

9. Aslam Siddiqi, *Pakistan Seeks Security* (Lahore: Longmans, 1961), p. 137.

10. This caused great anguish in Pakistan where neutrality had been denounced in strong moralistic terms. See for example, Mohammed Ayub Khan, "Strategic Problems of the Middle East," *Asian Review*, vol. 54 (July 1958), pp. 220–228.

11. So deep were the roots of Pakistani fears of India that the darkest interpretations were placed on studies of national and regional defense problems undertaken by Indians with official or semi-official standing, such as Indian Council of World Affairs, *Defense and Security in the Indian Ocean Area* (New York: Asia Publishing House, 1958), which in turn was based in part on K. M. Panikkar, *India and the Indian Ocean* (London: Allen and Unwin, 1945). See also Panikkar, *Problems of Indian Defense* (New York: Asia Publishing House, 1960).

12. This boundary settlement on March 2, 1963, was a reasonable territorial compromise, with many favorable aspects for Pakistan. The alarming aspect of it, from the perspective of London and Washington, was its anti-Indian orientation, as Pakistan cooperated with China to isolate New Delhi.

13. The Pakistani-Chinese meeting of February 1964 produced a communiqué endorsing Pakistan's demand for a plebiscite on Kashmir and supporting Peking's entry into the United Nations. The two countries also agreed to a second Bandung-type conference (*i.e.*, of all underdeveloped states)—as opposed to a second Belgrade-type of conference (of neutrals), at which the Indian view would hold a more dominant place.

14. From the American perspective, one favorable development in Pakistan's foreign relations, resulting in part from preoccupation with India, and in part from a change of regimes in Afghanistan, has been its settlement with the latter. See George L. Montagno, "The Pak-Afghan Detente," *Asian Survey*, vol. 3 (December 1963).

15. The Tashkent settlement of January 1966 exemplified constructive Soviet influence. Though neither belligerent yielded on the major issues at stake, Premier Kosygin succeeded in getting India and Pakistan to move toward normal relations, a maneuver that the United States firmly supported. In fact, Vice-President Humphrey, in promising to review aid to both states in February 1966, made this contingent on their adherence to the Tashkent agreement.

16. The central importance of India in Pakistan's view of foreign affairs and the resultant problems in its relations with the United States are most clearly illustrated in the speeches of its Foreign Minister and the writings of its President. See Z. A. Bhutto, *Foreign Policy of Pakistan* (Karachi: Pakistan Institute of International Affairs, 1964), and Mohammed Ayub Khan, *Pakistan Perspective* (Washington: Embassy of Pakistan, 1965).

Chapter 9

1. In *Hearings, Foreign Assistance of 1964,* House Committee on Foreign Affairs, 88th Congress, 2nd sess., 1964 (Washington: Government Printing Office, 1964) Secretary McNamara noted that Thailand came within the "Forward Defense" category of eleven states around the Communist periphery on whom the United States was concentrating the bulk of its military aid (p. 86). Deputy Assistant Secretary Frank Sloan described Thailand as the hub of the U.S. Southeast Asian defense effort, a key to SEATO and to American planning, an important center of a counter-insurgency program, and a locale for military construction work (p. 500).

2. The riots in Taipei, Taiwan, that led to the burning of a USIS library in 1957 ostensibly arose over resentment at the American retention of criminal jurisidiction in a particular case. Even if the real reason was antagonism over a U.S. decision against supporting a return to the mainland, the fact remained that resentment over SOFA existed near the surface, ready for political exploitation.

3. For the year ending November 30, 1963, the largest number of cases in non-NATO lands arose in Japan, but of the 3,433 total subject to local jurisdiction, 2,775 were traffic accidents. The Japanese waiver rate has been very high, reaching 89.11 per cent of the 2,747 alleged offenses by military personnel. Of the 340 cases tried, 274 resulted in fines, 29 in suspended jail sentences, and 29 in jail sentences. *Hearings, Operation of Article VII, NATO Status of Forces Treaty,* Senate, Subcommittee of the Committee on Armed Services, 88th Congress, 2nd sess. (Washington: Government Printing Office, August 7, 1964), p. 17.

4. To judge by the mild tone of these hearings in recent years, this problem has not proved as acute as feared, but American legislators remain alert to possible troubles in regard to trials or treatment in prison for all military personnel overseas. See, for example, *Hearings, Operation of Article VII, NATO Status of Forces Treaty,* Senate, Subcommittee of the Committee on Armed Services, 89th Congress, 1st sess. (Washington: Government Printing Office, June 25, 1965).

5. After six years of difficult negotiations, the United States finally reached a SOFA with South Korea. Dissatisfaction among Korean negotiators, as had been true of negotiators elsewhere, centered on opposition to a number of provisions over which American military officials retained legal authority.

6. The base and weapons understandings of 1959, the Bohlen-Serrano agreements, were made formally contingent on a settlement of the force jurisdiction question. Negotiations reached an impasse on this point in 1961, and were suspended until 1965, when, because of incidents in December of the preceding years, the Filipinos pressed for a resumption of talks. The complex American-Filipino relationship, especially in regard to trade and economic privileges for American nationals, combined with the question of bases and criminal jurisdiction to intensify the emotional atmosphere in which these issues could be negotiated. See Martin Meadows, "Recent Developments in

Philippine-American Relations: A Case Study in Emergent Nationalism," *Asian Survey*, vol. 5 (June 1965), pp. 305–318.

7. Deputy Secretary of Defense Cyrus Vance stressed the continuing importance of progress toward reducing the American balance-of-payments problem, noting that the adverse balance in billions of dollars in recent years had been reduced in the over-all defense program as follows: 1961-2.8; 1962-2.1; 1963-1.7; 1964-1.6. *Hearings, Military Posture and H.R. 4016 to Authorize [Defense] Appropriations during Fiscal Year 1966*, House, Committee on Armed Services, 89th Congress, 1st sess., Armed Services Paper no. 7 (Washington: Government Printing Office, 1965), pp. 161–162. Military assistance to Korea dropped from $161.4 million in 1963 to $147 million in 1964, with a further cut to $128.5 million in 1965, much to the dismay of the Korean National Assembly.

8. See W. D. Reeve, *The Republic of Korea* (London: Oxford, 1963), pp. 137–142.

9. The American shift from grants to loans has in fact put a strain on Korea's balance-of-payments position by necessitating a larger expenditure of foreign exchange for industrial raw materials. In exports, Seoul's striking growth rate saw this figure jump from $19.8 million in 1959 to $119.0 million in 1964, with manufactures accounting for over half the latter sum. However, the balance-of-payments and trade gaps remain large, with $530 million worth of goods needed for 1965 out of a total estimated national requirement of $1.67 billion. Exports, it is hoped, will rise sharply, to $170 million, but this is only one-third the anticipated import need. Ministry of Information, Republic of Korea, *Korean Economy Progress and Prospect* (Seoul, 1965), pp. 12–13, 23–24.

Chapter 10

1. See, for example, West German Defense Minister Kai-Uwe von Hassel's discussion of alliance relations in "Détente through Firmness," *Foreign Affairs*, vol. 42 (January 1964), pp. 184–186. Richard L. Worsnop, "American Troops Abroad," *Editorial Research Reports* (January 15, 1964), notes the concern Europeans felt about the possible removal of forces stationed in Europe to the American continent as a consequence of improved deployment capacity. Pp. 23–39.

2. What Americans considered prudent retreats from the doctrine of massive retaliation raised doubts in Europe. Pierre Gallois thus argued for national nuclear forces in "Force de frappe," translated in *Atlas*, vol. 5 (June 1963), pp. 342–344.

3. B-57s and F-102s were phased-out. In January 1965 two squadrons were removed, leaving six in Japan. General John P. McConnell explained that American squadrons were withdrawn from Clark Field and Japan as indigenous forces gained a greater capacity to provide for the defense of South Korea and Japan. However, he added that certain new fighter squadrons would undergo tactical rotation to both Japan and the Philippines. *Hearings, Department of Defense Appropriations, 1966*, Senate Subcommittees of the Committees on Appropriations and Armed Services, 89th Congress, 1st sess. (Washington: Government Printing Office, 1965), p. 964. The ex-

pansion of air facilities in Japan during the 1950s and their reduction in the next decade is a parallel case. The earlier effort aroused great hostility, and despite Japan's greatly enlarged capability, the withdrawal of viable American power in 1963–64 gave rise to considerable uneasiness.

4. Korean nationalist opposition to Japan manifested itself in the agitation against the 1965 treaty that allowed Seoul and Tokyo to resume full relations. Former President Posun Yun and former Premier Huh Chung led the substantial effort against ratification, arguing that this would open the way to the re-establisment of a Japanese hegemony in Korea.

5. Along with some sporadic action on the Korean front during 1964–65, there were vague Asian Communist threats about the opening of new theaters of combat as reprisals for American and South Korean participation in Vietnam. In the future, concern for the security of South Korea might well become an important aspect of a military crisis whose focus lies elsewhere in the Far East. The Koreans could cite airlift experiments, reduction of the American military establishment, and curtailment of expenses as indicating that the American commitment was a somewhat uncertain one. See, for example, Pyong Choon Ham, "Korea's 'Mendicant Mentality' A Critique of U.S. Policy," *Foreign Affairs*, vol. 43 (October 1964), p. 70.

6. Note, for example, the difficulties Premier Sato encountered during his 1965 visit there over the jurisdiction issue, and the unfavorable repercussions of this issue on national politics.

7. Robert Trumbull reports that almost all Okinawan leaders who favor a reversion to Japan want the American military bases to remain and to be treated differently from those in Japan. *The New York Times*, March 9, 1965.

8. Mendel, *op. cit.*, pp. 13, 134, 139; national survey conducted for Mr. Mendel by the Central Research Services, Inc., Tokyo, on file at the Roper Center, Williamstown, Mass.

9. However, the British-controlled islands in the Bay of Bengal and the Indian Ocean—like the "flyspeck" island bases in the Pacific—in general lack the space to support adequate facilities and their use may provoke objections centering on nationalism, neutralism, and jurisdictional controls. For instance, after receiving independence in 1965, the Maldive Islands assumed a distinctly neutralist coloration, making establishment of a base unlikely.

10. Secretary McNamara also referred to pre-positioned equipment as being in place in Okinawa and Thailand. *Hearings, Department of Defense Appropriations, 1966*, Senate, *loc. cit.* (Washington: Government Printing Office, 1965), p. 309.

Chapter 11

1. See, for example, a 1964 public-opinion study of American attitudes toward China, which reported that a large majority thought that we should be concerned about Communist China because of its aggressive intentions or its strength. Yet of those aware of the existence of two Chinese regimes, 34 per cent favored dealings with the Peking government as against 25 per cent opposed supporting a Nationalist attack against the mainland, as

against 10 per cent in favor. More respondents favored than opposed reciprocity in visits, discussion of problems, and exchanges of ambassadors, but a majority opposed the sale of wheat to Peking or its admission to the United Nations. *The American Public's View of U.S. Policy Toward China* (New York: Council on Foreign Relations, 1964), tables 2, 3, 7, 10, and 16.

2. A. M. Halpern, "Communist China and Peaceful Co-existence," *China Quarterly*, no. 3 (July–September 1960), pp. 16–31, stresses that Mao viewed the 1957 Soviet technological achievements as a far more extensive breakthrough in the struggle for power with the West than did Khrushchev.

3. In early 1964, Prince Sihanouk threatened to ally himself with China unless America and Britain agreed to participate in a conference to guarantee Cambodia's neutrality. However, a year later, when such a conference proved acceptable to Washington, Sihanouk had moved too close to China and therefore rejected the proposal, which the Chinese had opposed from the outset.

4. See Donald Hellman, "Japan's Relations with Communist China," *Asian Survey*, vol. 4 (October 1964), pp. 1085–92, and Ogata Sadeko, "Japanese Attitudes toward China," *Asian Survey*, vol. 5 (August 1965), pp. 389–98.

5. See *infra*, p. 28.

6. The rise of wheat as a major consideration in China's foreign policy is mirrored in the size of wheat imports. From 1960 to 1964, they totaled almost 22 million tons from all sources. For 1964 alone, Peking imported 5.6 million tons, of which Canada supplied 2.2 and Australia 1.8 million tons. *Statesman's Yearbook 1965–66*, p. 882.

7. A French policy clearly at odds with American objectives was set forth in a Statement on Vietnam by President Charles de Gaulle that recognized "the role [the Vietnamese people] would be capable of playing . . . once they could go ahead with their activities independently of the outside, in internal peace and unity and in harmony with their neighbors." August 29, 1963. He stressed, as conditions for peace, "an end to all foreign intervention . . . and . . . neutrality of the country." Thirteenth press conference, February 21, 1966. For the evolution of the French stand on neutralization, see *The New York Times*, February 26, 1965.

8. See the analysis by Drew Middleton, *The New York Times*, February 28, 1965.

9. A *Peking Review* discussion of the French-American "struggle" as a "focal point" in the "process of disintegration of the imperialist camp" was reported in *The New York Times*, April 4, 1964.

10. Pauline Lewin, *The Foreign Trade of Communist China* (New York: Praeger, 1964), p. 93, notes that Peking's trade pattern is increasingly centered on economic ends, due to its enormous needs and inadequate export strength. However, when the Chinese thought that they had the upper hand, as with Japan in 1958 at the start of the Great Leap Forward, they have tried to use economic negotiations to try to further their political objectives. The author considers a repetition of the 1958 experience improbable. See also the careful study of China's capacity for economic development and its relation to the problem of foreign trade by Alexander

Eckstein, *Communist China's Economic Growth and Foreign Trade* (New York: McGraw-Hill, for the Council on Foreign Relations, 1966).
11. See for example the summary of the Third National People's Congress (December 21, 1964–January 4, 1965), pp. 62–70. The turn toward optimism and renewed ideological extremism, already noted the previous year, became even more pronounced at the end of 1964. For an analysis of the less strident Second Congress meeting in the shadow of recent failures, see W. A. C. Adie, "Political Aspects of the National People's Congress," *China Quarterly*, no. 11 (July–September 1962), pp. 78–88, and the press communiqué, pp. 105–110; and George T. Yee, "The 1962 and 1963 Sessions of the National People's Congress of Communist China," *Asian Survey*, vol. 4 (August 1964), pp. 981–990.
12. *Statistical Yearbook 1964* (New York: United Nations, 1965), tables 47 and 117.
13. On the plans, changed policies, and performance record of the 1950s, see Liu Ta-chung and Yeh Kung-chia, *The Economy of Mainland China* (Princeton: Princeton University Press, 1965), for the years 1953–1959, and Chêng Chu-yuan, *Communist China's Economy 1949–1962* (South Orange, N.J.: Seton Hall University Press, 1963).
14. See Frank Robertson, "The 1962 Harvest," *China Quarterly*, no. 13 (January–March 1963), pp. 254–257. For the period immediately preceding, see W. K., "Communist China's Agricultural Calamities," *China Quarterly*, no. 6 (April–June 1961), pp. 64–75.
15. The Third Five-Year Plan, geared toward an independent economic development program, was first announced for 1963. When this proved beyond reach, the government moderated its pace and decided to begin this phase in 1966. But the emphasis throughout has been on heavy industry; only the marginal degree of emphasis has been modified when circumstances so demanded. See *The New York Times*, April 26, 1964, for a government statement that the state's investment in agriculture will be extremely limited and that peasants will have to rely on their own resources in developing production.
16. *China Quarterly*, no. 18 (April–June 1964), provides a valuable summary analysis of this and other important matters covered in "China's Secret Military Papers," a collection of documents captured in 1961.
17. Soviet aid in 1959–60 was well above that of 1956–58, which in turn was greater than in 1953–55. Edwin Jones, *loc. cit.*, p. 19. Cheng Chu-yuan, *Economic Relations between Peking and Moscow* (New York: Praeger, 1964); Chapter 5 is especially comprehensive on Soviet assistance through 1957.
18. Harold P. Ford, "Modern Weapons and the Sino-Soviet Estrangement," *China Quarterly*, no. 18 (April–June 1964), pp. 164–168.
19. See David A. Charles, "The Dismissal of Marshal P'eng Teh-huai," *China Quarterly*, no. 8 (October–December 1961). The purge of P'eng was strongly hinted at six years after the fact in a statement by Marshal Ho Lung emphasizing political control over the army. *The New York Times*, August 2, 1965.
20. Ellis Joffe, "The Conflict Between the Old and the New in the Chinese Army," *China Quarterly*, no. 18 (April–June 1964), pp. 124 ff, and Davis A. Bobrow, "The Good Officer: Definition and Training," *ibid.*, pp. 141–152.

21. International Commission of Jurists, *The Question of Tibet and the Rule of Law* (Geneva, 1959).

22. See John W. Lewis, *Leadership in Communist China* (Ithaca: Cornell University Press, 1963), Chapters 1 and 2.

23. A critical study of Mao's claims to originality of theory and doctrine, Arthur A. Cohen, *The Communism of Mao Tse-tung* (Chicago: University of Chicago Press, 1964) notes that such claims are valid in this category.

24. H. F. Schurmann, "Russia and China: The Roots of Social Policy," in Walter Laqueur and Leopold Labedz, eds., *The Future of Communist Society* (New York: Praeger, 1962), p. 161, cites this key difference and notes that it reflects the political structures of the Russian and Chinese societies.

25. Lecture by Allen S. Whiting at Williams College, October 1963.

26. According to the Chinese Communists, "The 'class struggle' . . . appears omnipresent in the international arena and . . . remains a constant in relations between 'socialist' and 'capitalist' countries." Allen S. Whiting, "China," in R. E. Ward and R. C. Macrides, eds., *Modern Political Systems: Asia* (Englewood Cliffs: Prentice-Hall, 1963), p. 142.

27. Chou En-lai reiterated this point in an interview with a French correspondent, reported in *The New York Times*, March 26, 1965, citing it as the basis for reaching any understanding with the United States. However, the Chinese adhered to "peaceful coexistence" in the realm of formal interstate relations, even offering it to the United States, provided America withdrew from the Taiwan area.

28. A major Chinese after-the-act assault on the Russian positions at the 1957 and 1960 meetings appeared in a comprehensive statement published in *The New York Times*, September 14, 1963.

29. Premier Khrushchev's famous statement of January 6, 1961, "For New Victories of the World Communist Movement," *Kommunist* (January 1961), pp. 3–37, in which he supported just wars of national liberation, contrasting them to the dangers of total and limited wars, has been repeatedly cited by American government officials as evidence of Soviet commitment in this regard. However, as the Chinese noted, later Soviet statements and Russian actions indicated a far from wholehearted support of this stand.

30. Ford, *op. cit.*, p. 170.

31. The main opening volley of this public attack was the editorial "Long Live Leninism!" *Hung Ch'i*, April 16, 1960, commemorating the nineteenth anniversary of Lenin's birth.

32. Harold Hinton, "The Sino-Soviet Dispute and the West: The Chinese Aspect," in Arnold Wolfers, ed., *Changing East-West Relations and the Unity of the West* (Baltimore: Johns Hopkins Press, 1964), p. 81, noted that provocation of "imperialist" acts would also serve Peking's purposes of heightening revolutionary tension and awareness.

33. Admitting that local wars might escalate, the Chinese also argued that in seven instances, American "aggression" had been checked, thus demonstrating that imperialist wars could be stopped short of dangerous escalation. *Hung Ch'i*, April 1, 1960. In a letter to the Russians of July 14, 1963, the Chinese again stressed the diminution of this danger.

34. Thomas Wolfe, *Soviet Strategy at the Crossroads* (Cambridge: Harvard

University Press, 1964), Chapter 10, noted that more recent Russian strategic writing allowed a role for limited war.
35. See A. M. Halpern, "The Foreign Policy Uses of the Chinese Revolutionary Model," *China Quarterly*, no. 7 (July–September 1961), pp. 1–16. Stuart Schram, "The 'Military Deviations' of Mao Tse-tung," *Problems of Communism*, vol. 13 (January–February 1964), pp. 49–56, holds that Mao tends to view the matter excessively in military terms.
36. And the statement along similar lines by the North Vietnamese, *The New York Times*, March 28, 1965.
37. The British analyst, C. P. Fitzgerald, in "A Fresh Look at the Chinese Revolution," *Pacific Affairs*, vol. 36 (Spring 1963), pp. 47–53, does not consider China inner-oriented to this extent, but he stresses the reactive nationalistic aspects of its revolution, its anti-Western and anti-Russian nature, its quest for a cohesive and embracing ideology, its deep desire for national unity, and its emphasis on organization and material progress. See also his pamphlet, *The Chinese View of Their Place in the World* (London: Oxford University Press, 1964), for a more sympathetic interpretation of Peking's orientation than is presented here.
38. Senator J. W. Fulbright pressed these views—at least for further examination if not advocacy—in his public speeches and comments in Senate Committee on Foreign Relations hearings during February and March 1966.
39. Compare Ralph Powell, "Everyone a Soldier—The Communist Chinese Militia," *Foreign Affairs*, vol. 39 (October 1960), pp. 100–111, with John Gittings, "China's Militia," *China Quarterly*, no. 18 (April–June 1964), pp. 110–116.
40. Samuel B. Griffith II, "Communist China's Capacity to Make War," *Foreign Affairs*, vol. 43 (January 1965), notes that the regular army now has command and training control over the militia, p. 228.
41. However, for an optimistic appraisal along with a summary of guerrilla raids, see Robert P. Martin, "Guerrilla War Hits Red China," *U.S. News and World Report*, vol. 54 (March 4, 1963), pp. 40–44, containing an interview with Generalissimo Chiang Kai-shek's son, Chiang Ching-kuo.
42. The specific issue of Taiwan and the general presence of the United States in Asia are closely linked in mainland Chinese thinking and propaganda. See for example, *Drive the U.S. Imperialists Out of Asia!* (Peking: Foreign Language Press, 1960).
43. George Patterson illuminates these problems in a review article in *China Quarterly*, no. 18 (April–June 1964). See also Margaret Fisher, and Leo Rose, "Ladakh and the Sino-Indian Border Crisis," *Asian Survey*, vol. 2 (October 1963), pp. 27–37; Surya P. Sharma, "The India-China Border Dispute: An Indian Perspective," *American Journal of International Law*, vol. 59 (January 1965), pp. 16–47.
44. W. F. Van Eekelen, *India's Foreign Policy and the Border Dispute with China* (The Hague: Nijhoff, 1964), in tracing the details of this argument, relates it to the erosion of the five principles of coexistence as a guideline for Indian foreign policy.
45. The effort of these neutralist states (U.A.R., Ghana, Ceylon, Cambodia, Indonesia, Burma) resulted in a meeting at Colombo on December 10–12,

1962, at which they devised a six-point plan for settling the border dispute. See "The 'Little Summit,' " *Far Eastern Economic Review*, vol. 39 (January 3, 1963), and *United Asia*, vol. 15 (January 1963), pp. 5–7. The formal positions of the two protagonists are detailed in India, Ministry of External Affairs, *Notes, Memoranda and Letters Exchanged between the Governments of India and China, November 1961–January 1963 and July 1963–January 1964* (New Delhi: White Papers, 6, 7, 8, 10, 1962–1964).

46. On the Burmese border accord, see Maung Maung, "The Chinese-Burma Border," *India Quarterly*, vol. 16 (October–December 1960), pp. 358–364, and Daphne E. Whittam, "The Sino-Burmese Boundary Treaty," *Pacific Affairs*, vol. 34 (Summer 1961), pp. 174–183. F. L. Greaves, "Thorns in the Dragon's Side," *U.S. Naval Institute Proceedings*, vol. 90 (November 1964), holds that the territorial gains in both settlements had strategic value for China, with little paid in return, p. 57.

47. For a recent illustration, see *The New York Times*, May 18, 1965.

48. Wolfgang Leonhard, *The Kremlin Since Stalin* (New York: Praeger, 1962), cites the new leaders' decision after 1953 to drop the mixed enterprise approach, and to trade, as Mao wished, on a strictly commercial basis for the products of the border regions, pp. 107–108.

49. See *The New York Times*, May 5, May 10, October 12, November 19, 1964 for instances of harsh words over the border regions. Norman Sklarewitz, "Frontier World War," *Wall Street Journal* (December 21, 1964), summarizes much of this debate along the frontier line from Sinkiang to Manchuria. See also F. C. Jones, "China's Irredenta: The North," *The World Today*, vol. 19 (November 1963), pp. 470–475, and more generally Oliver E. Clubb, "The Sino-Soviet Frontier," *Military Review*, vol. 44 (July 1964), pp. 3–13.

50. The American-Japanese treaty, a major target, serves as an example. See *Oppose the Revival of Japanese Militarism* (Peking: Foreign Language Press, 1960), published at the time of the treaty's revision.

51. Russell Fifield considers it possible that current Japanese and Indian policies may move in the direction of more cooperation and more energetic defense efforts. *Southeast Asia in United States Policy*, Chapter 11.

52. See J. M. Kaul, "Split in the C.P.D.," *India Quarterly*, vol. 20 (October–December 1964), pp. 373–390, Harry Gelman, "The Indian CP between Moscow and Peking," *Problems of Communism*, vol. 11 (November–December 1962), pp. 18–27, and Robert W. Stern, "The Sino-Indian Border Controversy and the Communist Party of India," *Journal of Politics*, vol. 27 (February 1965), pp. 66–86.

53. On the other hand, comparable threats by the Soviet Union have not had much impact on Japan in recent years. See, for example, its warning against Japanese bases becoming involved in the Vietnamese war, and Tokyo's response. *The New York Times*, April 7, 1965. Nevertheless, it is possible that Japan considers China, despite its far weaker nuclear arsenal, a more serious menace.

54. Naoi Takeo, "Sino-Japanese Deadlock," *New Leader*, vol. 41 (September 10, 1958), expressed the prevailing opinion when he viewed the stalemate primarily as a source of trouble for the Japanese economy. Warren Hunsberger, *Japan and the United States in World Trade* (New York: Harper

and Row, for the Council on Foreign Relations, 1964), p. 210, calculates that a combined Japan-China trade of $1 billion a year (about three times the 1964 level) is possible, and notes that imports of about $500 million from China in 1970 would amount to 5 per cent of the total Japanese imports projected for that year under Japan's income doubling plan.

55. It has already had some success with these two states. See Dai Shen-yun, "Peking and Rangoon," *China Quarterly*, no. 5 (January–March 1961), pp. 131–144, and Urmila Phadnis, "Ceylon and the Sino-Soviet Border Conflict," *Asian Survey*, vol. 3 (April 1963), pp. 189–196.

56. This, of course, makes their foreign policy vulnerable to elements beyond their control—particularly the cohesiveness of the neutralist world, the internal politics of distant states, and the ideological beliefs of its leading members—but which the Chinese can continually try to influence.

57. Kevin Devlin, "Rival Communist Parties," *The World Today*, vol. 20 (June 1964), pp. 262–269.

58. Seymour Topping, *The New York Times*, July 4, 1965.

59. See Donald Zagoria, "Communism in Asia," *Commentary*, vol. 39 (February 1965), pp. 53–58.

60. For examples of Chinese gains at Soviet expense in nine states during 1964–65, see summary of "an official British survey" in *The New York Times*, May 27, 1965. On the contest in Latin America, see *The New York Times*, May 25, 1964, and January 17, 1965.

61. In December 1964, Western observers even suspected that President Sukarno had agreed to suppress all but the pro-Peking party in order to gain Chinese diplomatic support for his confrontation with Malaysia. *The New York Times*, January 5 and 8, 1965.

Chapter 12

1. See, for example, Alice L. Hsieh, "Communist China and Nuclear Force," in R. N. Rosecrance, ed., *The Dispersion of Nuclear Weapons* (New York: Columbia University Press, 1964), pp. 164–168.

2. For example, in 1964 the Chinese identified a pilotless aircraft that they had shot down as a "plane of U.S. imperialism," and went on to claim the destruction of ten such U.S. or KMT planes over the past five years. *The New York Times*, November 17, 1964.

3. Whiting, *China Crosses the Yalu*, Chapters 5, 6; see also Panikkar, *In Two Chinas*.

4. Klaus Pringsheim, "China, India, and their Himalayan Border," *Asian Survey*, vol. 3 (October 1963), pp. 483–488.

5. Peking noted on innumerable occasions during 1963–65 that it would "absolutely not stand idly by" in case of American aggression. For one important instance before 1965, see the speech on foreign policy by Chou En-lai reported in *The New York Times*, December 30, 1964. After the bombings of the North were begun, this and other warnings (of "powerful rebuffs," "determination to fight to the end," joining in the war if asked, etc.) received a full airing, without Peking's actually committing itself as fully as in 1950 in Korea.

6. In a *Hung Ch'i* article celebrating the twentieth anniversary of the defeat

of Japan, Lo Jui-ch'ing, Chief of the General Staff of the PLA, noted that China would not go to war against America unless attacked, and then "we will reply on the same scale." See *The New York Times*, May 11, 1965.

7. This view appears to have been dominant in 1965 despite some indicators to the contrary. For example, an article signed "Observer" in *Jen-min Jih-pao* indicated that Hanoi could be justified in extending the war to Laos and Thailand and seemed to lend weight to the possibility of Chinese intervention. *The New York Times*, June 2, 1965.

8. Alexander Eckstein, "Russia and China: A Study in Economic Strategy," in Laqueur and Labedz, eds., *op. cit.*, pp. 146–155 argues that conceptually the stress on rural public works, rural industry and more efficient use of farm labor made sound economic sense. However, the frantic haste, the inadequate planning, failure to calculate the risks involved, and dogmatic assurance present a different picture with regard to actual operations.

9. It can be argued that a rational approach has a better chance of surviving in the domestic political context than in foreign affairs. In internal matters, objective reality can have an impact—albeit delayed—on doctrine, as in the case of the retreat from the communes back to smaller collective units and some private plots. International policies are determined in good part by "doctrinal validity," with reality more easily screened out in a government not noted for its objective search for the actual facts and issues involved. See John W. Lewis, "China's Secret Military Papers: "Continuities and Revelations," *China Quarterly*, no. 18 (April–June 1964), p. 78, for such a view based on study of these captured documents.

10. Hinton, "The Sino-Soviet Dispute," in Wolfers, *op. cit.*, p. 90, holds that the Chinese were willing to risk nuclear war in 1953 over the prisoner-of-war issue and that Stalin supported them before his death, to the extent of preparing for a possible conflict.

11. Premier Khrushchev was reported to have said to a Tass reporter on October 5, 1958 that "the Soviet Union will come to the aid of the CPR . . . if the United States attacks the CPR. . . . But we have not interfered in and do not intend to interfere in the civil war."

12. John Gittings, "Kosygin in Hanoi," *The World Today*, vol. 21 (March 1965), pp. 88–92. See also *The New York Times*, February 6, 1965.

13. Hanoi evidently became more interested in Moscow's moderate approach, at least to the point of agreeing that a conference over Cambodia would be useful. See the joint communiqué issued in Moscow at the end of a visit by a high-level North Vietnamese delegation, April 18, 1965. The Chinese opposed this meeting, precisely because it might broaden to include peace talks on Vietnam. Marshall Shulman holds that fear of Chinese criticism from the left has checked the Soviet drift toward a more stable relationship with the West. *Beyond the Cold War* (New Haven: Yale University Press, 1966), pp. 74–76, 82–83.

14. A. M. Halpern has argued somewhat along these lines: "A truly cautious man is not only prudent in his procedures but tends to direct himself to the safer rather than the maximum options. Chinese caution also depends on what is at stake and how seriously it is believed to be threatened. When the stakes are high and the threat is imminent, the Chinese are capable of

putting everything at risk." In "China in the Postwar World," *China Quarterly*, no. 21 (January–March 1965), p. 45.

15. The secret military papers (captured in 1961), covering the first eight months of 1961, revealed a clear Chinese recognition of military inferiority to the United States. The theme of Russian unreliability also received considerable stress. Still, they emphasized the existence of places where America could not bring its military superiority to bear and where Russian help would not be an important factor. In other words, the lesson was: opportunities for the effective use of force exist even under these unfavorable circumstances. See Alice L. Hsieh, "China's Secret Military Papers: Military Doctrine and Strategy," *China Quarterly*, no. 18 (April–June 1964), p. 99.

16. According to press reports in 1965, following Moscow-Hanoi accords on arms assistance, Soviet air-defense missiles destined for Hanoi had difficulty transiting China, because Peking opposed a major counseling role for Russia.

17. Abraham Brumberg, "The Cold Wind from Moscow," *The Reporter*, vol. 33 (October 21, 1965) notes this great Soviet dilemma, thinks that Russian vacillation has given Moscow the worst of the bargain on both counts, but concludes that a real *détente* with the West will, at best, be very slow in coming, p. 43.

18. Davis Bobrow, "Peking's Military Calculus," *World Politics*, vol. 16 (January 1964), pp. 287–301.

19. Though both the Taiwan Strait and Vietnamese confrontations involved "national liberations," in the latter case, the covert nature of the attack, territorial contiguity, and the proportionately larger commitment made the "just war" issue much more difficult for the Russians to evade.

20. Lee Chon-Sik, "Korea: In Search of Stability," *Asian Survey*, vol. 4 (January 1964), pp. 656–665, and "Korea: Troubles in a Divided State," *Asian Survey*, vol. 5 (January 1965), pp. 25–32.

21. Ferhat Abbas made great propaganda use of China's promise of aid-without-out-strings, following his visit to Peking in October 1960. In November 1964, in response to the Belgian-American paratroop operation in Stanleyville, Congo, Peking announced that it would take "all possible measures" and "never remain indifferent."

22. Hong Kong has considerable commercial and financial value for mainland China. In 1965, only Japan surpassed it as a market for Peking. Also, it provides Communist China with about 60 per cent of its fully convertible foreign exchange each year.

23. Secretary McNamara argued that the 1962 assault involved a staggering logistics effort and drained an already weakened economy. *Hearings on Military Posture and H.R. 2440*, p. 293.

24. See Robert B. Rigg, "Red China's Military Posture," *Army*, vol. 15 (October 1964), pp. 49–52, 54. It is interesting to compare this appraisal with an earlier study on China's shift from a guerrilla orientation, S. M. Chiu, "The Chinese Communist Army in Transition," *Far Eastern Survey*, vol. 27 (November 1958), pp. 168–175.

25. For China's militant *verbal* stance, see Department of State, Pbl. 7379,

Far Eastern Series 112, *Chinese Communist World Outlook* (Washington: Government Printing Office, 1962).

26. Tang Tsou, "Mao's Limited War in the Taiwan Straits," *loc. cit.*, stressed the theme of Peking's effort to undermine the Nationalists' confidence in the Americans. Lewis Gilbert, "Peking and Taipei," *China Quarterly*, vol. 15 (July–September 1963) notes that the Nationalists can indicate an interest in a deal with the mainland in an effort to keep the United States from adopting a policy inimical to Kuomintang interests, pp. 60–64.

27. Donald Klein has argued, however, that a vigorous and effective Nationalist diplomacy has contributed greatly to the ability of the regime on Formosa to hold its own in the diplomatic tug of war centering around recognition and representation at the United Nations. "Formosa's Diplomatic World," *China Quarterly*, vol. 15 (July–September 1963), pp. 45–50.

28. See Asher Lee, *loc. cit.*, Joyce Kallgren, "Nationalist China's Armed Forces," *China Quarterly*, vol. 15 (July–September 1963), pp. 35–44, estimated the Nationalist air force at 500 planes.

29. E. J. Cummings, "The Chinese Communist Navy," *U.S. Naval Institute Proceedings*, vol. 90 (September 1964) concludes that the Chinese Communist navy is facing hard times because of the low priority of resources assigned to it. However, he notes that it will continue to stress, at a minimum, fast torpedo and gun boats and submarines. P. 73.

30. Most frequently, attention focuses on a possible American strike against mainland bases involved in any engagement. There are other potential targets, however, at other sections of the coast or at vulnerable insular locations. It is difficult to judge which type of retaliation would be considered more escalatory, since much would depend on the diplomatic atmosphere, stated intentions, and the type of force used. It is also difficult to be confident the Peking regime could easily limit and control a new thrust in the Straits area to its own specifications.

31. Kallgren, *loc. cit.*, p. 39, estimated that over the years 1955–63, the Nationalists had 75,000–100,000 high-caliber troops on Quemoy and Matsu.

32. Two recent studies on Tokyo-Peking relations note Japan's growing interest in some regularization: Paul F. Langer, "Japan's Relations with China," *Current History*, vol. 46 (April 1964), pp. 193–198, 244, and Lawrence Olson, "Japan's Relations with China: Some Recent Developments," *American Universities Field Services*, vol. 11 (June 1964).

33. At the United Nations, Foreign Minister Shiina Etsusaburo denounced the first Chinese test as an "open betrayal" of mankind.

34. The antagonistic reaction of the Japanese Socialists at the time was intensified by the fact that the test occurred while a JSP delegation was in Peking seeking to improve relations between the two powers. As noted elsewhere, however, JSP leadership the following year nevertheless favored closer ties with Peking. The Vietnamese War served both as a cause and an opportunity for this policy orientation.

35. See G. F. Hudson, "Strains on the Japanese Left," *New Leader*, vol. 46 (September 16, 1963), pp. 12–13; Hans Baerwald, "Factional Politics in Japan," *Current History*, vol. 46 (April 1964), pp. 227–229, 243; A. Kashin, "The Defeat of the pro-Soviet Faction of the Japanese Communist Party," *Institute for the Study of the USSR Bulletin*, vol. 11 (November 1964), pp.

31–35. The letters of April 18 and June 11, 1964, from the Soviet to the Japanese party are in *Soviet Documents*, vol. 2 (August 31, 1964), pp. 3–35.

36. The 1965 upper-house elections witnessed moderate gains on the left— eight seats for the Socialists and one for the Communists. Though economic recession and concern with the government's involvement in America's Vietnam policies played a part in this outcome, a corruption scandal in Tokyo had a telling impact. In the popular vote, the Liberal-Democratic Party totaled about 50 per cent, actually gaining 5 per cent over its 1962 showing, and 10 per cent over the 1959 results. *The New York Times*, July 6, 1965.

37. As of 1965, Japan budgeted only around 1.5 per cent of its GNP for defense. This amount, almost $850 million, represented an increase of more than 9 per cent over 1964, but was far below its capacity.

38. In 1965, the ground forces stood at 171,500 with an additional 33,300 in the navy, and 39,000 in the air army. For 1967–72 only modest budgetary increases are contemplated, with manpower rising only to 180,000 in the army and proportionate increases in the other two services. Since all are volunteers, recruitments are not easy in a high-prosperity economy.

39. James W. Morley, "Japan's Security Policy in Transition," *Current History*, vol. 46 (April 1964), pp. 200–206, considers the problem of future defense policy. Compare the current situation with Hisachi Iwai, *Japan's Defense Strength* (Tokyo: Ministry of Foreign Affairs, 1958). Public opinion has come to accept a military establishment, rising from 58 per cent in favor in 1954 to 76 per cent in 1963. See *The New York Times*, November 5, 1965.

40. Robert Trumbull summarizes many of these arguments, by officials and intellectuals, which have appeared in such magazines as *Sekai to Nihon*, *Chou Koron*, and *Seisaku Geppo*. *The New York Times*, June 27, 1965.

Chapter 13

1. Quoted in P. J. Honey, *Communism in North Vietnam*, p. 170.

2. The Diem regime in Saigon exploited the oppressive actions of Hanoi against the peasantry, as for example, in response to the rebellion at Nghe An in November 1956. This helped the Saigon government in its rejection of an election on the question of unification that year. See Philippe Devillers, "The Struggle for the Unification of Vietnam," in P. J. Honey, ed., *North Vietnam Today* (New York: Praeger, 1962). Pp. 32–34. See also, P. J. Honey, "Revolt of the Intellectuals," *The World Today*, vol. 13 (June 1957).

3. See Hoang Van Chi, "Collectivization and Rice Production," in Honey, ed., *North Vietnam Today*, pp. 117–127.

4. The Lao Dong (North Vietnamese Communist party) congress in Hanoi during September 1960 was the occasion at which First Secretary Le Duan stressed the regime's objectives in the South, following a steady buildup of the insurrectionary campaign.

5. See Ellen Hammer, "South Viet Nam: The Limits of Political Action," *Pacific Affairs*, vol. 35 (Spring 1962), pp. 24–36. Western estimates of the total number of incidents during 1957–60 was 7,000. In 1961 this rose to 2,000 per month.

6. The strategic concept underlying guerrilla warfare in Vietnam was elaborated in a study by the D.R.V. Defense Minister, who had been military leader of the war against the French, Vo Nguyen Giap, *People's War, People's Army: The Viet Cong Insurrection Manual for Underdeveloped Countries* (New York: Praeger, 1962).

7. A general survey of the political and military aspects of the situation and the problems generated by 1965 is "The United States and the Situation in South Vietnam: Pros and Cons," *Congressional Digest*, vol. 44 (April 1965), pp. 99–128.

8. Edward G. Lansdale discusses the close relationship of political and military factors, so important in determining the staying power of the opposing indigenous forces in "Viet Nam: Do We Understand Revolution" *Foreign Affairs*, vol. 43 (October 1964), pp. 75–86.

9. The NLF won some sympathetic support in the West as a "national coalition" movement. It was, in fact, a transparent device undertaken for just that purpose. Its modest success was all the more puzzling because the Vietnamese Communists had used this same technique on three previous occasions within recent memory.

10. The rural-urban population ratio in South Vietnam is approximately three to one.

11. Both the D.R.V. and the Viet Cong rejected a treaty to guarantee Cambodia's frontiers and recognize a special status for the 50,000 Cambodians who reside in South Vietnam. *The New York Times*, January 6, 1965. Hanoi might hope for a sympathetic hearing in Peking, since China has territorial claims to a "traditional realm" whose border regions include many alien ethnic groups.

12. At a mass rally in Hanoi in May 1963, Liu Shao-ch'i stated, "Peaceful coexistence must not be used to abolish the socialist countries' duty to support the revolutionary struggle of oppressed nations and peoples. The foreign policy of socialist countries . . . must not be used to supersede the revolutionary line of the proletariat of various countries and their parties." New China News Agency, May 12, 1963.

13. For instance, at the start of 1964, China failed to echo D.R.V. claims that Peking was totally committed and would automatically swing into action in case of an American attack against the D.R.V. See *The New York Times*, February 24, 1964.

14. For general foreign-policy purposes as well as to enhance its position within the Communist world and improve and strengthen its political stance against the United States, Hanoi pressed for an extension of diplomatic relations with as much of the non-Communist world as possible. See Thomas P. Thornton, "Foreign Relations of the Asian Communist Satellites," *Pacific Affairs*, vol. 35 (Winter 1962–1963), pp. 341–52, especially on the quest for formal recognition.

15. ". . . in reality they [the Soviet leaders] are trying to gain political capital for their dealings with the United States imperialists and to carry out plots for 'peace talks' in a futile attempt to extinguish the revolutionary struggle of the South Vietnamese people." *Hung Ch'i*, March 22, 1965.

16. For the joint statement following the Kosygin visit to Hanoi and the joint

communiqué of April 18, 1965, see *Current Digest of the Soviet Press,* vol. 17 (March 3, 1965), pp. 9–11, and (May 12, 1965), pp. 13–15.

17. Sung An Tai, "The Sino-Soviet Dispute and Vietnam," *Orbis,* vol. 9 (Summer 1965) argues along similar lines regarding Soviet motives and hopes. He cites the carefully limited assistance offered, the mild and broad threats of retaliation for U.S. bombings, the absence of nuclear blackmail, and the lack of nuclear backing to Hanoi. Pp. 434–435.

18. On this, the Vietnamese Communists have been adamant. See for example, Le Quang Dao and others, *The Revolution in South Vietnam Will Be Won,* U.S. Joint Publications Research Service (JPRS 23,908), Department of Commerce, Office of Technical Services (Washington: Government Printing Office, 1964).

19. This must have been a staggering blow to Soviet prestige both inside the Communist camp and in the world at large. Soviet determination to press forward in other fields, particularly a treaty on nonproliferation of nuclear weapons, reflected Moscow's determination to adhere to its general foreign policy line. Typically, this did not indicate that the Russians would modify their traditional habit of bargaining as hard and as long as possible for the maximum number of concessions they could gain from whatever issue was under negotiation. On Soviet pursuit of disarmament talks in the face of Vietnamese war, see *The New York Times* November 7, 1965.

20. For a theoretical study of escalation, see Herman Kahn, *On Escalation: Metaphors and Scenarios* (New York: Praeger, 1965). Though reality is often more precise and complex, as well as laden with unexpected developments, this analysis has the merit of examining crises at various levels of rising intensity. It also addresses itself to the problem of de-escalation.

21. P.L. 88–408 [H.J. Res. 1145], 78 Stat. 384, approved August 10, 1964. This Southeast Asia Resolution expires either by concurrent resolution of Congress or when the President determines that the peace and security of the area is reasonably assured by international conditions.

22. For the Communist side, from an alleged indigenous, popular and progressive Viet Cong viewpoint, see Wilfred Burchett, *Vietnam: The Inside Story of the Guerrilla War* (New York: International Publishers, 1965).

23. See "U.S. Takes Measures to Repel Attack against U.S. Forces in Southeast Asia," *Department of State Bulletin,* vol. 51 (August 24, 1964), texts of documents relating to the incident, pp. 258–268.

24. The war effort was causing some economic strain as early as 1963. For a description of conditions in the D.R.V. before Hanoi intensified its war effort, see *Translations on North Vietnam's Economy,* JPRS 17, 415 (Washington: Government Printing Office, 1963).

25. George Carver, "The Real Revolution in South Viet Nam," *Foreign Affairs,* vol. 43 (April 1965), perceptively appraises the new, non-Communist nationalist surge that has occurred following long years of alien and authoritarian rule. Pp. 383–404.

26. Jeanne Kuebler, "Political Instability in South Viet Nam," *Editorial Research Reports* (May 26, 1965), pp. 387–404.

27. P. J. Honey reported that the North Vietnamese economy was suffering severely by the spring of 1965. See "Hard Times in North Vietnam," *U.S. News and World Report,* vol. 58 (May 31, 1965), pp. 56–57.

28. Though the Chinese continued to denounce the Soviet Union for its inadequate support of Hanoi and for seeking to end the conflict, the D.R.V. carefully expressed its gratitude for Russian support in 1965 and emphasized Moscow's constancy over the years. The Soviet Union used the fact that it was helping Hanoi as a weapon in its struggle against Peking within the Communist world.

29. Speaking in East Berlin on the twentieth anniversay of V-E day, Premier Kosygin said, "Some people contend that only a new world war can bring about the unity and solidarity of the Socialist camp and the international Communist movement. We decisively reject such a position. . . . We have no more important task than to prevent a new world conflagration."

30. The United States tried to drive a wedge between Hanoi and Peking by pointing out that China was willing to have North Vietnam suffer grave losses without coming to its help, simply to advance its own ideological cause. See, for example, President Johnson's speech of May 13, 1965, in *Department of State Bulletin*, vol. 52 (May 31, 1965), pp. 838–841, and the statement by Secretary of State Dean Rusk, *The New York Times*, June 24, 1965. This gambit did not have the effect sought, possibly because Hanoi had its own powerful motives for conducting the war and looked upon China as an essential support, either for a victory or in a compromise situation.

31. *The New York Times*, May 11, 1965.

32. The author disagrees with Samuel B. Griffith's relatively negative appraisal regarding China's capacity to make war beyond its borders. The Chinese could make a major military impact in Vietnam and generally hold their own as long as the war remained conventional. Cf. Griffith, "Communist China's Capacity to Make War," *loc. cit.*, pp. 233–236.

33. See President Johnson's speech at Johns Hopkins University, April 7, 1965, in *Department of State Bulletin*, vol. 52 (April 26, 1965), pp. 606–610. See also Ambassador Arthur Goldberg's speech at the United Nations, September 22, 1966.

34. Communist Party Secretary Brezhnev, speaking in Kiev just prior to the forty-eighth anniversary of the Bolshevik revolution, reflected the Soviet dilemma in denouncing Washington and Peking. "We see that the situation in Asia has become tense. . . . Tremendous responsibility falls on all peace-loving nations in that part of the world and on their political leaders. Any attempts to solve problems by the use of force offer the stranglers of the liberation movement new opportunities to increase their pressure on the freedom-loving peoples." See the analysis by Peter Grose, *The New York Times*, November 7, 1965.

35. Theodore Sorensen, *Kennedy* (New York: Harper and Row, 1965), pp. 548, 639–648, and Arthur M. Schlesinger, Jr., *A Thousand Days* (Boston: Houghton Mifflin, 1965), pp. 363, 365, 367–368.

36. For critical and supporting arguments, respectively on the value of neutralization, see Frank N. Trager, "Laos and the Defense of Southeast Asia," *Orbis*, vol. 7 (Fall 1963), pp. 550–582, and Arthur J. Dommen, "Neutralization Experiment in Laos," *Current History*, vol. 48 (February 1965), pp. 89–94.

37. Late in 1964, Souvanna did react against a published report that he had

agreed to allow American attacks on the so-called Ho Chi Minh Trail in eastern Laos, leading from North to South Vietnam. One might infer that he allowed air operations directed at the military struggle for Laos itself, and that these actions were being conducted on a sustained basis. *The New York Times*, December 22, 1965.

38. See E. H. S. Simmons, "Power Politics in Laos," *The World Today*, vol. 18 (December 1962), pp. 514–523, and "Breakdown in Laos," *The World Today*, vol. 20 (July 1964), pp. 285–292.

39. Eric Pace, "Laos: Continuing Crisis," *Foreign Affairs*, vol. 43 (October 1964), argues that 20,000 NVA troops hold together a Pathet Lao force of 80,000 against an opponent almost three times its superior, numerically. On the other hand, the American presence is crucial in preventing right-wing generals from overturning the neutralist regime and breaking up the fragile military coalition of rightists and neutralists. Pp. 73–74.

40. Edwin F. Black, "Laos: A Case Study of Communist Strategy," *Military Review*, vol. 44 (December 1964), pp. 49–59, views this situation in the broader setting of Communist operational concepts and efforts.

41. This point was made with considerable emphasis by Secretary of State Dean Rusk in a commencement address at Williams College, "Why Laos is Critically Important," June 14, 1964.

Chapter 14

1. Wu Yuan-li has considered two fundamental components in *Economic Development and the Use of Energy Resources in Communist China* (New York: Praeger, 1963), and *The Steel Industry in Communist China* (New York: Praeger, 1965). For a brief balanced appraisal of China's economy in the mid-1960s, see his "Communist China's Economy: Critical Questions," *Current History*, vol. 49 (September 1965), pp. 164–169. For a general survey see also Li Chohming, *Industrial Development in Communist China* (New York: Praeger, 1964), and Chao Kang, *The Rate and Pattern of Industrial Growth in Communist China* (Ann Arbor: University of Michigan Press, 1965).

2. See Leonard Beaton, "The Chinese Bomb: The ISS View," *Survival*, vol. 7 (January–February 1965), pp. 2–4; Robert Guillain, "Ten Years of Secrecy," *Bulletin of Atomic Scientists*, vol. 21 (February 1965), pp. 24–25; Morton Halperin, "China's Nuclear Strategy," *China Quarterly*, no. 21 (January–March 1965), pp. 74–76; Hanson Baldwin in *The New York Times*, May 20, 1965.

3. See the observations made by the U.S. Atomic Energy Commission, *The New York Times*, May 21, 1965.

4. For early reports of Soviet assistance to China in intermediate-range missiles, see Allen Nanes, "The Armies of Red China," *Current History*, vol. 39 (December 1960), p. 342.

5. Statement before the Armed Services Committee of the House of Representatives, *The New York Times*, May 15, 1965.

6. Malcolm Hoag, "Nuclear Strategy and French Intransigence," *Foreign Affairs*, vol. 41 (January 1963), pp. 286–298, and Drew Middleton, *The New York Times*, April 12, 1963.

7. See comments by Allen Whiting at ACDA-sponsored seminar on China and arms control, Airlie House, Warrenton, Virginia, July 9–10, 1964.

8. Halperin, "China's Nuclear Strategy," *loc. cit.*, p. 75.

9. See Leo A. Orleans, *Professional Manpower and Education in Communist China* (Washington: National Science Foundation, 1960), and Sidney H. Gould ed., *Sciences in Communist China* (Washington: American Association for the Advancement of Science, 1961).

10. During 1960–62, in the aftermath of the Great Leap Forward, 470,000 graduated from college, more than the total for the previous decade. China thus had over 1 million college graduates, but they lacked adequate training and proved difficult to employ. For earlier estimates of China's capacity in advanced fields, see John Berberet, *Science and Technology in Communist China* (Santa Barbara: General Electric Technical and Military Planning Operation, 1960).

11. *Pravda*, May 18, 1958.

12. *The Wall Street Journal*, July 12, 1965.

13. Testimony of March 5, 1965, before the Appropriations Committee of the House of Representatives.

14. Ouyang Hsing, "Imperialist Contradictions Around the Question of Great Nuclear-Powered Status," *Chinese Youth*, nos. 3–4, February 10, 1963, quoted in Halperin, "Chinese Nuclear Strategy," *loc. cit.*, p. 78.

15. This theme runs strongly through Dai, "Peking and the 'Third World,'" *loc. cit.*, with the—to me, premature—implication that China has achieved this result.

16. The Chinese emphasized this Soviet commitment in their bitter statements of August 14 and September 6, 1963.

17. Alice L. Hsieh, "The Sino-Soviet Nuclear Dialogue: 1963," *Journal of Conflict Resolution*, vol. 8 (June 1964), pp. 99–115.

18. On the danger of American nuclear blackmail, see the important pamphlet *The Differences between Comrade Togliatti and Us* (Peking: Foreign Language Press, 1963).

19. Cited in Hsieh, "Communist China and Nuclear Force," in Rosecrance, *op. cit.*, p. 166.

20. Ch'en Yi's news conference, October 28, 1963: "There is danger in being browbeaten by countries possessing atomic bombs, but to come under the protective wings of countries possessing atomic bombs would mean, in the final analysis, the loss of independence. Premier Khrushchev remarked sarcastically that 'a country that strains herself to produce atomic bombs will find itself unable to slip into its own trousers!' It is not clear whether he was referring to our country or not, but I feel like telling him that 'we will produce atomic bombs even though we may have no trousers to wear.'"

21. *The New York Times*, October 9, 1964.

22. Alice L. Hsieh, "Communist China and Nuclear Warfare," *China Quarterly*, no. 2 (April–June 1960), pp. 1–15.

23. This would apply particularly to Peking's support of wars of national liberation and to efforts to establish a Chinese hegemony in Asia.

24. For Indian and Japanese expressions of dismay at the United Nations over China's second test, see *The New York Times*, May 15, 1965.

25. Chou En-lai made these points unambiguously and emphatically in "Report on the Work of the Government" before the first session of the Third National People's Congress, December 21–22, 1964.

26. On several occasions during 1965, Peking denounced the United Nations, called for sweeping reforms, and even demanded the removal of "aggressor" members before it would join. Despite this hostile stance, its supporters managed for the first time to win a tie vote, 47-47-20, on November 17, 1965, on a resolution to seat Peking and oust the Nationalists.

27. See for example, A. Doak Barnett, "The Inclusion of Communist China in an Arms Control Program," *Daedalus*, vol. 89 (Fall 1960), pp. 831–845.

28. See Richard C. Bowman, "The Chinese Bomb: The Military-Political Implications," *Air Force and Space Digest*, vol. 48 (January 1965), pp. 32–34.

29. See John Gittings, "China's Bomb," *The World Today*, vol. 20 (December 1964), pp. 503–505.

30. See Leo E. Rose, "Sino-Indian Rivalry and the Himalayan Border States," *Orbis*, vol. 5 (Summer 1961), pp. 198–215, and A. R. Field, "Bhutan, Kham and the Upper Assam Line," *Orbis*, vol. 3 (Summer 1959), pp. 180–192.

31. It is difficult to project the position of Pakistan under such a dangerous, long-term threat as here posited. George L. Montagno, discussing its effort to move closer to Peking, notes with some bemusement Pakistan's equanimity in the face of mounting evidence of Chinese militancy and intransigence. "Peaceful Coexistence: Pakistan and Red China," *Western Political Quarterly*, vol. 18 (June 1965), pp. 309–317.

32. Malcolm Mackintosh argues that political considerations alone will keep Peking from using the bomb against other Asian states. "The Sino-Soviet Dispute," *Survival*, vol. 7 (October 1965), p. 250.

33. Perhaps to soften the image of a two-power protection, India has generalized its quest for guarantees by calling for U.N. guarantees to all non-nuclear powers. See B. N. Chakravarty, statement before the U.N.'s 114-nation Disarmament Commission, May 3, 1965, during a discussion of ways to prevent the spread of nuclear weapons.

34. In December 1964, Peking warned that as a consequence of America's "criminal scheme" (bombing Communist supply lines in Laos) "the flames of war will spread to the whole of Indochina . . ." *The New York Times*, December 25, 1964.

35. In addition, the Chinese were sharp in their commentary on the international Communist conference held in Moscow at the beginning of March 1965 in both *Jen-min Jih-pao* and *Hung Ch'i*, March 23, 1965. Only nineteen of the twenty-six invited parties attended. The Chinese, Albanians, North Koreans, North Vietnamese, Romanians, Indonesians, and Japanese boycotted the affair, even though it was downgraded to a consultative meeting in the quest for unity of the movement.

36. Initially, Peking ascribed Khrushchev's ouster to opposition to his revisionist view, as in the *Hung Ch'i* editorial "Why Khrushchev Fell," nos. 21–22, November 1964. Its March 23, 1965 statement on the meeting in Moscow reversed this interpretation in view of the adamant stand Khrushchev's successors took against Chinese demands, and ascribed his fall to the fact that he became a serious obstacle to the implementation of his revisionist program. P. B. Reddaway, "The Fall of Khrushchev," *Survey*, no. 56 (July

1965), cites as cause for his ouster the fear of Khrushchev's colleagues that his provocative policies toward China would precipitate a break with Peking. However, Reddaway noted no signs among those who succeeded to power of a desire to make significant ideological concessions to the Chinese.

37. With the escalation of the war in Vietnam in 1965, China intensified a major campaign to prepare its people for possible conflict. American radio broadcasts reported that residents of major southern cities were warned on November 23 and 24, 1965, to prepare for evacuation because of the mounting possibility of American air attacks.

38. On the dilemma confronting intelligence projections of the behavior of others and the twin dangers of excessive boldness and caution, see Roberta Wohlstetter, "Cuba and Pearl Harbor: Hindsight and Foresight," *Foreign Affairs*, vol. 43 (July 1965), pp. 691–707, and Fred Greene, "The Intelligence Arm: The Cuban Missile Crisis," in Roger Hilsman and Robert C. Good, eds., *Foreign Policy in the Sixties* (Baltimore: Johns Hopkins Press, 1965), pp. 127–134. For an appraisal of the Moscow-Peking relationship at a time when the Russians precipitated the crisis see Robert Crane, "The Sino-Soviet Dispute on War and the Cuban Missile Crisis," *Orbis*, vol. 8 (Fall 1964), pp. 537–549.

39. See note 34, *supra*.

40. Despite widespread belief to the contrary, China does have approximately fifty centers of industrial and economic significance. See Wu Yuan-li, "Can China Afford Wars?" *Orbis*, vol. 6 (Fall 1962), pp. 453–464.

41. This was Lo's long article commemorating the twentieth anniversary of the 1945 victory against Germany: "Commemorate the Victory over German Fascism! Carry the Struggle Against United States Imperialism to the End!" in *Hung Ch'i*, as reported in a perceptive summary analysis by Max Frankel, *The New York Times*, May 13, 1965.

42. Benjamin Schwartz has observed: "One makes a virtue of necessity . . . because the necessity is intractable. Where weapons and capital are scarce, what is to be lost in stressing the organization of human energy? Oddly enough, the official ideology also seems to stress the relation of virtue to necessity. . . . The fact that 'virtue' is associated with necessity by no means implies that the belief in virtue may not be genuine and fervid . . ." "Modernization and the Maoist Vision," *China Quarterly*, no. 21 (January–March 1965), pp. 14–15.

43. Several ambiguities in Chinese attitudes appeared from the very start of the nuclear era—in recognizing the bomb's importance but denying its decisiveness, in calling the Soviet bomb a great blow to the West but giving the achievement low-key coverage in the press, and in acknowledging but minimizing the nuclear danger during the Korean War. See William R. Harris, "Chinese Nuclear Doctrine: The Decade Prior to Development," *China Quarterly*, no. 21 (January–March 1965), pp. 88–95.

44. This theme received increasing emphasis and repetition later in 1965. For example, an article on bayonet fighting was published in seven major Chinese newspapers at the end of November. In its first section, titled "Defeat Atomic Bombs with Bayonets," it called for intermingling with the enemy in combat and so neutralizing the effect of atomic attacks, and cited the

combination of politics, courage, close combat, and bayonets as the formula for military victory in a "people's" war. Max Frankel in *The New York Times*, December 3, 1965.

45. Ralph Powell argues that the Chinese are well aware of the tremendously destructive power of nuclear weapons but believe that, since their opponents are doomed by the objective laws of history, these weapons cannot save them. In this sense, China's opponents—both "imperialists" and "revisionists"—and the weapons themselves are paper tigers. See his "Great Powers and the Atomic Bombs are 'Paper Tigers,' " *China Quarterly*, no. 23 (July–September 1963), pp. 55–63.

Chapter 15

1. See Ciro Zoppo, "France as a Nuclear Power," in Rosecrance, *op. cit.*, pp. 113–157. Compare with H. A. DeWeerd, "The British Effort to Secure an Independent Deterrent," *ibid.*, pp. 87–101; and Alfred Goldberg, "The Atomic Origins of the British Nuclear Deterrent," *ibid.*, (October 1964), pp. 600–618.

2. *The New York Times*, August 5, 1963.

3. See, for example, the statements by President de Gaulle at his press conferences on September 5, 1961, November 10, 1961, and May 15, 1962. On tests, he said, "The problem is disarmament . . . the reciprocal controlled destruction of weapons, beginning with vehicles." *Major Addresses*, p. 162.

4. This proposal was made in the midst of the great Sino-Soviet exchanges of polemics, which occurred at the time the test-ban treaty was being successfully concluded. See Griffith, *The Sino-Soviet Rift*, Chapters 14–16, and especially pp. 371–387, a Chinese reply of August 31, 1963, to a Soviet statement of August 21, 1963.

5. See Chiu Hungdah, "Communist China's Attitude Toward Nuclear Tests," *China Quarterly*, no. 21 (January–March 1965), pp. 96–107.

6. The statement added that "as a first step, the summit conference should reach an agreement to the effect that the nuclear powers and those countries which will soon become nuclear powers undertake not to use nuclear weapons, neither to use them against non-nuclear countries and nuclear-free zones, nor against each other." Chinese statement accompanying announcement of Peking's first nuclear test, October 16, 1964.

7. On several occasions during 1955–62, the Chinese, with Russian support, called for "an area of peace" in the Far East and the Pacific, though they never went into details as to territorial scope or problems of inspection. This might make sense even today, if parts of China were to remain free from such restrictions, since it would allow Peking to develop a nuclear capability without deploying such weapons along its sensitive eastern and southern frontiers. Such a development, and reciprocal American withdrawals, seem most unlikely; but while visiting Italy, Liao Chen-chin of the party's Central Committee proposed a regional pact to ban nuclear weapons "on either side of the Pacific." He stated that China was "ready to reach accords concerning geographically limited regions where, in view of existing friction, nuclear arms might be banned." See *The New York Times*, November 28, 1964.

8. For this reason, on December 31, 1964, the United States rejected China's proposal for a conference on nuclear disarmament.

9. For a discussion of this and related points of tension between America and French security and foreign policy outlooks, see Stanley Hoffmann, "Discord in Community: The North Atlantic Area as a Partial International System," in F. O. Wilcox and H. F. Haviland, eds., *The Atlantic Community: Progress and Prospects* (New York: Praeger, 1963), pp. 3–31.

10. For the Sino-Soviet rift to function in a pattern favorable to Chinese interests, the Russians will have to retain, with a very high priority, their commitment to the protection and propagation of the Communist realm.

11. Wolf Mendl, "The Background of French Nuclear Policy," *International Affairs*, vol. 41 (January 1965), pp. 22–36, notes how a policy begun to emulate Britain within the NATO system was used by President de Gaulle as the basis of his effort to move away from integration toward a loose coalition. The dilemmas of a French policy that opposes an American hegemony, seeks a "Europe of fatherlands," opposes any European control over French nuclear power, and yet somehow seeks to have France emerge as a leader of its neighbors, are clearly sketched by Raymond Aron, "Old Nations, New Europe," *Daedalus*, vol. 93 (Winter 1964), pp. 43–66.

12. At a press conference in Peking on September 29, 1965, Foreign Minister Ch'en Yi said that he favored the proliferation of nuclear weapons. But the gist of his argument was that China would not help other underdeveloped states acquire this capability and that the other states should first develop their over-all industrial plant and capacity to produce, since these strengths were China's "most effective atomic bomb."

13. A justification of French strategic concepts and a description of its armament program for 1960–1965 are provided in *France and Its Armed Forces*, distributed in 1965 by the Press and Information Service of the French Embassy in the United States.

14. This major Chinese statement published in both *Hung Ch'i* and *Jen-min Jih-pao*, continues as follows: "Not long afterward, in June 1959, the Soviet government unilaterally tore up the agreement on new technology for national defense concluded between China and the Soviet Union in October 1957 and refused to provide China with a sample of an atomic bomb and technical data concerning its manufacture."

15. President de Gaulle was particularly outspoken in this view of the Berlin crisis in his press conference, September 5, 1961, which he began with this topic. See *Major Addresses*, pp. 140–152.

16. In addition to the issue of an American confrontation, Peking felt itself betrayed by Soviet neutrality in 1959 in its conflict with India. This development may have seemed further proof of Soviet unreliability and of China's need for its own weapons in carrying out what Peking considered a proper foreign policy. *Jen-min Jih-pao*, November 2, 1963, took up the Indian matter in an editorial on the Sino-Soviet written exchanges of charges in 1963. Griffith, *The Sino-Soviet Rift*, pp. 225–226, discusses a particularly virulent Chinese statement of October 21, 1963.

17. This perspective on the importance of timing in negotiating with Moscow is stressed in Zbigniew Brzezinski, "Russia and Europe," *Foreign Affairs*, vol. 42 (April 1964), pp. 428–444.

18. Press Conference, March 21, 1963.
19. T.I.A.S. 5433, initialed July 25, 1963, signed August 5, 1963, in force October 10, 1963. Article I Section 2 enjoins the nuclear signatories from "causing, encouraging, or . . . participating in" nuclear tests or explosions in any of these three environments. Since underground tests were not prohibited, presumably a nuclear power could legally help another state test in this environment. See Egon Schwelb, "The Nuclear Test Ban and International Law." *American Journal of International Law*, vol. 58 (July 1964), pp. 642–670.
20. Masani, *loc. cit.*, illustrated this, referring critically to those, including Shastri, who professed that atomic bombs could not frighten India. He quoted *Mysindia* of Bangalore approvingly when it said, "We feel, every time we read in our daily papers the statement by some person in authority that India is not frightened by atom bombs, a cold shiver runs down our back, for the statement is blatantly false." p. 20.
21. The Soviet government expressed interest in the American disarmament approach set forth by William C. Foster, Director of U.S. Arms Control and Disarmament Agency, "New Directions in Arms Control and Disarmament," *Foreign Affairs*, vol. 43 (July 1965), pp. 587–601. Negotiations in the months that followed proved very difficult, but the Soviet government gave several indications of a desire to press for a nonproliferation treaty. It did not treat the Vietnamese war as a major stumbling block but focused its opposition rather on a multilateral force or any other mechanism that could move West Germany closer to physical control over nuclear arms.
22. The United States has consistently opposed these measures because it believes that their application would harm only American freedom of action, without affording adequate compensating controls over Soviet power.
23. See for example the statement of India's B. N. Shakravarty before the 114-nation U.N. Disarmament Commission on May 3, 1965. *The New York Times*, May 4, 1965.
24. It must also be recognized that any special concessions to China, however inadequate they may appear to Peking, will be very difficult for the United States to accept because of both domestic political pressures and fear that a government still committed to the advancement of its cause by means of guerrilla and other forms of "national" warfare will use these to unfair advantage.
25. India actually used the conventional-force argument in its rejection of China's call for a world summit conference to place a complete ban on nuclear weapons. Replying to Chou En-lai's letter of October 17, 1964, Minister of External Affairs Swaran Singh held that such a conference could not serve a useful purpose until substantial progress had been made on a draft treaty of complete and general disarmament. *Lok Sabha*, March 8, 1965. Apparently, a partial nuclear arms-control agreement is preferred by India to a total nuclear ban, in the absence of substantial progress in the conventional arms field.
26. Ch'en Yi's press conference of September 29, 1965, indicates a marked effort to dissuade others from following a nuclear-arms course. He is reported to have said, "If you are cold, you cannot wear an atom bomb;

if you are hungry, you cannot eat an atom bomb." Compare this to his October 28, 1963, retort to Khrushchev that "we will produce atomic bombs even though we have no trousers to wear."

27. R. S. Basai, "Communist China and India's Non-Alignment," *Social Science*, vol. 39 (October 1964), pp. 226–233, claims that China's border dispute is a device to force India to identify with the West and so enable communism at home to win wide gains among the masses. Werner Levi, "Indian Neutralism Reconsidered," *Pacific Affairs*, vol. 37 (Summer 1964), pp. 137–147, maintains that nonalignment is incompatible with Indian security requirements. This was quickly recognized by the Swatantra Party, which long bucked the tide of Indian opinion in opposing a foreign policy based on nonalignment and the principle of coexistence. Rather, it sought defense accords with neighboring states, including Pakistan, and with the West, if needed. See Howard L. Erdman, "India's Swatantra Party," *Pacific Affairs*, vol. 36 (Winter 1963–1964), p. 404.

28. This appears today to be far less likely in the case of Australia than Japan. The Australian labor party has in the past felt uneasy about SEATO because of Indian and Indonesian opposition. Also, it opposed the communications base agreement. But it has averred its loyalty to the ANZUS Pact. See Thomas B. Millar, "Australia and the American Alliance," *Pacific Affairs*, vol. 37 (Summer 1964), p. 157; Paul Hasluck, "Australia and Southeast Asia," *Foreign Affairs*, vol. 43 (October 1964), pp. 51–63; Shane Paltridge, "Australia and the Defense of Southeast Asia," *Foreign Affairs*, vol. 44 (October 1965), pp. 49–61. For a critical Australian perspective, see Coral Bell, "American Policy in Southeast Asia," *The World Today*, vol. 20 (June 1964).

29. In September 1965, eighty-six Members of Parliament in India, from all political parties, asked Prime Minister Shastri to make nuclear weapons since "the security of this country can no longer be left to the mercy or whim of so-called friendly countries, India's survival both as a nation and a democracy . . . casts a . . . duty on the Government to make an immediate decision to develop our nuclear weapons." In a public statement the following month, Shastri reiterated his stand against taking such a decision. *The New York Times*, October 20, 1965.

30. Statement before the Rajya Sabha (Upper House) on November 16, 1965. Dr. H. J. Bhabha, Chairman of the Atomic Energy Commission, in talking to the Congress Party's Standing Committee on Atomic Energy, supported the government's stand against proliferation but noted that China was now in a position to threaten the security of its neighbors. *Weekly India News*, December 3, 1965.

31. M. R. Masani held that "The idea of a deterrent is essentially that it must be unconditional and automatic. . . . The aggressor has to know that it is going to operate automatically." He thought that any guarantor had to say in effect: "Take note that such and such countries are immune from attack, *because we shall attack first.*" "The Challenge of the Chinese Bomb," *India Quarterly*, vol. 21 (January–March 1965), p. 24 (emphasis added).

32. Or the United States might take a more restrained course, expressing ap-

proval of a state's decision to forgo nuclear power without too much fanfare or intensive exhortations of others to follow suit.

33. Should the Japanese decide that Chinese nuclear power is a grave threat to their security, they would feel under considerable pressure to have some control or influence over the deployment and use of nuclear weapons. Note the tone of Prime Minister Sato's first public declaration on the Chinese nuclear threat. He stated that Japan was "deeply worried by a nuclear capability in the hands of a neighbor that had renounced the principle of coexistence with ideological rivals such as Japan." Also, "The policy of Communist China . . . is a threat enough without being armed with nuclear weapons." "Its threat to Japan is real now that she is a nuclear power." Statements before the Upper House, November 25 and 26, 1965, in *The New York Times*, November 28, 1965.

34. In an editorial October 16, 1964 on the first Chinese test, the *New Delhi Statesman* asked, "What will happen if our assumption that China will never use nuclear weapons turns out to be as facile and foolish as the earlier belief that a socialist country never commits aggression?" Quoted in *The Washington Post*, October 17, 1964.

35. Possession of nuclear weapons of course would comprise the most serious departure from the country's constitutional provision against rearmament, though nuclear AAA and ABM weapons could be justified on legal grounds as defensive weapons. Premier Sato Eisaku favored a nonproliferation treaty with guarantees of security by the nuclear powers. Recognizing the weight of public sentiment against nuclear arms, he held that Japan would not acquire nuclear arms, even if a multilateral nonproliferation agreement and guarantee against attack did not really give Japan security. *The New York Times*, December 25, 1965. He did not, however, directly confront what policy Japan would adopt in the absence of such an accord of guarantee and nonproliferation.

36. I am indebted to James Morley of Columbia University for his development and discussion of this point.

37. We must keep in mind that whenever Peking raises the possibility of a nuclear-free zone, its terminology is vague but implies a complete withdrawal of U.S. power from the environs of China and a ban on nuclear weapons "on either side of the Pacific." (See Note 7, *supra.*)

38. Japan's commitment to the alliance continued to receive plurality but not majority support during 1963–64. To the question, "Do you think Japan should join the Free camp, the Communist camp or remain neutral," the results were: "Free camp," 46 per cent; "Communist camp," 1 per cent; "neutral," 26 per cent; and "don't know," 26 per cent. Monthly surveys by Jiji Press, July 1963–June 1964, Roper Center, Williams College, Williamstown, Mass.

39. Robert Osgood, *The Case for the New MLF* (Washington Center of Foreign Policy Research, 1964).

40. Secretary McNamara estimated that China would deploy several launchers for medium-range missiles by 1969, with several dozen possibly by 1975. *The New York Times*, December 16, 1965.

41. See President Johnson's offer to all non-nuclear powers following the first

Chinese test. "The nations that do not seek national nuclear weapons can be sure that, if they need our strong support against some threat of blackmail, then they will have it." *Department of State Bulletin,* vol. 51 (November 2, 1964), p. 613.

42. Military aid from a variety of sources has been important to India for both material and diplomatic reasons. By May 1964, American aid over a five-year period had totaled about $500 million. Over the next year, the Soviet government promised India over $140 million worth of aid, including aircraft, tanks, and submarines; Britain offered about $40 million to help in dock-yard modernization and frigate construction. India has also purchased modern French aircraft. It also received help in developing its own factories to produce tanks, airplanes, and other war equipment. With a planned strength of 825,000 men, it was well on its way to equipping these forces with modern arms. See "Multilateral Indian Arms," *Economist,* vol. 212 (September 26, 1964), pp. 1207–1208.

43. It is an accident of history that nonalignment has brought India military aid from both superpowers. This is now a major justification for the policy, but as its critics have pointed out, it is a weak base to argue from. For if one of the donors stopped helping, would this require India to stop accepting desperately needed help from the other major camp? This could become a practical issue should Russia shift its ground. Moscow in 1965 gave some ominous signs that it was rethinking its pro-Indian policy. It took a neutral stand in the Pakistani war, halted its military aid at least temporarily, and put pressure on New Delhi to agree to the settlement at Tashkent. However, military aid was resumed the following year.

44. On December 9, 1964, Prime Minister Shastri stated that he wanted the United States and the Soviet Union to guarantee India and other non-nuclear powers immunity against nuclear attack from China. Indian spokesmen have repeated this request. For example, at the United Nations, B. N. Chakravarty called for international guarantees to protect countries that might be threatened by nuclear attack, calling them an essential element in any effort at nonproliferation. *The New York Times,* May 9, 1965. For supporting arguments see "India and the Bomb," *Economist,* vol. 213 (December 12, 1964), pp. 1220–1222.

45. Concern about the utility of an outside guarantee was expressed in India as soon as China exploded its first device. The *New Delhi Statesman* warned that India would lose its freedom of action "if we become dependent on the U.S. or the U.S.S.R. or both. And too much trust, let us face it, cannot be placed in our good friends either. Who can say what the international situation will be in ten or fifteen years hence?" Raj Krishna argued then, and has developed this theme since, that both America and Russia are horrified at the thought of involving their precious manpower in a major war between Asian states that can deploy huge masses of troops. He believes they would be basically unaligned in such conflicts. *The Washington Post,* October 17, 1964.

46. On the other hand, India does not feel obliged to support specific and vital Soviet interests. Thus the Russians could not win from New Delhi a vigorous denunciation of American policy in Vietnam. During Shastri's visit to Moscow in May 1965, he praised the Soviet Union lavishly, re-

ceived verbal support for his policy of nonalignment, and seemed to be moving toward greater dependence on Russian aid. The American connection then appeared to be wearing thin, what with a sudden postponement of the Prime Minister's scheduled visit to Washington and Pakistan's use of American arms in the Rann of Cutch incident. Yet the final communiqué called for a cessation of American bombings against North Vietnam, and a settlement based on the Geneva accords of 1954. See *The New York Times*, May 13 and 20, 1965. Similarly, a visit by Prime Minister Gandhi in 1966 elicited no firmer support for Moscow's position, save for a call on the United States to cease bombing North Vietnam, as noted in the joint communiqué of July 15, 1966.

47. In a historic reversal, Prime Minister Harold Wilson dropped the idea of converting Britain's nuclear arms into a NATO deterrent. He apparently concluded that sovereign control over such weapons was indispensable to the maintenance of Britain's status as a world power, which he quickly decided was very essential. In a prescient article, Anthony Hartley analyzed Britain's problems generally along these lines, with special emphasis on the need to keep France from gaining the upper hand in Europe. See his "The British Bomb," *Encounter*, vol. 22 (May 1964).

48. This and other unfavorable points are stressed by an original proponent of this solution who later changed his mind. Alistair Buchan, "The Security of India," *loc cit.*

49. B. K. Nehru makes a strong appeal against India's developing nuclear power, noting the Nth-country problem as one of his main arguments. In general, he argues that the new weapons are more significant politically than militarily for China. Political considerations also outweigh the military ones in the Indian case, he feels, but in this instance, this leads to a judgment to abstain. The root of his argument is the belief that so rudimentary a nuclear weapons system as China's will not pose a major threat, and even a general guarantee along the lines offered by President Johnson in 1964 will suffice to blunt this danger, without requiring India to depart from nonalignment. "The Challenge of the Chinese Bomb," *India Quarterly*, vol. 21 (January–March, 1965), pp. 3–14.

50. India has a more moderate industrial infrastructure capable of sustaining a nuclear weapons program. See Joseph A. Hasson, "Nuclear Power in India," *Indian Journal of Economics*, vol. 45 (July 1964), pp. 1–29, for a discussion of underlying economic and technical factors. To a 40 m.w. reactor at Trombay, headquarters of the industrial nuclear program, will be added a 380 m.w. reactor at Tarapur in 1967, a second of 200 m.w. in Rapasthan, and a third planned in Madras State. See Raj Krishna, "India and the Bomb," *India Quarterly*, vol. 21 (April–June 1965), p. 130.

51. Krishna argues that a nuclear weapons program, including a gaseous diffusion plant, would cost Rs. 200 crores (about $400 million) annually, at least in the early years, a sum he considers a tolerable addition to the Rs. 3,200 crores (about $6.4 billion) allocated to the public sector for each year of the fourth five-year plan. *Ibid.*, p. 131. However, Buchan calculates that it would cost India about $40 million to produce fifty 20-kiloton bombs. A delivery system would be of a different magnitude, requiring $4 billion, and amounting to a 45 per cent rise in the country's defense

budget over the long haul. "The Security of India," *loc. cit.*, pp. 213–214.
52. "India has greatly decreased its defense budget, improved its army and is probably—despite denials—making a nuclear bomb. It won't test this, but will probably confirm its existence after an operational warhead has been made." C. L. Sulzberger, *The New York Times*, April 21, 1965.
53. At present, India could move from its peaceful-uses stance to weapons production in 18 months. According to H. J. Bhabha, this is the time required from the point of inception of an arms program, for India has not taken any steps in that direction. Presumably it could close the gap as little as three months before making the final decision to proceed with the production of a military device. The last three months would also comprise the most expensive part of the program. *The New York Times*, November 29, 1965.

Chapter 16

1. It is altogether too easy to underestimate this problem, especially with regard to third-country opinions of the power ratio between America and its Communist rivals. In the Washington-Moscow arms race of the 1950s, for example, Indians in 1959 felt that Russia would be stronger than the United States by 1980. In 1962, public opinion in all the major countries of the free world placed the Soviet Union far ahead of the United States in the space race. Considering the image of power that China conveys despite its actual weakness, it might well be considered the equal of the United States within two decades in the neighboring states of Asia, though the facts as we see them would not warrant any such conclusion. For the public opinion studies, see U.S.I.A., "Free World Versus Communist Bloc Standing in the Four Major Cities of India" (February 1960), and "A Note on Recent Trends in U.S. Space Standings" (September 1962), Roper Center, Williams College, Williamstown, Mass.
2. Late in 1965, a strong sentiment for intensive military operations in Vietnam was already evident in American public opinion, though American combat losses were still relatively low, and China was not engaged in combat operations. In a poll taken for the Columbia Broadcasting System by Opinion Research Corporation, Princeton, New Jersey, 58 per cent favored more bombing as an effective way to bring about a settlement, against 21 per cent who advocated a temporary halt in bombing attacks. On nuclear weapons, 34 per cent favored their use in Vietnam if this would shorten the war, whereas 55 per cent disagreed. However, if China sent large numbers of troops into the fighting, 46 per cent then favored using nuclear weapons; 41 per cent were opposed. CBS broadcast, December 14, 1965, and *The New York Times*, December 15, 1965.
3. Masani, *loc. cit.*, p. 20 states: "What we want, whether we make the bomb or not, is to have a deterrent which would stop the bomb being dropped on Delhi, Janshedpur, Bengal, Bihar—the whole of our northern industrial belt." If his attitude is at all representative, India will seek an elaborate air defense network—all the more so if it does not have the surety of its own nuclear deterrent.

4. See Arthur Stein, "India's Relations with the USSR, 1953–1963," *Orbis*, vol. 8 (Summer 1964), pp. 357–373.
5. A monthly poll taken by Jiji Press during July 1963–June 1964 revealed that only 63 per cent knew that a Polaris submarine was slated to come to a Japanese port, and this percentage declined during the second half of the period covered. Among those who knew of the visit, 10 per cent approved, 38 per cent felt it inevitable, 17 per cent had no opinion, and 35 per cent disapproved. Roper Center, Williams College, Williamstown, Mass.
6. Royama Masanichi, "The Japanese Approach to World Affairs," *Japan Quarterly*, vol. 10 (April–June 1963), pp. 158–165; Ohira Masayoshi, "Diplomacy for Peace," *International Affairs*, vol. 40 (July 1964), pp. 391–396; and George Kennan, "Japanese Security and American Policy," *Foreign Affairs*, vol. 43 (October 1964), pp. 13–28, all place far less emphasis on military strength, even along the essentially defensive course suggested here.
7. Philip Quigg, "Japan Is Neutral," *Foreign Affairs*, vol. 44 (January 1966), pp. 258–259, asserts that Japan continues to follow an irresponsible course on security matters. "What most Japanese vaguely want is the best of all possible worlds: their national security assured and paid for by others with minimum risk to themselves and without what they feel to be the humiliating presence of foreign defenders. . . . Either the Japanese will have to provide entirely for their own defense as the price for getting us out of their islands or they will have to enter into a genuine partnership for mutual defense in which costs, risks and responsibilities are shared on a rational basis." It is my contention that only the latter choice for both the Japanese and ourselves is meaningful.
8. Former Prime Minister Kishi Nobusuke has advocated the step-by-step approach in tackling the problem of reasserting Japanese control. "Political Movements in Japan," *Foreign Affairs*, vol. 44 (October 1965), p. 94.
9. In Japanese public opinion polls, Korea was invariably ranked among the least liked and most disliked states during 1963–64.
10. American success in helping to bring such a regional system to life would strengthen fears that the United States was preparing to reduce its own military presence and involvement in the area. The price might be, again, renewed and even more binding security links with South Korea, the Philippines, and Australia.
11. This, however, has not prevented the growth of Australian trade with China, especially in wheat. J. Wilezynski argues that Australia should do more along this line, for he sees this as a favorable development that has been impeded by the American alliance. "Australia's Trade with China," *India Quarterly*, vol. 21 (April–June 1965), pp. 156–166.
12. See the analysis in *The New York Times*, December 26, 1965; Frederick J. Kroesen, "The Precarious Position of Thailand," *Military Review*, vol. 44 (December 1964), pp. 60–69.
13. As of 1966, Britain had 55,000 troops in the Malaysia-Singapore area, and planned to maintain this level of commitment "for the foreseeable future." Press reports indicated that the decision was taken in London because of American and ANZ pressures, for Washington in particular felt that the

British presence was vital as long as both the Vietnamese War and the Indonesian threat to Malaya persisted. For an account of an important Anglo-American defense meeting, see *The New York Times*, January 28, 1966.

14. D. P. Singhal, "Imperial Defense, Communist Challenge, and the Grand Design," *India Quarterly*, vol. 18 (April–June 1962), pp. 149–151.

15. Saul Rose considered the security deterrences facing Britain in the 1960s in *Britain and Southeast Asia* (Baltimore: Johns Hopkins Press, 1962), pp. 134–137, 194–197. See also M. A. Fitzsimmons, "British Foreign Policy and Southern and Far Eastern Asia," *Review of Politics*, vol. 24 (January 1962), pp. 109–140.

16. Compare this to Washington's determination not to become involved in Britain's security problems after 1950. See Dean McHenry and Richard Rosecrance, "The Exclusion of the UK from the ANZUS Pact," *International Organization*, vol. 12 (Summer 1958), pp. 320–329. And there were, nevertheless, divergences between Washington and London on the early stages of the Indonesian confrontation campaign. See Michael Leifer, "Anglo-American Differences over Malaysia," *The World Today*, vol. 20 (April 1964), pp. 156–166.

17. Coral Bell noted, during the worrisome days of 1963, that a joke then in circulation referred to Australia as "South Irian." See her studies of the tensions and strengths in the alliance, "Australia and the American Alliance," *The World Today*, vol. 19 (July 1963), pp. 302–310.

18. For a general discussion of the threat posed by Indonesia to its neighbors before the political upheaval of 1965 and the diplomatic policy choices open to Jakarta and to those opposing it, see George Modelski, *Indonesia and Her Neighbors* (Princeton University: Center of International Studies, 1964).

19. All this is quite apart from Australia's own difficulty in coping with its policy of racial exclusion and the barrier this creates against the close ties that Canberra seriously seeks to develop with many of its Asian neighbors.

20. The strategic importance of the rapid development of Thailand as a powerful base has generally not been widely appreciated. One aspect is considered in Denis Warner, "The Ho Chi Minh Trail and Our Thai Build-up," *The Reporter*, vol. 34 (January 27, 1966), pp. 26–28.

21. Even when the Vietnamese War escalated sharply in 1964–65, Washington adhered to its stand that it harbored no objectives—political or territorial—against North Vietnam despite "moving North" statements by premiers Khanh and Ky in Saigon.

22. A public opinion poll in May–June 1957 in the Bangkok area, heavily weighted with influential elements in the population, revealed that 45 per cent supported SEATO, whereas 30 per cent doubted its need, and 35 per cent opposed it. In terms of social classes, support in the upper range was 53 per cent, with 47 per cent in the middle, and only 32 per cent among the lower classes. A majority opposed further American military aid. Only 34 per cent favored it, 46 per cent held that it made Thailand a base for aggression and opened it to attack, and an additional 20 per cent were adamantly opposed. United States Information Agency, "A Note on Thai Attitudes towad SEATO, American Aid, and Relations with Communist

China," Report 12, August 13, 1957, at Roper Center, Williams College, Williamstown, Mass.

23. John P. Armstrong, *Sihanouk Speaks* (New York: Walker, 1964), has written a very sympathetic study that reveals, however unintentionally, the complexities and difficulties involved for Cambodian diplomacy in the personality of Prince Sihanouk. See also Roger Smith, *Cambodia's Foreign Policy* (Ithaca: Cornell University Press, 1965).

24. Michael Leifer, "Cambodia Looks to China," *The World Today*, vol. 20 (June 1964), pp. 26–31.

25. American aid totaled $355 million in economic and $84 million in military help between 1955 and 1963. See Armstrong, *op. cit.*, pp. 3–6, for a discussion of American and Cambodian objectives in this program.

26. Prince Sihanouk's belief in the value of neutrality and his lack of confidence in the reliability and effectiveness of the American security effort in Indochina led him to be an early advocate of Lao neutrality and a critic of SEATO. See Roger Smith, "Cambodia's Neutrality and the Laotian Crisis," *Asian Survey*, vol. 1 (July 1961), pp. 17–22, and Michael Leifer, "Cambodia and SEATO," *International Journal*, vol. 17 (Spring 1962), pp. 122–132. Armstrong, *op. cit.*, pp. 143–145, points out that Sihanouk had hoped to extend his neutrality to the Russo-Chinese split and the Sino-Indian confrontation, and recognizes that his task is becoming increasingly more difficult.

27. In 1965, permission was given to American military authorities at the "highest level of command" in South Vietnam to pursue enemy forces into Cambodia under special circumstances, to protect their forces. Department of State statement of December 21, 1965. Cambodia in turn emphasized that the ICC alone had authority to supervise the border area and could therefore check on the sincerity of Pnompenh's effort to remain neutral. It warned that it would respond to military violation of its territory by attack against South Vietnam and an appeal for help to countries prepared to assist it. See *The New York Times*, January 4, 1966, for a summary of three letters sent to the United Nations by Cambodia.

28. A statement made in a soberly worded lecture by H. M. Patel exemplifies this fear. "If a settlement with Pakistan [over Kashmir] can be reached and it would agree thereafter to adopt a neutral attitude in a conflict with China, our defense problem would be made appreciably easier. For the present, however, we must proceed on the assumption that we must face both these countries." *The Defense of India* (Poona: Gokhale Institute of Politics and Economics, 1963).

29. See S. M. Burke, "Sino-Pakistani Relations," *Orbis*, vol. 8 (Summer 1964), pp. 391–404. Note that even in the emotional response to Liu Shao-ch'i's visit of March 1966, Pakistan would not condemn American actions in Vietnam in the formal communiqué.

30. Thanat Khoman, "Which Road for Southeast Asia?" *Foreign Affairs*, vol. 42 (July 1964), pp. 628–639, reflects many of these hopes and doubts. David Wurfel, "The Patterns of Southeast Asian Response to International Politics," in William Henderson, ed., *Southeast Asia: Problems of United States Policy* (Cambridge: The M.I.T. Press, 1963), pp. 81–84, discusses the traditional reserve and emotional noninvolvement of Thailand's tradi-

tionally neutralist leaders, whose adjustments to reality have been in terms of great-power alignments, not ideological commitment.

31. Paul Martin reported these views as coming from military leaders whose names "are household words." *Berkshire Eagle* (Pittsfield, Mass.), November 14, 1964. Their views on matters not covered here include hopes that (1) Japan will take a greater role in its own self-defense, (2) India will display greater concern for its atomic security, and (3) neutralists will take a more favorable view of collective security.

32. *Ibid.* Guam has become a key target of Soviet political pressure, exerted through U.N. channels. Moscow has used the forum of the Assembly's Special Committee on Colonialism to call for the liberation of the Virgin Islands and American Samoa, as well as Guam. The United States has responded that it is fostering self-determination and economic development, and that it reports to the United Nations regularly. In 1964, a U.N. visiting mission found the people of the American-governed territories in the Pacific lacking sufficient political maturity for soundings on their wishes.

33. Morton Halperin, in his important book *China and the Bomb* (New York: Praeger, 1965), argues that the other Asian states have a sophisticated view of nuclear power and generally discount the threat that Peking can pose. See especially Chap. 4. My viewpoint is markedly different. However, though we may disagree in this and in other cases, I am indebted to the author of this pioneer work for his insights and analytical approaches, which helped me shape my own thoughts on this difficult subject.

34. It can be argued that the implementation of an $8-billion antimissile program that can effectively cope with a future Chinese threat against the American homeland will demonstrate the sincerity of the commitment to our Asian allies. It might, however, also emphasize the growth of Chinese power, underline our vulnerability and raise doubts about our willingness to run such risks to protect others on a distant continent. As in many similar instances, both strands of thought will probably "coexist," with the particular situation and the way it is handled determining which prevails.

Chapter 17

1. George Liska outlines—prematurely, in my judgment—what would be the impact of an integrated Western Europe's possible impact on global diplomacy, *Europe Ascendant* (Baltimore: Johns Hopkins Press, 1964), esp. Chapter 3.

2. A preliminary conference on economic aid was held by Japan and its former Asian enemies in April 1966.

3. For examples of caution in Okinawa, the Philippines, Taiwan, Laos, and Thailand, see the analysis by R. W. Apple, Jr., *The New York Times*, January 25, 1966.

4. Needless to say, one can remain convinced that this is a most vital issue without becoming unduly optimistic about the chances of eroding tradition-crusted anti-Western dogma in the near future. A most discouraging illustration would be the Japanese Socialist party and its rigid adherence to old images of the capitalist "enemy-failure." This persists despite Japan's own success in modernizing, the absence of a Communist party discipline

to impose orthodoxy, and the freedom of exposure to new intellectual currents in Europe and America. Yet these old Marxist answers no longer satisfy the new intellectuals, even if the West still remains suspect. See Adrath Burks, "Japan: 'The Kitchen and the Garden,'" *Current History,* vol. 46 (April 1964), pp. 230–237.

5. See Robert C. Tucker, "Russia, the West, and World Order," *World Politics,* vol. 12 (October 1959), pp. 1–23, and Marshall Shulman, *op. cit.,* pp. 250–271.

6. To go back to the founding fathers, see Sigmund Neumann, "Engels and Marx: Military Concepts of the Social Revolutionaries," in E. M. Earle, ed., *Makers of Modern Strategy* (Princeton: Princeton University Press, 1944).

7. The dreary and erroneous plaint that America wins wars and loses the peace settlements illustrates the need to iterate the simplistic point about the political consequences of wars. The preservation of Western institutions in Europe west of the Elbe and re-establishment of democracy in Japan are of such major significance that these alone prove the point.

8. General James Gavin seemed to reflect this view strongly in the wake of the major military commitment of 1965. See *Harper's Magazine,* vol. 232 (February 1966), and *The New York Times,* January 28, 1966 on Gavin's meeting with Pentagon officials who rejected his opinions.

9. See Fred Iklé, *How Nations Negotiate* (New York: Harper and Row, 1964), p. 190.

10. American public opinions, which has a considerably more flexible attitude than has generally been realized, will play a highly significant role in this context. See A. T. Steele, *The American People and China* (New York: McGraw-Hill, 1966).

11. A strong plea for a policy along these lines is made in Henry Schwarz, "America Faces Asia: The Problem of Image Projection," *Journal of Politics,* vol. 26 (August 1964), pp. 532–548.

12. On this point, see a letter by Arnold Beichmann, "Lowenthal's Errors: The Vietnam Argument," *Encounter,* no. 147 (December 1965), p. 91, and Richard Lowenthal's response to this and other criticisms in *Encounter,* no. 148 (January 1966), pp. 54–59.

13. A very interesting appraisal by Hanoi's strategist, Vo Nguyen Giap, in *Hoc Tap* is presented in excerpt form in *The New York Times,* February 2, 1966. Note especially his insistence that the crucial issues are support of the people, control of terror, and the creation of a viable army and government, objectives that he believes Washington cannot attain no matter how many troops it puts into the country.

14. A discussion of the disarmament issue from a perspective critical of American policy can be found in F. W. Neal, "U.S. China Policy and Disarmament," *Bulletin of Atomic Scientists,* vol. 19 (November 1963), pp. 5–8.

15. For more than a decade, many analysts have called for a more direct assault on the major issues separating the two states, sparked by a profound change in American policy, with Washington taking broad initiatives toward conciliation. See, for example, Nathaniel Peffer, "China in Reappraisal: Menace to American Security?" *Political Science Quarterly,* vol. 71 (December 1956), pp. 481–515; R. W. Alstyne, "Myth and Reality in the Far Eastern Policy of the United States," *International Affairs,* vol.

32 (July 1956), pp. 287–297; Harold Quigley, "Toward Reappraisal of Our China Policy," *Virginia Quarterly Review,* vol. 35 (Summer 1959), pp. 466–480; A. Brecht, "Fairness in Foreign Policy—the China Issue," *Social Research,* vol. 28 (Spring 1961), pp. 95–104. For a recent effort, see Report for American Friends Service Committee, *A New China Policy* (New Haven: Yale University Press, 1965).

16. For a strong argument in favor of a two-China policy as against other approaches see A. Doak Barnett, *Communist China in Asia,* Chapter 15, and the endorsement of this position in "Towards Two Chinas?" *Economist,* vol. 195 (June 18, 1960), pp. 183–184.

17. An imaginative approach to this problem by a senior Foreign Service officer was a speech by Marshall Green, "Communist China as a Problem in U.S. Policy Making," *Department of State Bulletin,* vol. 52 (March 29, 1965), pp. 449–453.

Index

COUNCIL ON FOREIGN RELATIONS

Officers and Directors

John J. McCloy, *Chairman of the Board*
Henry M. Wriston, *Honorary President*
Grayson Kirk, *President*
Frank Altschul, *Vice-President & Secretary*
David Rockefeller, *Vice-President*
Gabriel Hauge, *Treasurer*
George S. Franklin, Jr., *Executive Director*

Hamilton Fish Armstrong
William P. Bundy
William A. M. Burden
Arthur H. Dean
Douglas Dillon
Allen W. Dulles
William C. Foster
Caryl P. Haskins
Joseph E. Johnson
Henry R. Labouisse

Walter H. Mallory
Bill D. Moyers
Alfred C. Neal
James A. Perkins
Lucian W. Pye
Robert V. Roosa
Philip D. Reed
Charles M. Spofford
Carroll L. Wilson

PUBLICATIONS

FOREIGN AFFAIRS (quarterly), edited by Hamilton Fish Armstrong.
THE UNITED STATES IN WORLD AFFAIRS (annual). Volumes for 1931, 1932 and 1933, by Walter Lippmann and William O. Scroggs; for 1934–1935, 1936, 1937, 1938, 1939 and 1940, by Whitney H. Shepardson and William O. Scroggs; for 1945–1947, 1947–1948 and 1948–1949, by John C. Campbell: for 1949, 1950, 1951, 1952, 1953 and 1954, by Richard P. Stebbins; for 1955, by Hollis W. Barber; for 1956, 1957, 1958, 1959, 1960, 1961, 1962 and 1963, by Richard P. Stebbins; for 1964, by Jules Davids; for 1965 and 1966 by Richard P. Stebbins.
DOCUMENTS ON AMERICAN FOREIGN RELATIONS (annual). Volume for 1952 edited by Clarence W. Baier and Richard P. Stebbins; for 1953 and 1954 edited by Peter V. Curl; for 1955, 1956, 1957, 1958 and 1959 edited by Paul E. Zinner; for 1960, 1961, 1962 and 1963 edited by Richard P. Stebbins; for 1964 by Jules Davids; for 1965 and 1966 by Richard P. Stebbins.
POLITICAL HANDBOOK AND ATLAS OF THE WORLD (annual), edited by Walter H. Mallory.
FROM ATLANTIC TO PACIFIC: A New Interocean Canal, by Immanuel J. Klette (1967).
AFRICAN ECONOMIC DEVELOPMENT (rev. ed.), by William A. Hance (1967).
TITO'S SEPARATE ROAD: America and Yugoslavia in World Politics, by John C. Campbell (1967).
U.S. TRADE POLICY: New Legislation for the Next Round, by John W. Evans (1967).
TRADE LIBERALIZATION AMONG INDUSTRIAL COUNTRIES: Objectives and Alternatives, by Bela Balassa (1967).
THE CHINESE PEOPLE'S LIBERATION ARMY, by Brig. General Samuel B. Griffith II U.S.M.C. (ret.) (1967).
THE ARTILLERY OF THE PRESS: Its Influence on American Foreign Policy, by James Reston (1967).
ATLANTIC ECONOMIC COOPERATION: The Case of the O.E.C.D., by Henry G. Aubrey (1967).
TRADE, AID AND DEVELOPMENTS The Rich and Poor Nations, by John Pincus (1967).
BETWEEN TWO WORLDS: Policy, Press and Public Opinion on Asian-American Relations, by John Hohenberg (1967).
THE CONFLICTED RELATIONSHIP: The West and the Transformation of Asia, Africa and Latin America, by Theodore Geiger (1966).

THE ATLANTIC IDEA AND ITS EUROPEAN RIVALS, by H. van B. Cleveland (1966).

EUROPEAN UNIFICATION IN THE SIXTIES: From the Veto to the Crisis, by Miriam Camps (1966).

THE UNITED STATES AND CHINA IN WORLD AFFAIRS, by Robert Blum, edited by A. Doak Barnett (1966).

THE FUTURE OF THE OVERSEAS CHINESE IN SOUTHEAST ASIA, by Lea A. Williams (1966).

THE CONSCIENCE OF THE RICH NATIONS: The Development Assistance Committee and the Common Aid Effort, by Seymour J. Rubin (1966).

ATLANTIC AGRICULTURAL UNITY: Is it Possible?, by John O. Coppock (1966).

TEST BAN AND DISARMAMENT: *The Path of Negotiation,* by Arthur H. Dean (1966).

COMMUNIST CHINA'S ECONOMIC GROWTH AND FOREIGN TRADE, by Alexander Eckstein (1966).

POLICIES TOWARD CHINA: Views from Six Continents, edited by A. M. Halpern (1966).

THE AMERICAN PEOPLE AND CHINA, by A. T. Steele (1966).

INTERNATIONAL POLITICAL COMMUNICATION, by W. Phillips Davison (1965).

MONETARY REFORM FOR THE WORLD ECONOMY, by Robert V. Roosa (1965).

AFRICAN BATTLELINE: Amercian Policy Choices in Southern Africa, by Waldemar A. Nielsen (1965).

NATO IN TRANSITION: The Future of the Atlantic Alliance, by Timothy W. Stanley (1965).

ALTERNATIVE TO PARTITION: For a Broader Conception of America's Role in Europe, by Zbigniew Brzezinski (1965).

THE TROUBLED PARTNERSHIP: A Re-Appraisal of the Atlantic Alliance, by Henry A. Kissinger (1965).

REMNANTS OF EMPIRE: The United Nations and the End of Colonialism, by David W. Wainhouse (1965).

THE EUROPEAN COMMUNITY AND AMERICAN TRADE: A Study in Atlantic Economics and Policy, by Randall Hinshaw (1964).

THE FOURTH DIMENSION OF FOREIGN POLICY: Educational and Cultural Affairs, by Phillip H. Coombs (1964).

AMERICAN AGENCIES INTERESTED IN INTERNATIONAL AFFAIRS (Fifth Edition), compiled by Donald Wasson (1964).

JAPAN AND THE UNITED STATES IN WORLD TRADE, by Warren S. Hunsberger (1964).

FOREIGN AFFAIRS BIBLIOGRAPHY, 1952–1962, by Henry L. Roberts (1964).

THE DOLLAR IN WORLD AFFAIRS: An Essay in International Financial Policy, by Henry G. Aubrey (1964).

ON DEALING WITH THE COMMUNIST WORLD, by George F. Kennan (1964).

FOREIGN AID AND FOREIGN POLICY, by Edward S. Mason (1964).

THE SCIENTIFIC REVOLUTION AND WORLD POLITICS, by Caryl P. Haskins (1964).

AFRICA: *A Foreign Affairs Reader*, edited by Philip W. Quigg (1964).

THE PHILIPPINES AND THE UNITED STATES: Problems of Partnership, by George E. Taylor (1964).

SOUTHEAST ASIA IN UNITED STATES POLICY, by Russell H. Fifield (1963).

UNESCO: ASSESSMENT AND PROMISE, by George N. Shuster (1963).

THE PEACEFUL ATOM IN FOREIGN POLICY, by Arnold Kramish (1963).

THE ARABS AND THE WORLD: Nasser's Arab Nationalist Policy, by Charles D. Cremeans (1963).

TOWARD AN ATLANTIC COMMUNITY, by Christian A. Herter (1963).

THE SOVIET UNION, 1922–1962: A Foreign Affairs Reader, edited by Philip E. Mosely (1963).

THE POLITICS OF FOREIGN AID: American Experience in Southeast Asia, by John D. Montgomery (1962).

SPEARHEADS OF DEMOCRACY: Labor in the Developing Countries, by George C. Lodge (1962).

LATIN AMERICA: Diplomacy and Reality, by Adolf A. Berle (1962).

THE ORGANIZATION OF AMERICAN STATES AND THE HEMISPHERE CRISIS, by John C. Dreier (1962).

THE UNITED NATIONS: Structure for Peace, by Ernest A. Gross (1962).

THE LONG POLAR WATCH: Canada and the Defense of North America, by Melvin Conant (1962).

ARMS AND POLITICS IN LATIN AMERICA (Revised Edition), by Edwin Lieuwen (1961).

THE FUTURE OF UNDERDEVELOPED COUNTRIES: Political Implications of Economic Development (Revised Edition), by Eugene Staley (1961).

SPAIN AND DEFENSE OF THE WEST: Ally and Liability, by Arthur P. Whitaker (1961).

SOCIAL CHANGE IN LATIN AMERICA TODAY: Its Implications for United States Policy, by Richard N. Adams, John P. Gillin, Allen R. Holmberg, Oscar Lewis, Richard W. Patch, and Charles W. Wagley (1961).

FOREIGN POLICY: THE NEXT PHASE: The 1960s (Revised Edition), by Thomas K. Finletter (1960).

DEFENSE OF THE MIDDLE EAST: Problems of American Policy (Revised Edition), by John C. Campbell (1960).

COMMUNIST CHINA AND ASIA: Challenge to American Policy, by A. Doak Barnett (1960).

FRANCE, TROUBLED ALLY: De Gaulle's Heritage and Prospects, by Edgar S. Furniss, Jr. (1960).

THE SCHUMAN PLAN: A Study in Economic Cooperation 1950–1959, by William Diebold, Jr. (1959).

SOVIET ECONOMIC AID: The New Aid and Trade Policy in Underdeveloped Countries, by Joseph S. Berliner (1958).

NATO AND THE FUTURE OF EUROPE, by Ben T. Moore (1958).

INDIA AND AMERICA: A Study of Their Relations, by Phillips Talbot and S. L. Poplai 1958).

NUCLEAR WEAPONS AND FOREIGN POLICY, by Henry A. Kissinger (1957).

MOSCOW-PEKING AXIS: Strength and Strains, by Howard L. Boorman, Alexander Eckstein, Philip E. Mosely, and Benjamin Schwartz (1957).

RUSSIA AND AMERICA: Dangers and Prospects, by Henry L. Roberts (1956).

THE LIBRARY
ST. MARY'S COLLEGE OF MARYLAND
ST. MARY'S CITY, MARYLAND 20686

080616

DS
33.4   Greene, Fred.   '78
.U6   U.S. policy and the
G7   security of Asia.

DATE DUE			

Library of St. Mary's College of Maryland

St. Mary's City, Maryland   20686